# PISTOL & REVOLVER DIGEST

## 3rd Edition

## By Dean A. Grennell

DBI BOOKS, INC., NORTHFIELD, ILLINOIS

**About Our Covers:** We are proud to show-case Harrington & Richardson's Double Action 903-6" and 904-6" revolvers on our front cover. Both guns are chambered for the .22 Long Rifle and feature 6-inch barrels, fully adjustable sights, walnut grips and a nine-round cylinder capacity. The 904-6" is equipped with a target bull barrel. Our back cover features another pair of .22 Long Rifle H&R revolvers — the 904-4" and the 905-4". The 904-4" is the same as described above except for its shorter barrel. The 905-4" is a nickel finish version of the 904. **Photos by John Hanusin.**

**PUBLISHER**
Sheldon Factor
*EDITORIAL DIRECTOR*
Jack Lewis
*ART DIRECTOR*
Sonya Kaiser
*ART ASSOCIATE*
Dana Silzle
*ARTISTS*
John Vitale
Denise Hegert
*PRODUCTION*
Betty Burris
*COPY EDITOR*
Dorine Imbach
*CONTRIBUTING EDITORS*
Claud S. Hamilton
Charles W. Karwan, Jr.

**Produced by**

*Charger Productions*

ISBN 0-910676-49-6                    Library of Congress Catalog Card Number: 76-23196

# CONTENTS

# ACKNOWLEDGEMENTS

**A**LTHOUGH THIS appears near the front of the book, it's the last item out of the overheated typewriter and, as on many similar occasions, I'm keenly aware of and humbly grateful for the invaluable assistance that several others have contributed.

As in previous editions, Claud S. Hamilton's contributions made the vital difference between a book that made the printer's deadline without a lot of blank pages and I trust the reader will share my gratitude for avoiding that painful contretemps. I believe I've termed Hamilton genial — which he certainly is — but the only photo in which he appears here is rather atypically cold-eyed in appearance so I'd like to include a photo on this page that comes much closer to depicting the real Red Laig in all his urchin *joie de vivre*.

Tom Ferguson is not the direct author of any of the text here, but his touch is clearly apparent in many places, provided you know where to look. Over the past many happy years, I've derived inestimable benefits from an informal correspondence network that includes Ferguson, Hamilton and which included William H. Corson until his untimely passing in early 1981. A likeness of Ferg appears in chapter 4 and the taut confines of caption space did not quite enable me to get the point across that I had in mind: The late Gen. George Patton is said to have held pearl stocks in scalding contempt, meanwhile packing the ivory-handled sixguns that served as his trademark as distinctively as Gen. MacArthur's corncob pipe. Ferguson and I found it considerably chucklesome that the ornately gussied-up gat of an authentic New Orleans ponce did in fact carry stocks of ivory, rather than pearl.

I'd be painfully remiss if I didn't give proper credit to Jack Lewis for aid and assistance too broadly ramified for any hope of detailed listing.

Col. Claud S. Hamilton (USA, Ret.)

Then there is Sheldon Factor, the book's publisher, who also read the raw copy personally and caught any large number of fluffs, practically all of which have been rectified (I hope!).

Dorine Imbach and Betty Burris, as on many such projects, made yeowomanly and successful efforts to get the words into type, all neat and Bristol-fashion.

Jean Grennell, my wife and helpful helpmate of thirty-seven memorable years contributed by monitoring the daily papers, calling pertinent items to my harried attention and leaving me helpfully undistracted as I hunched over the typewriter in the den/office at home, where most of these words seeped onto paper.

As for many years, cherished friends in the shooting/reloading industry were of great help and assistance. To mention only a few, that would include Dave Andrews of CCI-Speer, Steve Hornady of Hornady Manufacturing, Jim Hull and Mike Bussard of Sierra Bullets, Dick Lee of Lee Precision, Fred Huntington of Huntington Die Specialties, Stan Newman of Colt's Firearms Division, Roy Jinks of Smith & Wesson, Bill Siems of Federal Cartridge, Dick Dietz of Remington, Warren Center of Thompson/Center, Wayne Gibbs of Hensley & Gibbs, Walt Stevenson of S&S Precision Bullets, Tony Sailer of C-H Tool & Die Corp., and Steve Herrett of Herrett Stocks. I'd even include Bill Jordan, were it not for the fact that he never sent the requested photo in full trickshooting regalia. Oh foosh, let's include him anyway, okay? That is only a pallidly partial listing of such noble souls and profuse apologies to any and all whose names are omitted! Comes to that, Chuck Karwan's notes on gun values deserve recognition and hereby get it!

Last but far-far from least, we have Sonya Kaiser, without whose devoted efforts and remarkable abilities, this and several other books would never have gotten off the ground. Time after time, she'd transfix me with steely topaz gaze and decree that she needed this or that by such and such a time, with unstated but implicit alternatives if it didn't materialize. I'd planned to dedicate this book to the Rogers kids — Ginger, Buck & Roy — but I've decided that Sonya Kaiser is more worthy of the honor.

The final note of gratitude is to you out there: the gun-loving, book-buying public, without whose support, none of this would be possible. May your tribe proliferate prodigiously.

With cordial best regards,

*Dean A. Grennell*

Dean A. Grennell

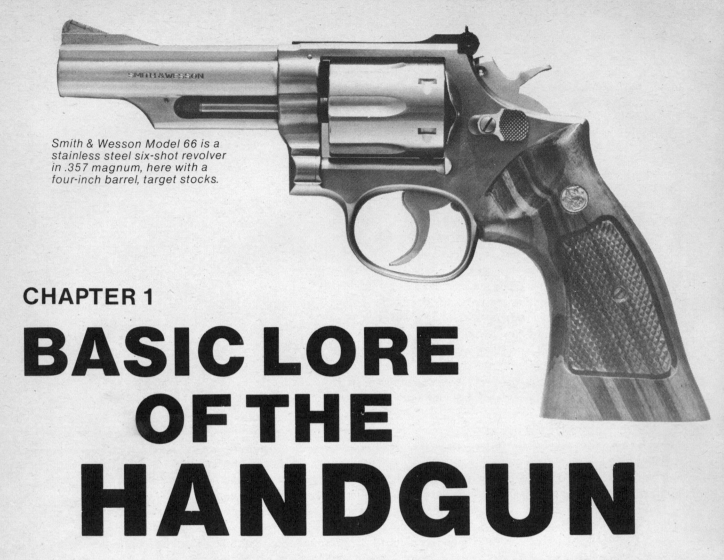

Smith & Wesson Model 66 is a stainless steel six-shot revolver in .357 magnum, here with a four-inch barrel, target stocks.

# CHAPTER 1

# BASIC LORE OF THE HANDGUN

## Classifying The Handgun Species Into Sub-Groups, With Notes On The Unruly Exceptions

*"All mankind can be divided into two basic categories: those who divide things into two basic categories, and those who don't."*
— *Jim Bianchi*

HANDGUN, as a term, seems to become more difficult to pin down and define as the years march along. Nearly any definition that comes to mind has exceptions that tend to confuse the issue. If you'll be so kind and understanding as to accept that the comments here are not unfailingly valid, and that not every possible exception will be noted, detailed and ramified, we'll have a go at kicking the subject about.

Ostensibly a handgun — sometimes written hand gun — is a firearm or allied device for launching projectiles, capable of being operated while held in one hand. It does not (usually) incorporate an extended stock intended to be held against the shoulder when being shot. Its barrel is (usually) less than sixteen inches in length. Its overall length is less than 26½ inches. It has a rifled bore that can, does, and will impart a rotational force to the projectile(s).

It should be noted that we are talking in terms of handguns as viewed by laws of the USA. Other countries can, may, and quite probably do see things in any number of different lights.

By those standards a rifle has a barrel measuring sixteen inches or more in length; a shotgun has a barrel eighteen inches or more in length; and both must measure 26½ inches or more in overall length. Shotguns and rifles can and usually do have shoulder stocks. Rifles have rifled barrels, while shotguns are smoothbores. There are no legal restrictions as to maximum barrel length for a handgun, nor on minimum barrel length, comes to that. If it pleases your fancy you can have, own and operate a handgun with a forty-eight-inch barrel, or one even longer. You

Top, as discussed, the Remington Model 600 rifle was designed from the action of their XP-100 pistol.

Although the Wilkinson Arms Terry carbine resembles their Linda pistol (both in 9mm) the latter has an action different from the Terry.

may have a little trouble locating it, but if you find one it's perfectly legal.

It is not legal to convert a rifle or a shotgun into a handgun by shortening the barrel and/or removing the shoulder stock. With a few qualifications it is not legal to attach a shoulder stock to a handgun. Exceptions here are certain curios, as defined by the authorities in charge of such things, for possession by collectors. A shoulder stock can and may be attached to a handgun if it has a barrel more than sixteen inches long and if that barrel is rifled; or eighteen-plus inches long for a smoothbore. Again, the final assembly must be 26½ inches or more in overall length.

Exceptions to the foregoing and other restrictions are not necessarily illegal, *per se*. It is, rather, that they fall under the conditions of the Federal Firearms Act of 1934 and are thus subject to payment of a $200 transfer tax, along with the requisite paperwork, permits, forms and associated red tape. That is the federal viewpoint, subject to quibbles from the state of your residence.

There are no specific restrictions against converting a handgun into a rifle or, for that matter, a shotgun. As an example of how that works, back in the early Sixties Remington designed their Model XP-100 pistol and, once that was done, went on to produce their Model 600 rifle based upon and around the same basic action. Had they brought out the Model 600, then the XP-100, *that* would have been a federal no-no. If you begin to perceive a fine, foamy froth of illogic in all this, I'm relieved that you've noticed it.

Let us move away from the arrant perplexery, before your eyes and mine become permanently crossed, and go on to review some of the basic categories and sub-groups of

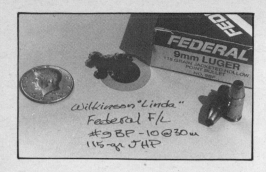

The 9mm Linda fires from a closed bolt with exceptional accuracy and a half-dollar hides 10-shot 30-meter group entirely, using Bushnell scope.

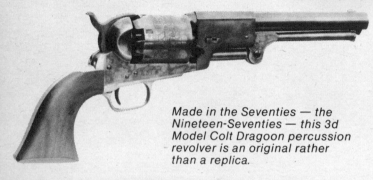

Made in the Seventies — the Nineteen-Seventies — this 3d Model Colt Dragoon percussion revolver is an original rather than a replica.

handguns. The first fork in the road is the one that separates the muzzleloaders and their conceptual kin from those handguns that operate with what is termed fixed ammunition or, more commonly, cartridges. You'll find that the hand-stuffed guns using old-fashioned black gunpowder come under a somewhat different set of rules than those applying to cartridge guns. As we're not concerned with the former here we'll move on to look at the latter.

Or should we make note of the distinction between firearms, including the black-powder burners, as contrasted to powderless guns such as air guns and the like? The latter would include those that propel projectiles by releasing controlled amounts of carbon dioxide or by the harnessing of other forces. Let's keep it to cartridge-using firearms, lest we get hopelessly lost in a sea of tangents.

Having settled that here comes another fork in the road: We have single-shots, and then there are repeaters. The latter are capable of firing two or more shots before needing to be reloaded. In the outer examples there are repeaters capable of shooting 177 times before requiring

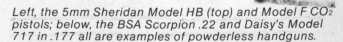

Left, the 5mm Sheridan Model HB (top) and Model F $CO_2$ pistols; below, the BSA Scorpion .22 and Daisy's Model 717 in .177 all are examples of powderless handguns.

*Nearly a pistol but technically a shotgun, the .410 bore Snake Charmer can be fired effectively with one hand.*

replenishment of the magazine, and guns of greater capacity may be just around the corner.

That's one way of dividing things, but then we have the consideration as to whether the gun uses ammunition that is of the rimfire or center-fire persuasion. Center-fire ammo in turn breaks down into Boxer-primed and Berdan-primed sub-groups, and we'll beam a bit of light on that difference a bit later.

That gives us two possible variants of the single-shot, which we'll put on hold for the moment and press on to the repeaters, both rimfire and center-fire. Yes, if you were about to ask, I regard it as insensately illogical to use a hyphen in one and omit it in the other, but that seems to be the sanctioned usage.

I guess we could break down the repeaters into two sub-groups: manually actuated and self actuated. In the former we'd have nearly all the revolvers (except for the Webley-Fosbery automatic revolver, long since extinct), as well as a few of the eccentric designs that more or less resemble autoloaders but aren't quite. One fast example of that uncommon breed is the Semmerling Model LM-4 pistol that handles the .45 Automatic Colt Pistol (ACP) cartridge. After firing the round in the chamber the shooter must shuck the slide forward and then back again to eject the spent case and chamber a fresh round from the magazine. You could term that a pump-action pistol I guess. The principle is quite common in shotguns and less so in rifles, but extremely rare in handguns.

Let's take up the revolvers and come back to the autoloaders in just a bit. They subdivide into rimfire and center-

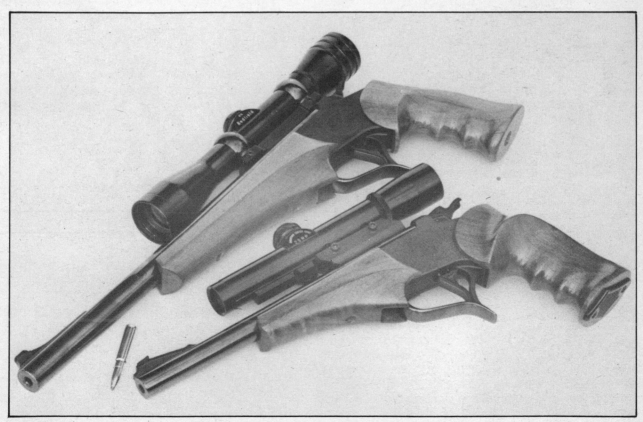

*A brace of Thompson/Center Contender single-shot pistols with 10- and 14-inch bull barrels, scopes by Redfield and T/C; both handling the 7mm T/CU cartridge lying between the muzzles. The Contender swaps barrels for great versatility.*

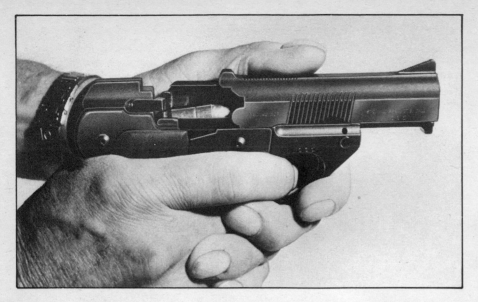

Semmerling LM-4 in .45 ACP is a novel pump-action repeater, not an autoloader. Photo left shows how its slide is shucked forward to function. Below, for size comparison, the LM-4 and .38 Spl Colt Detective Special with its two-inch barrel.

fire, of course, and split up further into single-action and double-action variants.

Briefly the difference is that the single-action must be cocked manually, by thumbing its hammer back to full-cock position for each shot. With a double-action, you can do it that way or, as you wish, you can just give a longer, harder pull of the trigger and that makes the hammer move rearward and drop to fire the cartridge after it's reached the let-off point.

Again we have exceptions: The police department of at least one major city had so many problems with officers who cocked their double-action revolvers and then fired them unintentionally that they converted all of their nom-inally double-action (DA) revolvers to single-action (SA) mode. That doesn't mean what you might assume. The modification involved removal of the nominal SA notch on the hammer so that the revolver could be fired solely by the long pull of the trigger that is usually termed DA. Since the modified guns had only one option they were SA, with a

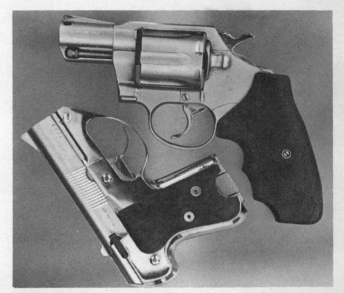

long, hard pull. As I understand, it did reduce the number of incidents involving accidental discharges of duty weapons, but it certainly didn't simplify discussions such as this one.

If the hammer of a normal DA revolver is cocked and fired in the SA mode, the trigger pull is much shorter and lighter, usually increasing its potential accuracy to a useful extent. That is not to insinuate that accuracy is a hopeless dream if the firing is done in DA mode. Some DA revolv-ers have amazingly smooth and easy trigger pulls in that mode. If you inch the shooting hand around a little, so as to get the tip of the trigger finger to make contact with the frame just prior to let-off, it is possible to fire a good DA revolver with accuracy rivaling that of nearly any SA

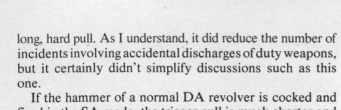

A New Model Ruger Super Blackhawk .44 magnum single-action, here in limited custom Mag-na-port Classic edition, with gold-plated touches.

*Five photos above and at right show a stop-action sequence of a revolver being fired in double-action mode. Gun has just "fired" in photo number 4, followed by letting the trigger go forward for the next shot. Note how cylinder moves 1/6-turn during sequence.*

design. Yes, it does take practice, but it can be done and it is a most useful aptitude:

Broadly speaking — that is, ignoring possible exceptions — a SA revolver is usually loaded by swinging out the loading gate and stuffing a cartridge into each chamber in turn as the cylinder is rotated. The loading gate is located at the rear of the cylinder on the right-hand side, with few if any exceptions. The hammer must be drawn to the rear slightly to facilitate cylinder rotation. After firing, the empty cases are punched out of each chamber in turn by means of an ejector rod located beneath the barrel.

To load or reload a DA revolver the cylinder latch is actuated, permitting the cylinder to pivot outward to the left on its crane. If fired cases are in the chambers a rearward push of the ejector rod expels them by moving the extractor star. The fresh rounds are inserted into the chambers, either one at a time or with the aid of a speedloader, and the cylinder pivots back into place for further firing. As you may imagine, reloading a DA revolver is considerably faster than the same chore for a SA desgin.

*Here's the same customized Chuck Ward .38 Special, aka Li'l Montgomery, with its hammer cocked in readiness to be fired in single-action mode. The tiny gap visible here between trigger stop and trigger guard is all the movement required to fire this gun in SA mode.*

On S&W revolvers, the small catch just below the hammer is pushed forward to release the cylinder so it can be swung out to eject fired cases or reload with cartridges.

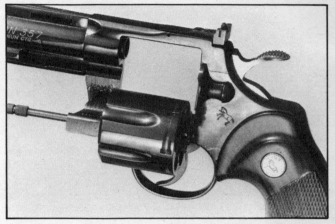

A similar catch on Colt revolvers, such as this Python, is pulled rearward to release the cylinder. As discussed, the cylinder of a revolver should be opened and closed gently to avoid serious wear and damage; never with a snap.

Cylinder latch of DA Rugers, such as this Redhawk .44 mag, is pressed inward at rear to unlock cylinder, as here.

Charter Arms revolvers open either by pushing the catch forward or by pulling forward on the ejector rod.

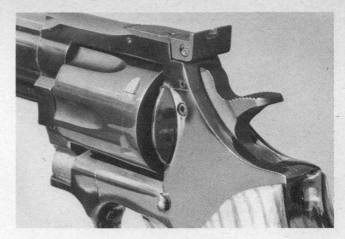

Revolvers from Dan Wesson Arms open by pressing down on the small catch visible here just ahead of the cylinder.

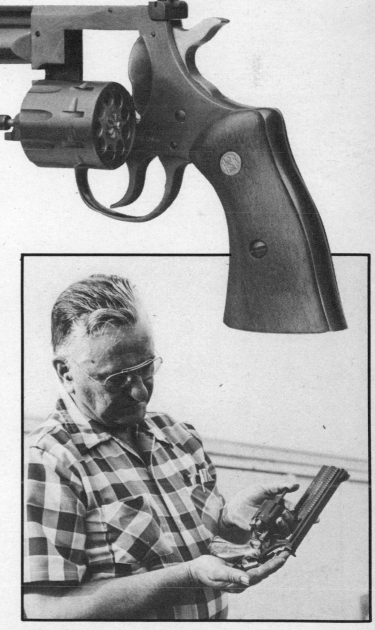

Harrington & Richardson revolvers such as this one open by pulling forward on the ejector rod, visible here beneath the barrel and just ahead of the cylinder.

The cylinder latches on DA revolvers present an appearance that suggests they could be safety catches, a device commonly found on autoloading pistols. Presumably that accounts for the unsettling frequency with which characters in mystery stories pause to check the safety on their revolvers, or perhaps pull out the clip and look at that. As a group mystery writers appear to know less about firearms in general and handguns in specific particular than, for example, nasturtiums know about the theory of relativity. One needs but to read a few mystery stories to have this observation redundantly proven.

Curiously enough there have been a few revolvers that did actually have safeties in the true sense of the term. None of these proved popular or saw wide purchase and use. A revolver has little or no need of a safety, as such. If the hammer is down — on the majority of modern revolver designs, and note the following exceptions! — it can't fire without a deliberate pull of the trigger. If the hammer is back it can be lowered — with all possible care! — if the shooter decides not to fire, and once down the revolver is back in as safe a mode as it's apt to get.

As discussed in the next chapter the older SA revolver designs are most prudently carried with an empty chamber beneath the hammer, since a blow in the hammer spur can and sometimes has set off a live round beneath it. Newer

Ejecting spent cases from a .44 mag Chuck Ward bowling pin gun on Model 29 S&W frame. Note how the gun is held to avoid dropping it; bad news with a $2400 gun!

Safety catch on this pre-WWII Colt Woodsman .22 auto prevents firing when pushed upward (left) and unlocks sear to permit gun to fire when pushed down (below). Other auto pistols have varying arrangements for the safety catch, but this is typical.

**CRUSADER**
**LARGE FRAME**

The High Standard Crusader was designed and is in limited production; one of the rare modern revolvers having a safety catch.

SA designs incorporate a transfer bar arrangement that neutralizes this particular hazard. As a gunowner it is your responsibility to learn the details regarding your gun(s), handling it or them accordingly.

As a category revolvers are probably the most reliable and troublefree type of repeating pistol. They are not totally so — hardly any mechanical device is. The tip of the firing pin can break off unnoticed, leaving you with a formidable-looking paperweight. Experimental lubricants employed injudiciously can solidify inside the works, freezing up the mechanism that rotates and/or locks the cylinder in position. Unburned granules of powder can and sometimes do get beneath the extractor star preventing easy rotation. A primer on a reload seated insufficiently can interfere with cylinder rotation, and a loosely held

Above, most modern revolvers such as this S&W K-frame are designed with blocking devices to prevent firing if the spur of the hammer is struck. Others such as the Ruger Redhawk, left, have a transfer bar that must be raised (arrow) for gun to fire by deliberate trigger pull.

Although revolvers usually are more reliable than auto pistols, defects can put them out of action too. Arrow indicates broken tip of the firing pin, left, as contrasted to normal pin in the photo above. Tip of pin must protrude through recoil plate (photo below left) in order to strike the primer of the cartridge and fire it.

bullet in the neck of the case can migrate forward from stress of recoil to project form the front of the chamber, effectively preventing the cylinder from rotating when its turn comes to fire and thus tying up the gun. As if that were not enough the ejector rod can come partially unscrewed on some makes and models, again causing difficulty in closing the action or in cylinder rotation, or both.

A good feature of the revolver is that a dud round does not cause a stoppage the way it would in an autoloading pistol. A second DA pull brings the next round into position and fires it. That is not unalloyed good news, sad to say. If the dud had sufficient spunk to drive its bullet up into

the barrel, firing a normal round against the lodged bullet quite probably would cause damage to the gun and perhaps to the shooter or bystanders as well.

Some of the revolvers designed for use with the .22 long rifle — a rimfire cartridge — have cylinders with up to nine-shot capacity, Most revolvers hold six rounds, although one is wise to restrict the old SA designs to only five as noted. A few of the smaller revolvers have five-shot cylinders and the Freedom Arms miniatures for the .22 rimfire magnum cartridge have four-shot cylinders.

The majority of autoloading pistols offer magazine capacities exceeding those of comparable revolvers. In most

Here the arrow indicates the amount of protrusion of the tip of the firing pin during a normal firing cycle. When the trigger is released firing pin retracts and is blocked.

Circle indicates a granule of unburned powder that got under the extractor star to prevent cylinder from being closed properly. Loose ejector rod has same effect.

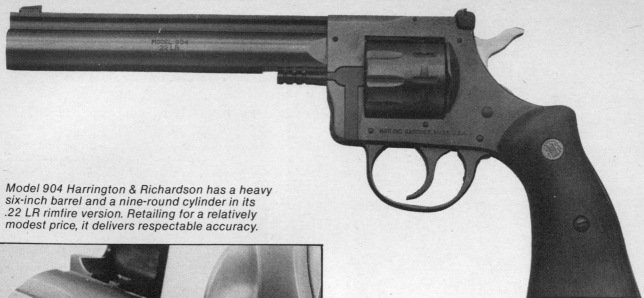

Model 904 Harrington & Richardson has a heavy six-inch barrel and a nine-round cylinder in its .22 LR rimfire version. Retailing for a relatively modest price, it delivers respectable accuracy.

instances the magazine holds some given number and you have the option of carrying one more round in the chamber. Thus the familiar Colt Model 1911-type service pistol can be loaded with seven rounds in its magazine and an eighth in its chamber. Other auto pistols can handle a lot more than that, usually by means of a staggered-column magazine that makes the butt of the gun a trifle difficult to grasp comfortably, especially if you have a small hand.

While there are the inevitable exceptions here is how a typical autoloading pistol operates: One or more cartridges are loaded into the magazine, the magazine is inserted into its well — usually a tunnel up through the handle — and pushed upward to lock it securely in place by the magazine catch. The slide or bolt of the gun is grasped and dragged rearward to the full extent of its travel, then released. The recoil spring, which was compressed further when the slide was dragged back, drives the slide forward and scoops a cartridge out of the magazine, pushing it up the feed ramp and into the chamber. In the process of doing all that the hammer or striker has been cocked so that only what we'd term a SA pull of the trigger is needed to fire the round.

Upon firing the force of recoil drives the slide rearward, ejecting the empty case, coming to a stop, then moving forward to repeat the chambering cycle, once again cocking the hammer.

Most auto pistol designs have a small device usually

Astra's Model A-80 is an example of the DA auto with staggered-column magazines that are becoming quite popular. This one's in 9mm; also in .38 Super, .45 ACP.

*No longer made, The Auto Mag was a large, powerful auto that required its magazine catch be fastened securely lest recoil lift the gun, leaving the magazine neatly suspended in midair, as in this 1/1000-second shot below!*

termed a disconnector. Its function is to prevent the next round from firing until after the trigger has been released and pulled again. If the gun continues to fire as long as the trigger is held back, you have a fully-automatic design. Those are rather difficult to control and they are subject to the same Firearms Act of 1934 as the stocked handguns discussed previously. Again, a $200 transfer fee and a lot of paperwork are involved but it can be done if you live in one of the more permissive states. Arizona is such a state, for example, and California is not.

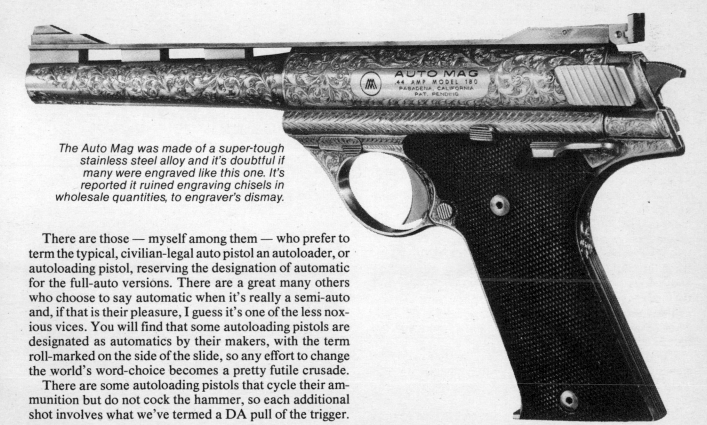

*The Auto Mag was made of a super-tough stainless steel alloy and it's doubtful if many were engraved like this one. It's reported it ruined engraving chisels in wholesale quantities, to engraver's dismay.*

There are those — myself among them — who prefer to term the typical, civilian-legal auto pistol an autoloader, or autoloading pistol, reserving the designation of automatic for the full-auto versions. There are a great many others who choose to say automatic when it's really a semi-auto and, if that is their pleasure, I guess it's one of the less noxious vices. You will find that some autoloading pistols are designated as automatics by their makers, with the term roll-marked on the side of the slide, so any effort to change the world's word-choice becomes a pretty futile crusade.

There are some autoloading pistols that cycle their ammunition but do not cock the hammer, so each additional shot involves what we've termed a DA pull of the trigger.

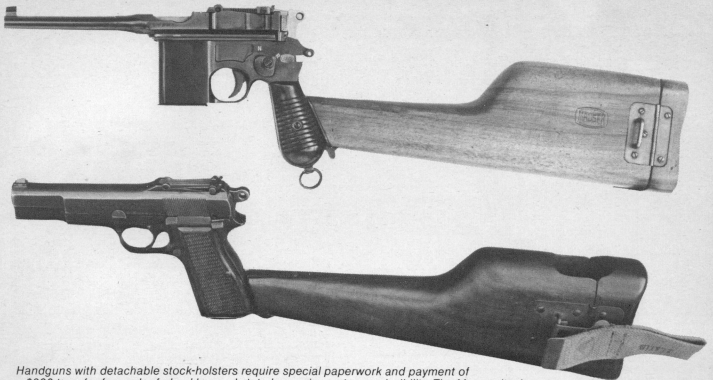

Handguns with detachable stock-holsters require special paperwork and payment of a $200 transfer fee under federal law and state law varies as to permissibility. The Mauser (top) has a fire-selector lever to change from semi-auto to full-auto mode. The Browning Model 1935 Hi-Power in 9mm (lower) is straight semi-auto but has an adjustable rear sight for long-range work. (J. Curtis Earl Collection.)

Examples of that would include the Thomas .45, now discontinued, and the Heckler & Koch Model VP70Z chambered for the 9mm Luger cartridge.

As may be discussed in the following chapter on handgun safety, it is prudent practice to make certain that the muzzle of an autoloading pistol is pointed in a safe direction when you let the slide bang forward to put a live round into its chamber. There is always the outside chance that worn and/or defective parts could allow the chambered round to fire. This does not occur frequently, but it does

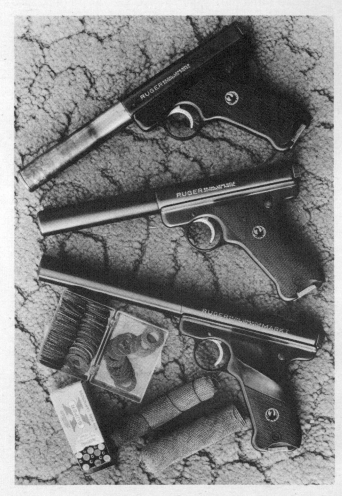

Above and at right are samples of Ruger .22 auto pistols fitted with silencers, aka suppressors. They are from the collection of Phoenix, AZ, machine gun dealer J. Curtis Earl, who is holding the one in the photo above.

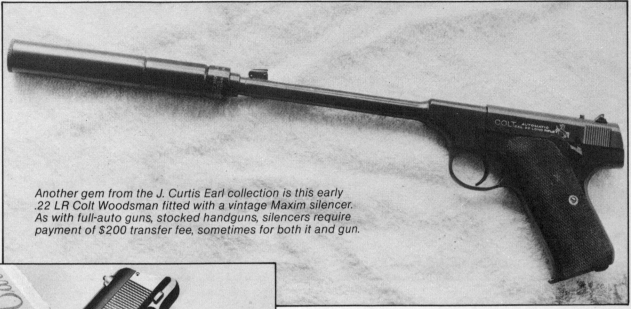

*Another gem from the J. Curtis Earl collection is this early .22 LR Colt Woodsman fitted with a vintage Maxim silencer. As with full-auto guns, stocked handguns, silencers require payment of $200 transfer fee, sometimes for both it and gun.*

*The now-discontinued Thomas .45 cycled its loads in the semi-auto mode by means of a locking lug operated by what one might take to be the grip safety (it wasn't). Each shot was fired by a full double-action trigger pull.*

occur sometimes. For example, it happened to me exactly once in the past fifty-eight years and a bit, but I'm still deeply grateful that the muzzle wasn't pointed where a hole would have caused anguish or discomfiture. I note that here, perhaps redundantly, on the chance that some reader may skip over the next chapter.

If you reload your own cartridges, as discussed in chapter 6, it is possible and sometimes advantageous to load down to levels that will not actuate the feeding cycle. In such an example the spent case remains in the chamber after firing and can be ejected manually by retracting the slide, with the next live round being chambered when the slide is released. Odd as it may seem that can be useful if, for example, you are at pains to avoid the loss of any spent cases. Ejected brass tends to gravitate toward the tallest, thickest cover it can reach, or so it seems. If you're working with cartridge cases that have to be made up with consider-

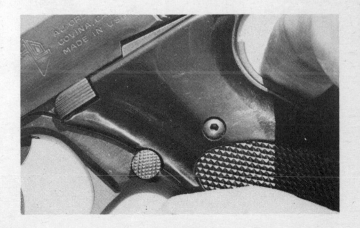

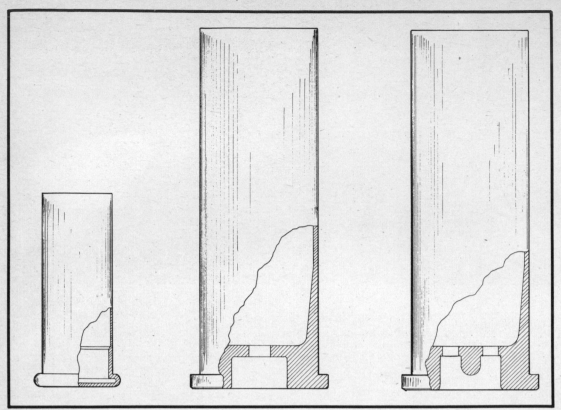

Courtesy of Omark/CCI-Speer, here are cross-sectional drawings illustrating the concept of rimfire cases (left), and center-fire in the Boxer (center) and Berdan (right) types. Since the Boxer primer has its own integral anvil, it's the only type that's practical for reloading.

able effort — such as the .38-45 Clerke, discussed in chapter 6 — the loss of even one tends to taint your entire day unpleasant.

To this point we've said little about the distinctions between rimfire and center-fire beyond grumbling about the arbitrary inconsistency of terminology. The difference is clearly shown in the accompanying set of line drawings. A rimfire round has its priming compound distributed about the entire periphery of its hollow rim. Priming compound has the useful property of taking fire when crushed abrupt-

ly, producing a flame that ignites the main powder charge. The molecules of the powder contan enough atoms of oxygen in their makeup to burn most vigorously, with no need of oxygen from the surrounding air. That happy state of affairs is what makes firearms operate. Modern powders are usually based upon a chemical compound called nitrocellulose, often wth some percentage of nitroglycerin added. Powders that contan nitroglycerin are termed double-base, those without are called single-base. Both types usually incorporate small amounts of other chemicals,

*Since recoil-operated auto pistols require a solid hold to assure reliable functioning, they must be gripped securely and sometimes even that is not enough as in this case. The shooter, Magali Akle, is using the proper "weasel choking" hold, but this round hung up anyway.*

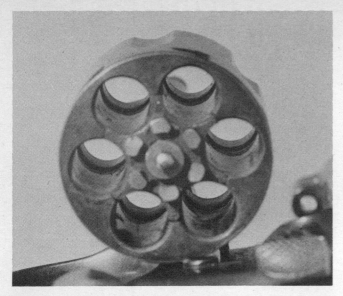

Revolver chambers have sections of smaller diameter ahead of the case mouth to prevent bullet expansion at that point, as in photo, delivering bullet intact to cone.

Here's a view of the forcing cone at the rear of a revolver barrel, designed to ease the bullet into the rifling as gently as possible. Fouling buildup here will degrade accuracy.

added to modify the burning properties and other ballistic characteristics. Such powders are properly termed nitro powders and more popularly, if less precisely, "smokeless" powders, despite the obvious fact that some amount of smoke is usually visible when they are fired.

The basic principle of the center-fire cartridge is quite similar to that of the rimfire. A wafer of priming compound is positioned in the shallow metal cup of the primer and upon being seated is held against an anvil under some amount of pre-stressing pressure. The tip of the firing pin strikes the center of the outside of the primer cup, indenting it to crush the priming compound against the anvil, causing

the priming compound to detonate and ignite the main powder charge.

The foregoing applies to both the Boxer and Berdan types of center-fire primers. The distinction is that the Boxer primer carries its own anvil, whereas the Berdan primer is designed for use with a cartridge case that has an integral anvil. Cases intended for use with Boxer primers have a single, central flash hole. Cases for Berdan primers have at least two smaller flash holes, off-center within the case head.

Curiously enough the Berdan primer was invented and developed in this country, while the Boxer primer is an

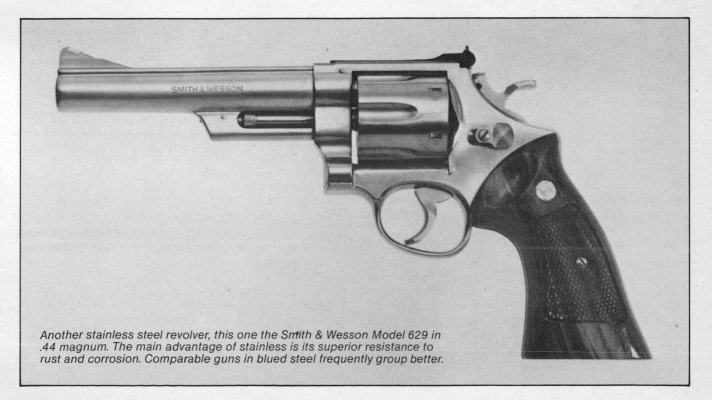

Another stainless steel revolver, this one the Smith & Wesson Model 629 in .44 magnum. The main advantage of stainless is its superior resistance to rust and corrosion. Comparable guns in blued steel frequently group better.

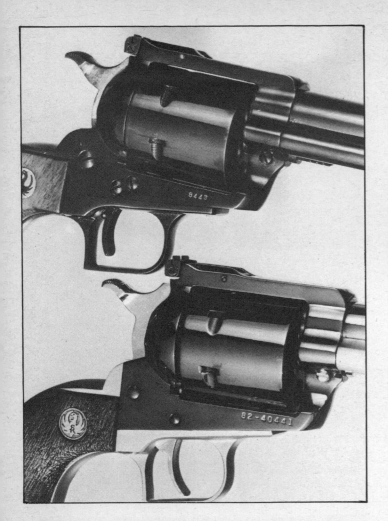

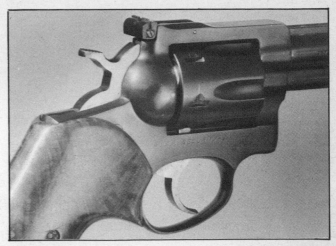

An Old Model Ruger Super Blackhawk (top) of about 1962 vintage, compared to the New Model. Note distinctive three screw heads in OM vs. two pin ends in NM and comparative positions of the triggers. The NM has the transfer-bar modification (as on page 14) permitting safe carrying of a live round beneath the hammer: A practice that is extremely dangerous on SA revolvers without the transfer-bar feature, as discussed in Ch. 2. Below, it's important to be thoroughly familiar with the direction of cylinder rotation in any given revolver. The round visible here is next-to-fire in Ruger Security-Six.

Weight at muzzle steadies aim, tames recoil. Muzzle of regular bull-barrel for T/C Contender at left, untapered "Full-Bull" at right, both in ten-inch barrel lengths.

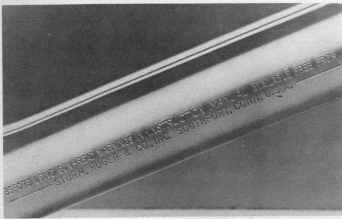

Recent production of Ruger handguns carries a notice roll-marked on the barrel to read the instruction manual, noting they'll send a free copy if you don't have one.

European creation. Paradoxically the Boxer primer is now in wide use here, while the Berdan primer is the one commonly found in European center-fire ammo, as well as that produced in most other areas of the globe.

The significant distinction is that Boxer-primed cases are readily reloadable, by means of a decapping pin that goes down through the center of the case to knock out the spent primer when the spent case is put through a loading press. It is fairly obvious that a loading die for decapping Berdan primers would have to have two or more decapping pins and they would not work unless the case was properly oriented to the die when put into the loading press.

It is possible to reload Berdan-primed cases, but it is damnably difficult and tedious, requiring special equipment to get the spent primers out, specialized primers and additional equipment to reprime the case. Reloading Berdan-primed cases, as a direct result, is not a widespread practice.

As I've noted in several previous books and, with a bit of good fortune, may say again in some yet to come, it is not impossible to reload rimfire cases. It is, however, an even bigger bucket of snakes than reloading Berdan-primed brass. It is also a pursuit somewhat fraught with peril, and most emphatically not recommended!

*Called the COP, for Compact Offduty Pistol, this is a novel four-barrel derringer in .357 magnum, firing each barrel in sequence by means of a full double-action trigger pull. Bottom, the Wildey is an innovative gas-operated auto. It fires two Winchester magnum cartridges of 9mm and .45 diameter. Not as yet in production, its future is a little uncertain to the present.*

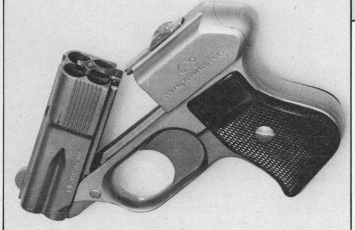

Rimfire cartridges have been made in a wide variety of different sizes and bullet diameters and weights. Some of those are long-gone, some remain in more or less good supply and popular use. The king of them all is the .22 long rifle, packing a bullet that weighs around 39 or 40 grains, in the longer of the two common case lengths. The .22 short carries a bullet of about 29 grains, in the shorter of the two common lengths. At one time there were BB caps and CB caps in a case even stubbier than that of the .22 short, but they are seen little if ever these latter days. A further variant, not especially popular and perhaps doomed to early extinction, is the .22 long, which puts a 29-grain bullet in the longer case without accomplishing much of a

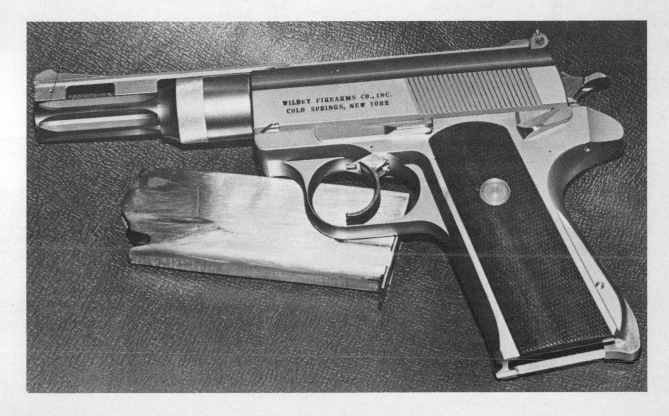

*Originally made in .380 auto, AMT now has their little Back Up auto in .22 LR; it holds more and kicks less!*

useful nature. As a further offshoot we had CCI's Mini-Caps, a 29-grain bullet put up in the longer length of case with a truly miserly ration of propellant so that velocities are quite diffident. They subtitle these as *zimmer patrone* (not *patronen*), which my dubious *ausland Deutsch* roughly translates to "room cartridge," as for firing indoors.

There are fully double-gaited guns that can shift with cheerful aplomb from rimfire to center-fire and back again, as the shooter's fancy wills. The Thompson/Center Contender is a prime example. It features a pair of firing pins, one for each use, along with a circular inset in the business

*A recent handgun trend has been what we might term the assault pistol such as Model KG-9 Interdynamic in 9mm modeled by Magali Akle, really wearing ear-muffs! The KG-9 fires from an open bolt, delivering large groups.*

*Here's one of two Mag-na-port recoil-cutting ports on Model 29 S&W customized by Austin Behlert. As the beefy snubbie uses .44 mag, you need all help possible.*

Various views of the un-numbered prototype for the Mag-na-port Classic series, with the others numbered 1 to 200. Such guns are created more as objets d'art than shooters, with touches of gold and, of course, Mag-na-porting at the muzzle. Produced in 1978, this gun has never been cocked. If I want to shoot a Super Blackhawk, I've got good old #8448, a super-tackster!

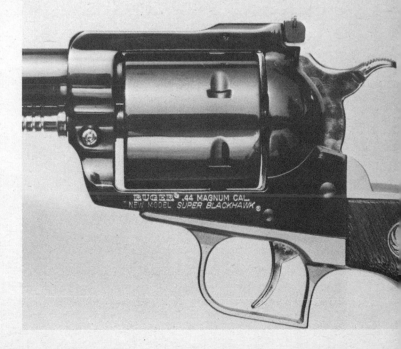

end of the hammer that can be rotated half a turn with a screwdriver to strike one firing pin and not bother the other. If the Contender is not the world's most versatile handgun, I can't imagine what might ace it out. Its barrels are interchangeable and available in a bewildering profusion of standard and more or less unlikely chamberings.

I can, if the fancy goads, pick up one Contender receiver, fit it with a .22 long rifle barrel and use it to fire the CCI Mini-Cap or someone else's .22 short. Then, in the space of hardly over a minute, I can swap barrels, flip the hammer insert and come roaring forth with a 400-grain behemoth of a bullet at close up around 2000 feet per second (fps). The first you can hardly hear; the second you can barely bear, if that. Versatile? Umm, yass!

Rimfire cartridges as a class do not muster impressive amounts of put-down. Their intrinsic potential for accuracy at moderate ranges can hardly be faulted. I have a High Standard Victor that carries a 4X Leupold scope.

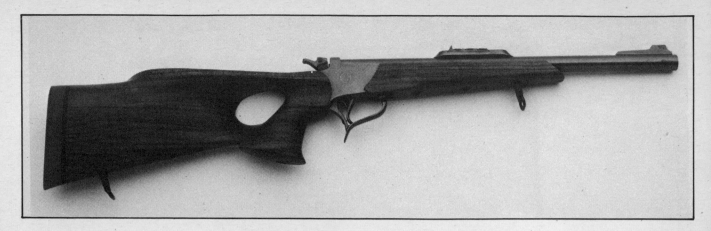

A while back Lee Jurras made up some Howdah pistols on the T/C Contender, chambered for monster loads. A few were fitted with 16-inch barrels and stocks to make into burly little carbines. Yes, the kick is pretty fierce!

With its favorite fodder, the CCI Green Tag target load, it will usually clump them inside an inch at a distance of fifty yards. It will do about the same with any of several other precision-grade .22 long rifle loads. If you can condone a mention of long guns, I have a Winchester Model 75 — the poor man's Model 52 — that will put them into .25-inch at fifty yards, practically everything into one caliber .38 hole. It has a long barrel, out to around twenty-six inches or so, and some of the CCI Mini-Caps out of that rifle are barely audible, at least if you're burdened with ears like I have. It is about the closest thing to a legal silencer that I know about.

Speaking of silencers, that brings us to another mystery writers' favorite. Sinister characters in the corpse-opera genre are forever pausing to screw a silencer into the muzzle of their revolver before pressing on to commit their deeds of darkest dastardy. To purloin a choice term from friend Tom Ferguson, that is pure roachmilk.

A revolver has — with the inevitable exception — some perceptible amount of gap between the front of its cylinder and the back of its barrel. As the bullet sizzles past that point, the pressures from the burning powder are still quite close to their peak. The leakage comes roaring out of both

The .44 magnum is a versatile round used in all four guns above: Ruger carbine, Super Blackhawk, S&W Model 29s in 6½ and 4-inch barrel lengths. Best grouper is the SBH.

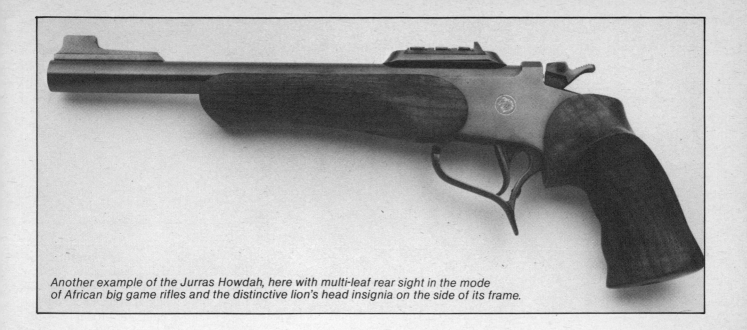

*Another example of the Jurras Howdah, here with multi-leaf rear sight in the mode of African big game rifles and the distinctive lion's head insignia on the side of its frame.*

sides. It is quite possible to photograph the fiery plumes on fast film if the revolver is held on its side and fired in total darkness. They gush forth a foot or more to each side. If you screwed the world's greatest silencer onto the muzzle, it wouldn't begin to mute down the uproar from the gas leak at the gap.

The exception just noted would be a revolver set up to handle Robert Olsen's Invicta cartridge. A typical example of that would have a .44 magnum case that holds a .357 bullet neatly centered in a sort of bushing made of plastic. The cylinder would be for .44 magnum, but the barrel

*A recent offering from Colt was this cased Python Hunter kit with a scope on an 8-inch Python, retailing for $1095.*

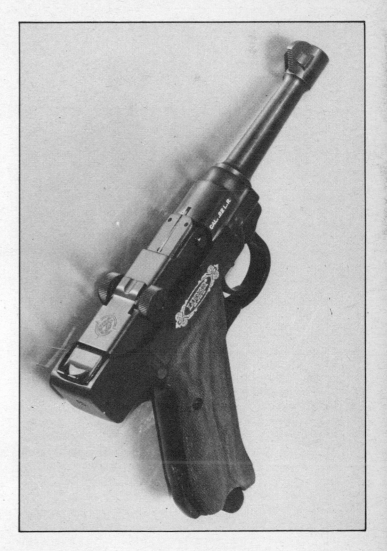

*The .22 LR Luger, made in the USA by Stoeger. It follows the general looks of its German namesake closely and is a better grouper than any original I've tried!*

The gun started its career as a Model 28 S&W Highway Patrolman in .357 mag. Leon Smith of Redding, CA, used Dan Wesson Arms barrel shrouds to convert it to .41 mag with 3 interchangeable barrels. Not shown is a 16-inch barrel which, once installed, makes a shoulder-stocked carbine. I call this my SS&WW...

would be of .357 dimensions. When the round is fired the plastic sleeve or bushing moves forward and effectively seals the gap at the front of the cylinder as the bullet continues on down the barrel.

Silencers, sometimes called noise suppressors, are not too effective if the velocity of the bullet exceeds the speed of sound. A fairly close approximation of the speed of sound through atmosphere can be obtained by subtracting 32 from the temperature reading in degrees Fahrenheit, then adding 1086. As an example, if the ambient temperature is 74°F, you'd subtract 32 and add the remaining 42 to 1086, arriving at a figure of 1128 feet per second.

A muzzle velocity of 1128 fps is relatively small cheese in terms of fairly high-performance handgun loads, although many of the milder ones fall below that level. If the bullet goes faster than the speed of sound through air, sometimes termed MACH One, it produces a small-scale but highly audible sonic boom in its passage through the air. Even if you muted every last decibel of sound from the escaping powder gases, the whippy crack of the bullet's flight could still be heard and nothing much can be done about it.

As with stocked handguns and full-automatic guns silencers are not illegal in themselves, but subject to the $200 transfer tax and attendant red tapery. There are at present no restrictions against silencers when installed on air guns, and a few enterprising manufacturers have marketed air-gun silencers. I have no information on how many they've sold, but suspect it is something less than a land-office business.

It is faintly ironic to reflect that a defective muffler on your motor vehicle can earn you a citation for excessive noise, but on the other hand an effective muffler on a firearm, if not backed by the appropriate paperwork, can get you some deep rumbles with the law. Since a sound level of ninety decibels is usually regarded as the point at which noise becomes hazardous to hearing acuity, it would be nice if silencers were permissible, provided they muted the report of the gun down to around ninety decibels, which is still far from sneaky, soundwise. I do not expect to see such a sensible approach adopted in the foreseeable future.

Being engaged in my slightly unlikely line of work, it is a fairly frequent occurrence for friends and acquaintances to quiz me as to my recommendations on the best handgun for them to purchase to have on hand in the event of dire need.

My instinctive reaction on being asked such a question is somewhat akin to that of the late, great Louie Armstrong when someone asked him to define jazz music. His response reputedly was, "If you have to ask, you'll never know."

I've never actually given that answer because I consider it objectionably flip and non-responsive. A question honestly and sincerely asked deserves an answer in kind.

In sober truth, however, I've yet to formulate an answer

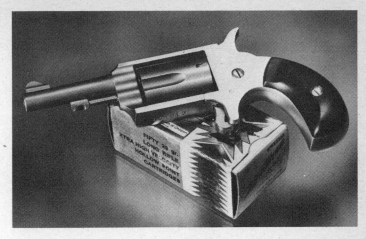

*Nearly as small as they get, here's Freedom Arms' Model FA-L for .22 Short/LR, weighs just 4¼ ounces.*

with which I feel entirely satisfied. Since most such questioners are not malodorously wealthy, cost is an obvious consideration. Handguns as a general category have become *expensive* little dingbats at this point in the inflationary spiral.

If the questioner is of the personality matrix that is apt to go out and fire the gun for the sheer fun of doing so, it sim-

*The four-inch barrel length is a popular choice in revolvers since it is a good compromise between compactness and capability. The Model 15 S&W at right in .38 Special is termed their Combat Masterpiece; Model 24 next to it in .44 Special is the Model 1950 Target; the hard-chromed specimen is a considerably reworked Model 1917 in .45 ACP or .45 Auto Rim. Model 66 S&W at left in stainless is for .357 magnum, will also handle the .38 Special.*

S&W Model 25 above fires either .45 ACP or Auto Rim cartridges. Twin fitted cylinders for Ruger Blackhawk left are chambered for your choice of .45 ACP or the .45 Colt, aka .45 Long Colt. Both offer flexibility.

A close look at the novel front-locking system on the Ruger .44 mag Redhawk. Recess in the frame below the barrel, left, accepts the locking lug, right, that is retracted when the cylinder locking catch is depressed, permitting the cylinder to swing out for loading.

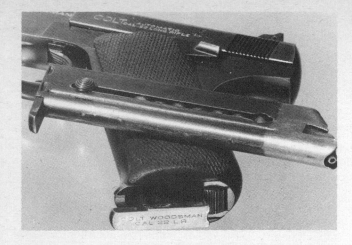

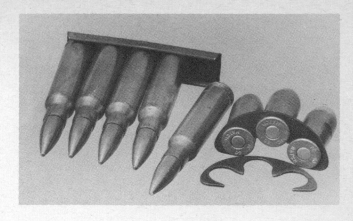

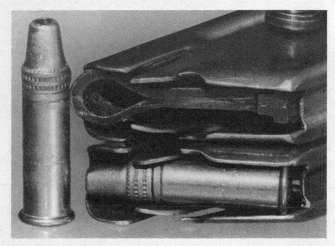

Although often called "clips," the items left and below are more accurately termed magazines. A true clip is a gizmo that grips cartridges by the heads, as in the photo above. Design, shape and condition of magazine lips is crucially important for reliable functioning and this pair for the old Colt Woodsman work very well. The .22 LR ammo shown here is Remington's remarkable Yellow Jacket which exits the 4½-inch Colt at 1195 fps.

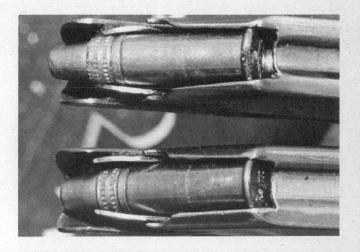

plifies the matter greatly. If it seems likely that they will buy one gun and one box of cartridges and fire the first round out of it in the throes of a dire, last-ditch emergency, I experience qualms and reservations about recommending any gun at all. If an assailant threatens and you produce a gun, but can't muster the necesary visceral determination to use it, the aforesaid assailant may wrest it away from you. If that happens the odds are good that you will then be assailed by your own gun, causing you to regret that you ever bought it in the first place.

These are the things I think about when hit with that question, which happens about a dozen times in the average year. If the person has little or no familiarity with firearms I am reluctant to suggest an autoloading pistol for the simple reason that such a gun requires a technical familiarity that's apt to be beyond their easy grasp. The auto pistol expects and requires a minimum level of expertise on the part of its user.

I prefer to suggest a competent revolver in the vicinity of .38 Special or .357 magnum with a barrel length around three or four inches. As a usual thing I go on to suggest something along the lines of a Ruger Speed-Six with its fixed sights. At this point I'd like to note that I own no stock in Sturm, Ruger and Company, Incorporated. My motive is entirely altruistic. There are cheaper guns and there are guns I'd prefer personally if price were no object. Nevertheless the Ruger Speed-Six strikes me as the best compromise I know of in terms of reasonable cost and acceptable design and workmanship.

As noted, that's what I suggest if I have reason to believe the questioner would be better off owning a gun than not. If I do suggest it I go on with earnest recommendation that they take the time and trouble to become decently familiar with its operation and maintenance. By that I mean they should fire some adequate number of rounds through it so as to get intimately acquainted with the procedures for loading and reloading it, as well as the subjective sensations of firing it. They should also make a realistic determination of the competence and effectiveness of the gun/shooter combo in their specific case. If they can't manage to pink a man-sized target across a distance of six feet or so, it is better to learn that in practice than after push has come up against hard shove, agree?

Another suggestion I make, in the matter of defense guns, is to consider the possibility of shot loads for the first chamber or two to come under the hammer. The remaining

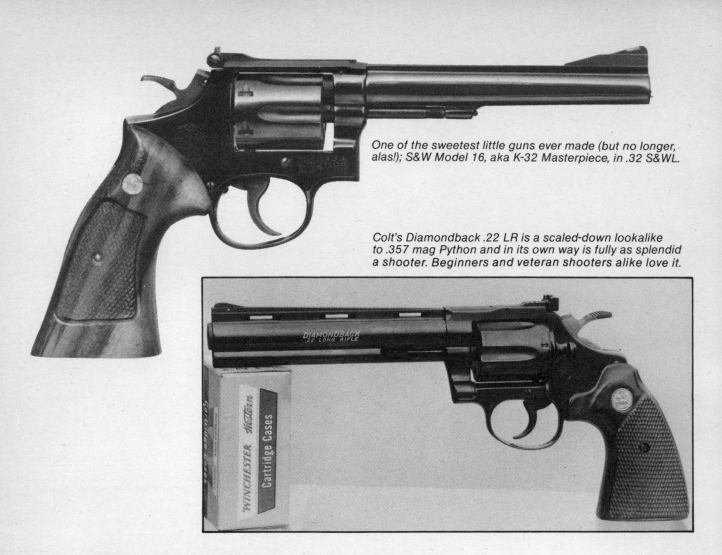

One of the sweetest little guns ever made (but no longer, alas!); S&W Model 16, aka K-32 Masterpiece, in .32 S&WL.

Colt's Diamondback .22 LR is a scaled-down lookalike to .357 mag Python and in its own way is fully as splendid a shooter. Beginners and veteran shooters alike love it.

The Model 36 S&W Chiefs Special is a tiny but capable 5-shot revolver in .38 Special, here approximately lifesize. Some of these are capable of slightly incredible accuracy although it's quite a challenge to get it out of them.

The Browning Model BDA, made for them in Germany by SIG-Sauer in 9mm, .38 Super and .45 ACP is probably the most trouble-free auto pistol I've encountered. Left, perfectly legal for air guns, Crosman's stock for their Model 1377 pneumatic: an engaging little gun! Below: If you look closely, you'll see a thin gap between cylinder and barrel on M24 S&W .44 Special target model.

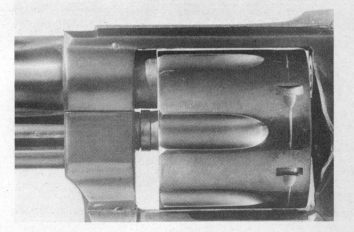

three or four chambers can be stuffed with jacketed hollow-point loads at a weight of 125 grains or so, in the event that further firing may be required. The virtue of the shot load for the first one or two rounds is that it is a to-whom-it-may-concern proposition, with a spread that asks little aiming skill on the part of the shooter. Even when fired in the starkest kind of panic, it will probably pepper the target with several pellets that sting memorably. More, the shot loads won't penetrate partitions of an apartment to imperil innocent occupants of adjoining suites.

Shot loads are made up for the .38 Special and marketed in six-round packs by CCI-Speer. They work just fine out of .38 Specials or .357 magnums. Most gun stores stock them or can get them on request. For those capable of assembling their own cartridges from raw components it's possible to purchase empty capsules in packages of fifty, which can be filled with shot pellets in the size of your choice and reloaded into previously fired center-fire cases.

The package is imprinted with suggested load data, and these are likewise available from CCI-Speer. The empty capsules are also available in .44 size, which can be filled with shot and put up in .44 Special cases for use in .44 Special or .44 magnum guns. As far as I know, CCI-Speer does not offer ready loads in .44 Special, perhaps due to limited likelihood of demand.

The shot loads in the CCI-Speer capsules are remarkably effective at short range, thereby deserving a trial and

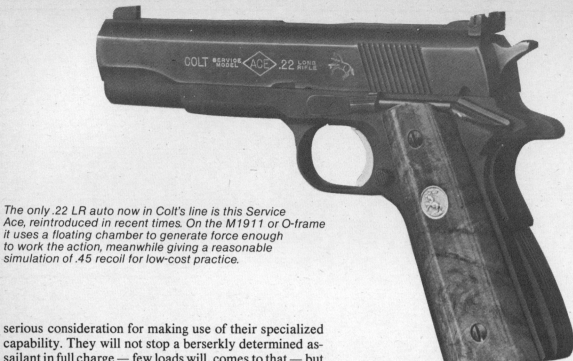

The only .22 LR auto now in Colt's line is this Service Ace, reintroduced in recent times. On the M1911 or O-frame it uses a floating chamber to generate force enough to work the action, meanwhile giving a reasonable simulation of .45 recoil for low-cost practice.

serious consideration for making use of their specialized capability. They will not stop a berserkly determined assailant in full charge — few loads will, comes to that — but field trials are quite apt to prove that they'll put some highly distracting tiny perforations in a man-sized piece of cardboard from a distance of ten feet or so, even if fired in the most desperate, scrabbling, stab-shot kind of haste.

Brief mention was made of the matter of the first one or two shots to come under the hammer of a revolver and that needs further discussion. The thing that makes a revolver fall within the definition is that its cylinder revolves as the hammer is cocked and/or its trigger is pulled in DA mode. Depending upon the make and model, some cylinders rotate one way, some the other way. If you propose to team up with a revolver you need to determine and memorize the direction its cylinder rotates during operation. If, as but one example, you neglect to burn that useful bit of lore into your mental circuitry, you could load up with one or two rounds of shot cartridges only to discover that they were the last one or two to be fired in your particular gun. That might not be as helpful as you'd optimistically hoped.

The time has come to tie off this chapter and move on to other topics. To those readers painfully familiar with all

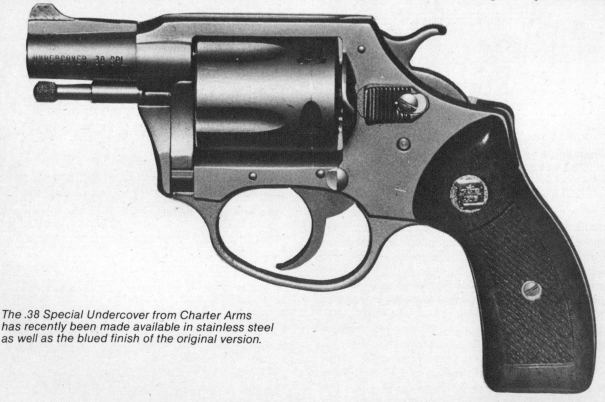

The .38 Special Undercover from Charter Arms has recently been made available in stainless steel as well as the blued finish of the original version.

As noted in the text, when quizzed as to a good choice for home defense, I usually suggest something along the lines of the Ruger Speed-Six as in the 4-inch blue or 2¾-inch stainless examples here. They handle .357 magnum, have fixed sights and probably represent the best balance between quality, accuracy, reliability, simplicity and moderate price.

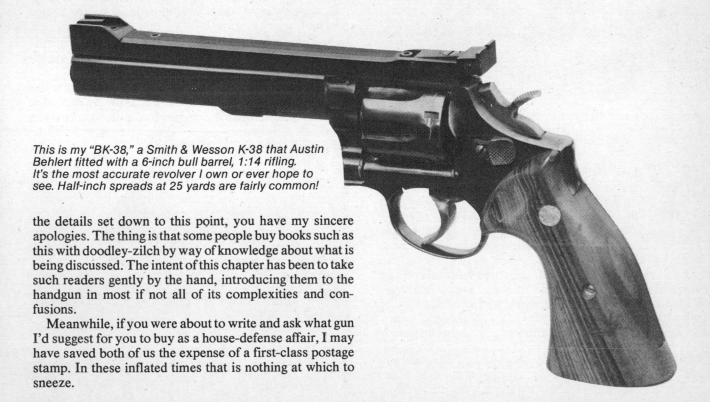

This is my "BK-38," a Smith & Wesson K-38 that Austin Behlert fitted with a 6-inch bull barrel, 1:14 rifling. It's the most accurate revolver I own or ever hope to see. Half-inch spreads at 25 yards are fairly common!

the details set down to this point, you have my sincere apologies. The thing is that some people buy books such as this with doodley-zilch by way of knowledge about what is being discussed. The intent of this chapter has been to take such readers gently by the hand, introducing them to the handgun in most if not all of its complexities and confusions.

Meanwhile, if you were about to write and ask what gun I'd suggest for you to buy as a house-defense affair, I may have saved both of us the expense of a first-class postage stamp. In these inflated times that is nothing at which to sneeze.

# CHAPTER 2

# VITAL ASPECTS OF HANDGUN SAFETY

## *The First Mistake Is The One You Want To Avoid!*

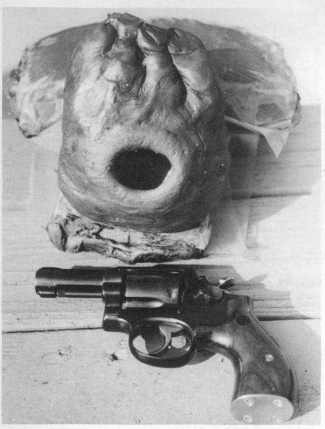

*Even small handguns make big ugly holes and do so in the bat of an eye. That is exactly why you must handle them with all possible caution and foresight; see lower right!*

**Y**OU CAN GET INJURED, painfully or fatally, by almost any artifact of our contemporary civilization, from the abacus to the zither, and perhaps beyond. The handgun, due to its compact dimensions, poses serious potential hazards because it is so treacherously easy to lose track of where it's pointed at any given time.

I learned that fact in a harsh and unforgiving school. For quite a few months of WWII, I was an instructor on a range for the .45 pistol at Tonopah Army Air Base, near the tiny town of the same name in Nevada. It was by no means uncommon for a trainee to whirl from the firing line, complaining, "Hey, Sarge! I pull the trigger and it won't shoot. What's wrong?" The ominous muzzle, roughly 7/16-inch in span, would be quite apt to be lined up with the instruct-

or's more vulnerable viscera. It tended to hone your reactions to a keen, cutting edge.

You became acutely muzzle-conscious. Several years after the war, while riding home from the office on bicycle, a small boy on the sidewalk spotted me, threw popgun to shoulder and let off an imaginary round at me. I nearly fell off the bike from over-reaction.

The price of security is eternal vigilance, and I do mean *eternal.* Toward the end of my stint as a .45 instructor, one of the permanent-party officers from the base came out, needing to fire his required qualification round. There were no students on hand at the time, so I ran him through one-on-one. He was a pleasant gentleman and, between us, with a bit of coaching he racked up an impressive score. With the firing completed, we talked for a while about the .45 auto and I plucked my pet pistol from the pliers pocket of my GI coveralls, where I customarily carried it. I was quite proud of that gun, as I'd spent a lot of attention swapping parts and stoning the trigger to crisp perfection. I cocked it, reversed it, handing it to him butt first. "Just try that trigger," I urged.

He held it meditatively, muzzle upward by about forty-five degrees, gently and carefully squeezing the trigger ...POW!

As I was standing there facing him, the big slug missed my right ear by hardly more than a foot. It's anyone's guess which of us was the more startled.

Now, the thing of it is, I *knew* that gun was loaded, with a round in the chamber. It was the way I always carried it. Rattlesnakes were fairly common to the area and a ready

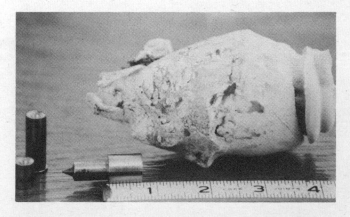

*Here's a plaster-preserved reproduction of the entire cavity from the shot at upper left. The bullet was a .38 Spelunker at 1048 fps; see bulletmaking chapter on that.*

Shooters and nearby spectators require protection for eyes and ears to ward off long-term hearing loss or short-term sight loss. Plugs, as worn by Grennell here, may not be readily visible in such photographs.

.45 was a useful thing to have. How can you possibly explain a lapse of attention that lets one cock a loaded .45 and stand there beaming fatuously while someone squeezes the trigger, with the muzzle practically looking you in the face?

Shift up to late 1964. I was visiting the home of some friends and one of the other visitors, hearing that I was reasonably familiar with firearms, noted that he'd just bought a Luger, but didn't know how to load it. Would I show him, please? I had owned nominally identical guns a few times for short intervals, so I agreed to show him. I demonstrated how to insert the cartridges into the magazine, then shoved the magazine up into its well, holding the gun in my right hand with the muzzle well elevated as I grasped the two knurled toggle knobs between the thumb and forefinger knuckle of my left hand, drawing the toggle upward and rearward to the limit of its travel, releasing it...POW! I should hastily note that my right index finger was lying alongside the trigger guard, extended and not touching the trigger. I removed the magazine, ejected the second round remaining unfired in the chamber, and told him to run it past a good gunsmith before attempting to fire it again.

I've a rueful suspicion that the Luger's owner solved his problem by selling it to someone else, though I'd hope not. A gun such as that is a ticking time bomb. The Luger, or *Pistole '08* is one of the few guns that can fire while partially disassembled.

It's probable you've heard occasional accounts of people who shot themselves, often fatally, while engaged in cleaning a handgun. I've often been puzzled as to how this could happen because the first thing I do when I clean a gun is to open the action and make certain it's entirely empty of

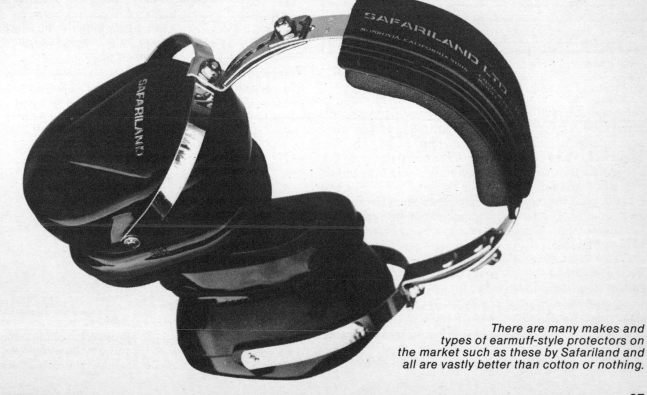

There are many makes and types of earmuff-style protectors on the market such as these by Safariland and all are vastly better than cotton or nothing.

# HEARING PROTECTORS MODEL D325

Designed for low frequency attenuation characteristics (up to 1000 cycles) for reverberating gunshot noise most often found in closed firing ranges.

- Best hearing protection for the range of frequencies found in the use of firearms.
  - Excellent for those high pitched magnum pistol gunshot reports.
  - Excellent for heavy rifles and their low and medium frequency sounds.
  - Excellent for the low frequency sounds of shotguns. Helps reduce flinching due to noise.
- Adjustable with self locking cadmium plated nuts.
- Comfort: Afforded by resilient cushions that conform to head and ear.
- Durable: Domes constructed with patented rib of high impact polycarbonate.

## ATTENUATION CHARACTERISTICS

| FREQUENCY (Hz) | 125 | 250 | 500 | 1000 | 2000 | 3000 | 4000 | 6000 | 8000 |
|---|---|---|---|---|---|---|---|---|---|
| ATTENUATION (dB)* | 22.9 | 26.4 | 26.1 | 31.0 | 31.5 | 33.6 | 35.5 | 35.8 | 35.8 |
| STANDARD DEVIATION | 3.8 | 3.5 | 3.7 | 3.7 | 3.3 | 4.2 | 4.7 | 4.9 | 4.3 |

*Real ear attenuation tests were performed by an independent laboratory and certified to American National Standards Institute, Inc. Standard S3.19—1974.

➤ No product affords total hearing protection over extended periods of exposure to high noise levels. Care should be taken to avoid these conditions.

*Here's some pertinent information from the carton for the Safariland muffs overpage. Note the attenuation in dB varies with the frequency of the sound; note arrow!*

*Small foam plastic plugs are compressed, stuffed into ear and expand to seal the opening. These offer about as much protection as most, are inexpensive also.*

cartridges. A well documented incident is reported on pages 508-9 of *Firearms Investigation, Identification and Evidence,* by J.S. Hatcher, Frank J. Jury and Jac Weller, 1957 edition. I'd like to quote briefly from the account for the sake of spreading the word on a little known but deadly hazard:

"The disassembled parts comprised a 9mm Luger automatic pistol and subsequent identification proved it to be the fatal weapon. The side plate and locking bolt had been removed and placed upon the bed; the frame was lying on the floor. The barrel with its attached receiver, breechblock and firing mechanism were found together — with a partially extracted fired cartridge case in the chamber.

"The ensuing investigation revealed what some owners of the Luger pistol may know — that the barrel and receiver assembly alone can fire a cartridge loaded into the chamber. (...)

"In this particular case the victim had obviously left a

cartridge in the chamber and then started to 'take down' the pistol for cleaning. By accidentally pressing on the exposed sear mechanism he caused the pistol to fire — and what first appeared to be a possible murder was settled for as an accidental shooting."

The thing to remember is that a gun can — and sometimes does — go off when you do not expect or intend for it to do so. The sensible and effective antidote for that state of affairs is to handle it in such a way that the muzzle *always* points in a direction so that, if it does go off, you will not mind the consequences unduly.

A little knowledge is a dangerous thing: not original, but true, nonetheless. I recall reading a newspaper account several years ago, concerning a visitor who was shown an auto pistol belonging to his host. The guest commented that, if threatened by such a gun, all you had to do was to push the muzzle back a little and it would not go off. To prove this, he inserted a live round in the chamber, pressed his left palm over the muzzle, pulled the trigger and blew a gaping hole through his palm, along with other tragic consequence I'm going to beg off recording here.

Several designs of autoloading pistols have a feature termed a magazine disconnector or magazine safety. The intent of such devices is that a live round in the chamber cannot be fired when the magazine has been removed. It is a well-meaning concept, but it poses a few disadvantages. Like any other mechanical device, such systems can get out of order, tending to create false and dangerous confidence in the minds of the users. Moreover, in a tense and

*Here's my well-used pair of Norton Sonic II plugs that do not interfere much with normal sounds but block off the louder noises. That can be advantageous at times.*

trying situation, if the shooter has kept careful count and knows the magazine has gone dry, with one round remaining in the chamber, that round is not capable of being fired once the empty magazine has been removed. It cannot be fired unless a loaded or empty magazine is replaced in the magazine well. That, in itself, can pose a serious tactical disadvantage.

Many — not necessarily all — such magazine disconnectors can be defeated and bypassed if you know the secret. It involves putting some amount of pressure upon the trigger and holding it as you remove the magazine and maintaining the same careful pressure until you get a fresh magazine back into place. The hazards of such a procedure are formidable, as should be obvious. A trifle too much pressure and the chambered round goes off. Should you feel impelled to try this, for the love of liverwurst, do so with a gun carefully verified as empty! And then, by all means, point it at something in which you can tolerate a hole, should it go off despite all your precautions.

If the discussion to this point seems to have put undue

*Suitable safety glasses or a good pair of shooting glasses are at least as necessary for casting as for shooting.*

emphasis upon the vagaries of the autoloaders, it should not be assumed that revolvers are paragons of safety. A round carried beneath the hammer of the old-time single-action six-shooters is apt to be set off by any solid blow upon the hammer spur, as when the gun might be dropped, for but one example. It became the prudent practice to carry such guns with an empty chamber beneath the hammer, converting them into five-shooters, as it were. Development of the double-action revolver in the early decades of the Twentieth Century saw many designs that provided a respectable margin of safety against inadvertant discharge of a round beneath the hammer, when the hammer was lowered. Despite that, some traditionalists persisted in carrying an empty chamber under the hammer, even if the odds against an accidental discharge were highly unlikely.

In more recent times, several revolver deigns have incorporated a feature called the transfer bar. When the hammer is down, it can't even touch the firing pin. As the hammer is cocked, the transfer bar rises up out of the action so that when the trigger is pulled the hammer hits the bar and that, in turn, transfers the blow to the firing pin, setting off the cartridge.

The Colt Model 1911 .45 service auto, and quite a number of other auto pistols and revolvers, incorporate a feature called a floating firing pin, also known as an inertia firing pin. With the hammer fully against the rear of the firing pin, the tip of the pin still does not make contact with the primer of the chambered round. When the hammer is cocked and the trigger pulled deliberately, the hammer slams down and hits the rear of the firing pin with such force that

*Bill Jordan, photographed while plotting fresh deviltry, contributed the illustrative anecdote that's on page 42.*

it drives the pin forward to fire the cartridge by sheer inertia.

As was noted about the magazine disconnect, that is a well-intentioned concept, but it can be — and has been — defeated by unusual circumstances. A really solid and vigorous blow against the muzzle of the gun can drive the gun rearward with enough force to let the firing pin course forward against the restraining force of the firing pin spring to fire the chambered round anyway, even if the hammer is fully down, or if the gun is carried in cocked-and-locked mode, with the hammer back and safety catch up. Examples include cavalry troopers falling off their horses, or guns falling from a respectable height to land muzzle-down on a hard surface. In the latter instance, the slug can pose a serious hazard as it ricochets off the surface.

The only positive way to nullify that hazard is to carry such guns with a loaded magazine and the chamber empty. It is true that such a cautious approach will lengthen the time for getting off the first shot by some small amount. Sometimes, that can pose a hazard even more objectionable. It is a situation where you have to make your decision and accept the consequences, either way.

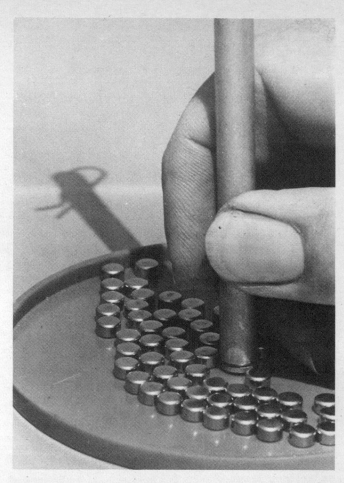

*Automatic primer feeding systems with brass tube magazines should be treated with great caution. If they are dropped, it can set off a violent chain explosion.*

Speaking of dropping things, and getting back to revolvers, you should be aware of the hazard posed by revolver designs in which the entire cylinder is removed for reloading or extraction of remaining live rounds. If such a cylinder is dropped, with one or more live cartridges in the chamber(s), the round(s) can be set off if they strike a hard object. Even a .22 rimfire short, set off in the limited confines of a revolver cylinder, can generate enough velocity to inflict a fatal wound if it strikes the wrong place. Most such revolvers are chambered for .22 rimfire cartridges, but the same applies if they accept center-fire ammunition. It is not the intent to condemn such guns, but rather to emphasize the precautions required in their use.

Revolvers are distinguished by a cylinder that revolves as the trigger is pulled and/or as the hammer is cocked. From one make and model to another, the direction of the cylinder rotation may vary. As but two examples, Colt revolvers usually have cylinders that rotate in a clockwise direction, while Smith & Wesson revolvers have cylinders that rotate counterclockwise in every example I've encountered to date.

It is quite important to become intimately, instinctively familiar with the direction of cylinder rotation for any given revolver you anticipate using. It is a common practice for target shooters to load five rounds into a six-shot cylinder for purposes of firing half of a ten-round course. In either make, swinging the cylinder shut with the empty

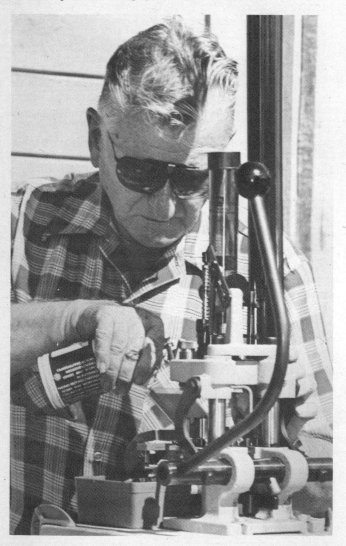

*Spilled powder around the reloading area can pose safety problems. Here a pressurized can of Dust-Off is being used to blow away loose granules on The Green Machine.*

chamber under the hammer puts you in readiness to fire all five, as planned. If, for some reason you only propose to fire a single cartridge, the cylinder has to latch into place with the given round at 10 o'clock, for a Colt, or 2 o'clock for the S&W.

Ponder that last sentence for a brief bit. We've discussed accidental discharges in some depth, but it must be borne in mind that handguns are sometimes employed in lieu of life-preservers, and an ineffectual click when you hoped for a lusty boom can and quite possibly may get you seriously traumatized.

The trained handgunning expertise of any given person becomes sharply apparent when they hand a gun to another or, in turn, have a gun handed to them. Properly, the hander should verify the empty status of the gun before relinquishing control and, rightly, the handee should perform the same cautious ritual as an instinctive reaction.

With revolvers, the correct drill is to actuate the cylinder latch and ease the cylinder open tenderly, push the ejector rod rearward and close the cylinder gently. If, for any inexplicable reason, you wish to brand yourself as a witless neophyte in handguns, all you need to do is work the latch, letting the cylinder bang open, and then slam it back into place with a sharp snap of the wrist. There is hardly anything that can be relied upon with greater certainty to ruin what may have been a fine revolver, up to that point. Just a few such maneuvers will spring the crane out of its delicate and critical alignment, converting a fine shooter into junkerdom.

Long ere this I've grimly made it a practice to deliver a brief but pointed lecture on the subject before letting *anyone* get their hands on a revolver I own and cherish. Every single time I've assumed the other party knew better, that party has gone *wham-snick* before I could even begin to get my mouth open. The practice of closing revolver cylin-

*A split lip on an auto pistol magazine can render gun inoperative to pose a severe safety threat if you're depending upon it to preserve your personal hide!*

ders with a facile snap of the wrist is fostered extensively by the nincompoop actors on television, who perform this idiot maneuver so assiduously that the great viewing public thinks that's the way it's done.

With auto pistols, the checking procedure is to remove the magazine first, then draw the slide fully to the rear, visually verifying the empty status of the chamber. If you leave the magazine in place, pulling the slide back usually will lock it in open position or, if the magazine contains cartridges, the gun will be loaded and ready when you let the slide bang forward, even if it wasn't before. Recall please the disturbing incident of the rickety Luger that went off as the round was chambered. At the risk of seeming tediously redundant, all such operations should be done with the muzzle pointed so that an accidental discharge would not have painful consequences.

Suitable protection for eyes and ears should be regarded as mandatory when shooting and when engaged in several other shooting-related activities, with special emphasis upon casting bullets. When thus engaged, not many are apt to be so cautious as to continue wearing ear protectors, but the eye protection certainly should be retained. Speaking personally, I can recall at least four incidents in which the fact that I was wearing durable shooting glasses spared me from serious, painful eye injury or perhaps the loss of one or both eyes. Three instances were while shooting, one while casting bullets.

In the latter instance, the alloy was getting low in the pot. Looking about, I spotted a box of dubious old cast bullets, decided to recycle them, dumped them into the top of the electric pot and there was a loud report accompanied by a Vesuvius of silvery spatters. A bit later, I found an empty .22 short case on the ground nearby, but with no slightest trace of a firing pin indent in its rim which led me to theorize it had gotten mixed in with the shopworn bullets to end up amid the molten alloy.

The Bausch & Lomb shooting glasses I was prudent enough to have been wearing at the time bore conclusive evidence that I was lucky they were in place, since each lens had a sizable splat of frozen alloy that would have hit the pupil of the eye had they not been in the way. I think of

*Small quantities of powder can be stored in a chest such as this with a carrying handle on top to permit rapid evacuation from danger in the event of a fire or the like.*

*A gun lock is a nice idea, but if you can't find the key when you need the gun right now, that can also be hazardous. A good solution was this keyless affair from Safariland that opened by pressing a catch that required a considerable amount of strength in the thumb. Tension was adjustable to taste. See photos on facing page.*

that incident often and make doubly, triply certain to put the glasses on. Up in the rafters over the shop, I've a frightfully shopworn motorcycle helmet that, on the afternoon of April 26, 1967, extended my longevity to the present. Like the safety glasses, when you need such protection, it's already too late to hunt it up and put it on. Ponder that, if you please.

The intensity of sound is measured in units called decibels, commonly abbreviated as dB — not db and certainly not Db as it wound up in another book I did! — somewhat in the manner of the Richter scale for rating earthquake intensity, decibels progress in logarithmic proportion, so that a 60 dB noise is vastly more than twice as loud as a 30 dB noise. It is not the intent of this discussion to probe deeply into the intricacies of audiometry, but rather to note that your ears need protection from the loud sounds of gunshots only slightly less than your eyes need shields against against hurtling debris.

Bill Jordan, mentioned elsewhere here, is not only a marksman of supernatural skills, but a *raconteur* whose repertoire bristles with goodly gems, not all of which I

could hope to get away with quoting here, but I'd like to stir in one innocuous and pertinently illustrative filch from the lofty BJ: Two old gun writers met for the first time in a number of years. One was volubly enthusiastic.

"Hey, I've got this new hearing aid and it's the greatest thing you ever saw! Why I can hear as well now as I could when I was just a kid!"

"Is that so?" the other responded, "What kind is it?"

The first one glanced at his wrist and replied, "Quarter after four."

Massive overexposure to the sound of gunshots deadens the auditory nerve and causes a problem termed nerve loss. You lose ability to detect sounds of the higher frequencies, short of noon-whistle ferocity. That makes it very difficult to distinguish the subtle difference in the sound of consonants that render speech decipherable. Fifty and sixty sound much the same; so do government pension and Doberman pinscher and so on. Such problems respond poorly if at all to hearing aids. I once blew $500 an ear to find that out and yes it's a lavish price to pay for sweet corn. The tiny amplifier only transmuted softly muted gibberish

In writing up an earlier edition of this unlikely work, a reviewer made a great federal case out of the fact that the text said one should wear shooting glasses and ear protectors while some of the illustrations showed people shooting without the benefit of one or both. If the same gent is assigned to coat this edition with curmudgery, permit me to note that there are photos in which the shooter is wearing Norton Lee-Sonic ear plugs and the fact may not be clearly apparent after the engraver and printer have dealt with the photos. If an illustration turns up here in which a shooter is foolishly risking ears and/or eyes, or seems to be, it is hereby clearly and specifically set down that they are stupid to do so and their example should not be followed.

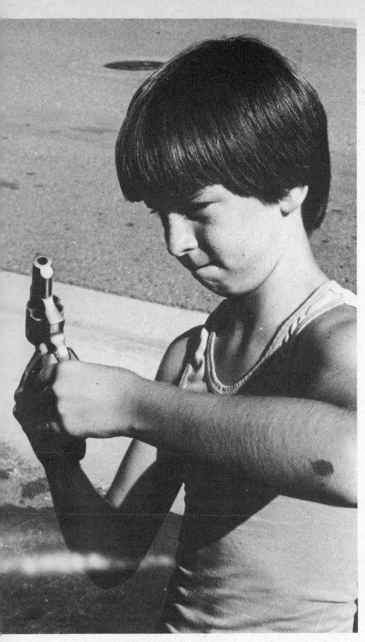

*By way of checking out the Safariland lock I gave it to son Bill in an (empty!) Colt Detective Special. Look on his face is indicative of the degree of determination used.*

into harsh, unbearably strident gibberish, but gibberish it remained. Placidly pushing a cart about the supermarket, a shrill squall from a toddler in a nearby cart could nigh take the top of your head clean off before you could claw for the volume dial.

After a year or so, the Sturgeon General's herring aide — forgive, please? — went on the bunk and the supplier claimed it was my fault because I'd perspired about the ears; a *faux pas* difficult to avoid during Southern California dog-days. He wanted about the original tab to put them back into working order so I said foosh and went back to begging a lot of pardons.

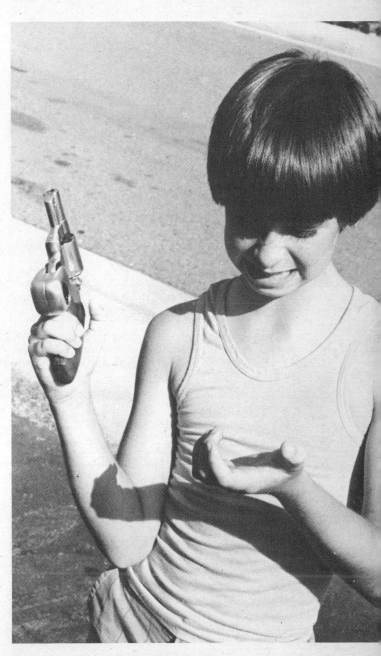

*Note his expression and that the lock remained in place. These are old photos and Bill's now six foot three and a safe gun handler, so the lock's no longer needed!*

Smokeless powder requires great care in use and storage while black powder requires a great deal more. Note the cautionary notices on this can of black and heed them well.

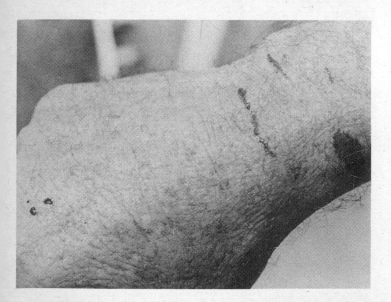

Revolvers can shoot to the side as well as to the front as shown by oozes of Type B Rh + gore. Another potent argument for shooting glasses and updated tetanus shots!

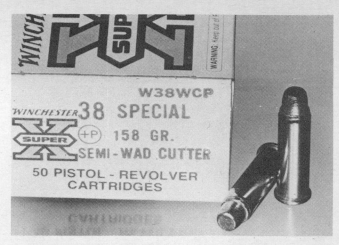

Before using +P loads in a .38 Special you must be certain that its maker sanctions the use of such ammo. If in doubt, ask the dealer who sold it or write to the manufacturer.

Curiously enough, the prestigious publication that ran the dour review has carried accounts with the dubious assurance that loaded ammunition poses no serious threat if set off unconfined. In my humble opinion (imho) that is Grade A mule milk. I've clear recollections of an incident in the barracks I occupied at Tonopah. One of the co-occupants, hoping to liven the proceedings, peeled back the lid atop one of the oil-fired barracks heaters and dumped a whole fifty-round box of GI .45 ACP ammo down into the fire. Barracks dwellers made their exits from the doors at either end in a manner reminiscent of bullets from a caliber .30 Browning machine gun, both as to velocity and cyclic rate. Some were even observed to hit hummocks of desert sand and ricochet upward with eerie whines.

It was a goodly while before the first intrepid soul ventured back into the barracks and as he did so the stove emitted one more *whump!* so that a further long interval ensued before anyone got that brave again.

The stove was a total loss and the wonder is it didn't set the barracks ablaze. Its main drum of perhaps 22-gauge steel was riddled with caliber .45 holes in several places and badly nubbled in a lot of others. Film was not to be had at the time so I can't supply photographic evidence but you have my solemn word, should you care to accept it.

A lot of thoughtful consideration needs to be taken in the matter of storing and handling such brisk combustibles as powder, primers and loaded ammunition. It should be well protected from routine fire hazards and, if possible, should be kept in containers that are readily capable of being evacuated in the event that a fire might start elsewhere in the building. I recall that the late George Nonte once published a dour account of the time his house caught fire and as the trucks rolled up one of his neighbors in near-terminal hysteria went dashing out to warn the firemen to flee for their lives since Nonte's house was one great bomb and it could take them all away just about any instant. Nonte commented that his gratitude for the neighbor's concern was sharply limited.

A five-foot shelf filled with books such as this could hardly approach listing all of the pitfalls of which to beware and no pretense is made that this chapter does much more than scarify the surface of the matter. It is hoped that it will

The same .38 Spelunker load shown on page 36, out of the six-inch barrel of this Colt Python, virtually detonated the water that filled this aluminum beverage can to provide further motive for avoiding holes where not wanted.

As noted in chapter 1, there are a few revolvers that do have safety catches such as the little stud at the front of the grip on this unlikely specimen from the Tom Ferguson collection. Guns like this are prime examples why such rounds as the .32 S&W are loaded to such diffident levels and, even so, it may get more than slightly iffy to try firing them. If in doubt, don't do it is a good attitude.

serve to alert the reader to the potential hazards so that a basic attitude of disaster avoidance can be set up and buttressed.

Chapter 6 of PARD's first edition covered the same topic and I've been terribly tempted to quote from it *en masse* but have refrained lest some reader cry foul and class me with Dear Abby and Ann Landers. I would however like to beg your indulgence and drop in a brief quote, admittedly recycled:

"It boils down to this for the bottom line: Firearms safety is a kissin' cousin to firearms courtesy and the golden rule plays a part. If gun muzzles make you uneasy — as they damned well should — do not let others see the muzzle of a gun you are holding. Be as brusque and positive as may seem necessary in inculcating the principles of firearms safety in your associates, keeping ever in mind that the eraser for guns has yet to be invented. If the associate can't seem to get the message, take such steps as will assure cessation of association. Getting shot is no fun. At worst, it's so bloody permanent."

I can't wish anyone much better than to hope they never learn the truth of all that the hard way. Watch it, hmm?

# RECENT TRENDS IN HANDGUN AMMUNITION

*Discussing What We'd Like To Have And Speculating On Why We Haven't Got It.*

## CHAPTER 3

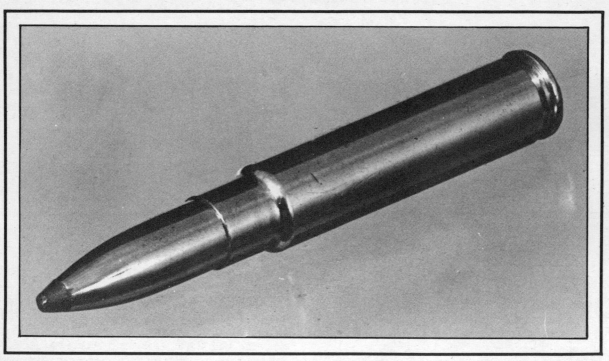

*One of the most potent handgun cartridges around these days is the 7mm Thompson/Center Ugalde or T/CU to use its customary abbreviation. A wildcat — not sold as factory ammo — it is made from the .223 Remington case to use bullets of .284-inch diameter in weights from 115 to 175 grains. Factory barrels are available for the T/C Contender pistol in lengths of ten and fourteen inches. The 7mm T/CU has held groups under one minute of angle at one hundred yards, with energies that approach the 1700 fpe level.*

IT'S INTRIGUING at times to chart progress in various areas, plotting the state of the art as to performance over an extended interval of time on a graph. If you try that with handgun performance, you'll usually end up wondering where we went wrong.

Take the top speed of aircraft as an example. Wilbur and Orville Wright got us started with a prototype that went a bit over 40 mph. By the end of WWI, 125 mph in level flight was still considered fairly awesome. Along in the Thirties an Italian seaplane — the Macchi-Castoldi, as dubious memory has it — hit 440 mph. In the late Thirties there was a brief flap when it was reported that the deer botfly could hit 660 mph or so in brief sprints, but that was followed by an embarrassed admission that the calculations were in error.

During the six-year span of the Hitler/Tojo Fracas, the propellor drive more or less reached its plateau of performance and the jet engine came along about the end of it. Supersonic flight became an everyday reality and I really don't know what the top aircraft speeds are running these days: perhaps somewhere in the 2500 to 3000 mph brackets. Meanwhile, we've gone into space and left footprints on the moon's gritty pumice and that involves paces that make even 4000 mph seem pretty picayune.

Out in my front driveway rests a little Opel GT that could have ruled the hallowed bricks of Indianapolis in the

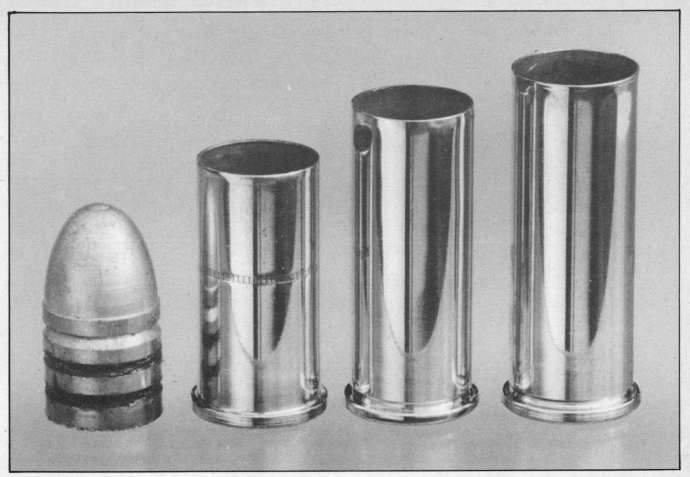

Growth of a cartridge: At left is a 255-grain cast bullet from the Lyman No. 429251 mould, initially designed for use in the .44 Smith & Wesson Russian case (second) which was lengthened to create the .44 S&W Special and, later the .44 Remington magnum. All three cases have the same basic head dimensions except that the .44 S&W R usually is found with the old balloon head design. The Special and magnum remain on the market.

early years of the present century by virtue of the fact that — a bit over seven years ago — it proved eminently capable of covering measured miles in a tad under thirty seconds. Certainly it could have eaten the lunch of the fabled Auburn Speedster that generated vast awe about 1936 by the fact that it was guaranteed to top the 100 mph mark.

So how does the present-day state of the ballistic arts stack up against the progress of passenger vehicles in the air and on the ground? Alas, it is a thing to make one blush in contemplation.

Quite early in this century a gent name of Gabbet-Fairfax dreamed up a pistol he called the Mars and whomped out some cartridges for it that delivered velocities on the order of 1400 fps or so, and that was with bullets of respectable girth and grainage so that the equivalent foot-pounds would seem respectable by today's standards.

We had a stimulating burst of instant progress right around the turn of the century when nitrocellulose-based propellants superseded the traditional foom-fodder comprised of charcoal, saltpeter and sulfur that had ruled the shooting roost for the previous several centuries. Eight decades or so have elapsed and where are we now? It's humiliating, galling and frustrating, but we're still hard-

pressed to deliver much more foot-pounds out of a hand-held firearm than Gabbet-Fairfax got from his Mars way back when.

Today's revolvers are essentially identical to those of the early 1900s. One of the most-admired autoloaders of the present came off Browning's drawing board more than seventy years ago and today's designers are still busting their gussets trying to improve upon it significantly.

In terms of progress in any number of other fields it would seem logical to assume that by this time we should have handguns capable of delivering a nice round foot-ton — 2000 fpe — of energy, without subjecting the shooter to undue punishment and with the capability of holding one minute of angle (moa) when fired from a steady rest. They should hold a dozen or twenty rounds and have a net bulk not much larger than the remarkable Model 1911 Colt.

By the standards of progress in other fields, those are pretty modest expectations. Recall that we're thinking in terms of hundred-fold gains in speeds of aircraft and spacecraft and land vehicle speeds have trebled or quadrupled in the past eighty years or so. For firearms, we're wistfully looking for a two-fold gain, and we certainly do not have it; not that I can see, for sure!

Considering rifles for just a bit, the .220 Swift came along in the latter Thirties to put a 46-grain bullet out at

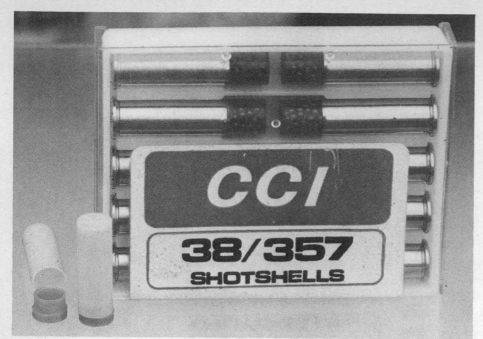

CCI markets a loaded shotshell for use in .38 Special or .357 magnum guns. A second load is offered for .44 magnum only. They also market empty shot capsules in both diameters for use in reloading such ammo.

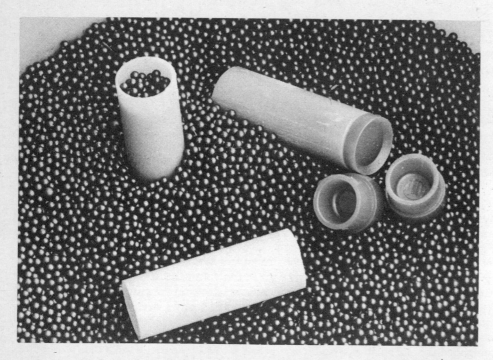

Here are a few of the .38 size CCI capsules in the process of being filled. The .44 capsule can be loaded in .44 Special cases for optional use in the Special or magnum and the capsules can be used with two or three buckshot pellets of the appropriate diameters.

4140 fps; 1751 fpe. As the Sixties were merging with the Seventies, there was a brief flurry of faddish fascination for the sub-caliber bullets with accent upon the caliber .17 or .172-inch jobs. Velocities for some of those edged beyond the .220 Swift mark, but with considerably lighter bullets. I recall clocking a load out of a .222 Remington magnum necked down to .17 with a fleaweight bullet at just 5280 fps: a nice round mile-per-second starting pace. At that speed, for every grain of bullet weight, you get 61.91897655 fpe so that a bullet weighing about 32.3 grains would pack a foot-ton of ka-powie. The bullet in question weighed perhaps half that.

It's entirely true that there are rifles that pack a foot-ton of sock with quite a bit to spare and some of the burly-bred behemoths that buck and bellow along the firing lines at the unlimited handgun silhouette matches these days probably can top that arbitrary figure. They are not, however, anything that Honey West might consider suitable to pack in her garter holster.

There are at least two handguns on the current market capable of topping 3000 fps: Remington's XP-100 in .221 Fire Ball and Thompson/Center's Contender in .223 Remington. The Remington needs a 40-grain bullet and crafty reloading to do that from its ten-inch barrel while the T/C can do it with the better factory loads from the Super-14 barrel.

Let's be specific: I clocked five rounds of the military .223 load made by Poongsan Metal in the Republic of Korea and distributed by Hansen Cartridge Company, Southport, Connecticut. Velocities were 3076.9, 3016.6,

3110.4, 3044.1 and 3081.6 fps. That brings the average velocity to 3065.92 fps and the standard deviation to 36.24. I pulled one of the bullets from the same batch and weighed it at 55.3 grains. That put the average energy at 1154.52 fpe or so. The loads grouped quite well, but we're still 845.48 fpe shy of that dream foot-ton, right? More, we're still thinking in terms of big single-shots, not compact repeaters.

Most of us think of a minute of angle as representing one inch of center-center spread for every one hundred yards. If you care to drift that through a few decimals, it's closer to 1.047197551 inches at that distance, but 1.05 inches is certainly close enough for government work.

A good XP-100 with a good load will crack a moa barrier with light-hearted insouciance, even with a modest

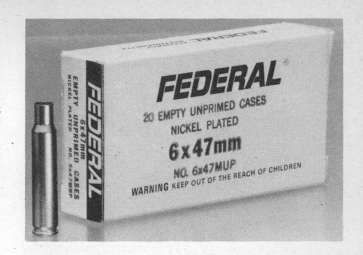

*Above, Federal marketed empty unprimed cases in 6x47mm at one time, recently discontinuing them so that little or no info is to be had on possible use as a handgun cartridge. A 6mm Ugalde, similar to the 7mm T/CU is said to be under development. Right and below, Ruger's revolver for the 9mm Parabellum (Luger) can be used with clips from Ranch Products, Box 145, Malinta, OH 43535 as a handy form of speedloder with clips available to handle two or six rounds. The Model 547 Smith & Wesson 9mm revolver will not accept such clips.*

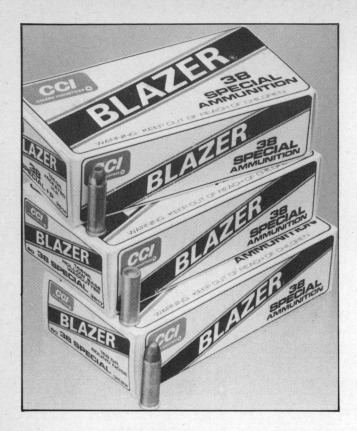

2X scope topside. The latter-day Contenders will do the same with cartridges such as the 7mm Thompson/Center Ugalde usually termed T/CU. I've gotten one of the latter down to .914-inch between centers for five at one hundred yards and the nettlesome thing was that four of those holes were within less than half an inch in spread. The same cartridge in the same gun has mustered readout energies to as much as 1698 fpe without displaying alarming pressure signs.

If you launch a 40-grain bullet at 3000 fps, you're only delivering about 800 fpe at the muzzle so the 7mm T/CU clearly represents a goodly gain in accurate power. Right at this moment, as research time can be surreptitiously snitched, I'm working with the 6.5mm Ugalde that is an as-yet unadopted variant of the 7mm T/CU, being made up on the same .223 Remington or 5.56mm NATO parent case. Dropping the bullet diameter by a half a millimeter,

from .284-inch to .264-inch, gives a usefully more distinctive shoulder that clears up some of the petty problems that plague the 7mm T/CU such as curtailed reloading life from incipient head separations.

I do not know if Wes Ugalde — a gunsmith in Reno, Nevada — has looked into the possibilities of a .223 case necked to .257-inch for the caliber .25 bullets or, for that matter, a 6mm Ugalde that takes the .243-inch size. There is a 6x47mm cartridge made up on the .222 Remington magnum case opened to .243-inch that has won some popularity among benchrest rifle competitors to the extent that Federal offers a nickel-plated factory case for it. Would the 6x47mm be the wowser of all time for the Super-14 Contender barrels? The prospects seem likely, but data to

From left, a .380 ACP, 9x18mm Ultra and the 9x19mm Parabellum or Luger. The 9x18 is not commonly encountered here and is essentially used in Europe in the countries that forbid military calibers such as the 9mm Parabellum.

The .357-.44 Bain & Davis is a .44 magnum case necked to .357-inch bullet diameter. At one time Bain & Davis would rechamber Model 27 or 28 S&W revolvers for this round. T/C used to offer it as a Contender barrel and Rock Pistol, 704 E. Commonwealth, Fullerton, CA 92631 chambered the Merrill Sportsman for it.

Left, the .451 Detonics magnum is slightly longer than the .45 ACP, with stronger head to take higher loads. The .41 Avenger, right, uses a similar case necked to .410 diameter in barrels from SSK Industries for use in existing auto pistols of the M1911 pattern.

confirm or refute it are not available at this time, unfortunately.

All of which is hardly Damon nor yet Pythias in terms of our hypothetical dream-gun. The only guns that can begin to approach the stipulated foot-ton at one moa performance are single-shots, hobbled to a cyclic rate of fire not much beyond four aimed shots per minute or so.

There are bottleneck rifle cartridges in bounteous profusion, but not nearly as many of such for handguns. Several of the Contender offerings are bottlenecks, but how many can you suggest that are readily digestible among the revolvers and autoloaders? Yup, we have the .30 Luger and the 7.63mm Mauser, and that feckless fancy, the .22 Jet for a revolver discontinued these many years. With a bit of finagling you can have a .357 magnum rechambered to take the .357-.44 Bain & Davis wildcat that is created by necking a .44 magnum case to accept .357-inch bullets. With a lot of intent and canny browsing about, you might luck onto some reasonably sturdy revolver to take the old .32-20 WCF cartridge; a round that has to be some kind of unappreciated sleeper of all time. Yes, we have the .38-40 and .44-40 WCF, but both are not used in any revolver suitable for hotrodding. Beyond that, what? Have I overlooked anything?

Let's take a keen look at that necked-down .44 mag

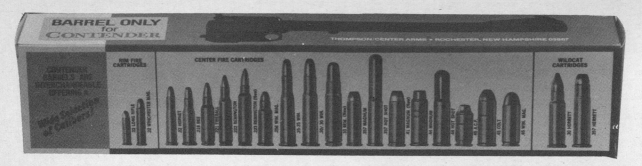

A recent T/C Contender barrel carton shows this array of cartridges although some have been dropped from the catalog because they drew but limited sales figures.

round. The lab crew at Hornady, bless their dedicated hearts, cranked a couple pages of listing for it into the third edition of the Hornady Handbook, pages 374-5, terming it the 357/44 Bain & Davis, working from a ten-inch Contender barrel. They max' it out at 2400 fps/1047 fpe for the 110-grain bullet, 2200/1344 for the 125 and 2100/1548 for the 158-grain. Put it into a revolver with a sixteen-inch barrel and the cylinder-gap handicap and you might just possibly shade those figures a trifle, but it's unlikely that

From left, .357 mag, .30-30 WCF, .30 Herrett, .357 Herrett, .35 Rem, .444 Marlin necked to .35, .41 and .44 mag. All but #1 and #6 can be had as Super-14 T/C barrels plus .222 Rem, .223 Rem 7mm T/CU, and .45 Win mag, making a fairly extensive offering.

you're going to hit the foot-ton landmark. Sorry about that.

As this is being written I'm still waiting to put hands upon one of the few new concepts that's been offered in the repeating hangun marketplace to the present time. As the book at hand is being produced in a reasonably sequential format, it's entirely possible that I may have solid data on it by the time the final pages close. With that in mind, I'm reserving the final chapter for a catch-up/close-out effort and you're welcome to cheat and skip forward to see what the bear did in the buckwheat and where, if you wish.

The cartridge in question is the Olsen Invicta, currently under development in two distinct versions. One fires a .257-inch-diameter bullet out of a .357 magnum case; the other launches a .357-inch-diameter bullet with all the foom and fury that the .44 magnum case can supply. Both versions are intended for use in a Dan Wesson Arms revolver having a cylinder of the given size mated to a barrel with bore dimensions scaled to the specified bullet diameter.

Both versions operate upon the proven principle of a big push exerted upon a bullet of modest diameter. Unlike the

The .22 Rem Jet, left, was made on a .357 mag case for .222-inch bullet diameter and foundered in seas of shooter apathy. The .221 Rem Fire Ball uses the standard .224-inch bullet and has won moderate success. As noted here, the Fire Ball operates at high pressure.

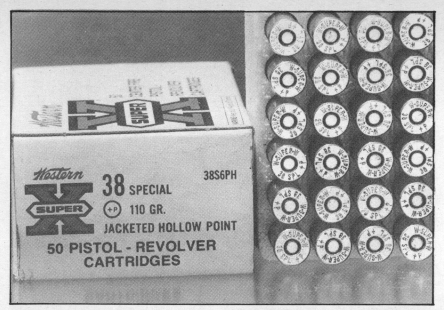

The +P .38 Special loads have proved popular for use in the sturdier guns of that caliber, as sanctioned by gun's maker. Note that the headstamp also carries the +P labeling in the event the round gets away from the original carton.

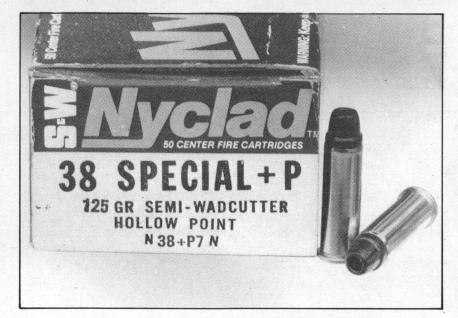

A good idea was the S&W Nyclad which covered a soft lead bullet with Nylon to avoid fouling and air pollution. Federal took over the Nyclad when S&W discontinued ammo manufacture. Below right, the 6.5mm Ugalde next to a 7mm T/CU. Former is a promising performer, as is latter. Note the stronger shoulder of the 6.5 case.

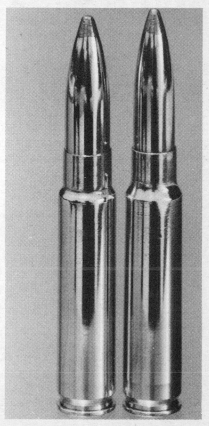

B&D entry, the Invicta is not a bottleneck case. Rather, it encases the smaller diameter bullet in an adapter bushing made from sophisticated plastic to center it in the mouth of the launching case. Upon being fired, both bushing and bullet move forward quite smartly. As the bushing gets to the front of the cylinder it stops, sealing the cylinder gap and guiding the bullet into the forcing cone of the smaller barrel designed to fit it. In so doing, the collar seals off virtually all of the gas that leaks to bleed away pressure in conventional revolvers.

Based upon a just-arrived communique from Robert Olsen, it appears that the version that uses a .44 mag case to get a .357 bullet out the muzzle can muster about 2580 fps with a 110-grain bullet for 1626 fpe; 2100 fps for a 125-grain bullet for 1224 fpe; or 2180 fps for a 158-grain bullet at 1668 fpe. We are still somewhat shy of a foot-ton from a repeater and never mind the stipulation about one moa.

It should be noted that the figures quoted here for the

From left, .22 rimfires in CCI Mini-Mag Long; CCI Stinger; Federal #514; Remington Yellow Jacket; and W-W Xpediter. Last four are of the new ultra-hot loadings for the .22 LR.

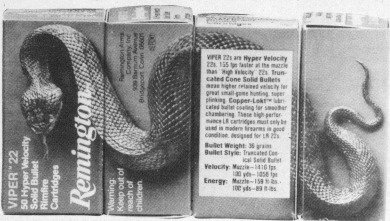

VIPER 22s are **Hyper Velocity** 22s. 155 fps faster at the muzzle than "High Velocity" 22s. **Truncated Cone Solid Bullets** mean higher retained velocity for great small-game hunting, super plinking. **Copper-Lokt™** lubricated bullet coating for smoother chambering. These high-performance LR cartridges must only be used in modern firearms in good condition, designed for LR 22s.

**Bullet Weight:** 36 grains
**Bullet Style:** Truncated Conical Solid Bullet
**Velocity:** Muzzle—1410 fps
100 yds—1056 fps
**Energy:** Muzzle—159 ft-lbs.
100 yds—89 ft-lbs.

The newest offering from Remington in what they term Hyper Velocity for the .22 LR is the Viper, packaged in the rather spooky-looking carton shown at left in full wraparound grisliness. Data from lower panel of the carton is reproduced above for easier reading.

Olsen Invicta, according to Olsen, represent the absolute top of his tests to date and probably will be reduced when recommended load data is offered.

What level of effort does it take to get a foot-ton from a handgun, even at point-blank distance, before the turgid atmospheric medium has a chance to drag the speed down to ho-hum paces? Let's cite a few examples, keyed to bullet weight:

A 40-grain bullet at 4745 fps;
A 50-grain bullet at 4244 fps;
A 55-grain bullet at 4046 fps;
A 60-grain bullet at 3874 fps;
A 75-grain bullet at 3465 fps;
A 90-grain bullet at 3163 fps;
A 100-grain bullet at 3001 fps;
A 110-grain bullet at 2861 fps;
A 125-grain bullet at 2684 fps;
A 140-grain bullet at 2536 fps;
A 158-grain bullet at 2387 fps;
A 170-grain bullet at 2302 fps;
A 200-grain bullet at 2122 fps;
A 225-grain bullet at 2001 fps;
A 240-grain bullet at 1937 fps.

Any of the listed combos pack a foot-ton and a trifle to spare and all of them are somewhat out of our reach to the present moment, so far as I know. It's true that we're getting tiny bits closer, decade by decade, but where are the galloping strides that can be readily cited in comparable areas of human endeavors?

There is of course a simple explanation — if not an excuse — for the problem. As the powder charge burns it is converted into a given volume of gas that is compressed to as much as 40,000 or more pounds per square inch (psi) in the example of some of the magnum handgun cartridges. Some of the more energetic rifle calibers range as high as 53,000 psi or more. The No. 10 Speer Manual lists the maximum working pressures specified by the Sporting Arms and Ammunition Manufacturers Institute (SAAMI) for several of the handgun cartridges for which it includes load data:

| Cartridge | psi |
| --- | --- |
| .221 Remington Fire Ball | 55,500 |
| .30 Carbine | 40,000 |
| .380 ACP | 18,900 |
| 9mm Parabellumn (Luger) | 35,700 |
| .38 Colt Super | 35,700 |
| .38 S&W | 14,900 |
| .38 Special (standard) | 18,900 |
| .38 Special (+-P) | 22,400 |
| .357 magnum | 46,000 |
| .41 magnum | 43,500 |
| .44 Special | 15,900 |
| .44 magnum | 43,500 |
| .45 Auto Rim | 16,900 |
| .45 ACP | 19,900 |
| .45 Colt | 15,900 |
| .45 Colt (for Ruger or Contender) | 25,500 |

Those figures represent the leash that limits the operating range of the given cartridge. The pressure of a compressed gas varies inversely in proportion to the volume it occupies and as a further factor we have the extremely high temperature at which it is applied to the base of the bullet, increasing the effective pressure many times over the equivalent amount of gas were it at ordinary room temperature.

As the bullet commences to move up the barrel, a proportionally greater amount of volume becomes available for the gases to occupy and pressure begins to drop off. The

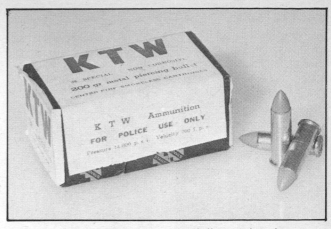

The original KTW loads were carefully restricted to police use only but recently stirred up furor when TV stations campaigned against their use. The bullet was solid brass coated with Teflon, and it did show a most impressive capability for getting through things.

duration over which the powder burns is quite short although by no means instantaneous. Thus we have the situation in which the peak pressure is developed perhaps as the bullet has moved an inch or so from its starting point. After that the accelerating bullet makes more volume available for the gas to occupy and the pressures drop off at a comparatively rapid rate.

If it were possible to maintain a uniform pressure upon the bullet base for the entire duration of its travel up the barrel, some extremely interesting velocities could be obtained; far in excess of any handgun ballistics possible to the present. The powder companies have plowed a lot of

Here's an early developmental prototype of the BBM Hard Cap shot load for use in .45 ACP pistols, with a much earlier paper-patched .45 ACP shot load for use in the Thompson submachine gun. The Hard Cap load will feed and cycle through any reasonably capable M1911 auto for part or all of its eight-shot total capacity.

As discussed, any drastic enhancement of the .357 magnum cartridge will probably require letting out the cylinder length by a generous amount. The .357 is still operating on cylinders proportioned for the .38 Special (far left). The .357 at near left is shown in a Colt Python chamber above and you'll note it has little or no nose-room to spare; a decided handicap.

research and development into improving the burning qualities of the propellant by modifying the size and configuration of the granule or by coating with compounds that retard combustion slightly so as to keep the peak lower, meanwhile maintaining the push at helpful levels.

There appears at this time little possibility of a dramatic breakthrough that will upgrade the performance of smokeless powders sharply. That's not to say it couldn't happen, but any realistic view of the odds is quite discouraging. Borrowing a lyric from the show *Oklahoma,* "They've gone about as far as they can go."

I mention the matter of multi-powder loads with a considerable degree of hesitancy because there is a fairly unanimous consensus that duplex loads should be avoided as assiduously as cobras with rabies. Put bluntly for emphasis: *Do not mix powders!* Sooner or later I suppose nearly any reloader gets the idea that some of this plus some of that loaded together might deliver improved performance. The ballistics and resulting peak pressures of such mixtures are unacceptably unpredictable and far too hazardous to be considered.

Alternative approaches have been tried out. In the area of larger artillery they are perfectly willing to go to a great deal of bother if results more or less justify it. Experimental cannon have been designed in which auxiliary powder charges are located downbore — if I may coin the word — to be set off by hot gases from the primary charge as the projectile base passes the opening, thus injecting added boosts of pressure to offset the increased chamber volume and maintain pressures around permissible peak levels. The concept has shown velocity gains, but the approach has not been regarded as practical.

Every now and again some experimenter turns back to the concept of frontal ignition in which the flame from the primer is carried down a slender tube integral to the flash hole for delivery to the front of the powder charge near the base of the bullet. The idea is that you start the fire up front and let it burn rearward instead of vice versa in hopes of getting some increase in velocity without a corresponding boost in peak pressure. As with the multi-charge artillery load, it helps somewhat, but not enough to justify the increased complexity.

If the progress of single-bullet ballistics is earthworming instead of skyrocketing — and we'd have to sigh and admit that such is the case — some cheering words can be reported in the area of multi-projectile load for handguns. The president of BBM Corporation (221 Interstate Drive, West Springfield, MA 01089) reports they're ready to commence production of the cartridge that will probably be marketed under the name of .45 ACP Hard Cap.

I have a few sample rounds on hand of an earlier Hard Cap prototype, but the final configuration is essentially identical to a .45 ACP round carrying the standard 230-grain round-nosed full metal jacket bullet, appearance-wise. It is reported that it packs about half an ounce of shot and the chief advantage is that the Hard Cap rounds can be loaded into the magazine of the typical .45 ACP auto to feed and work the action in the manner of conventional cartridges.

BBM Corp. reports that current development of the

Hard Cap has reached the point where it holds a remarkably close pattern to extended distances from a revolver such as the Ruger Blackhawk: "Patterns the size of a grapefruit at fifteen feet," is about the way they phrase it.

The hard problem with shot loads in handguns has long been that the rifling imparts a considerable amount of rotation to the shot charge so that centrifugal force causes the pattern to open up rapidly upon leaving the muzzle. The Hot Shot barrels and loads for the Thompson/Center Contender bypassed that handicap quite neatly by use of a removable choke tube in the muzzle. The choke carries a short section of non-helical lands and grooves that serve a two-fold purpose in arresting the rotation, also shredding the rather long shot capsule to deliver a pattern that is quite acceptably tight. Made in .357 and .44 magnums, the Contender Hot Shot barrels can be used with solid-bullet loads by simply removing the choke tube. Ballistics of the .44 Hot Shot load compares quite favorably with a standard .410 shotshell out of a .410-bore shotgun of conventional barrel length.

The past few years have seen marked improvement in performance for .22 rimfire ammunition, specifically in the long rifle size. That was initiated by the CCI Stinger load that made its debut late in 1976. It was followed by the Xpediter from Winchester-Western and the Remington Yellow Jacket. Early in 1982 Remington added a .22 LR load they call the Viper which is a solid-bullet version of the Yellow Jacket's truncated-cone hollow-point bullet.

Remington lists rifle ballistics for both loads on the box:

| | |
|---|---|
| Yellow Jacket: (33-grain bullet) | 1500 fps/165 fpe muzzle 1075/85 at 100 yards |
| Viper: (36-grain bullet) | 1410 fps/159 fpe muzzle 1056/89 at 100 yards |

Ballistics in handguns are proportionally lower of course due to the shorter barrels. The Yellow Jacket in the 4½-inch barrel of my Colt Woodsman averages about 1195 fps for 105 fpe at muzzle.

*Checking with a vernier caliper shows that the .357 round on the opposite page would have its nose protruding if the overall length gets much beyond 1.6 inches. Extending the cylinder beyond the conventional lengths is going to take a great deal of expensive retooling and the question as to whether or not the potential sales would balance such production costs is one of those agonizing high-level executive decisions you read about!*

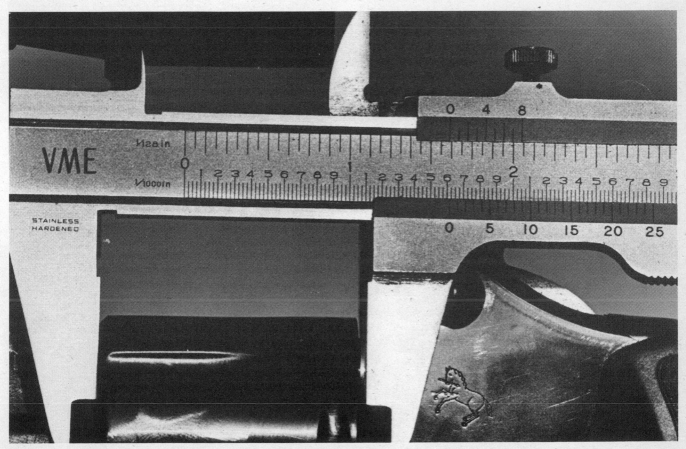

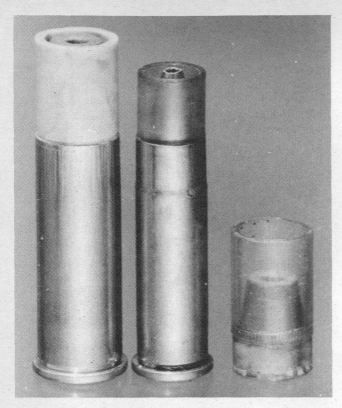

The .358 Invicta is made up in a .44 magnum case and its .257 counterpart is in a .357 mag case. Translucent sleeves center and right let you see the bullet inside.

It is a curious fact and none too well known that typical .22 LR cartridges attain their peak velocities in relatively short rifle barrels, down around sixteen inches or so. When clocked out of twenty-six-inch target rifle barrels, they are quite apt to show a marked decrease in velocity as compared to the figures from the shorter barrel. The reason for that is obvious. There is only a small quantity of powder and it's consumed early in the cycle. The last ten inches of

the longer barrel only slow it down by the effect of friction.

That points up a further problem to plague the ballistician bent upon improving the breed. In terms of what you put in compared to what you get out, the firearm is a woefully inefficient mechanism. If the latent energy in the powder charge could be harnessed so as to be delivered to the target without loss, the figures would boggle credulity by quite a margin. The losses in the system include but are not necessarily limited to heat dissipated through the cartridge case wall to the chamber, heat imparted to the barrel by direct conduction of the burning gas plus more heat transferred to the bore through projectile friction; the energy consumed in driving the weight of the powder gas itself from the muzzle; the energy used up in igniting the powder granules and raising the temperature by a few thousand degrees in the space of mere microseconds, and so on, *ad infinitum*.

If you've ever had occasion to remove a bullet that lodged in the bore due to an improper load you're quite familiar with the large amount of frictional resistance encountered.

These and a whole gaggle of other interlocking factors combine to keep us from getting the sort of performance from handguns that we might wish and dream about. Back around 1965 a maverick handgun called the MBA Gyro-Jet appeared on the market. It launched small rockets that consumed their charge of solid fuel on the way to the target venting the gas through a series of helically-angled tail jets

*Here are cross-sectional drawings that illustrate the concept of the .358 and .257 Invicta cartridges quite clearly. The concept is from Olsen Development Lab, 307 Conestoga Way, Eagleville, PA 19408.*

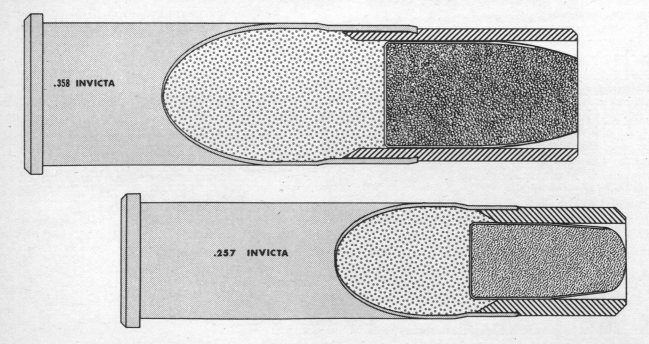

The Hot Shot barrels for the T/C Contender have gone through a number of modifications and revisions down the years and the .44 mag one here is of fairly recent vintage. The wrench at left is used in removing the straight-landed muzzle choke that's shown removed here with a .44 Hot Shot capsule and .357 loaded round.

that were intended to supply the rotational spin for stabilization. Since the bullet presented much the same manner of fire hazard as a tracer load it was immediatley forbidden for use in those areas where dry vegetation posed fire problems. The ammunition was expensive and accuracy was depressingly casual. The gun and load faded off the market in just a short while: another idea whose time was not yet.

As the book goes together there are rumors that a major manufacturer is working on a .357 cartridge provisionally dubbed the super-magnum, but no hard facts are available just yet. At one time the Great Western single-action revolvers were offered for use with a cartridge called the .357 Atomic, likewise marketed by Great Western. The .357 Atomic was dimensionally identical to the regular .357 magnum cartridge, but loaded to somewhat more intrepid levels of performance in a manner more or less comparable to the .38-44 load once put up for use in the Smith & Wesson Outdoorsman revolvers. That was an early-day equivalent of today's plus-P load for the .38 Spe-

cial and it is pertinent to note that I've encountered a few examples of .38Special designated as +P+, presumably operating at levels above the 22,400 psi of the plain +P; just how far, I've not been able to find out.

In plain point of fact, the .38 Special cartridge has enough internal volume to be capable of giving the .357 magnum a brisk run for its money, provided comparable peak pressures could be tolerated. The .357 in turn is handicapped by the fact that most if not all of the revolvers for it have comparatively short cylinders so that the overall length of the loaded round must be kept within maximum dimensions not much greater than those of the .38 Special. If anyone is going to get a .357 super-magnum off the ground the first order of the day will have to be the creation of a revolver with a cylinder sufficiently elongated to eliminate the present .357 magnum's severe shortage of space up front.

Well, as we're sometimes wont to remind ourselves, no one ever claimed it was supposed to be *simple,* did they now?

*Both the First and Third Model of the Hand Ejectors had the sturdy under-barrel lug to protect the ejector rod. They differed in that the First Model had the triple-lock feature and the Third Model omitted the expensive item.*

**M**OST AMERICAN shooters today know immediately what you mean when you mention the .44 magnum. It's that great massive Smith & Wesson revolver that only the very few are tough enough and rough enough to handle. Yet, it's that gun that has been in such demand for the last decade that the factory still has not been able to catch up and that can command just about any price a dealer wishes to place on it. How many, though, know how it all began?

The modern .44 revolver as we have known it was first visualized by the engineers at Smith & Wesson in 1905. That was the year when work began on the last of the S&W series of swing-out cylinder revolvers, the large N-frame models. Because of the great success of the Smith & Wesson .38 Special cartridge introduced a few years earlier, it was determined that the new .44 should be an almost exact enlargement of that cartridge. The .38 Special had already achieved a notable reputation for fine accuracy and the one real change that was made in the .44 was to load it down

slightly in velocity in the belief that this might make accuracy better. The first version had a charge of 26 grains of black powder behind a 246-grain lead round-nosed bullet.

Our in-house historian, Claud Hamilton has spent a great deal of time in researching the background and has presented us with his findings, which follow:

One factor which influenced Smith & Wesson was the call by a few prominent target shooters of the day for the heavier caliber. These shooters were influential far beyond their numbers and many of them believed that the larger caliber would improve their scores. From the outset, the .44 Special, as the cartridge became known, was first and foremost a target round. No real effort was ever made to push it for military service, nor was much done to interest law enforcement agencies in the caliber. When, soon after its inception in 1909, the old formalized style of target shooting fell from favor, the cartridge languished for a number of years in a condition of benign neglect. Nothing, it seems, better illustrates this than the total numbers of revolvers made for the cartridge by Smith & Wesson during the entire fifty-seven years while they were catalog items; 1909-1966: about 45,000! Less than one thousand a year on the average. What were these revolvers like?

The official factory name for the first of the line was The .44 Hand Ejector, First Model 1909-1915. It was also called the New Century and the Triple Lock. This last because of the unique and expensive three-point locking system incorporated to insure true barrel and cylinder alignment. Those familiar with modern Smith & Wesson revolvers know that they feature a pin locking system which fastens the cylinder axis at the rear in the breech face and at the front under the barrel. This revolver had a third locking point where the yoke meets the frame. A tremendous amount of hand fitting was required by today's standards, so that the revolver sold for $21! This revolver was available in barrel lengths of five and 6½ inches, and in blue or nickel finishes. Target sight versions were available as well, though

it seems that only a few of the professed target shooters of the day used them. In addition to .44 Special, the revolver was offered in .38/40, .44/40, and .45 Colt calibers.

The cost of the triple lock feature made the revolver noncompetitive, and the decision had already been made to terminate this model in 1915 when a large order for heavy frame revolvers was received from the Government of the United Kingdom. These were to be in the British Service .455 caliber, and the British Army did not much care for the heavy under barrel lug which, they felt, was likely to catch dirt in rough service conditions and result in jams and damage. The circumstances, however, were urgent so that some three hundred .455 revolvers were made for the UK in this model before the new British Service series was begun.

The .44 Hand Ejector, Second Model 1915-1917, 1920-1940, except for minor changes and internal improvements, was the same as the First Model but for the barrel. The heavy under barrel lug was discontinued along with the triple lock feature and the price was lowered to

*The Second Model Hand Ejector did away with the under-barrel lug, considered undesirable by the military.*

$16! The barrels retained their beautifully contoured shape and were available in the same lengths. Blue and nickel finishes were offered as were target sight models and the other calibers could still be had on special order. Production was interrupted when the entry of the United States into the First World War demanded the entire effort of the plant to produce .45 ACP revolvers, the now famous 1917 Army model. These guns were numbered in a separate series and the frames and cylinders were slightly enlarged to better handle the large cartridge.

Unfortunately, Smith & Wesson's best efforts were not good enough and the plant was taken over by the government. This was the first time the factory had not been under the control of a member of the Wesson family. To put things in proportion, it is worth noting that the total production of .45 ACP 1917 Army revolvers for the Army during 1917 and 1918 was approximately 163,000 units.

Production of the Second Model was resumed in 1920 and continued until July 1940.

Despite what the British thought of it, the heavy under barrel lug of the First Model was popular particularly in the West and in Mexico, and in 1926 Wolf and Klar of Fort Worth placed a special order for .44s having this feature. Since the order was large, the factory listened and the .44 Hand Ejector, Third Model of 1926, 1926-1941, 1946-1950, was born. It had the same characteristics as the Second Model but the heavy under barrel lug was there, without the triple lock feature. This model remained a special-order-only gun until 1940.

Although it is one of the rarest models, some feel it is the most important of the .44 Hand Ejector series, for it was with one of these that Elmer Keith began his experimental work in the 1930s and '40s which led directly to the inception of the .44 magnum. Production was interrupted by World War II and resumed in 1946.

For some unknown reason the factory began to separate The .44 Hand Ejector, Fourth Model, 1950-1966, into a target and a military version and special effort went into development of a ribbed barrel version with fine new target

*The Model 29 in .44 magnum with 6½-inch barrel is mounted in the Ransom Rest for Hamilton's firing tests. The Model 29 is somewhat larger than the earlier models and weighs 7½ ounces more than its predecessors.*

Ed Presser shoots the four-inch Model 29 with .44 magnum test loads. It should be noted that firing the .44 magnum revolver without suitable eye protection is not at all a good idea as some of them are lead-spitters.

sights. This is the rarest of all the predecessors of the .44 magnum. Only 6250 were made and the model was discontinued in 1966.

Almost no one was much interested in the .44 Special. Elmer Keith, in the years between the wars, did extensive work with his Third Model, developing long-range hunting loads that greatly exceeded the capabilities of the factory cartridge. He began to write about these loads and the results he had achieved in the NRA's *American Rifleman* and other gun magazines. The factory was disturbed by the loads he was proposing in print but the evidence was there; his gun was giving good service with them. One of the first innovations Keith made was to load using a bullet of his own design, the flat-point Keith lead semi-wadcutter. This hard cast bullet does not expand much and is a deep penetrator on game. It is also more destructive to tissue than the lead round nose style.

Smith & Wesson's post-war President C.R. Helstrom had read Keith's work extensively and became interested in his new loads for the .44. They met and, as a result, Helstrom approached Remington offering to produce a new .44 magnum revolver if the .44 magnum cartridge were produced by Remington. In July 1954, four Fourth Model .44s were produced in the new caliber and went into a test program. By December 1955, the first .44 magnum revolver

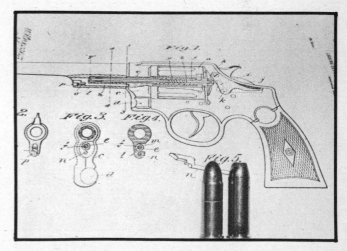

The original .44 Special cartridge is at left above, with its usual 246-grain round nose lead bullet. The .44 magnum at right is .125-inch greater in case length and beefed up to take the higher pressure.

*Martha Penso loads one of the .44s in preparation for a test firing. Ear protection is mandatory with these noisy cartridges to avoid irreversible hearing loss. Hamilton spots the previous group in the background.*

*Hamilton is firing some double-action groups from the 4-inch Model 29 off the sandbag rest, handheld.*

was completed. It was both larger and heavier than its predecessors. Frame height is .03-inch greater while the frame cut is shorter by .02-inch, making for more metal in the frame. The cylinder is .17-inch longer and .015-inch larger in diameter. Cylinder walls are .013-inch thicker; all in all a definitely beefed-up version of the earlier .44s.

Gone forever was the beautifully contoured barrel of the old .44s and in its place was a straight, bull barrel with a broad rib. Overall, the weight increased some 7½ ounces. The new .44 magnum received tremendous press coverage, probably more than any single new gun since World War II ended. As a result, sales got off to a good start and were sustained at a much better rate than had been the case with the earlier models.

As did the .357 magnum, the .44 magnum started out as a lead bullet load featuring the hard cast Keith-style lead semi-wadcutter. Unlike the early .357s, it did come with a gas check on the base of the bullet but this proved to have little effect. Both guns were notorious when it came to leading with full-house loads and this limited their potential to the few rounds a hunter might fire before a good cleaning must take place.

*As charge weights approach the maximum listings in manual, each charge needs to be hand-weighed.*

It remained for Lee Jurras to shake up the factory ammunition makers with his new line of expanding bullets for handguns before the full potential of the .44 magnum was realized. Along with this came the great upsurge of interest in handloading so that more and more shooters became able to take full advantage of the tremendous flexibility of the .44 magnum. It can, quite literally, do anything that the .44 Special, .45 ACP or .45 Colt can do, and much more. You can load it down for target work, a little higher in power for law enforcement or defense, and all the way up for hunting tough game at long range.

Recently, we fired a Second and Third Model .44 Hand Ejector against a Model 29 using factory ammunition and handloads of my own concoction. At twenty-five yards off the Ransom Rest, here are the results:

"Nothing really remarkable here but then my rest was not well and solidly mounted. I was somewhat surprised at how well the old Second Model did; it is 55 years-old and has a badly pitted bore. I believe that this illustrates the loss in accuracy that generally accompanies power pushed to the limit. The worst groups I obtained were made by the full-house .44 factory load in the magnum," reports Hamilton, who did the shooting.

| | Group size in inches, center to center | | |
|---|---|---|---|
| Load | .44 Hand Ejector Second Model | .44 Hand Ejector Third Model | Model 29 |
| .44 Special R-P 246-gr. LRN (factory load) | 1.29 | 1.01 | 1.85 |
| .44 Speer 200-gr JHP, 7.0-gr. Unique | 1.50 | 1.83 | 2.10 |
| .44 Speer 200-gr. JHP 5.1-gr. 700X | 1.41 | 1.65 | 1.05 |
| .44 Speer 200-gr. JHP 10.0-gr. AL-7 | 2.98 | 2.35 | 2.20 |
| .44 Speer 200-gr. JHP 5.3-gr. Red Dot | 2.85 | 2.08 | 2.55 |
| .44 Magnum R-P factory LSWC | | | 3.15 |
| .44 Magnum Speer 200-gr. JHP, 11.0-gr. AL-7 | | | 2.66 |
| .44 Magnum Speer 200-gr. JHP, 12.0-gr. AL-7 | | | 1.78 |

# CHAPTER 4
# RESTOCKING YOUR HANDGUN

*Improving The Interface Between Gun And Palm Can Offer Many Benefits, And Here Are Notes And Comments On Shopping For Replacement...Or Building Your Own!*

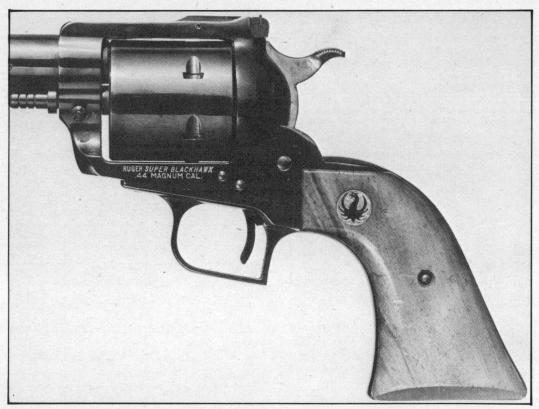

*The plow-handle contours of single-action revolvers such as this Old Model Ruger Super Blackhawk are well suited for softening recoil, but double-action guns require a different shape for best results as discussed in the text.*

THE DESIGNERS of any given handgun usually make every earnest effort to fit it out with a handle of such contours and dimensions as to fit all hands equally. With hardly an exception that comes to mind, factory handles end up misfitting nearly everyone equally. They may be too big, too small, too thin, too fat, too short, too long, too steep, too sloping, too abrasive, too slippery, or any number of combinations of the defects just listed, plus possible others.

A properly fitted handle makes any handgun easier to fire with speed, accuracy and comfort. The heavier the recoil, the more important the handle becomes. The plow-handle shape of the traditional single-action revolvers — such as the Colt or the various SA Rugers, the Virginian

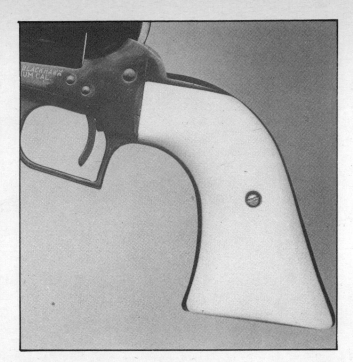

The SBH on the facing page here wears a set in moulded epoxy that bear a marked resemblance to ivory although much more durable; sadly they're no longer made. Below, a set of mother-of-pearl stocks on a vintage Colt SAA.

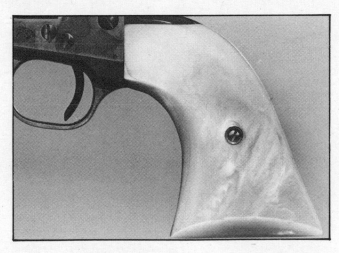

Most of the classic and traditional revolver designs fall far short in another area, in regard to the gripping area: They do not provide for supporting the weight of the gun on the upper surface of the second finger of the shooting hand — that is, the middle finger; the one next to the index or trigger finger. That fact has led to the sale and installation of a great many grip adapters, such as the rubber one made by Pachmayr or the aluminum version by Tyler. Many shooters find that such accessories are quite helpful on typical DA revolvers using the original factory stocks.

Let us pause briefly to clarify a confusion in terminology. In this discussion I am using *handle* to refer to the

Standard S&W Colt M36 Chiefs Special stocks are by no means easiest to use, but any of the many alternatives sacrifice much of the compactness that's the design's virtue.

Dragoons and all the rest — have the virtue of transmitting hard recoil gently to the shooting hand, inflicting minimal discomfort even with the largest cartridges and heaviest loads. Upon firing, the handle slides back in the hand to spread the kick over a longer interval, so that you can absorb it without ill effect.

That's fine up to a point, but if you wish to fire further shots, as quickly as possible, you must reestablish your hold on the handle. It's not a serious matter with the SA revolvers because you have to cock the hammer again anyway. Most DA revolvers assume that you may wish to fire additional shots quickly in the DA mode, so they provide a hump of varying size and dimensions at the top of the gripping area that serves to anchor the gun in your hand all right, but it can maul your hand rather fiercely with some of today's hotter loads. Such punishment is highly conducive to flinching, and that can wipe out any hopes for accurate bullet placement.

entire portion of the handgun gripped by the shooting hand, including the exposed or hidden parts of the receiver and the outer covering of wood, plastic, rubber, or whatever. The wooden (etc.) attachments go by many terms in common usage. They are called stocks, grips, slabs, plates, scales and perhaps other things as well. I have fallen into the practice of calling them stocks, out of deference to a good friend name of Steve Herrett, president of Herrett Stocks up in Twin Falls, Idaho. If you refer to them as grips in Herrett's presence, he will make plain his disapproval, and perhaps his nausea: "I pack my clothes in a damned *grip!*" he will snort.

The production blueprint for the O-frame Colt Model 1911A1 pistol covering specifications for the detachable hand-fillers also terms them stocks. A large number of other people persist in calling them grips, just as a lot of people keep on referring to detachable box-type magazines as clips, despite the fact that a true clip is something

Right, Philippine monkey-pod wood on a Colt Python. While pretty, these loosen with humidity change. Below, two versions of the Pachmayr rubber or Neoprene stocks on Colt M1911.

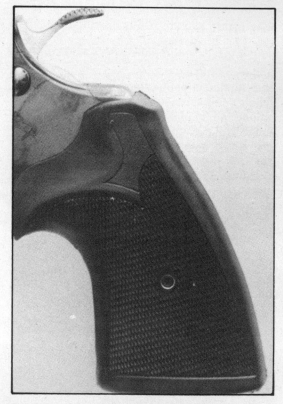

entirely different. The minor objection to *stock* is that it conveys an image of a shoulder stock, as on a rifle, which would be less than legal on a true handgun. It boils down to this: You have to call them something, and you should be consistent for the sake of easy understanding. Therefore, here and in the rest of the book, we'll use *stocks* as the term for the detachable parts and *handle* or *grip area* for the entire portion grasped by the shooting hand.

The gap between most factory handgun handles and total shooter satisfaction has provided a lot of prosperity for a number of people engaged in production of add-on stocks to suit shooters' tastes. If you shop about with enough diligence you can find almost anything by way of replacement stocks, and you may come to agree that some

Pachmayr stocks on M15 S&W Combat Masterpiece.

Pachmayr stocks on 2½-inch Colt Python.

are considerably worse than those supplied as factory originals. Some stocks are produced under the supervision of people who are themselves ardent and enthusiastic handgunners. Others are made by people with little or no personal interest in firing pistols. In the latter example the fact may be painfully apparent.

I winced as I used the word *interface* in the sub-head for this chapter. It is one of the trendy modern tic-words in the same class with *parameter* and *lifestyle.* "Avoid cliches as you would the plague" has long been one of my guiding

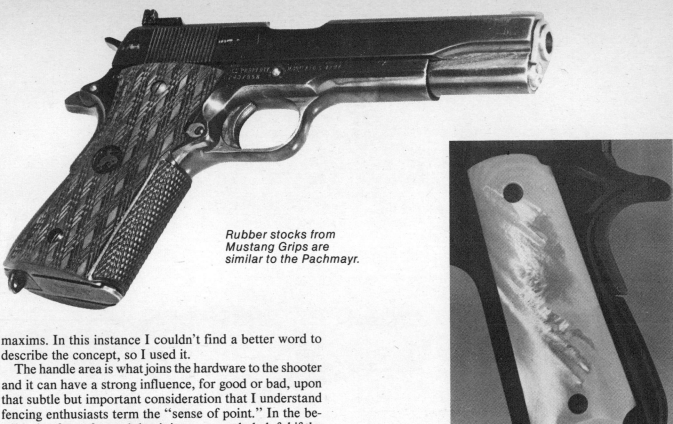

Rubber stocks from Mustang Grips are similar to the Pachmayr.

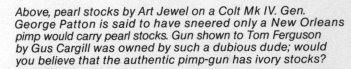

Above, pearl stocks by Art Jewel on a Colt Mk IV. Gen. George Patton is said to have sneered only a New Orleans pimp would carry pearl stocks. Gun shown to Tom Ferguson by Gus Cargill was owned by such a dubious dude; would you believe that the authentic pimp-gun has ivory stocks?

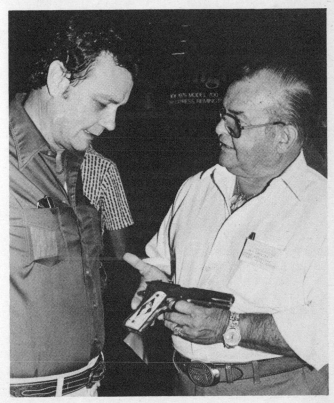

maxims. In this instance I couldn't find a better word to describe the concept, so I used it.

The handle area is what joins the hardware to the shooter and it can have a strong influence, for good or bad, upon that subtle but important consideration that I understand fencing enthusiasts term the "sense of point." In the bewildering fury of swordplay it is enormously helpful if the fencer has a keenly accurate and instinctive awareness of just where the point of his/her blade is at any given instant.

In much the same manner it is a state of things to be sought and valued if the handgunner has a keen sense of where the hole will turn up if a shot is loosed at any given moment, *without visual reference to the sighting system.*

Against targets close enough to be seriously threatening, it is an extremely useful thing to have the ability to look at a given point, regardless of where or how the gun is held, get off a shot and see a hole appear *right there*. In the hard and

Set of .45 stocks carved from laminate of walnut and birch, with thumb rest; not made at present.

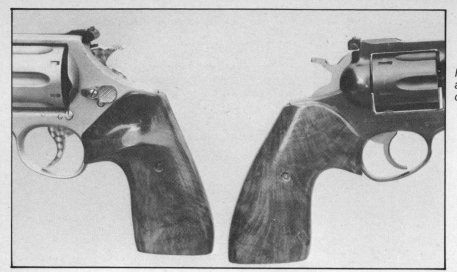

Herrett's Jordan Trooper stocks are almost completely symmetrical and comfortable to use with either hand.

A very early Thompson/Center Contender with the woodwork used at that stage of production. The 6-inch .22 LR barrel is not often seen.

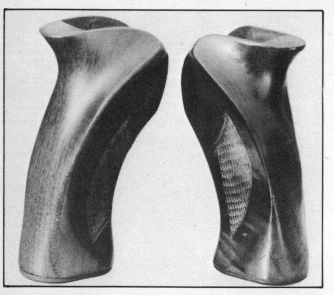

Above, LH and RH Contender stocks from the late Seventies. Right, Herrett's Handgun Hunter stocks for Contender are ambidextrous, with memory groove for the fingers.

unforgiving emergency situations in which you either survive or get converted into a statistic, such instinctive accuracy — sense of point, if you will — is just one awfully nice advantage to have.

Nearly anyone has the ability to point at something with an extended index finger to an impressive degree of precision. The fact can be proven readily by taping to the finger a small flashlight, focused to a tight beam and controlled by the tester to turn on when the subject is pointing. Regardless of the position of the hand the spot will turn up acceptably close to the intended mark. It is just one of those happy, built-in capabilities of the human mechanism that, once known, can be harnessed usefully.

The problem lies in developing a handgun that can be grasped in the same manner to duplicate the same uncanny accuracy of the index finger. It can be done, but it may take a substantial amount of doing.

There are some gifted and inspired individuals who have perfected this ability to entirely incredible degrees. It takes a lot of practice and it helps if you start with a superior set of neural circuitry in the first place. I have a good and valued friend name of Bill Jordan who can whip a revolver

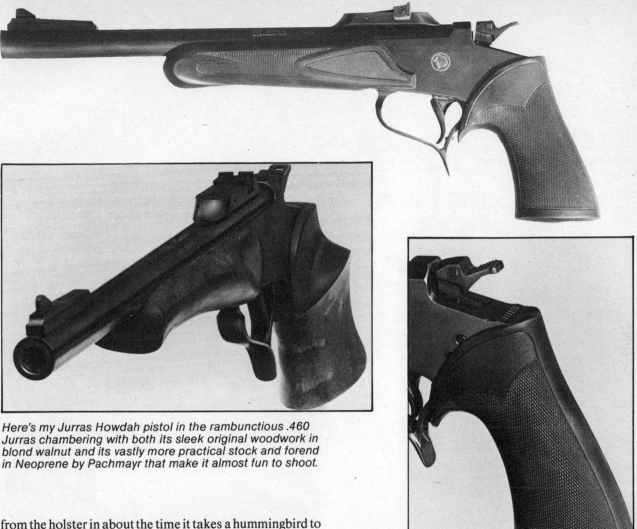

Here's my Jurras Howdah pistol in the rambunctious .460 Jurras chambering with both its sleek original woodwork in blond walnut and its vastly more practical stock and forend in Neoprene by Pachmayr that make it almost fun to shoot.

from the holster in about the time it takes a hummingbird to beat its wings twice, and demolish an aspirin tablet from six feet away, firing wax loads from hip level. I've watched him do it on various occasions and he never misses. Despite that I still don't believe it can be done. I claim that nobody can be *that* good; but Jordan surely is.

Jordan along the way designed a set of handgun stocks which Herrett markets as the Jordan Trooper. I have sets of those on a six-inch Ruger Security-Six and another on a Model 1917 Smith & Wesson in .45 ACP/AR that John Williams trimmed back to four-inch barrel length. Both are magnificent performers. Both guns have that charming trait of making me look like a much better shot than I know I really am. It is terribly difficult to refrain from admiring such accessories, intemperately. I do not even attempt to do so.

The Jordan Trooper stocks, as supplied by Herrett, are quite ambidextrous. That is, they are just about as comfortable, efficient and pleasant to fire out of one hand as the other, assuming you have a functional hand on either side. Some of my shooting buddies do not. One was born without a right hand, and an amazing number of others are southpaws, far more than the fourteen to twenty percent of the entire population that one might expect from supplied statistics.

I have long since built up a considerable amount of dis-

like for handgun stocks that force you to fire from one hand or the other. I am reasonably ambidextrous myself. Back in the Hitler-Tojo fracas my first firing encounter with the .45 service pistol was quite humiliating. I didn't even come close to making Marksman with it. Despite that I wound up as a gunnery instructor — having turned up an unexpected flair for operating flexible machine guns — and spent a lengthy while as an instructor on a .45 pistol range, as noted elsewhere here.

I devoted a lot of intent practice to getting reasonably proficient with the .45 auto and finally worked my score high enough to qualify as Expert with the right hand. Once that was accomplished it took me less than two weeks to qualify as Expert firing left-handed! It is my dogged contention that handguns are fired more with the brain than with the hand that happens to be holding them.

I can recall any number of hunting situations in which I had to switch sides to get the shot off properly. I can envision emergency situations in which the favored side gets disabled, so that your only hope is to use the weak hand. Carry a gun that can be fired from one hand and not from the other? I simply can't see it. For that reason I'd rule out a

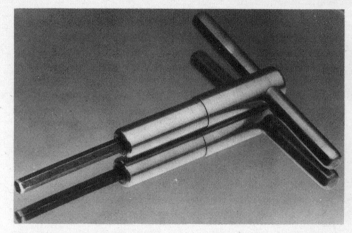

Left Bianchi's Lightning stocks on S&W M36 and M19 snubbies. Note how the ramped upper portion keeps the hammer spur from snagging. Below, a homemade hex wrench, 3/16-inch across the flats, is a most handy item for changing Contender stocks and getting them tightened.

lot of designs with impressively bulky thumb rests and the like. If you can't fire it with equal ease and efficiency out of either hand I want no part of it. Certainly not if it gets down to a hard choice between living through a given tomorrow or missing it entirely.

I mentioned the optimistic goal of designing a set of stocks that fit any hand and every hand. Curiously enough I own and enjoy a gun with a set of woodwork that comes acceptably close to fulfilling that dream. I customarily refer to it as Li'l Montgomery, by way of admiring acknowledgement of its maker, Chuck Ward, who takes his mail out of Box 610, down in Raymore, MO 64083. Ward built a similar gun for my friend Tom Ferguson, who christened his Georgie Patton, apparently in the belief that I'd named mine for Lord Montgomery.

I should note that I no more than rarely bestow names upon guns I own. I've a 1918 vintage Model 1911 Colt I call Ol' Loudmouf, and a six-inch Colt Python that is often referred to as Monty, as well as a Model 600 Remington in .35 Remington caliber that is called Pa Barker. That is the sum total of my excesses along such lines, to the present.

Li'l Montgomery started his career as a fairly mill-run, garden-variety Model 10 Smith & Wesson Military & Police revolver in the usual .38 Special chambering. Ward installed a three-inch heavy barrel, worked his way through the action in an operation he terms blueprinting, installed a fixed trigger stop, and made up the remarkable set of stocks from a regulation set of S&W target stocks. He even removed the original S&W medallions, replacing them with circles of black plastic which he terms "mother of screwdriver handle."

A further Ward trademark, appearing on most of the stocks he turns out, is the inclusion of a stainless steel buttplate, held in place by four Phillips-head screws. In the course of the handle remake, he removes some amount of metal from the rear face of the receiver, fairing it into the wood with exquisite precision.

I'll try to provide a series of photos of the Chuck Ward stocks on Li'l Montgomery for the helpful guidance of any-

one who wishes to duplicate their subtle magic. Magic is the only word that fits in this instance. Having owned the gun for upward of four years, I've allowed a number of friends to fire it. In all that time I've yet to find anyone who didn't marvel at the uncanny way it fitted their hand. In every instance the introducee started right out firing it as if they'd had years of intensive practice, despite the fact that many had little or no prior experience in firing handguns. I have large hands with abnormally long thumbs — a great boon for handgunning — but people with hands even larger, as well as those with much smaller ones, all marvel at the perfect fit of those Chuck Ward stocks in their hands.

The Thompson/Center Contender single-shot pistols have gone through a great many modifications since their primary introduction back in 1967. Along the way they were fitted with a number of different stock designs, varying rather broadly as to acceptability. Since the larger cartridges handled by this ultimately versatile pistol deliver prodigious amounts of recoil, the muting of that punishment can be welcome, indeed. I have one of the custom versions of the Contender that Lee Jurras made up a few years back in limited quantities, calling it the Howdah. Mine is in .460 Jurras chambering, by no means the lust-

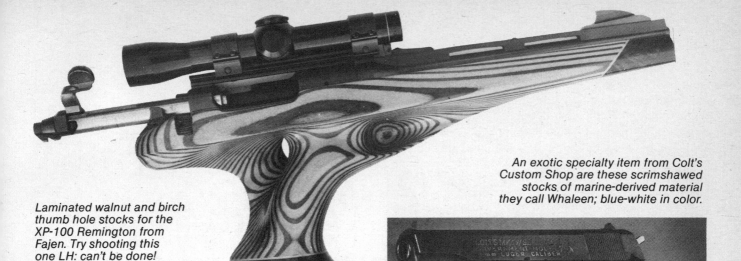

Laminated walnut and birch thumb hole stocks for the XP-100 Remington from Fajen. Try shooting this one LH: can't be done!

An exotic specialty item from Colt's Custom Shop are these scrimshawed stocks of marine-derived material they call Whaleen; blue-white in color.

iest of the roster, but it surely kicks as viciously as anything I care to encounter in a handgun.

My Howdah came with a lovely set of woodwork in blond walnut. After making up and trying out perhaps as many as eight rounds I swapped the issue stocks for one of the Pachmayr rubber ones, with a matching rubber forend for the sake of looks. I will not go so far as to say that substitution of the Pachmayr rubberwear made it a pleasure to fire, but it certainly took a helpfully large amount of the sting out of the operation.

Pachmayr developed their rubber stocks some few years back, and have added designs for several guns since the original introduction. One of the first designs was for the M1911 Colt autos. They are extremely practical and efficient. What they are not is pretty. They are now offered in patterns to fit quite a number of handguns, including such gentle kickers as the Ruger .22 autos in .22 long rifle. As far as I know, you can get the Pachmayr rubber stocks in any

color you wish, so long as your preference happens to be black.

Getting back to the T/C Contender, Steve Herrett has been supplying the stocks for those in recent times, and the standard factory offering comes with a thumb rest on one side or the other; for right-handed firing unless otherwise ordered. Available from Herrett, however, is an ambidextrous version called the Handgun Hunter with finger grooves up front. The Herrett Handgun Hunter comes

A .22 LR Colt Diamondback with factory stocks installed below and an assortment of replacement stocks that can be substituted to taste. Finger groove pattern is by Fuzzy Farrant. Stock at right is by Herrett, refined to shape by exhaustive field-testing research program.

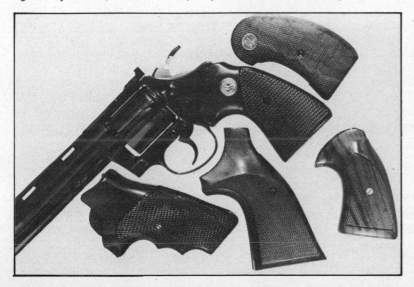

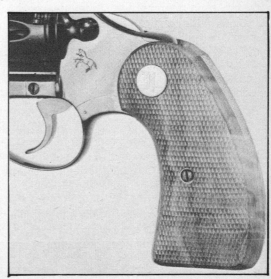

Tully, NY, silversmith Sid Bell makes these elegant fancies out of what he terms jewelery-grade pewter for installation by Colt's Custom Shop. RH side carries "Colt of arms."

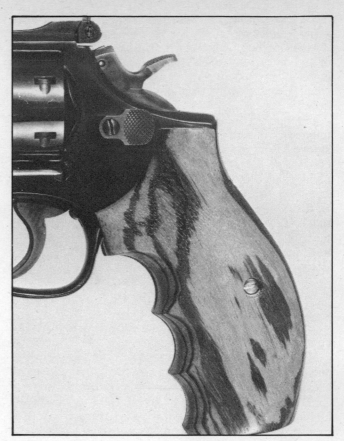

A set of zebrawood stocks by Mustang Grips enhances this short-barreled M19 Combat Magnum in .357 mag.

awfully close to my estimation as to the ideal woodwork for the Contender. It is quite symmetrical on either side; no thumb rest, but that's okay in my book because I don't find my thumbs getting all that tired.

The directory section at the rear of the book carries the names and addresses of all the firms offering replacement stocks, and accompanying photos illustrate several examples of these.

There are a number of the small pocket revolvers that come out of the box with handles that are quite small, for the sake of keeping their overall bulk to the barest minimum. As a rule most shooters find it difficult to fire effectively with these, so a number of stockmakers offer larger patterns. These may aid the pointing qualities or accuracy as compared to the original stocks, although at a cost of sacrifice in compactness.

An exception to that generalization is a set of stocks in Maccassar ebony made up by Fuzzy Farrant for a Model 1972 Colt Detective Special. These are handsome to behold, they feel great in the hand and they are probably a trifle less bulky than the original factory stocks. I hope I can scavenge up a photo of that gun to include here, because the gun is in custody of one of my sons, who's a full-time park ranger. A few months ago he fired the Colt DS for his required monthly qualification, rather than his issued Model 66 Smith & Wesson, and met his qualification requirements with a goodly number of points to spare. I

think that speaks well for the Farrant stocks, as well as for the Colt DS, and it doesn't greatly malign his shooting ability either.

There are a few handguns whose stocks are simple enough to permit restocking by workshoppers of rudimentary skills such as (sigh!) myself. Many others require a quantity of highly precise inletting and working of the woodwork to fit the hardware properly. Some of the more thoughtful makers of such guns will supply inletted blanks on special order, with plenty of surplus wood left so that the buyer can shape the finished stock(s) to personal taste and preference. One such maker is Dan Wesson Arms and another is Thompson/Center Arms.

About the only facilities needed for shaping such inletted blanks are a suitably padded bench vise, a few wood rasps and some sandpaper of appropriate grades and grit sizes, plus a suitable final-finish medium, and patience, manual dexterity, etc.

If you happen to own or have ready access to a drill press, a table saw, a belt sander and perhaps a metal lathe, it becomes possible to fashion some fairly decent looking stocks for the old Model O Colt auto, of which the M1911 pattern of .45 auto is the commonest example. Quite a lot of years ago my brother Ralph tried his hand at making .45 stocks for a brief while and during that interlude gave me a set I've enjoyed extravagantly ever since. Made of dark, plain walnut they are somewhat bulkier than the standard factory sets. Blueprint thickness at the base is .25 inch, while Ralph's set is .35 inch for the right hand (RH) and .33 inch for the left hand (LH). That may not seem like a lot of difference, but it made them feel and fire incomparably better in my large, long-thumbed hand. They were the standard set on Ol' Loudmouf for the better part of two decades.

During most of that period, and with ever-mounting intensity, I nursed a yen to try my own hand at making .45 stocks. Quite recently I reached the point where I could hold off no longer. Ralph very kindly dug up and passed along a set of four layout templates he'd made up in stainless steel. Other friends provided invaluable assistance, advice, and technical details. I happened upon a local store that retailed exotic hardwoods and maintained a rummage table of small scraps at fairly friendly prices. You don't need much wood to fashion a set of .45 stocks.

I had long suspected that making such things would pose some problems, which turned out to be correct. The problems were not insoluble, however. Without keeping close track, I'd guesstimate I've turned out over one hundred sets in the past half-year or so, several of which were — in Steve Herrett's neat phrase — "good enough for who they were for." I'd like to share the general *modus operandi* with you, along with the bypasses I found around the problems that came up.

Lacking one of Ralph's layout templates you can use a pair of factory stocks to good effect. I suggest making up the first few sets in some relatively humble and inexpensive wood as you iron out the kinks in your production technique.

You start by working the basic wood into slats of convenient size. I tend to think of this as "slatting out." The thickness should be 5/16 inch or just a trifle more, and the

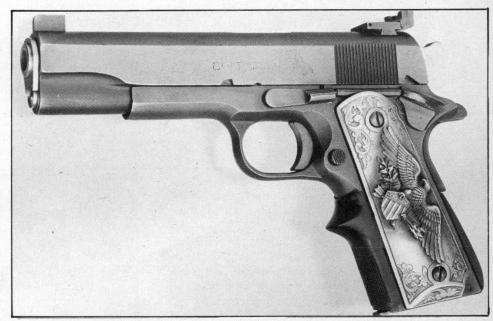

Another example of Sid Bell's artistry in metal and yes they are a touch impractical for hot loads! The neat little finger-nub up front is no longer on the market to the best of my knowledge.

Bell also produced this set of pewter stocks to grace a limited run of Aces for the Colt Custom Shop.

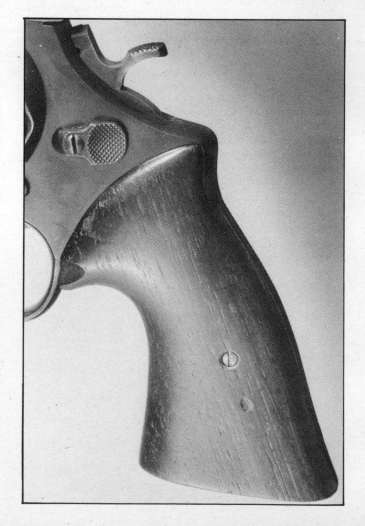

*Buffalo motif on Sid Bell stock left is the other half of the eagle and shield pattern on previous page and the old bull's horn can gouge you a crafty one if incautiously gripped as a hot load is fired. Below, one of the prettiest revolvers stocks I've seen, in rosewood by a maker long out of business, sad to say.*

width 1⅝ inches; again a touch of surplus doesn't hurt a thing. Govern the length by the fact that you need about 4½ inches for each side, so work in multiples of that, if the length of the original wood permits.

With slats on hand use a spring clamp to hold the template in a position selected with an eye to getting the choice cut of the grain pattern. I like to align the front edge of the template with the slat, or back from it just a wee trifle, and parallel to the edge. Mark around the top, bottom and rear edges of the template with a sharpened pencil or fine pen; the brand called "Le Pen" works well for this. Mark the two holes for the stock screws at the same time.

Take it to the drill press and drill the upper hole as closely as you can manage to the marked location as laid out with the template. Then insert the guide pin through the hole-spacing guide and on into the first hole you drilled...

Ah yes, the hole-spacing guide: We hadn't mentioned that, right? Let's backtrack a bit. Both of the screw holes need to be pretty close to .238-inch diameter, which requires a letter B size drill bit. That is, of course, a bit primarily designed for drilling holes in metal. Move the drive belt on the drill press to one of the higher rotating speeds, put a piece of scrap wood beneath the workpiece to keep the exit opening of the hole clean and sharp, then secure the workpiece and the scrap stop to the drill press bed with a C-clamp. That prevents the workpiece from climbing the bit as you break through, which can be pretty heartbreaking when you're working with a really choice hunk of wood.

A good alternative is if you can latch on to a letter B size drill bit that has been reground to brad-point format. It makes a much cleaner hole and it doesn't need to be C-

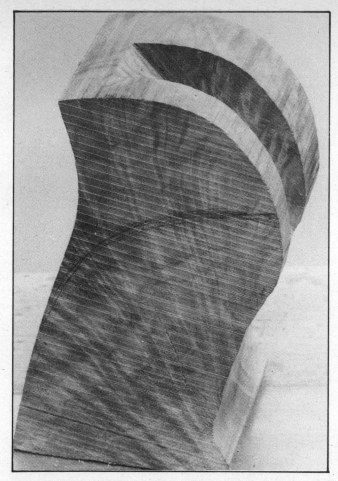

*Inletted blanks such as the one shown here in two views are generally available from Thompson/Center Arms, with the fairly complex inletting neatly performed so that the Contender owner can shape and finish it to the final details of personal taste. This specimen is a remarkably handsome hunk of feather-crotch walnut for RH thumb rest.*

clamped down as you drill, although the scrap stop beneath is still helpful. The only source I know is the one from which I obtained mine. You buy a regular B-size bit and send it to Ron Perry at 471 Pittsford-Henrietta Townline Road, Henrietta, NY 14467. He will grind it to brad-point pattern and return it to you. His current fee for this useful service is two dollars with your furnished bit, and he'll do it for other sizes, as well, for about the same price. That price is subject to change without notice, of course, inflation being how it is. You might wish to inquire first, and a stamped, self-addressed envelope would be an appreciated courtesy.

As to the hole-spacing guide, you'll have to make that yourself. The one shown here was made from ⅛x1¼-inch steel bar stock, which is a standard offering, in three-foot lengths, in most local hardware stores. You drill the holes with a B-size bit that has not been converted to brad-point mode; that is, with one in the standard pattern as purchased from the more elaborately supplied hardware stores. If no local source can be found letter-size drill bits are stocked by Brownell's, B-Square, and most other suppliers of gunsmith gear.

The guide shown here is a touch over four inches long; could be longer, but that's enough. The spacing of the two guide holes — and here comes the tricky part — is just exactly 3.074 inches between centers.

I don't know how many four-inch pieces of bar stock I wasted in futile efforts to get the holes properly spaced via careful measurement, layout, prick-punching and drilling; let's say several. You may be able to bring it off and, if so, you're a better man than I am, Gunga Din!

Ultra-precise hole-spacing is a lead-pipe snap if you happen to have a milling machine; I don't. What I do have is a luvverly 10x24-inch Jet metal lathe, from Corbin Manufacturing and Supply, Box 758, Phoenix, OR 97535. It took an embarrassing amount of furious wheel-spinning and cogitation before it occurred to me that holes could be spaced with exquisite precision using the metal lathe. Here's how it's done:

I C-clamped a piece of teak board, one inch thick and a bit, to the tool post; then C-clamped a hacksawed-off piece of the ⅛x1¼-inch band stock to that. I installed a #2 countersink in the headstock chuck of the lathe. I cranked the tool post crossfeeds toward me about as far as it would go, then turned the crank back the other way until the dial centered on a zero. That done I cranked the clamped workpiece over against the rotating countersink, made a small hole through it, backed the tool post away, replaced the countersink with a B-size drill bit and brought the work-

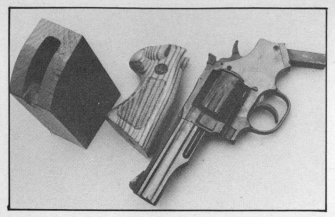

Left, a Dan Wesson Arms .357 showing the tang of its receiver, with factory stock in zebrawood and an inletted blank offered by DWA for shaping a stock to your own taste. The blank is installed at right and it's obvious there's a good abundance of wood!

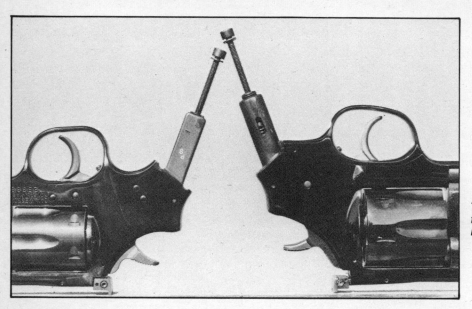

Tangs of the DWA .44 right and their .357 are somewhat different in contours and dimensions.

piece back against that to make the first hole, .238-inch in diameter. I swapped the B-bit for the countersink again, moved the tool post assembly back to the right, and then...

Mindful that the crank of the crossfeed moves it just 125/1000 (.125) inch with each full revolution — which is exactly equal to ⅛-inch — I gave the crank a carefully counted twenty-four turns, which should have advanced the workpiece by twenty-four eighths, or three inches. Then I turned it just seventy-four thousandths (.074-inch) beyond that, brought the workpiece back up against the rotating counterbore, backed it away, substituted the B-size drill bit, brought the workpiece back for the second hole of that size, and switched the big gizmo off. The lathe has a name. Being a Jet by brand I call it Mister Atkins, in honor of my favorite guitar-picker. Sorry 'bout that!

The locating pin was made from ⅜-inch cold-rolled bar stock. It's not quite 1-3/16 inches in length. That isn't terribly critical; if it fits and works, use it. The pin was knocked out on Mister Atkins, an elementary exercise even for a machinist with eleven left thumbs.

So let's turn back to the original basic procedure. We take our hole-spacing guide and drill the second hole the pluperfectly correct distance from the first one. The tolerance here is pretty sparse. When done properly the stock blank will drop onto the two stock screw bushings of its own weight, and will fall off the same way when inverted. I tend to think of this as a "plock-fit" and strive for it. I do not always achieve it and a few sets have required minor force to install and/or remove.

So we now have a pair of .238-inch holes of exquisite precision and symmetry, acceptably close to 3.074 inches between centers, in each of the blanks. Let me hastily note that the lower holes need to be centered to the laid-out marking from the template. I've a set here in handsome pau ferro where the guide slipped perhaps a sixteenth on one side. They can be salvaged if I fill the vagrant hole with epoxy and redrill and I intend to do just that as soon as I can figure out how to make epoxy look like pau ferro.

Is it all that simple? I hate to have to break the news, but not quite. We have now come to the point where the four holes, two in each blank, need to be counterbored.

The original .238-inch holes have to accommodate the

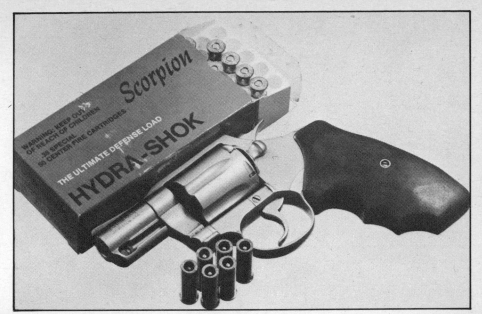

*Right, the exceptionally satisfactory set of combat stocks by Fuzzy Farrant, 1235 West Vine Avenue, West Covina, CA 91790, on a Colt Detective Special. Below the A.M.T. Hardballer has stock screws with slightly larger head diameter than those used by Colt.*

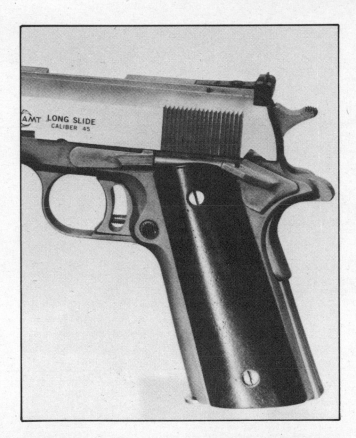

it rises above the receiver surface by about .040 inch or so. Here, for once, we needn't fit to fanatical precision. It only needs to clear the metal surfaces, not to kiss them passionately in so doing. We can counterbore from the underside by a diameter of as much as .308 inch or so, to a depth of .055 inch, give/take a trifle. As long as the inner surface of the stock snuggles down flat against the receiver, that's all we really need, unless we're all-out to impress contemporary craftsouls.

We accomplish all this crafty counterboring by means of a small bit of tooling that can be made up with the aid of a metal lathe and a clumsily-wielded three-cornered file. It doesn't take much skill, machinistwise. As proof I cite the fact that I made the examples shown here and, as machinists go, I ruefully must rate myself as the klutz of all time. I am not proud of this; merely aware of it, okay?

*A fairly standard Chuck Ward trademark is this stainless butt cap: "Handy for tacking up wanted posters," he says.*

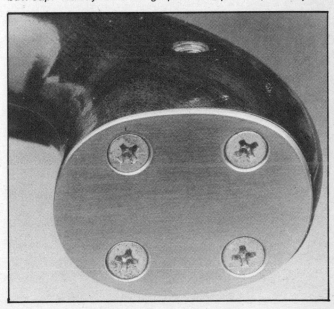

heads of the stock screws, which are about .273 inch in diameter; slightly larger in some examples, such as the AMT Hardballer. The .273-inch counterbore needs to go in from the outer surface to a distance of about .177 inch from the inner surface of the stock. That leaves a small amount of wood in the shoulder for the screw to compress upon before it encounters the top of the stock screw bushing, which is roughly .175-inch above the plane of the handle portion of the receiver.

At the same time we must provide clearance for the shoulder of the stock screw bushing from the inner surface of the stock blank. That is about .270 inch in diameter, and

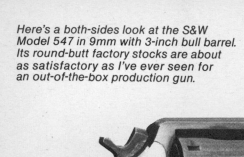

*Here's a both-sides look at the S&W Model 547 in 9mm with 3-inch bull barrel. Its round-butt factory stocks are about as satisfactory as I've ever seen for an out-of-the-box production gun.*

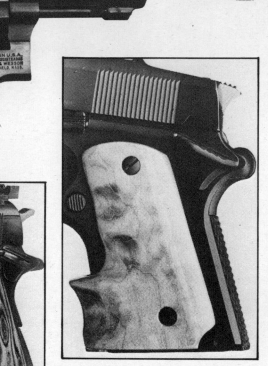

*Bullshooter's Supply of Tucson, AZ, makes these remarkably effective combat stocks: bocote on M1911, quilted maple on .45 Detonics.*

*Factory target stocks for the S&W N-frame series, such as these on a vintage M57, have a look and feel of just-rightness.*

Illustrations show the counterbore taking shape, and dimensions are indicated. You can make this from ⅜-inch cold-rolled rod, available in one-yard lengths from nearly any hardware store or ironmongers. Better, you can make it of oil-hardening drill rod of the same diameter, hardening it after filing the teeth. It will perform splendidly for a long time, even if not hardened. I get my o-h drill rod stock from Manhattan Supply Company, 151 Sunnyside Boulevard, Plainview, NY 11083. I'm sure there are other sources, but that's at least one, and a pretty good one, I think.

Note that to accept the head of the stock screw the cutter for counterboring from the outer surface incorporates a guiding pilot that also serves to stop the cut at just enough above the inner surface to leave some wood to compress for a satisfactory fit. The tip of the pilot wants to be projecting about .177 inch or so beyond the cutting faces of the counterbore. In counterboring you put a piece of leftover scrap ⅛x1¼-inch bar stock beneath the workpiece for the pilot to stop upon.

I've become partial to making up the counterbores as a double-ended affair. Thus, in the typical confusion of shopwork, if you find the one, you've likewise found the other. If you lose both, you mutter unprintable comments and make up a fresh one. The counterbore for use on the underside can have a cutting shoulder of as much as .308-inch diameter, if you wish. It has a guiding pilot tip, but the length is not critical. You merely steer the .238-inch-diameter pilot into the predrilled hole and gnaw downward until you have at least .040 inch of clearance. If you end up with .057 or .063 inch, it really doesn't hurt a thing. Ending with only

*Here are three examples of homemade stocks for the .45 auto and its kin produced by the methods and techniques described and shown in the accompanying text and illustrations. From left, there are Osage orange, sandalwood from Australia and a nicely burled specimen of walnut.*

.033 inch may send you back for another try.

The piloted tip of the counterbore to create clearance for the head of the stock screw serves a most useful function: No matter how thick or how thin the slab may be, you always end up with a clearance cut that gives you just precisely the engagement for the stock screw that is needed.

In making the double-ended counterbores, I've found it useful to add a touch of color-coding to stave off potential goofs. The parts of the shank that are gripped by the drill press chuck are of the same diameters — about .314 inch, not critical — so that you can reverse them without a lot of chuck-twirling. I have color-coded the shank above the end for the outer counterbore blue, and the other one green, by holding felt-tipped marking pens against them while rotating. Thus, if the end with the visible blue marking is in use, I know that it goes against the top of the stock blank, because the sky is blue (usually), and it's overhead. Conversely, if the green end of the counterbore is visible, that means it's for the underside of the stock blank, corresponding with green grass, which is underfoot.

If all that strikes you as silly, may I note that you've probably not yet had the chagrinful experience of making the bigger counterbore inward from the top, so as to provide a painfully generous amount of clearance for the head of the stock screw—? As it happens, I've done so, which is why I took the approach noted, to forestall future shemozzles.

So, we now have the crucial holes spaced and counterbored. If you've not stopped reading by this point, let's go on with the rest of it, serene in the assurance that most of the worst is now to the rear.

Cut the blanked portion out of the slats on the table saw, leaving a bit to spare. Trim to the upper curvature at the top. A good, easy way to do that is by means of one of the inexpensive sanders powered by an electric drill, such as the model by Black & Decker, shown here. You still need to trim the rear edge of the blank to the marked line. Originally, I did that by fastening both blanks to a piece of board using screws and inching in upon the marked cutline by cautious passes on the table saw, with fine readjustments of the miter gauge as required. After a frustrating while at that approach I made up the pin-locating guides, likewise illustrated. These ride in the two channels cut into the table saw bed. The blanks are positioned by means of the steel pins inset into the guide, and a single cautious pass removes the excess wood from the rear edge with gratifying precision and a minimum of futzing-about.

A similar guide, also shown, is used to make the relieving cut across the top of the LH stock to clear the plunger tube. That's also done on the table saw, and it requires precise adjustment of the height of the blade. Once adjusted, a piece of scrap wood can be relieved to serve as an adjustment guide on future sessions.

Once the plunger tube relief cut has been made in the top of the LH stock, both stocks can be tried on the gun to check for general fit, and to mark the lower edge by outlining it against the butt of the receiver with a sharp knife. The surplus wood can then be cut from the lower edge of the stock to the scribed line on the table saw by adjusting the miter gauge of the saw and using extreme caution if the blade guard is not in place. It's better to approach the scribed line in two or three passes, adjusting the miter

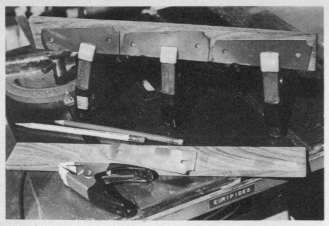

Basic slats are cut 1⅝x5/16 and outlines are traced on them from metal templates held by spring clamps.

Each blank uses about 4½ inches of basic slat. Laying them out as shown here avoids waste of the wood.

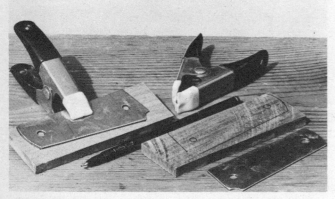

Note that holes are located by tracing circles in the template as a reference point for drilling them later.

Layout in this manner assures the closest possible match of grain from one side to the other. Note that patterns are laid out to the front edge, as discussed.

gauge as necessary to get the final cut exactly lined up with the metal of the receiver.

I should note that I use a hollow-ground planer blade on the table saw for applications such as this, as well as for slatting out the wood to the dimensions given. When such a blade is good and sharp it leaves a cut surface that is almost glass-smooth, requiring no more than moderate final sanding to get the inner surface of the stocks dead flat and smooth. As the blade loses its edge — which happens rather soon with some of these woods — it will begin to leave burn-marks on the cut surface, requiring considerable additional sanding to remove.

Although the procedure just given can be used to trim the lower edge, you'll note that the cutting gauge used to trim the rear edge of the blanks has another set of guide pins at the opposite end, so that it can be reversed in the grooves of the saw table for trimming the lower edges. Trimming gauges such as these are not hard to make, and they are wondrous time savers. The steel locating pins are made from .25-inch cold-rolled bar stock in the lathe, with the outer ends turned down to .238 inch and press-fitted into B-size (.238-inch) holes drilled in the board, using the hole-spacing guide to assure the correct distance between centers.

Note that both of the cutting guides have a generous-sized piece of scrap wood running crosswise in the center. Those serve two purposes, both good. They add rigidity to the guide, and they help to keep absent-minded fingers away from the cutting edge of the blade, thereby saving a small fortune in Band-Aids!

With the two blanks completely drilled, counterbored, and outlined, there are a few further operations that should be completed before going on to round off the outer surfaces. The front edge of the RH blank needs to be marked for the clearance cut to allow free movement of the rear tip of the magazine release, after which the wood is removed at that point. For this I use the Dremel Moto-Tool in one of the small drill press holders Dremel makes for it with a .25-inch router bit installed. I've become rather partial to making this clearance cut from the inside, as shown here, so that the front edge of the RH stock retains a straight line, once installed.

If you decide to make that clearance cut clear through the wood, in the manner of the factory stocks, the outline can be followed when laying out the blank from the original pattern and cut away. A further possibility is to mark the front edge with the point of a knife and center a cut with the Dremel router bit on the marking. The crescent cut on the

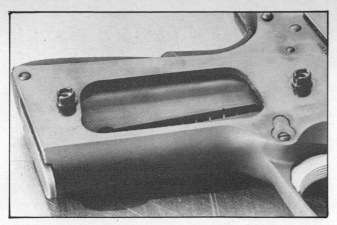
*Here's a good look at your two stock screw bushings and the magaizne release that requires clearance cut on RH.*

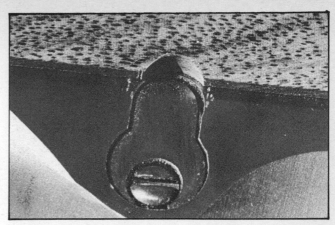
*Still with the RH stock, here's one way to mark the edge and cut the relief with a Dremel Moto-Tool router bit.*

factory stock is considerably more generous than it needs to be.

Factory stocks have a vertical edge around the front, rear and lower sides, measuring .062 inch, and there is a forty-five degree bevel cut along the lower edge, leaving the vertical edge. As you prefer, the lower edge can be beveled or left at a ninety-degree edge entirely. This is a matter of taste and choice, as is the inclusion or omission of the clearance cut at the lower rear corner to give access to the mainspring housing pin. If you don't mind having to remove the stocks to get at the housing pin, the resulting effect is attractive and somewhat more comfortable in firing, since you don't have all those sharp edges digging at the heel of your hand.

The housing pin cut, if made, is a .344-inch radius, centered at the intersection of the rear and lower edges. A router with a .75-inch straight bit installed can be used to make this cut within acceptable tolerances, using guide and stop strips held to the router bed with C-clamps. Obviously, this is an operation requiring extreme care and

caution to avoid routing incautious fingertips! I don't recommend that approach. It's considerably safer to make the cut with a coping saw to the marked outline and smooth it with a piece of sandpaper wrapped around a length of .75-inch-diameter dowel.

If you omit the housing pin relief cut it's a good idea to make a pair of shallow relief cuts on the inner surface to avoid interference betweeen the stock and slight protrusions of the housing pin, as shown in the nearby illustrations. This will avoid distracting gaps when the stocks are installed.

All of the proeceding operations are done much more easily when the outer surfaces are still flat. With those attended to it is time to form the outer surface of its final, rounded contours. The curvature has a nominal radius of 1.031 inches on both sides, to a final thickness of .25 inch. Those are blueprint specs, but you are free to follow your personal fancy in departing from them, making the stocks thicker or thinner, as desired.

Another indispensible tool for .45 stockmaking is the

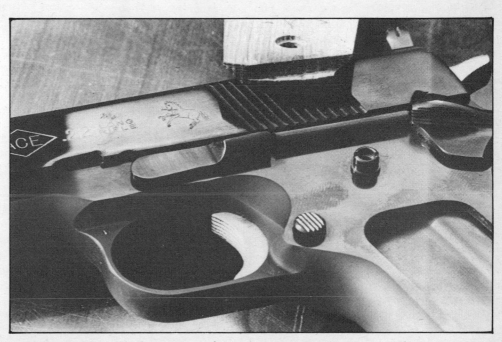
*LH stock would be a simple project if it weren't for the need to make a relief cut to clear the plunger tube at the upper edge as in the relieved blank visible in the upper portion here.*

If using standard letter B bit, workpiece should be held to drill press bed with C-clamp. Brad-pointed bit reground by Ron Perry cuts cleaner and does not need clamping.

Hole spacing guide and locating pin have holes 3.074 inches between centers of .238-inch diameter. Steel band stock and cold-rolled rod were used in making these items.

holding block, as illustrated here. It's made from a piece of scrap two-inch plank with two holes drilled in one edge spaced 3.074 inches between centers using the hole-spacing guide described here. Two pieces of .25-inch cold-rolled rod are turned down to .238 inch at one end and press-fitted into the .238-inch holes in the plank. Position the projecting ends of the steel pins so that a drilled stock blank will be held by them, without the ends of the pins protruding. You will be using this handy item extensively, both for holding the blanks during the rounding step and later clamping the holding block in the bench vise for final sanding and finishing.

Lacking a belt sander the blanks can be rounded by simply putting them on the holding block in the vise and using a wood rasp, sandpaper and a great deal of careful, patient elbow-grease. If you have to go that route I'd suggest cementing some Open-Coat sandpaper in various grits such as 100 and 220 to a piece of board, gluing the handle to the opposite side of the board and using that. Cut the original sheets of sandpaper in two pieces, across the middle, so as to have working surfaces about 5½x8½ inches. The advantage of this is that it maintains a straight line in one direction. This is a good way to use up leftover scraps of particle board, since that is usually flat and warp-free, regardless of its other shortcomings.

The approach I much prefer is to fasten the belt sander,

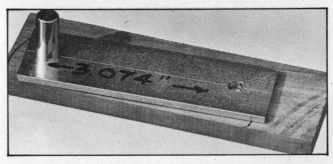

With the first hole drilled, pin is installed as here and guide is aligned to mark for lower hole to assure the desired spacing that is quite important for good fit.

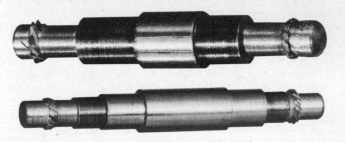

Two examples of the double-ended homemade counterbore used to finish upper and lower surfaces of the two stock screw holes in blank.

A piece of scrap wood beneath the blank will help to assure a cleanly cut exit opening as the bit goes through.

inverted, in the bench model Black & Decker Workmate. The latter is bolted to the top of a small but fairly heavy stand. The trigger switch of the belt sander can be locked on, providing a moving surface of sandpaper that is large enough across the flat to shape the stock blanks in straight longitudinal lines, provided they are sanded somewhat diagonally across the belt.

Let's note another point here. In rounding the blanks you are going to produce a substantial amount of sanding dust. For the sake of your health avoid inhaling the wood dust. That means wearing a breathing mask of suitable design or, alternatively, directing a fairly powerful stream of air across the sanding operation to carry the airborne dust away from your face. You can use an electric fan or, if available, a small squirrel-cage or centrifugal blower.

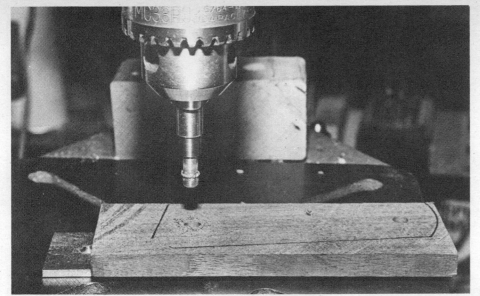

*Pilot tip of topside counterbore stops the cut just .177-inch from lower surface as it touches the steel plate beneath the workpiece to locate the shoulder at the ideal height to engage screw head.*

*Above, the .273-inch counter bore to clear head of the stock screw. Note the small ledge thus made for the screw head to bear against. Right, clearance cut for the shoulder of the bushing is about .308-inch diameter, .055-inch in depth and for one welcome time, a bit bigger doesn't hurt a thing!*

Note also that the wood dust from some of these exotic hardwoods may be more or less allergenic, irritating to the skin and membranes. Cocobolo, African padauk, pau ferro and zebrawood are among but by no means all of the possible offenders in this respect. With that in mind, you may wish to wear a long-sleeved shirt and perhaps rubber gloves, as well. It will soon become apparent if any of the woods are irritating to your skin, and you can take the needed precautions henceforth.

The fallout of the sanding dust makes an ungodly mess, suggesting that the sanding is much better conducted outdoors, so as not to coat everything in the shop with the pesky stuff. Use discretion in directing the airstream from the fan or blower, to avoid coating the family sedan with wood dust, for example.

I prefer the medium grade of paper for the sanding belt, about 80-grit, although 100-grit or 120-grit will do a good job, at the expense of taking longer. Avoid the coarse grades, such as 50-grit, except perhaps for initial roughing to shape of the more difficult woods. The coarse paper may cause you to remove more wood than you wanted to, and it's awfully hard to put it back on!

With the fan going and the belt in motion seat yourself to view the operation from about eye level. Wearing safety glasses, place the blank on the holding block and commence rounding the outer surface of the blank. Again, it's better to use up a few blanks from inexpensive scrap wood for initial familiarization, until you acquire the basic knack of this operation. Round a little off one edge, then about the same off the other, pausing frequently to take a keen survey of the progress. Pay special attention to the remaining depth of the holes that will accommodate the heads of the stock screws. Keep a firm image in your mind as to the thickness of these screw heads, so as to avoid taking off so much wood that they'll protrude when the stock is installed. If in doubt leave a bit of extra wood to be removed during final finishing by hand.

We noted that the blueprint curvature is an arc with a radius of 1.031 inches. You are by no means confined to maintaining a perfectly circular cross-section. You may

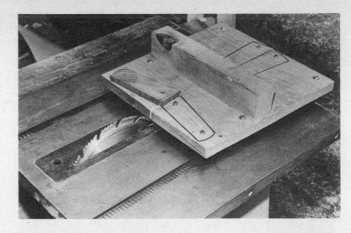

*Above left, the two trimming jigs that ride the bed groove of the table saw, locating the blanks by steel pins in the screw holes to make the trimming cuts on the lower and rear edges of the blanks, as well as the jig for relieving LH blank for plunger tube clearance. Lower edge is trimmed first (top right, lower left), jig is reversed for rear edges.*

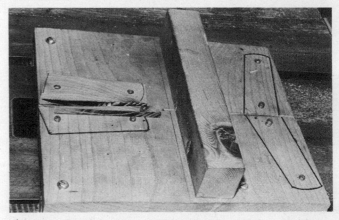

wish to experiment — preferably with scrap samples — in modified cross-sections more or less parabolic in format. For example, if you're right-handed try thinning down the front edge of the RH blank a little more, either doing the same on the LH side or letting it build up a bit. If your fingers are quite short you can remove a little extra wood on both front edges to achieve a better hold of the gun, which can prove extremely useful. In short, explore the possibilities and if it feels good, do it!

Final finishing is done with each blank in turn being held on the holding block in the bench vise. Use progressively finer grits of sandpaper until no slightest trace of the

scratches from the rounding can be seen or detected by a thoughtful fingertip.

A handy wrinkle is to fold the full-sized piece of sandpaper into thirds, across the shorter dimension. In so doing you'll discover it's much easier to control in hand-sanding, giving you a secure holding surface with little or no tendency for the sandpaper to weasel about and get wrinkled.

The finer — white colored — grade of 3M Steel Wool Substitute is an excellent material for the final polishing of the sanded surface, prior to applying the finish. Take pains to avoid dishing the area around the screw holes, such as by

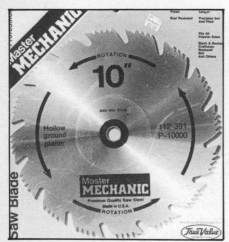

*Hollow-ground planer blades give delightfully smooth clean cut for such uses. Blade height is adjusted for plunger-tube cut by use of gauge cut from scrap. Please note and remember that most of these operations cannot be performed with the saw blade guard installed so the greatest of care is needed in working.*

With blade set we're ready.

After preliminary cut.

Held against guiding edge.

Kerf is widened by making extra cuts, until excess wood is removed...

...like so!

Check to be sure it fits to taste, adjust if needed.

Some blanks may stick to the pins. A putty knife works well to dislodge them, but shut off the motor!

Clearance cut can be made just as well on a blank after it's been rounded-over; this one's in Oregon myrtle wood.

using a sanding block during the work with the coarser grades.

There is hardly any limit to the finishes that can be applied, and you're the final judge as to what's preferred. My own choice, after having tried many possibilities, is Flecto Varathane in the pressurized spray cans. As has been noted regarding alcohol for curing the common cold, "Nothing else fails half so well." A further choice is between the satin and high-gloss versions of this and several similar products. In general my taste favors the glossy, but I have a set of bocote stocks on Ol' Loudmouf that were originally finished in high gloss and then rubbed down to a mellow satin appearance, and they look and feel almost painfully elegant. To some extent the final selection of finish will depend upon the wood.

You will encounter some woods that are highly reluctant to accept a coat of spray Varathane. African padauk and pau ferro are two outstanding examples of this. Both have a content of oil that keeps the Varathane from setting up to its usual durable hardness. It will usually be necessary to apply some other finish as an initial sealing coat in such instances. Spray-on shellac works well since it also tends to seal the open pores in the wood, and the first few coats can be sanded down between sprays to produce a superbly smooth surface that will be a great asset when you move on to the Varathane. Another possibility is Flecto Varathane II, which seems reasonably compatible with most if not all woods, though it is quite unsuited as a final finish, being prone to water-spot in the presence of moisture. Base coats of Varathane II, topped by final applications of plain Varathane, seem to work quite well. If you have an unwanted surplus of satin finish, it can be used up in the preliminary

Left, rounding upper edge to marked line with belt sander. Above, it works well to take several sets through the steps as a batch, doing one operation on each set in turn.

coats, followed by a final coat or two of high-gloss, resulting in the same degree of gloss obtainable by coat after coat of the high-gloss.

Nearby illustrations show the simple setup I use for supporting the blanks during spray finishing. Some #6x½ sheet metal screws are of a perfect size to drop into the screw holes to keep unwanted finish from ending up there. The blocks have small relief holes in their upper surfaces to provide clearance for the tips of the sheet metal screws. These also serve to keep the freshly sprayed stocks from slipping off the support blocks.

After spraying, the stocks are carefully lifted off the supports and placed on small pieces of scrap wood for support, whereupon they are put on the dashboard in the car for dry-

Colt medallions go 1 inch below upper hole on #12 bit with use of another piloted homemade bottoming counterbore that looks scruffy, but inlets pinstripe bocote to perfection.

ing in the warmth of the sunlight. I think of the cars as my solar-powered drying ovens and, since they face more or less to the south, the inside temperature can get anywhere up to 160 degrees Fahrenheit or so on a sunny day.

Note that African padauk is somewhat photo-sensitive, particularly when unfinished. The blinding-bright scarlet color will quickly darken to a pleasant reddish chocolate shade when exposed to light. I suspect you could probably hold a photo negative to it and make a sort of contact print. If you wish to retain its full brightness, protect it from the light while the finish sets up.

Quite accidentally I stumbled upon a handy approach for getting the last bit of Sunday-morning shine to the glossy Varathane. I'd applied a protective coat to the inner surface of a set and some of the spray wafted around and settled upon the outer surface. Understandably reluctant to apply a further complete coat to the outer surface, I put the stocks in the holding block in the bench vise, folded a piece of paper towel down to slightly larger than the stock, applied a few drops of Ronsonol lighter fluid to the towel and tried to rub off the unwanted overspray. It came off

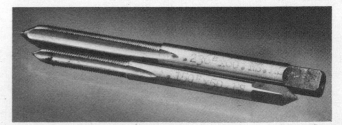

Brownell's can supply the special taps for stock screw and bushing thread, both of which can be quite handy.

quite nicely and in the process I noticed that it considerably improved the looks of the rest of the stock as well.

That was the fortuitous and independent discovery of what I call solvent-polishing, which has since become a routine step of the production cycle. Lighter fluid is prin-

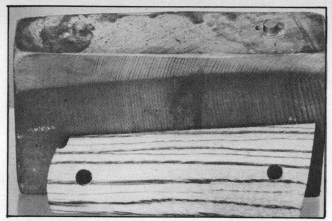

Holding block from scrap wood with locating pins is one of the handiest, most indispensible of all the tools. The blank here is a semi-finished LH stock in zebrawood.

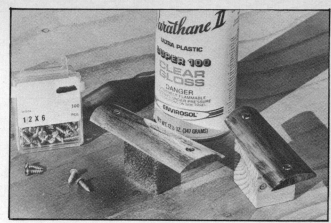

#6x½ sheet metal screws are perfect to keep the finish out of the screw holes. Varathane II is okay for priming coat but exterior Varathane is needed for the final coat.

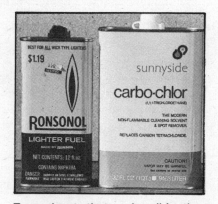

Two solvents that work well for the crafty solvent-polishing technique described here. Right, shallow reliefs to clear tips of pin.

cipally composed of naphtha — a highly flammable petroleum distillate — and further checking turned up the fact that another solvent, with the brand name of Carbo-Chlor, works even better for this purpose. Carbo-Chlor is non-flammable, but the vapors are hazardous if inhaled — as are those of all solvents — requiring that it be used with excellent ventilation.

I devised and built several improvised presses for edge-gluing and laminating pieces of suitably contrasting wood together in making up stock blanks for something beyond the common appearance. Apart from a huge crusher affair, the smaller presses depend upon a series of bolts and nuts to exert their urgent force. The nuts are secured to the lower surface of the upper crosspiece in the manner shown, which seems to work extremely well. The nuts and bolts are ⅝-11 NC thread on the largest press, and ½-13 NC on all the rest. The threads on such inexpensive hardware store items may be a trifle rough, and I found it helpful to run a die of the appropriate size over the bolts, and a matching tap into the nuts, resulting in usefully easier turning.

The important thing here is to get the lower crosspiece sufficiently rigid and massive as to resist warping under pressure. Laminated workpieces from the first two models tended to show a painfully detectable curvature upon completion. The third press has its lower crosspiece laminated of Honduras mahogany and some extremely tough fir, and it has been notably free of that problem.

Nearby illustrations show some experimental blanks laminated from four strips of African padauk and three strips of Osage orange. Respectively bright scarlet and vivid yellow, these are probably too painfully colorful for most tastes, even including mine. As I wanted to end up with a final width of 1⅝ inches, I divided that distance by seven to arrive at .232 inch as the desired thickness for the basic strips. The rip fence of the saw was adjusted by trial settings, followed by a micrometer check of the thickness of cut pieces of scrap. After their session in the laminating press, the resulting seven-decker sandwich was sliced into slabs about .25-inch thick. The slabs were smooth-sanded on one side and that was laminated to a thin slice of rock maple for durable support, with the maple serving as the inner surface of the blank. I had tried Honduras mahogany as the support of similar sets, but found it objectionably prone to chip and fray at the edges during cutting to shape on the table saw. Maple presents much less problems in this respect, although good, clear birch serves about as well.

A further interesting possibility is to cut some end-grain slices from wood with an arresting figure, edge-gluing

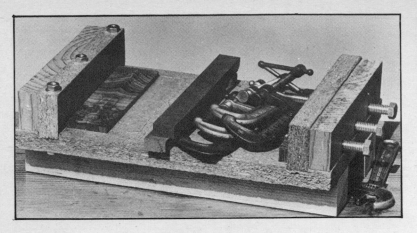

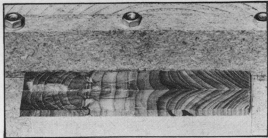

Edge-gluing press for joining bookmatch pattern of end-grain East India teak, above.

Details of homemade laminating press used to join teak panel to maple underlay for a stock of striking appearance and grain pattern.

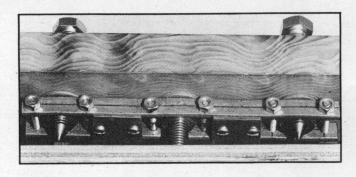

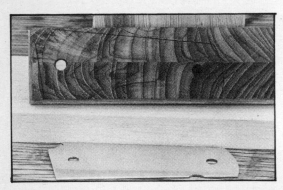

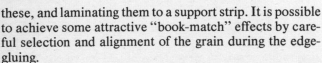

Ends of thrust bolts have 60° taper to match guide holes in steel plate. The nuts are anchored as in photo above.

these, and laminating them to a support strip. It is possible to achieve some attractive "book-match" effects by careful selection and alignment of the grain during the edge-gluing.

Many factory stocks for the .45 auto carry small medallions on each of the outer surfaces. Nominal location for such medallions is on the line between the two stock-screw holes, and centered one inch below the center of the upper hole. Vertical orientation of the medallion should be to the centerline, rather than on a line parallel to the axis of the gun barrel.

One approach for improvised medallions was to cut the head from a .45 ACP spent case and inlay that into the surface of the finished stock. I made up a small, piloted cutter on the lathe to route out the .480-inch-diameter relief cut for the medallion. In use, this works well, although you have to pause a few times to clear the wood fibers from the cutting teeth. It's made from cold-rolled steel rod, not tempered. The hardness of the steel is enough greater than that of any wood to permit cutting several holes before the edges of the bit dull detectably.

Cutting a thin wafer off the head of the .45 ACP case was a minor challenge, finally solved by removing the

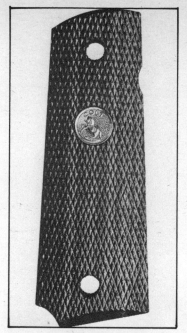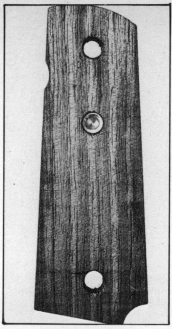

*Above, outside and inside views of RH factory stock for general guidance on how they handle pertinent details. Right, a set in pau ferro, skillfully checkered by Steve Fischer, cut to traditional patterns.*

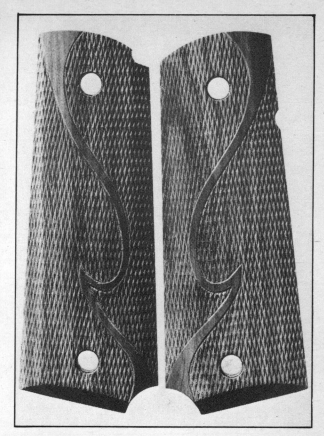

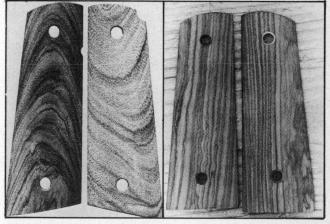

*No two sets of pau ferro ever look much like any others. Gorgeously grained and of colorful brown tones, it's one of the nicest-looking, meanest-working of all woods.*

collet assembly of my Forster Brothers case trimmer, knocking out its handle rod and chucking the collet into the headstock of the lathe. That held the case perfectly centered, and quite securely. I used cases that were nickel-plated, headstamped "FEDERAL .45 AUTO," since that seemed a suitably fitting medallion for use on a Government Model pistol. If you anticipate marketing such things commercially, you'd be wise to inquire from the given ammomaker to obtain their permission for such use.

You could leave the fired primer in place. I do not recommend the seating of a live primer, for reasons that should be obvious. What I did was to prevail upon the friendship of Dave Andrews at the Omark/CCI plant. He sent me a moderate supply of the large pistol size of primer cups, procured from that point in production before the wafer of primer mix and the anvil were added. These look realistic, but are entirely inert and safe to handle. If you feel an urgent need for such dummy primers, I suggest you write to me for a few — they're as mailable as anything ever gets — rather than pestering Dave Andrews for them. These are also nice for use in dummy cartridges, provided you don't let them get mixed in with some live rounds.

I've probably employed forty or so different woods in making .45 stocks to the present, finding wide variation as to suitability and satisfaction between them. Many of these are extremely hard, in comparison to typical woods, so they're best slatted out with a saw blade having teeth tipped with tungsten carbide. Carbide blades are the only type that should be used in cutting the various teaks, for example. In the process of growth, teak trees seem to pick up silicates from the soil and incorporate quantities amid the wood fibers. If cutting teak with a steel saw blade in fairly dim light, you'll probably note occasional flying sparks as the teeth encounter pockets of silicates and the like. You can readily imagine what this does to the cutting edges of steel saw teeth! Tungsten carbide, being second only to the obdurate diamond in hardness, alleviates such problems.

Here, in no significant order, is a listing of some — by no means all — of the woods suitable for use in handgun stocks, with a few notes on characteristics of each.

**Pau ferro** is a tropical species, as are many of the hardwoods listed. The term means iron wood, and that's fairly descriptive. It shows a broad variation as to color

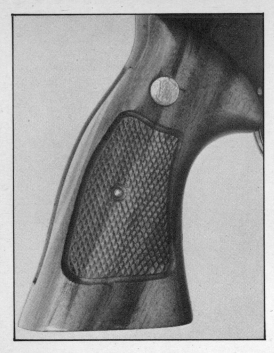
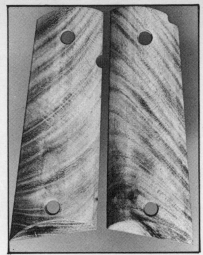
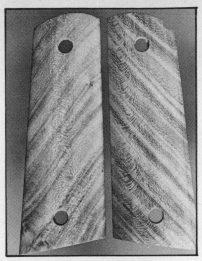

*Goncala Alves, left, is well known to S&W fanciers; makes nice .45 stocks if you can find the stuff. Above, two sets in Osage orange, a bright yellow wood of handsome grain. One set has lower edges cut to 45° bevel; other set has concealed RH magazine release relief.*

and grain pattern, with hardly any two samples ever looking much the same. Color varies from a pleasingly tawny middle-brown to a rich, reddish shade of burnt umber, often with spectacular and/or pleasing grain pattern. Properly selected and finished it results in stocks of immensely attractive and elegant appearance, so as to compensate the worker for its intractable toughness to work, its reluctance to accept finishes, and its proclivity for causing rashes on the skin closely similar to poison ivy/oak/sumac, et al.

**Cocobolo** is another extremely hard, dense, fine-grained wood, resembling pau ferro in that respect. Usually it's a deep shade of darkest brown to nearly black with reddish streaks of grain. It finishes to a surface almost without visible pores. It's hard to find in good grades and is rather expensive. Like pau ferro, as noted earlier, its dust may prove highly irritating to the skin and inhalation must be avoided entirely.

**Goncala Alves**, as I understand, is not a botanical term but a person's proper name, for whom the wood was named. I won't swear that's true, only that I heard it was. This is the wood extensively used by Smith & Wesson for their revolver stocks, thus familiar to many firearms enthusiasts. It often shows vivid grain patterns, ranging from red through orange and yellow to brown, with a fairly grain-free surface.

**Tulipwood** is a real grabber in color and grain pattern; usually a pinkish-orange in background color with grain pattern in bright reddish-brown. It works to a hard, smooth surface and accepts nearly any finish superbly and easily. The tree is prey to some manner of fungus that leaves areas of greenish-gray rot, usually where you want them the least. It's hard to find in suitable grades and is roughly $5/pound if you can find it.

**Osage orange** grows in the lower Midwest, from about Kansas on down to Texas, where it's often termed *bois d'arc*, French for "wood of bows," being equally well suited for use in archery. When freshly worked its usually a bright lemon to chrome yellow with good but not vivid grain pattern. Once made up it's notably hard, tough and

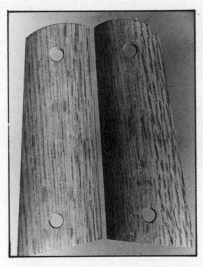

*Quartersawn red oak makes a nice set with tawny hue and rugged grain pattern.*

durable, resisting surface damage extremely well. It accepts nearly any finish quickly and easily. If left unfinished it gradually darkens to a pleasant middle-brown color from exposure to the air.

**Bocote** is a dark, brown-and-black wood, usually with highly striking grain pattern that varies according to the direction of sawing. It may show a neat pinstripe or, cut the other way, a mad profusion of loops, whorls, lakes, and rings. Quite hard, it saws well to a surface nearly resembling milled metal, and it sands to glassy smoothness. Varathane sets up on it fairly quickly, as do most other finishes.

**Padauk,** pronounced "pah-DOOK," occurs in varieties from Africa and Burma, perhaps other sources as well. As noted here the African padauk is a blinding, day-glow scarlet when freshly finished, darkening to reddish brown on exposure to light and/or oxygen. The Burmese padauk is much less prone to color change, remaining a fairly constant muted orange. When freshly cut, Burmese padauk will exude white powdery deposits from the pores for a considerable time, requiring patient removal with

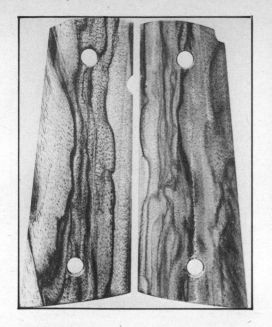

Left and above are two examples of what the more carefully selected examples of walnut can offer. Even the straight-grained humdrum examples of walnut take checkering extremely well, do not look bad.

lighter fluid on bits of paper towel before applying the finish. Of the two the African padauk is found more frequently and it has a grain that is generally more showy and attractive than that of the Burmese.

**Sandalwood** is another that's purely a joy to work. Also used in perfumes and incenses its fragrant aroma is a minor side benefit. Ranging in color from a soft oyster white through rich tans and light browns, its surface texture is one of the finest I've ever encountered. Although extremely hard, it cuts and finishes with delightful ease. Quite often

Bocote is a colorful, flamboyant wood, colored in bright yellow and burnt umber brown. Its grain pattern varies to a great extent by the way it's cut as in these two examples.

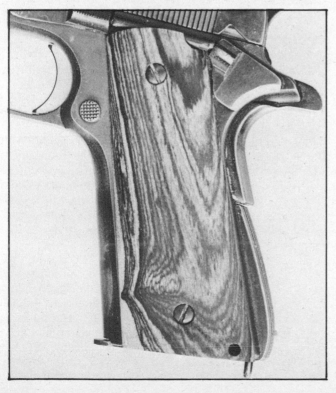

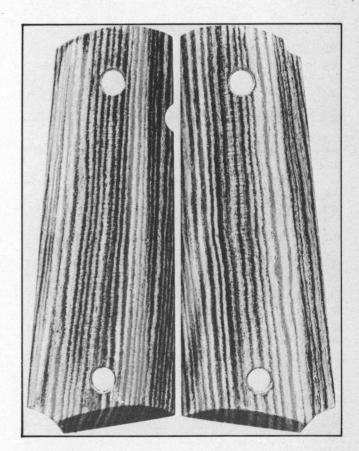

the grain shows a rippling iridescence as the viewpoint is shifted, which a friend compares to satin moire.

**Putumuju** is a rare and costly tropical hardwood ranging in color from orange-yellow to yellow-orange with a highly attractive grain pattern. It works easily and finishes superbly.

**Zebrawood** is reasonably common as a material for handgun stocks. Its usual background color is a pale, creamy yellow with striking grain pattern in deep brown or nearly black. Fairly hard, it works moderately well, albeit with an odor reminding one of a livery stable. It finishes

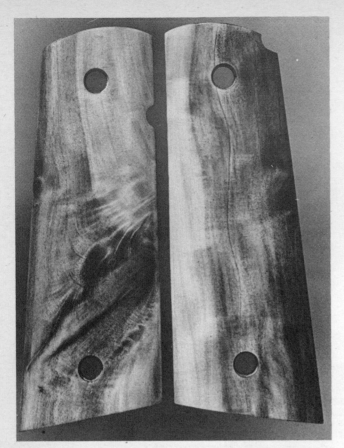

*Australian sandalwood offers vivid colors, spectacular grains, finishes up as smooth as optical glass and, as a further delight, it smells sensuous while being worked!*

with some amount of open grain that requires careful filling and sealing before applying the final finish.

**Canarywood** isn't quite as bright a yellow as its name might lead you to expect and its grain is fine and subdued. Apart from that it works and finishes fairly well. You may wish to try enhancing its color by applying a few wipes of yellow food coloring prior to final light sanding and application of finish. That results in an appearance that's quite attractive on a blued gun. Food coloring is available in most grocery stores in yellow, blue, red, green, and sometimes orange. The colors do not seem to fade on prolonged exposure to light, and use of these stains to enhance appearance of the wood is by no means unknown among various gunsmiths.

**Maple** occurs in many varieties, including the bird's-eye patterns and some gorgeous stuff usually termed quilted maple. In color it ranges from creamy white to pale beige. Its grain is nearly poreless in most examples. It needs to be cut with a well sharpened blade, otherwise it blade-burns badly, requiring a lot of sanding to eliminate the marks. It serves well as a basic stock material, and because of its tough nature it is well suited for support of laminates and similar uses. In moderation staining may improve the final appearance.

**Mahogany** comes in several variations, of which the Honduras species is fairly common and marginally suitable for .45 stocks. Colored a warm orange-brown it shows little by way of interesting grain pattern, and it finishes with

a lot of open pores that require more time and effort to fill and seal than the appearance of the finished stock set is apt to justify.

**Teak** occurs in at least two distinct varieties: Burmese and Indian. The Burmese is usually more uniform in grain pattern, compared to the Indian (often termed East Indian to help pinpoint the source). The usual color is a soft middle-brown with darker brown graining. Once in several blue moons you may luck onto an example of the figured India teak with the stunning burl markings of the example illustrated here, but don't hold your breath, okay? The difficulties of sawing teak were noted earlier. In addition, when you sand the stuff the sanding dust is oily and stubbornly sticky, clinging to everything with incredible tenacity. Once you get it smooth and wiped down clean with lighter fluid and paper towels, teak of either type accepts finishes such as Varathane quickly and well.

**Locust** appears in several varieties, and it isn't encountered too commonly in sources of commercial woods. Most locust trees grow to small stature, hardly thick enough in the trunks to interest lumbermen. The wood is hard, heavy and one of the toughest I've ever encountered. It finishes to a surface as smooth as elephant ivory, accepting finishes magnificently. Colors vary, although a soft, light yellow is often seen. If available it would be a fine wood for use on blued guns.

**Mesquite**, like locust, may be difficult to find. Once located it's a fine stock material. The base color is a pleasant yellow with beautiful graining in dark reddish browns. It is uncommonly impervious to warpage from humidity changes, thus superbly suited for rifle stocks. Worm holes are all too common, requiring filling with suitable tinted fiberglass.

**Myrtle** grows only in Oregon and in the Holy Land. An

*Quilted rock maple is a gorgeous pinkish-orange in hue with rippling grain pattern sort of like boiling taffy.*

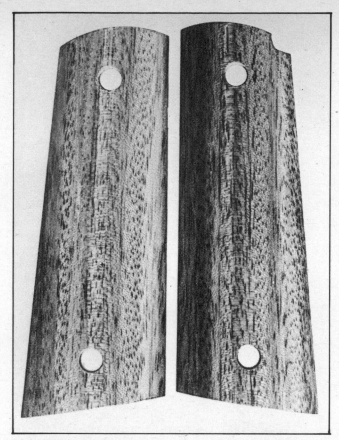

*Okan: Rich, elegant, burnt-sienna brown with brilliant streaks of reds and yellows running through it; quite hard and rugged, it works well and accepts finish nicely.*

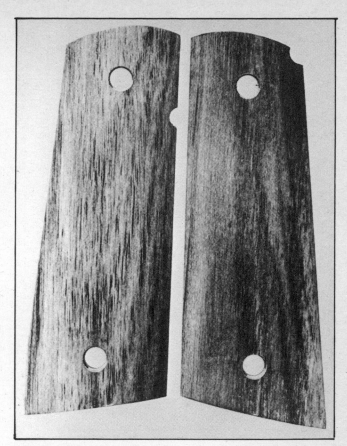

*A real sleeper, this is persimmon wood boasting classy grain and a tawny warm grayish-brown background color.*

evergreen variety its wood is accordingly classed as a softwood, but soft it certainly is not! Wayne Gibbs, of Hensley & Gibbs bullet mould fame, sent me a hunk of Oregon myrtle and it has to be the toughest stuff to cut I've ever seen; even worse than purple heart. It sometimes occurs in the so-called tiger-stripe variety, as illustrated on the set by Paul Holguin shown here on the Star Model PD. Even the common type of myrtle will make a good set of handgun stocks or a nice rifle stock, if you can manage to shape it to your will, that requiring some doing.

**Philippine mahogany** or **lauan,** is so coarse in grain structure and so insipid in color as to deserve little or no consideration for handgun stocks.

**Oaks** are a class of hardwood readily purchased and comparatively inexpensive in the modest quantities required for a use such as .45 stocks. Oak occurs in many varieties, quite a few of which are pleasantly well suited for such purposes. I've used quarter-sawn red oak with exceptionally satisfactory results, both as to working qualities and appearance after finishing.

**Walnuts** are another large group with several subspecies, all of which show fine promise for stockwork. The plain, straight-grained pieces will finish up to a competent if not spectacular set of stocks. If you can scavenge up a piece with a singular, curly-burl grain pattern, such as the set shown here, it's one of the best of all materials. Walnuts sand to leave a moderate amount of pores to fill and seal, after which they will accept nearly any suitable finish in a cheerfully cooperative manner.

**Koa** is a hardwood from Hawaii and, like pau ferro, it is rare to find any two pieces showing a marked resemblance to each other. Although not exceptionally heavy, koa is extremely hard, sawing with moderate difficulty and requiring the sharpest possible blade to avoid burn marks. Once cut it shapes and sands down nicely, requiring moderate filling and sealing, and it goes on to finish easily and well. The pieces that are somewhat muted in color respond well to discreet applications of suitable stains before final finish.

*Left, pitomba changes color with viewing angle; nice wood if you can get it! Right, skipline work by Browning.*

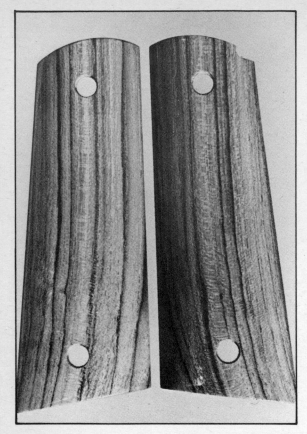

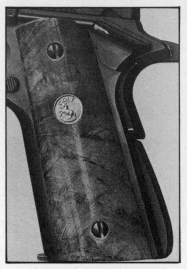

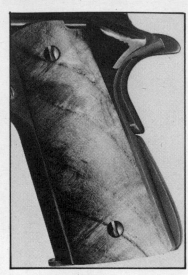

Teak takes many forms and the set at left in India teak is typical. Above are two examples from an unlikely piece of crotch-burl India teak that works up looking like choice brown marble; about as nice as wood gets

**Ebony** is another super-hard wood, occurring in Africa and in certain parts of southern Texas. Carbide-tipped blades are a must for cutting it and patience is needed for further shaping. Its color is dark brown to nearly black usually with quite subdued grain. For that reason it may be better suited for inlays or laminates than for use in a complete set of stocks.

**Purple heart** is one of the heaviest and hardest of all known woods; that's the good news. The bad news is that it's an absolute devil to cut or work. It tends to warp as it dries and cures. You get splinters in your fingers by merely looking at it. The grain is usually quite subdued and the color may seem pretty to those who are color-blind. By that I mean that it's a strong purple. I made one set of .45 stocks from purple heart and they ended up looking at least as dreadful on the gun as I'd expected, although the owner, who'd begged for a set of them, professed himself quite delighted. Beauty is in the eye of the beholder, for sure!

**Rosadillo,** (pronounced *rosa-DEE-yoh*) is a pleasantly tight-grained wood, ranging from medium brown to fairly bright red. The colors mute down quickly if left unfinished. It cuts and works with delightful ease and I suspect it would accept checkering superbly. The redder examples finish out to a decided crimson hue in the bare wood, but that shifts toward scarlet under finishes such as Varathane, with an attractive appearance, despite rarely having much by way of grain pattern. The browner pieces finish up to a rather ho-hum or utilitarian appearance that does little to repay the effort expended.

**Rosewood** is another broad category with a host of sub-species. These range in color from a deep purplish-brown which ends up nearly black under the finish, to several slightly lighter shades of brown or pinkish-brown,

some of which display some reasonable amount of subdued but attractive grain. Most if not all types are hard, heavy, tough and considerably on the costly side. Several years ago I shaped something out of a hunk of some manner of dark rosewood on the disc sander. I don't recall the exact date, but I can pinpoint it as the time I learned the folly of inhaling sanding dust. I swear I sneezed purple for at least a week after that!

**Okan** is hard, heavy, tough, and a medium-dark reddish brown. Depending upon the direction in which it is cut, you can obtain a pleasant and subtly elegant final effect. It cuts and works with no more than moderate difficulty, and the surface pores will require some amount of sealing and filling.

**Persimmon** is another wood that may be hard to find, but its appearance is singular. The usual color is a warm, grayish beige, often with a grain pattern that is quite visible and attractive. It's fairly hard but cuts and works down nicely, and its qualities in the finishing phase are excellent.

**Pitomba** is a dark, reddish brown tropical hardwood that may display remarkably attractive grain patterns. Like tiger-eye gemstone the grain changes with the viewing angle, and as you rotate the finished stock the appearance and color will shift from dark brown to a much lighter shade. Again, it's a challenge to track this one down and, once found, paying for it is the next problem. I have a set made from pitomba that was too thin for a stock set as obtained, so I laminated it onto sheets of rock maple and made up the resulting blanks to put on a stainless, long-slide AMT Hardballer. This, along with some of the other darker woods, is a fine choice on guns that are made of stainless steel or nickel-plated.

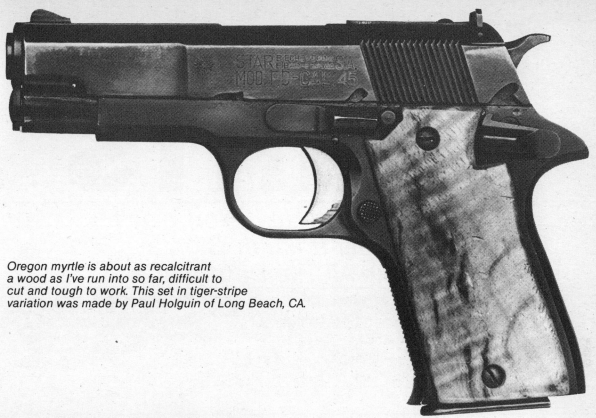

*Oregon myrtle is about as recalcitrant a wood as I've run into so far, difficult to cut and tough to work. This set in tiger-stripe variation was made by Paul Holguin of Long Beach, CA.*

*The laminating press was used to join up seven layers of alternating African padauk and Osage orange after which they were sliced to make blanks of red and yellow stripes and relaminated to a maple underlay for a striking effect.*

I'm told that there are at least 70,000 known woods, of which about 10,000 varieties see some amount of commercial use. It's obvious that the foregoing list hardly touches the surface, but it should provide useful guidance as to some of the more or less promising possibilities. Making handgun stocks is a lot of fun, immensely rewarding when they turn out the way you had in mind. The .45 auto is a good starting point, being simpler than most. There are several other guns for which the stocks are not unduly nightmarish to cut and fit.

Quite recently I've been exploring the possibilities of using carbide router bits in my drill press to create a sort of poor-man's milling machine for use on woods. With the workpiece held securely in the drill press vise and moved along the press bed against guiding straightedges secured by C-clamps, it seems possible to perform some pleasantly precise milling and shaping, even on the hardest, toughest woods in the rack. Needless to say, it is an operation not unfraught with peril for the heedless and unwary. You must keep the rotation of the bit in mind and avoid making a cut so that it can grab and seize the wood.

To make that approach practical it was necessary to take up about eighteen years' accumulation of end-play in the quill of the drill press, but that proved to be a simple matter once I discovered that a small collar carried a little hex-socket set screw for just that purpose. I think this will enable me to attack some of the harder projects, such as fitting for the Browning Hi-Power and similar examples. It makes an intriguing prospect to contemplate!

# CHAPTER 5

# HANDGUN SIGHTS

*If You Can't Hit It, You Won't
Bother It Much: Sights
Make All The Difference!*

*Scope sights on handguns can tighten group sizes remarkably although they are at their best when firing off a steady rest as Buck Coulson is doing with my six-inch Colt Python here. Scope is an early prototype of the Thompson/Center RP at 1.5X magnification on B-Square rings and bases. One-inch 25-yard groups are not uncommon with it.*

**B**ACK IN THE DAYS when I was studying to become an aerial gunner in an all but forgotten war — the Global Disagreement of 1939-45 or so — I encountered a thought in an army tech manual that sticks in memory to the present. It observed something along the lines of, "A BB shot that hits packs more effect than a shell from a sixteen-inch naval cannon that misses." Some might feel inclined to argue the point, since a near-miss from one of those potent projectiles can be pretty distracting. The basic philosophical concept still seems quite valid.

Your typical handgun is not notable for the ease with

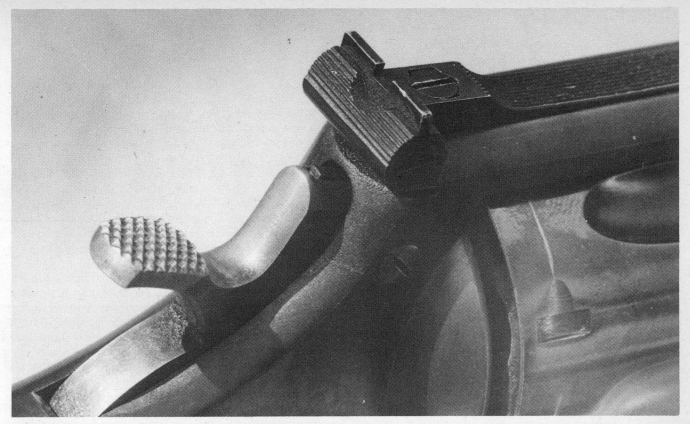

*Two click-detented setting screws adjust the rear sight used on Smith & Wesson revolvers. This is an excellent sight and about all you have to do is make certain the front holding screw (not visible here) is kept tightened.*

which it can be employed to score hits upon the intended impactee. In the old, classic, idiotically impractical mode of firing, the handgun is extended in a single hand, wavering heroically about and in the general area of the target. It is as if some diabolical rulemaking committee addressed their attention to the challenge of making it as difficult as possible to score a hit on the target. One can but wonder why they didn't decree that handguns must be gripped by the toes of a single bare foot, as the shooter lay prone, facing the other way and aiming by a small mirror, directed over the shoulder. That might have made it a bit tougher and, if difficulty was the intended goal, it would all have been quite logical.

At least as recently as the distant days of WW-Deuce, any shooter who dared to brace the aim by introducing the free hand into the grip would and did get roundly screamed-at by the range officer. I cannot say if the situation prevails down to the present. I severed my connections with the armed forces in 1946, early in the year, doing so with whoopingly joyous zest and relish.

If you're seriously bent upon pinking something with a handgun, be it a tin can or an adversary intently bent upon effecting your personal demise, the two-handed hold makes the best possible sort of sense. If you can utilize a solid rest for bracing the aim, that's all to the better. For a northpaw to stand picturesquely erect, left fist exquisitely snuggled into left hip, with the pistol wavering hypnotically in the unbraced right hand, it is the faintly preferable mode to clenching the gun in your toes; but just barely. Clearly, the gifted souls who decree such idiocy have never had the experience of being strafed by hostile fire.

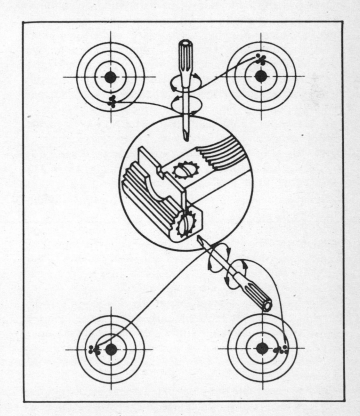

*This diagram from Smith & Wesson gives a graphic explanation of which direction either screw should be turned to move the holes toward center of bullseye.*

Here is a recent pattern of adjustable rear sight used on the Thompson/Center Contender, complete with a helpful marking to indicate turning direction.

I've been tacking toward the laying-on of the idea that the handgun is a difficult instrument with which to execute a useful hit. With that in mind, any strategem that aids in accuracy is well worth embracing. Paraphrasing, it matters not how you play the game; what really matters is that you win the sucker.

Sights of some sort have been found on handguns for the past two or three centuries, at least. In the earlier examples, there was some manner of bead on the end of the barrel, just above the muzzle, perhaps with a notch filed in the nose of the hammer to afford a point of aiming reference when the hammer was cocked. As double-action revolvers came into general use, the hammer notch was superseded by an open notch at the rear of the top strap of the receiver or frame. Such sights, termed open iron sights, or fixed sights, remain in use down to the present and, quite probably, on into the future for some while.

A set of open iron sights that are dead on the precise money are a wondrous goodness and a thing to cherish tenderly. Short of truly stark catastrophe, they cannot be knocked askew and will deliver the coal to the center of the chute without fail. It is a source of significant sadness that such dead-on sight systems are rather a rarity. With most such things, your only hope of securing a center-on hit is to employ some judicious amount of what is commonly termed Kentucky windage. That is to say, you have to obtain a sight-picture that is some canny quantity of high-left, low-right or whatever at the given distance in order to make a hole at the point you had in mind.

Handgun designers became sharply aware of this distressing state of affairs rather early in the game and came up with the solution of a movable rear sight. In some instances, they offered a rear sight that was movable in azimuth — right/left — along with a front sight movable in elevation.

It is a regrettable but palpable fact that hardly any two handgun loads deliver the hits to precisely the same point. That's what makes adjustable sights so uniquely useful. By judicious diddling of the adjustment, you can calibrate the point of impact to exquisite congruity with the point of aim. At that point, if all else is favorable, you can make a hole at the exactly intended locus. In the final essence, that is the vast majority of what handgunning is entirely about.

Most modern handguns boasting adjustable sights incorporate all of the movement in the rear sight. That simplifies the situation quite usefully. If the point of impact is off the intended mark, you have but to move the rear sight in the direction you wish the holes to move. If the holes strike low, you raise the rear sight. If they hit too far to the left, you move the rear sight to the right; just exactly that clearcut and simple.

Telescopic sights have been in use on rifles since some time around the American Civil War, or the War To Establish The Southern Confederacy; whichever term pleases your fancy. Scope sights were used little if at all on handguns until quite a number of years later. They began coming into sporadic use in the 1950s, with a gradually mounting acceptance on through the Sixties, Seventies and the still-current Eighties.

Scope sights for handguns offer certain undeniable advantages, meanwhile laboring under certain handicaps. They enhance the potential accuracy of the handgun, often to extents that boggle credulity. On the other hand, they add to the bulk and offset the compact contours that are the special charm of the handgun.

When employing any manner of open iron sights, the shooter must try to focus the aiming eye upon the rear sight, front sight and target, all simultaneously. That is a challenge to which no human eye is equal; never has been/ never will be, alas. As a canny compromise, the shooter can try to focus upon the front sight, letting the rear sight and target blur as they will, and do.

When a scope sight is properly adjusted, its reticle or crosshairs will be in crisply beheld focus, superimposed upon an aiming point that is about equally sharp in visual focus. The fact that the target area is magnified to some extent is purely a bonus. Even a scope that didn't magnify the target at all would offer a solid gain in aiming acuity.

Handgun scopes have gained popularity by leaps and bounds in recent times. At one time, putting a scope on a handgun involved some amount of drilling and tapping to get the mounts and rings in place. That state of affairs, too, is phasing away. The newer state of the art includes mounts that take the place of existing adjustable iron sights, with no need for drilling and tapping additional mount holes.

There is a ready-made and accepted standard for rating and comparing potential accuracy in any manner of firearm. It is the minute of angle, commonly abbreviated as moa. It is usually regarded as one inch of spread between centers of the holes at a distance of one hundred yards. In point of fine fact, it's a trifle more generous than that, more like 1.05 inches and, if you wish to really split nits, closer to 1.047197551 inches. With that established, you can go on and calculate the dimension of one moa at any given distance. As but one example, one moa at a distance of one mile (1760 yards) is 18.43067690 inches.

Rifles are tenderly regarded if they can group within one moa at a given distance. Quite a lot of them can't quite cut the mustard. Handguns that can bring off the feat are even more rarely encountered, but some few can do it. I own two handguns that have made the grade, along with a few others that have come quite gratifyingly close. The first to

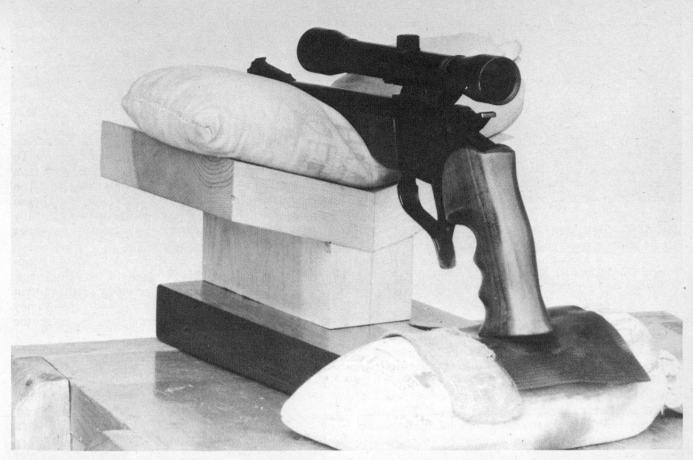

*A sandbag rest greatly eases and simplifies firing handguns from a benchrest. Holder shown is simple and easy to make from small scraps of two-inch plank. Table saw is set at an angle of about 74° to cut ends for the platform and two pieces for the support are cut at the same angle, all being glued together, as here. It should be noted that the Contender pistol gives its finest accuracy if the wooden forend is supported.*

bring it off was the Remington Model XP-100, chambered for the .221 Remington Fire Ball cartridge and sporting a Leupold M8-2X scope. That heartwarming feat was executed a decade or so ago. Only within recent months, a second gun made the grade. That was a Thompson/Center Contender with a fourteen-inch bull barrel, topped with a Redfield 4X scope, which put four holes into a spread of about one-half-inch, with the fifth blowing it to .914-inch between centers. Still cozily within the bounds of the moa figure quoted previously. The cartridge that turned the trick in the T/C Contender was the 7mm Thompson/Center Ugalde, or T/CU; a wildcat on the .223 Remington case, with the neck opened to accept 7mm (.284-inch diameter) bullets.

Such feats are heart-warmingly gratifying, and I should make all reasonable haste to note that they are not done in the classic offhand stance. Rather, they are done off the sandbag benchrest, with all of the human factor errors scrubbed from the equation. Even so, groups that size are not easy to obtain. The fact remains that I have at least two handguns that are capable of out-grouping nearly any rifle in my racks, and I'd hate to bet loosely on a face-out between any of them.

*This group was fired at 100 yards from a Contender with 7mm T/CU Super-14 barrel and 4X Redfield scope on Conetrol mount and rings, per load data.*

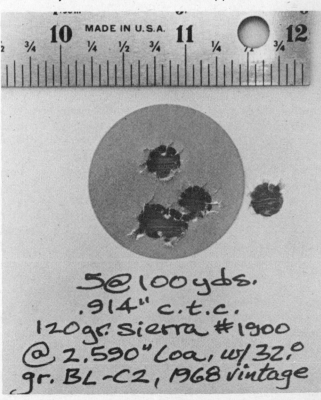

5 @ 100 yds.
.914" c.t.c.
120 gr. sierra #1900
@ 2,590" Loa, w/ 32.0
gr. BL-C2, 1968 vintage

A popular modification is to install the adjustable Smith & Wesson rear sight on the slide of a Model 1911 auto. Collectors may wince at the desecration of a rare Springfield Armory slide, but it reached my hands that way!

Does that suggest and affirm that scope sights on handguns are the outermost be-all, do-all, end-all? By no manner of means. Even so, the humble iron sights retain some significant edge in certain circumstances. I still have vivid recollections of a hog-hunt in southern Texas nearly a decade ago. Steve Herrett was introducing me to his then thrillingly new .30 Herrett wildcat pistol cartridge for the T/C Contender pistol. The test gun carried a scope in lieu of open ironmongery sights.

It was early in that year and we were slogging through the coarse brush, not far from the city of Hondo, Texas, with a pack of highly trained hoghounds doing their dedicated thing. The time came for me to take my turn with the notable new pistol and I found myself confronted with a madly churning maelstrom of black hog and equally black hounds, all a-hugger-mugger in a thick stand of brush, with no slightest clue as to which hunk of hurtling hide was porcine or canine. For redundantly obvious reasons, I much preferred not to test the efficacy of the new .30 Herrett round on one of our host's pack members. Had I pinked a pooch, I feared I might be compelled to take it home as a tagged trophy and I was certain the family recipe shelf had no directions for hog-hound en brochette, or whatever.

At that troubled moment I would have given one of anything of which I had at least two for the use of any manner of the coarsest possible open iron sight on the gun in hand. The hog was perhaps fifteen feet from the muzzle of the gun, so pinpoint precision was the least of all worries. Through the scope, hog-hide and hound-hide were utterly indistinguishable, all in a seething, raucous ferment.

I hope you never find yourself in a predicament quite that engrossing and involving. What I did was to open both eyes and concentrate with all available ferocity upon steering a slug to the hog, not a dog. I was lucky, as were the pooches. It was an adventure I'd go far out of my way to avoid savoring again.

I recall all this traumatic experience by way of putting the picture into realistic perspective. Scopes are purely ducky if you're bent upon scalping a pocket gopher 129

Tom Ferguson snapped this photo of me as I was trying to nail a Texas wild hog engaged in a mad fandango with our guide's (left) highly trained pack of hounds.

yards off and away. Open iron sights are just awfully handy if you have the objective of hitting one hunk of hurtling hide in a highballing horde of hog and hounds. In the latter instance, there is much good that can be said of the humble notch and blade system.

Putting a scope on a handgun tends to complicate its convenience as to carrying about. The holster that fitted so neatly before will no longer accommodate it. There are various holsters made up for carrying scoped handguns, but they use up a lot of leather; an expensive commodity in today's marketplace. One solution has been to use some manner of sling, which or may not double as a steadying device for use while aiming. Hunting in rough and/or vertical terrain puts a lot of value on some manner of gun-carrying device that leaves both hands free for use and it's nice if it also protects the gun from savagely abrasive encounters.

In his earlier days Henry Ford is said to have observed that his customers could have any color of Model T they

Here is the remarkably smooth and compact adjustable rear sight that comes installed on the Llama Omni auto in caliber .45 ACP only; 9mmP version has fixed sight.

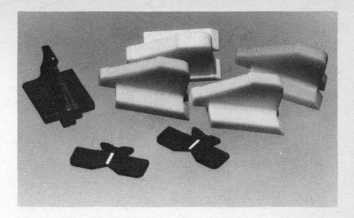

Here's an assortment of red, white, yellow and sky blue front sights plus a gold bead and rear sight inserts that can be had from Ruger for use in the .44 mag Redhawk.

fancied, so long as they wanted black. For quite a lot of years black was the prescribed color for open iron sights and, if you wanted some other hue, you could apply nail polish, model airplane dope or whatever your fancy preferred. Having grown up and more or less learned to shoot in a world where black handgun sights were the accepted commonplace, I find I still favor that color over just about anything else that's available. I have encountered a few handguns that were either stainless steel or nickel plated, up to and including both front and rear sights. Trying to hit something with a set of silver sights is a tougher challenge than anyone really needs, in my book.

At some point along around the Sixties there came a penchant for putting red inserts in the rear surface of the front sight and/or a white outline around the notch of the rear sight. In theory, this was supposed to enhance the sighting capability in unfavorable lighting conditions. In the years since, we've also had a proliferation of putting icebox white inserts into, onto and around both front and rear sights. If you have ever tried to use such things in blazing broad daylight, with the sun coming from behind you, there is no need to offer my comment on them. If you've been spared that experience, I can but note it's pretty miserable. It might be great if you have to take potshots at something in a dimly lighted alley, but it's a lousy system for daytime use. As a tangential sidenote, one should make every effort to avoid firing any of the larger handguns in a narrow alley, particularly one with brick walls on both sides. The resulting sound effects are intensely traumatic.

The mounting popularity of multicolored handgun sights has given rise to a number of firms offering do-it-yourself kits for applying the inserts. The best of these, in my experience, are the ones put out by Rich Brokken, from Bullshooters' Supply in Tucson, Arizona. These are available in various gaudily visible shades of red, orange, yellow, white and pale blue, but in honest black, as well, so that one can rectify the silver-sight atrocities. I hope you didn't snicker when I mentioned pale blue. Oddly enough, it's one of the better shades for a front insert.

Another sidenote here — cosecantal, if not tangential — concerning the effect of judiciously chosen color on the visibility of the aiming point, or target: Black isn't all that

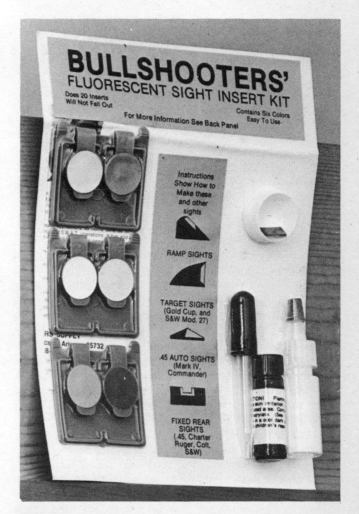

Bullshooters' Supply, Box 13446, Tucson, AZ 85732 makes and markets this excellent kit for doing your own color inserts in choice of six colors, also available in black or a night-luminous yellow shade if desired.

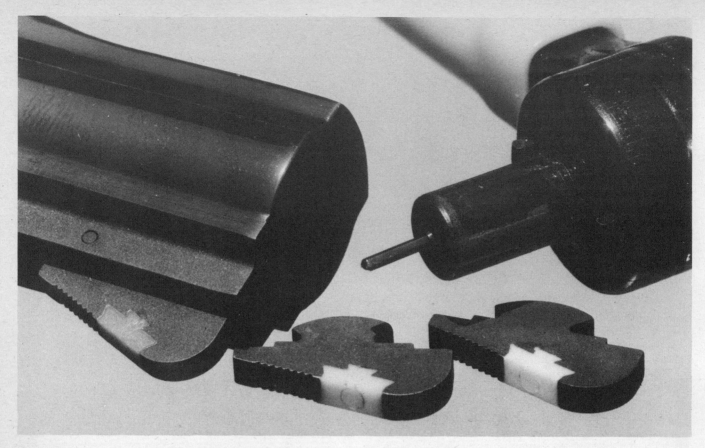

Front sights for the Dan Wesson Arms revolvers can be removed by means of the hex-wrench furnished with the gun for replacment in your choice of red, yellow or white inserts shown here left to right in that order.

bad as a color for the sights, as redundantly noted, but it is less than ideal as the hue for the bullseye. A circular black aiming point is acceptable if you plan to employ the six o'clock holding picture. That presupposes that your sights are adjusted to place the actual holes somewhat higher, so that — if all goes well — they end up in the exact center of the X-ring.

Candidly, such a concept runs contrary to my sense of fitness and propriety. In my book, the hole should appear precisely at the upper tip of the front sight, as it was viewed in the sighting picture. In other words, if I take a six o'clock hold, I want the hole to turn up at the lower edge of the black aiming circle. I do not want it to strike high by a distance equal to the radius of the circle: I want it right, damned-well where I *aimed* it.

Some few years back I had a fairly decent but by no means super-outstanding S&W K-38 in the locker and Austin F. Behlert offered to do his number on it and turn it into a combat competition gun, so I put it into his hands and, in the fullness of time, it came back. All in an eager quiver, I took it to the range and found that there was simply no possible way that I could bring the sights even close to congruity with the point of impact. With the rear sight clear to the lower limit of its travel, the holes wound up in the paper the better part of two feet below where I'd aimed.

I have never been into combat competition nor, comes to that, any other manner of handgun competition what-

soever, even up to and including metallic silhouette. Pursuits such as those are for lucky souls who have leisure, of which I have none at all. I have a boss who keeps asking when he's going to see some copy, and keeping him partially placated and marginally mollified takes the greater part of 168 hours in any given week. That is an explanation, not an excuse, okay?

I got Behlert on the phone and told him that the gun was quite nice, except that it shot low by an unacceptable margin. With suave gentility, he explained the facts of life to me: It seems that the usual practice is to take a twelve o'clock sight picture at the silhouette target, aiming for the scalp, so as to place the holes in the 10-ring, located somewhere down around the solar plexus or perhaps the lunar one. That is the way it's usually done, Behlert assured me.

With all the soft-sell diplomacy I could put hands upon, I explained my crank views on the matter and we ended up agreeing that I should send the gun back for a revision to my maverick prejudices. It came back again, icily capable of putting holes just exactly where the sights were looking when it went off. It carries a Douglas Premium barrel rifled to a pitch of one turn in fourteen inches, rather than the 1:18.75 pitch that's standard for most S&W .38 Specials. The difference the sharper pitch makes is awfully close to incredible. Just about any decent load at all groups into half an inch at twenty-five yards, and some do somewhat better.

Faithful readers will recognize that as my BK-38, mentioned frequently since it is one of the two guns I employ routinely any time I'm working with the .38 Special cartridge, which is to say fairly frequently. The other is the Chuck Ward Street Gun, also known as Li'l Montgomery.

We started to discuss strategically suitable color for the aiming point, itself. We got as far as noting that black bullseyes worked but poorly with all-black sight systems. If you drop by your local dealer in office supplies, you'll find that various manufacturers put up circular self-adhesive stickers in a variety of sizes and colors. The .75-inch and 1.25-inch are common diameters and the colors range through fluorescent shades of yellow, red, orange and green, perhaps others. The choice in shades is a subjective thing and, if you happen to be color-blind, all bets are off.

In coarse theory, black-on-yellow is the most vividly visible of all possible color combinations. We have that on the word of a dedicated gent name of Bustanoby, who ranked something like sixty-six combinations in terms of relative discernability.

Along the way, I've plowed a fair amount of research into the matter and can report that — for my personal pair of orbs — the day-glo green or screaming chartreuse seems to fare better than any other color tested to date. It picks up the intersection of a scope reticle in starkest clarity, and delivers just about as good a sighting image when used with open iron sights of a black hue. It isn't even all that bad with an iridescent red insert on the front sight.

The fluorescent colored circular pasters are at their best when surrounded by an area of dead flat black. I like to make up instant aiming points by affixing a colored .75-inch circle in the center of a one-inch square of black target paster, so that the whole thing can be peeled off and stuck to a large piece of white paper, perhaps a dozen aiming points at a time, to conserve the strenuity of chasing back and forth to replace targets.

Sighting clarity, like beauty, is in the eye of the beholder. Fizzy-green may not be the ideal choice for your eyes. The pertinent point here is that it's productive to check out the possibilities, so as to settle upon one that works best for you. If you can't see it clearly, you can't hit it precisely; just that pellucidly simple, no?

*The indispensible Ransom Rest ordinarily requires anchoring to an utterly immovable support for optimum accuracy, but the place where I shoot has no such facility so here are two solutions. The Robot Pistolero, left, carries a 4X Lyman rifle scope that's harmonized to the gun in the rest so that each shot can be aimed by lining the reticle of the scope with the bullseye. Corson-type base, right, is anchored by a Buick wheel on the two-inch plank at its bottom. Note the tensioned length of ⅜-inch threaded rod at the front for bracing.*

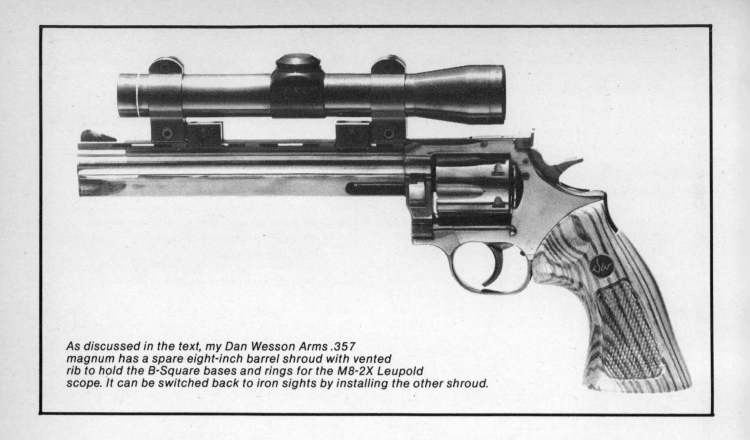

*As discussed in the text, my Dan Wesson Arms .357 magnum has a spare eight-inch barrel shroud with vented rib to hold the B-Square bases and rings for the M8-2X Leupold scope. It can be switched back to iron sights by installing the other shroud.*

My retching distaste for sights set for a six o'clock hold that puts the holes some inches and fractions above the actual aiming point stems back to the days when I formulated a lot of my pistoleering prejudices. It was an era when I was doing a lot of dump-shooting; mostly at rats and the like. A scurrying dump rat, intent on its daily rounds, offers an elusive aiming point at best. It is a situation where you want to aim there and, by-golly, *hit* right exactly-precisely *there.*

Any revolver or pistol that was sighted to hit something like 2.4 inches above point of aim at fifty feet or twenty-five yards was strictly a rubber crutch under those trying circumstances. It is just a terribly trying challenge to locate an imaginary six o'clock, just that far beneath the scalp of a sprinting dump rat. It is a lot simpler and better if you don't have to scramble and scrabble and try to cope with such problems.

There are sighting systems that endeavor to provide the best of both worlds by incorporating open areas in the front and rear scope mounting bases so that you can squinch down and use the iron sights if desired. The idea seems to offer a lot of attractive merit except that I've yet to encounter one that really worked in the intended manner. In the ones I've tried, the notch and blade just do not line up with the holes in the scope mounts. I could note that's almost painfully typical of the way my life often seems to have been laid out.

Another approach that seems to operate more dependably is to arrive at a state of affairs in which the scope can be removed and/or replaced with minimum fuss and bother, requiring little if any sight adjustment when reinstalled. I have such a setup for the eight-inch barrel on a Dan Wesson Arms .357 magnum revolver that seems capable of really excellent accuracy with either sighting system. The scope is on one of the B-Square mount and ring sets available from the same maker for other guns such as the Colt Python and Mark V Trooper; the T/C Contender, the Ruger .22 Standard Auto and so on. For DWA revolvers it needs to go on the heavy shroud with the ventilated rib. As my eight-inch barrel came with the standard shroud that has the solid rib, it was merely a matter of obtaining a second shroud with the vented rib and installing the scope on that. Changing shrouds on the DWA revolver takes only a minute or so and the sight setting seems to stay pleasantly close to the money during the shroud changes.

I have a pair of scoped .22 auto pistols — a bull-barrel Ruger and one the High Standard folks call The Victor. Both are capable of remarkable accuracy and since I have other .22 auto pistols there is no need to fret about getting the scopes off or back on.

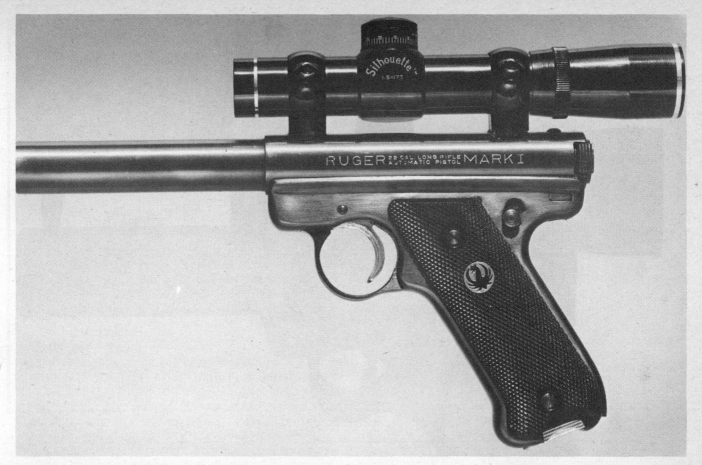

This Mark I bull-barrel Ruger .22 auto carries an M8-2X Leupold scope in a pair of ring bases, once but no longer available from Weaver. They are mounted to holes drilled and tapped in the receiver and the front sight was removed and stored away carefully, together with the rear sight against the time of future need.

One thing you discover quite early in working with scoped .22 handguns is that they tend to make their preferences as to ammunition highly evident. The choice of loads makes a lot of difference in the size of the group which is of course something that .22 rifle fans have known for a long time. With the aid of a scope, it's a quick and pleasant chore to winnow out the most promising loads for the given gun.

Peep or aperture-type rear sights have never won much popularity with handgunners, perhaps due to the intrinsic design of the guns. With a rifle you can get your aiming eye within a couple of inches of the rear sight, but that's not usually practical with a handgun. Williams has produced a few rear sights with fairly large apertures for use on the T/C Contender, but the majority of pistol shooters seem to prefer the open notch.

Handgun scopes do not seem to require a high degree of magnification and it's doubtful that it would be much help. An M8-2X Leupold was entirely adequate for getting groups of one inch or tighter at one hundred yards with the Remington XP-100 and that seemed a little hard to believe, even as it was happening, because the center of the reticle seemed to cover the aiming point completely. Burris

The Victor by High Standard is one of the most accurate .22 auto pistols I've ever encountered and the M8-4X Leupold scope makes 1-inch 50-yard groups not uncommon. These are the same Weaver rings and easily removed.

Simple rack holds 4X Redfield pistol scope on tripod for fine-tuning eyepiece adjustment as described in text. Lens in Canon A-1 is a zoom but normal lens is okay.

Another view of setup at left. Arrow indicates tip of power pylon about 400 yards away. Our fascinating mama hawk was away on patrol when this photo was made; see at left.

But she returned in time to pose! This red-tailed hawk has her nest atop the pylon. Note how the adjustment has left reticle and distant subject in simultaneous sharp focus. That's a tremendous help for shooting.

makes a 6X pistol scope, but most other makers stop at 4X.

The one factor that seems to offer the greatest benefit in getting optimum accuracy from a scope is to get the eyepiece adjusted properly. There are optical bore-sighting devices such as the Bushnell or the Sweany and they are invaluably helpful in making the preliminary adjustment of the turrets after installing the scope. I've been using one of the Bushnell jobs for years and right gratefully. On nearly every occasion, it has put the first shot within about four inches of the point of aim at one hundred yards and it's a simple matter to walk it in from that close.

Several of the more sophisticated rifle scopes feature adjustable objective lenses — that's the one up front — to permit setting them to eliminate parallax at any desired distance. Without parallax, you can move your eye about and the reticle (crosshair) will remain exactly on the point of aim. When parallax is present, the reticle moves as the eye moves, even if the scope remains motionless. By turn-

Standard sights for the .44 magnum Ruger Redhawk (no relation to hawk in photo above) are black with a white outline and adjustable for both elevation and windage.

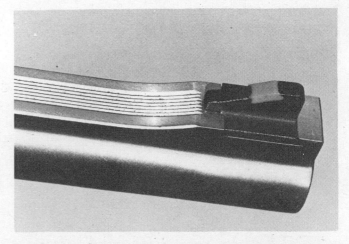

Here's the front sight of the same gun as at left. It has a bright red insert in the rear face with the rest black.

At right and above are the adjustable sights used on the Colt Officers Model Heavy Barrel .38 Special target revolvers into the Thirties. The rear sight is movable from right to left and can be locked in its setting.

The front sight handled adjustment of the Colt system for elevation and, as with the rear, had a screw that had to be loosened and retightened after adjustment.

ing the adjustable objective, such a condition can be corrected although you may need to repeat the process when firing at some different distance.

Few if any handgun scopes have adjustable objectives, but most of them have eyepieces that can be rotated and locked in the selected setting by means of a knurled or serrated ring ahead of the eyepiece. An adjustable eyepiece enables you to arrive at a sight picture in which both target and reticle are crisply and simultaneously in focus; a state of affairs very much to be desired and pursued. Any disparity of focus between one or the other causes the eye to focus and refocus on one then the other; fatiguing and highly unproductive.

Most scope sights are shipped from the factory with the eyepiece set well forward. We can think of that as the near-sighted adjustment and there is a fairly obvious reason for it. Most scopes are bought by people who walk up to a clerk in a store and ask to see this one or that one. Once it's in their hands, they take a speculative look through it, usually at an object that's fairly close. If the image seems sharp to them, there is a good chance they may buy the scope. If they see a fuzzy image they hand it back perhaps asking to see some other make or model.

A close-in focus may help to sell a scope, but it doesn't work too well later on for use at the longer ranges. The instruction sheets usually furnished with the scope offer a few suggestions, but I've seen few such that were as clear and direct as one might wish.

You could prop the gun on sandbags or perhaps on something such as the Ransom Rest with the reticle centered on an object at a suitable distance and try to get it and the reticle into precisely matched focus. The trouble with that approach is that the human eye is just too helpful and anxious to please. You look at the aiming point and the eye focuses on that, shifting back to the reticle as you turn attention to it.

The approach that works extremely well, simplifying and streamlining the whole bogglesome chore, is to line up the scope and aiming point as described, then take a look through the scope with a single-lens reflex camera. You

Bushnell's optical bore sighter comes with three sizes of mounting spuds to fit various calibers. It makes quick and astonishingly easy work of boresighting scopes.

Omega Sales, same address as Mag-na-port Arms, has these two-bar peep blades to replace conventional open notch for several guns such as this single-action Ruger.

Bushnell's Model 74-2800 Power-Booster pistol scope is of 1.3X magnification, but accesory lens can be installed up front to convert it to 2.5X magnification if desired.

Two mounting rings by Weaver for scopes of one-inch body diameter to be used on bases below. Ring at right is of the extended pattern for use in difficult installations.

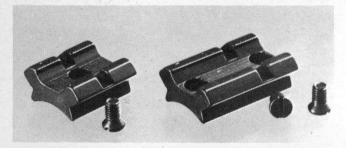

Weaver's Quick-Detachable bases come in many models to accomodate the holes already drilled and tapped in a wide variety of rifles and, more recently, in handguns.

may have to move about a bit to obtain a good view of the scope image in the camera finder and, having done so, rotate the focusing ring on the camera lens until the reticle is in sharp focus. Make a note of the number on the camera focusing scale: typically four to six feet. At the same time, refocus the camera lens until the image of the aiming point is sharp, as seen through the scope, making a note of the camera lens setting for that also.

Loosen the locking ring ahead of the scope eyepiece slightly and back the eyepiece rearward — counterclockwise — by a couple of turns. Return to the camera and focus on both the reticle and aiming point, recording the camera lens settings for both as you did before.

Here is the Thompson/Center RP — for Recoil Proof — scope with super-handy target knobs on a set of rings and base by Conetrol. You're right: That's an early receiver as denoted by scroll behind the etched puma.

Repeat the entire process, recording the settings as you go until you reach the eyepiece setting with the least possible disparity between the focus for the reticle and aiming point or preferably with none at all. Turn back the eyepiece locking ring and secure the eyepiece in that adjustment. Take a look directly through the scope with your eye to verify that both are in razor-sharp simultaneous focus as viewed in normal shooting mode. While you're at it, move your eye slightly and note if the reticle remains motionless in relation to the aiming point or if it shifts as your eye moves. That is of course your check for the presence or absence of parallax.

The eye relief of a scope is the distance from your eye to the rear lens or eyepiece at which you see a full-sized image that seems to fill the entire rear scope lens. As you move your eye rearward from that distance, the image will shrink and appear smaller than the lens.

If you have some amount of parallax and no ready means to get rid of it through scope adjustment, you can minimize the problem with most scopes by merely pulling your aiming rearward slightly to reduce the apparent size of the image seen in the rear lens. From that position moving your eye up/down or left/right will cause the center of the reticle to appear off-center in the image. With the scope held motionless, simply move your eye until the crosshair is centered in the reduced image and maintain that approach from shot to shot. It will usually minimize or eliminate parallax error.

Much of the foregoing may seem like a lot of needless complication and bother, but a properly adjusted scope sight is a joy to use whereas one that's off merely sets your teeth on edge and helps you miss. Who needs that?

Open iron sights are not as readily correctable. It may prove helpful to attach a small aperture to the appropriate lens of your shooting glasses at a suitable point so you can squint through the tiny hole and on through the sights to the target. That operates on the fairly familiar principle of stopping down the iris diaphragm of a camera lens to increase the depth of field or overall sharpness from near to far. It may help or it may not, depending somewhat upon your shooting situation, but it's worth a try.

Arrow indicates the distance the eyepiece had to be turned back from its locking ring to bring the reticle into satisfactory focus with the target as discussed here.

Millet Industries, 16131 Gothard St., Huntington Beach, CA 92647 makes replacement sights and novel 4-bladed screwdriver for the cross-slotted adjustment screw heads.

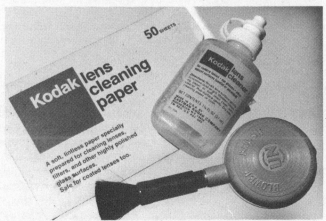

Soft camel-hair blower brush, cleaning fluid and lens-cleaning tissues are only thing to use on scope lenses. Such items are readily available from camera stores.

An adjustable peep or aperture rear sight made by Williams for use on the Thompson/Center Contender.

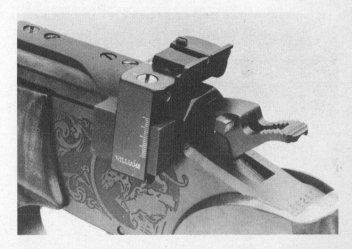

Same maker's open-notch rear sight for the Contender.

Weaver's tip-off rings made it a simple operation to install an M8-4X Leupold pistol scope on this Merrill Sportsman single-shot pistol in .357/.44 Bain & Davis.

# CHAPTER 6

# RELOADING
# HANDGUN
# AMMUNITION

## This Absorbing Pursuit Offers Savings, Versatility And The Possibility Of Exceptional Performance

*A round of 7mm T/CU takes its raucous and boisterous departure from a Contender Super-14 barrel and the camera records the muzzleflash and if you look closely you may see a faint ghost image of the barrel where it ended up after recoil. If you hanker to plink with this super-potent pussycat, you have no choice save to roll 'em yourself as it's a wildcat round, not as yet available commercially. You may not see the ear plugs but you can bet your sweet bippy they are installed, being needed here!*

I T'S A COMMON belief that reloading will save money and pay for the cost of the equipment in a short time. In most examples, that is not quite the way it works. I suspect that most reloaders spend a greater amount, over the long haul, than do those who buy their ammo across the counter. The big plus benefit you can get from reloading is that it enables you to fire a substantially greater number of rounds for a comparable amount of cash outlay.

There are other advantages to reloading, too. It gives you access to ammunition that simply is not available commercially. There are several of the less popular handgun cartridges for which the ammomakers offer but a limited choice of loads. As an example, consider hollow-point bullets: Within recent times, Federal Cartridge Corporation has made hollow-point loads available for a few cartridges of marginal popularity, such as the .45 Long Colt and, later, the .44 Special. That still leaves a few others, such as the .45 Auto Rim, .44-40 WCF, .38-40 WCF, .32-20 WCF, and .32 S&W Long as examples where you're lucky if you can find a store with a box of plain lead bullet loads. Hollow-point bullets, suitable for reloading in most of the calibers mentioned, are reasonably available, or you can cast your own and go on from there.

Let's say you happen upon a nice Colt New Service revolver in .44 S&W Russian. Factory loads are not to be had but you can trim down .44 Specials and put it back on the line if you're a reloader.

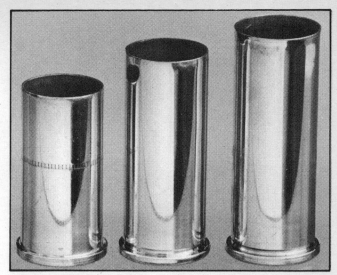

Fired .44 S&WR case left is .950-inch in length, in case you need to know. Book length is 1.160 for the .44 Special, 1.285 for the mag. If longer cases are trimmed down, loads should be reduced somewhat.

If you've a yen to fire wadcutter bullets for target practice in your .44 Special, .38 S&W, .32 S&W, or .32 S&W Long, reloading is your only out, and you may have to cast them yourself. Wadcutter mould blocks are available from one or more makers, suitable for use in all of those and many others, as well.

Let's suppose you want to fire bullets heavier or lighter than the factory offerings. As a reloader, you have easy access to several choices from either end of the scale; as a shooter of factory fodder, what you see on the shelf is what you can have, and that's it!

Those are the obvious tangible values. Some of the intangibles are quite attractive, as well. It is not always easy and simple, but it is sometimes possible to isolate and make up a load that your particular handgun will fire with accuracy that cannot be matched by any factory load that you can buy. When such happy combinations come along, it's enough to fair make you glow in the dark, and beam upon your personal munition works with ineffable contentment.

If we are going to discuss the reloading of handgun ammo, it would be well to define the term, and that is getting less simple with each passing year. Such sports as handgun metallic silhouette competition have produced a state of affairs where it's quite difficult to categorize a given center-fire cartridge as a handgun load or a rifle cartridge. Some of the more intrepid silhouette-smackers consider the full-bore .458 Winchester magnum as a dandy pistol cartridge. Having once owned and occasionally fired a large rifle chambered for that round, merely contemplating firing the .458 Win mag from a handgun turns my complexion mottled chartreuse, but you see my point, no?

Cartridges such as the .30-30 WCF or the .35 Remington are now standard chamberings for the Thompson/Center Contender, and I own barrels for both, as well as .22 Hornet, .22 K-Hornet, .218 Bee, .222 Remington and .223 Remington; all of which would have been automatically classified as rifle rounds not too many years ago. I do not deplore this state of affairs; merely noting it as a minor complication for purposes of our discussion at hand.

It should be noted that rimfire ammunition is not reloadable as a convenient and practical operation. Neither is the CCI *Blazer* center-fire ammo, with its cases drawn from aluminum and fitted with one-shot Berdan primers of a diameter not available commercially.

While we're nailing down definitions, let's touch briefly upon a couple of potentially puzzling points: There is a bountiful abundance of books that offer data for making up reloads, specifying the proper amount of this powder behind a bullet of that weight for a given cartridge. About half such works are termed manuals, while the rest are called handbooks. As far as I've ever been able to determine, the words are fully synonymous, across the board. I've sometimes tried to evade the dilemma by saying manuals/handbooks, but that's a rather awkward usage. In the book at hand, if I say manual, I also mean handbook, and vice versa.

Then we have the matter of handloading/reloading. You can build up your supply of cases by saving them after firing factory loads, or you can purchase them in the form of virgin brass, primed or unprimed. If you install primers, powder and a bullet in virgin brass, that's handloading. Once fired, if you repeat the process with the same deflowered case, it becomes reloading. Since it's pretty much a manual operation, you could build a case for calling it handloading exclusively, as many do. Put another way, it's always handloading, but it's usually reloading. It is a fine point, to which most shooters do not assign vital importance. I prefer to call it reloading because the word falls more trippingly from my tongue.

The fact that you've read this far into the chapter can probably be interpreted as evidence that you have some degree of interest in reloading. That being the case, I'd urge you to save all of your spent center-fire cases — also known as brass, hulls, empties, and so on — against the possible day when you decide to acquire the capability of resurrecting such things. Until you reach that personal

continental divide, you can store the accumulation in old coffee cans, cigar boxes, Zip-Loc plastic bags, or any other container you regard as suitable and convenient. Whatever you do, never discard reloadable, center-fire brass! It is an artifact of tangible and escalating value, as can be readily proven if you check the price tags on boxes of virgin brass at your nearby gun store.

Reloading cases that have been fired at least once is a bit more complex than handloading virgin brass, so let's review the basic steps involved. Inspect the fired cases, checking for cracked necks, presence of foreign material inside, live primers, massive corrosion and/or similar contamination, or ay other characteristic that affects the reloadability.

You may have noted that a factory round is a slightly loose fit in the chamber of a pistol or revolver; it drops into place easily, and the base of the bullet is gripped quite securely by the case neck. That is not true of fired cases. They fit the chamber snugly, or they may not fit at all. A bullet of the proper diameter drops easily into the case mouth, and falls back out when you invert the case, usually. As a further consideration, the primer has a dent in its center, having shot its wad, thus needing to be replaced.

So the next step in reloading a case that has passed inspection is to get it back down to a size that will enter the chamber easily, with the inside diameter of the neck small enough to grip the bullet base securely. Meanwhile, you've got to get rid of the spent primer and put a live one in its place.

These and subsequent operations are performed with the aid of a reloading press and set of reloading dies. Likewise required is a shell holder of proper size, which goes in the top of the ram of the press to grip the head of the shell, or case.

Die sets for typical, straight-sided handgun cases — such as the .38 Special, to cite the commonest example —

*Above left, a .357 Herrett with a .35 Remington, both standard chamberings for the Super-14 T/C Contender. The .30 and .357 Herrett are based upon .30-30 WCF brass. Both cartridges shown will handle .358-inch jacketed rifle bullets, as here, or they do a good job with .357 pistol bullets. Below, match brass is some of the nicest you can get for .45 ACP and the FC (Federal Cartridge) is one of my all time favorite varieties.*

*An excellent way to store cases until needed, this keeps dust out and makes the contents readily visible. An identifying tag can be put in the bag to record data. Below, the indispensible case holding block is easy to make if you have a drill press. Holes ½-inch in diameter at ⅝-inch spacing work quite well for most cartridges.*

usually comprise three dies. The first die performs a full-length resizing of the case, usually expelling the spent primer in the process. The second expands the case mouth back up to its proper inside diameter or ID, meanwhile providing a slight flare to accept the base of the bullet for easy seating. The third die seats the bullet to its correct depth, turns the case mouth flare back in, and perhaps crimps the case mouth around the bullet base in the same operation. Alternatively, some three-die sets will full-length resize on the first die; decap, expand and flare the mouth on the

second; and seat/crimp on the third. The specific details for the die set at hand should be obvious, given basic familiarity with the necessary procedures.

It is a minor problem we have to endure, but you'll find that there is some variation in size and specifications from one make of case to the next, even if all are of the same nominal caliber. This is particularly true of the 9mm Luger and, to a lesser extent, of the .45 Long Colt. Case head diameters may vary so much that some cases cannot be put into some shell holders. At the other extreme, some cases may not be gripped securely by other shell holders. Those are rather extreme examples, however, and most cases will work okay in most holders.

Variation also occurs in the thickness of the brass at the case neck, and that is the consideration that dictates the usual approach of case resizing. Since the ID is the critical dimension, in terms of bullet fit, uniformity is obtained by

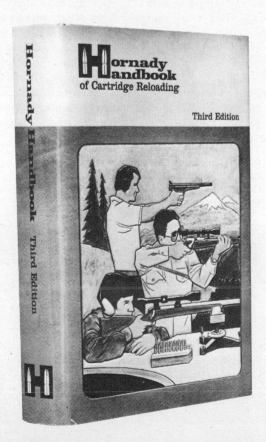

**Hornady Handbook** of Cartridge Reloading

**Third Edition**

*There are a number of excellent books on the market such as this one from Hornady, others from Speer, Sierra, Hodgdon, Lyman and so on. They should be consulted to verify safety of powder charges being used.*

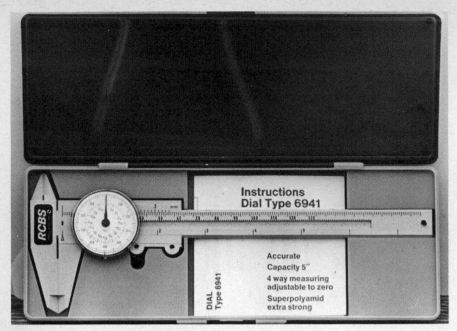

*RCBS has this dial caliper that measures to a bit over five inches to entirely acceptable precision.*

first reducing the outside diameter or OD to bring the ID well below bullet diameter. When the case is pushed back up around the second — mouth-expanding — die, its ID is enlarged to exactly the correct size, so that all cases processed will provide the necessary secure grip of the bullet base.

A properly made mouth-expanding die can be turned up or down on the top of the press to the point where it executes a small but necessary flaring of the case mouth to permit seating the bullet without shaving or gouging metal from the sides of the bullet. If you can see bits of scraped-off bullet metal at the mouth of the loaded case, you are doing something wrong. Such loads will be considerably less accurate than those seated without damage to the bullet.

Brass is an alloy of copper and zinc; it has the property of becoming harder and more brittle as it is worked back and forth by the passes into the loading dies. For that reason, it is well to avoid extravagant flaring of the case mouth. The trick is to flare it just enough, and not any more beyond that point.

Jacketed bullets do not require as much neck flare in the case, and some dies may provide no flare at all. In such examples, it's a good idea to deburr the inside edges of the case neck by using one of the inside/outside neck deburring tools offered by many makers of reloading equipment. Lacking such an accessory, a tapered reamer can be used, or a carefully wielded pocket knife.

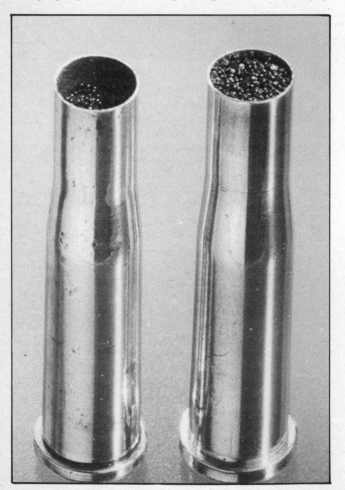

*Far left, a Remington .22 Hornet case next to a W-W case, both holding identical charges. This points up the need to sort cases by headstamp. Below left, .38 Special with roll crimp and a taper-crimped one. The latter tends to deliver the bullet with less distortion.*

A specialty item for removing Berdan primers, this may still be available from Huntington Die Specialties, Box 991, Oroville, CA 95965, but you'd still need the new primers and a punch for getting them installed.

Loading dies are made of steel and then heat-treated to harden them to impressive degrees. Even so, the brass case must be lubricated before full-length resizing. Following that, the lube must be removed from the case before firing. A popular and convenient way to apply lube is to roll the case across an uninked rubber stamp pad that has been lightly coated with lube. Several makers also offer case neck brushes for applying lube to the inside of the case to ease its passage over the expanding plug. The bristles of the case neck brush can be lightly coated at the tips by stroking the brush across the lube pad. Avoid applying too much lube to the inside of the case neck, since most lubes will deactivate both powders and priming compounds to some extent if they come into contact with them.

Failure to apply lube — or use of incorrect lubes —

before resizing will cause grit and metal particles to embed in the inner die surfaces, scoring and scratching the cases in a most unsatisfactory manner. In extreme cases, particularly with bottleneck cases, the case may stick in the die with such tenacity that the head is wrenched off by the shell holder on the ram downstroke, leaving the case stuck in place. Several diemakers offer stuck-case removing kits for coping with such misfortunes. The kits usually consist of a No. 7 drill bit, a ¼-20 tap, a hex-socket cap screw of the same thread and a small, cup-shaped chamber.

In use, the die is removed from the press and the expanding stem is backed upward enough to get the decapping pin out of the flash hole. At that point a hole is drilled up through the flash hole and threaded with the ¼-20 tap. The cap screw is put through the hole in the cup and threaded into the tapped hole and torque is applied with the hex wrench to loosen the stuck case. Needless to say, the case is ruined and the operation requires enough time and fuss to help you remember not to repeat the mistake.

At the instant of firing, the brass case will expand outward to grip the walls of the chamber quite securely, thus easing some of the rearward thrust of the case due to the high-pressure powder gasses. Sizing lube left on the outside of the case defeats this ability to cling to the chamber wall, causing much greater — possibly damaging — stress upon the action of the gun. That's the reason for removing the case lube after resizing.

The sizing lube can be removed by wiping each case with a piece of rag or paper towel, but it's a tiring and tedious operation. There is a quick and easy approach, but no manufacturer to date has ever shown any inclination to produce the little gadgets for doing the job. I refer to the little gizmos I call K-Spinners, illustrated nearby. These usually have a .25-inch-diameter shank, for use in small electric hand drills, with the business end slightly tapered to accept the case mouth in a friction fit. The K-Spinner is secured in the chuck and the case is pressed over the end. A

Forster Brothers can supply these little reamers for their case trimmer in most diameters and I like to put a light cut as shown into the necks of cases before seating jacketed bullets. One treatment usually will suffice for the next several loadings, but it gets the base of the bullet into place without scraping jacket metal.

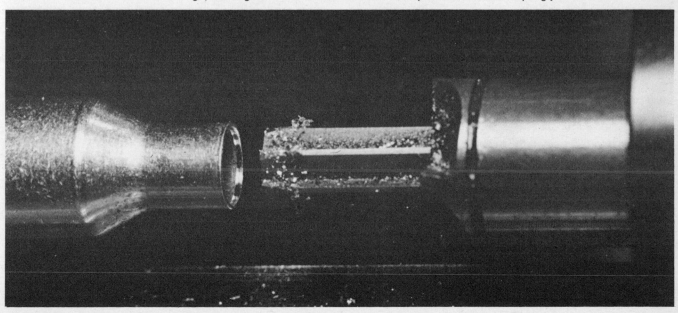

Candidates for the scrap heap are these split .45 ACP cases and the .218 Bee case with a severe example of incipient head separation. These are just two of the things to check for in prior inspection.

squeeze of the drill trigger switch rotates the case as the paper towel is held against it, whisking off the lube in a second or so.

If you happen to have access to a drill press, the K-Spinner can be put in that and the motor turned on. Cases can be pushed onto the end, wiped, and pulled off with no need to turn off the motor. If the case has been decapped at that point, it is a simple matter to push a primer pocket cleaner up into the pocket to remove primer residue at the same time.

The nearest thing to a K-Spinner to appear on the market is made by Lee Precision as an accessory for their handy little case-trimmer sets. It's one of their regular holding plugs with a short piece of .25-inch shaft extending from the outer end. That permits using a small electric drill to perform the trimming, followed by a wipe of the paper towel to remove the lube. After that, you have to shut off the motor, loosen the little aluminum holding collar, remove the cleaned/trimmed case, replace it with another, and so on. It's okay if you're trimming the cases, but rather a lot of bother if you just want to get the lube off.

It is possible to make up the K-Spinners with the business end stepped to handle two or more basic calibers simultaneously or, rather, alternatively. If you work with a drill press having a .5-inch chuck, you can dispense with the .25-inch shanks and just cut short pieces of cold-rolled steel rod of the appropriate diameter, chuck them into the press and use a flat file to dress the business end down to the right dimensions, using a case of the given size to check your progress. I usually make these so as to handle either as-fired cases or resized ones. The K-Spinners can be used to remove corrosion, by means of fine steel wool and perhaps a dab of automotive chrome cleaner, 3M Steel Wool Substitute or similar cleaners. If it pleases your fan-

cy, a dab of Happich's Simichrome metal polish will leave them glittering like a newly minted gold coin. Most motorcycle shops carry Simichrome in stock, or it can be ordered from Brownell's, Incorporated, 210 South Mill, Montezuma, IA 50171.

There is a shortcut around the bother of lubing and delubing the cases, and it consists of using resizing dies that have inserts of tungsten carbide or, in the instance of Redding-Hunter dies, titanium carbide. Such dies require no lube, and work just fine without it. They usually cost a bit more, but they save an awful lot of time and bother, more than enough to justify the added tab over the long haul. Carbide dies for straight-sided cases such as .38 Special, .357 magnum, .41 magnum, .44 Special/magnum

Here's a powder trickler being used to dribble it into the pan a granule at a time until the pointer is dead-even with the zero line. Some prefer these.

*Stamp-crimped primer pockets may be encountered on military cases such as .308, 5.56mm, .45 ACP or 9mmP. The stamped crimp must be removed to permit the seating of the new primer. C-H Tool & Die Corp. offers the set here to take care of that. The shell holder goes in the top of the die body and the proper size of the two punches snaps into the ram to swage away the crimp.*

and .45 ACP/AR are not a great deal more expensive from most makers. Some even carry them for the .32 S&W Long. When it comes to tapered cases, such as the 9mm Luger or .30 GI carbine, the price goes up by a goodly margin. As far as I know, at this time no one offers carbide dies for any bottleneck cartridge.

With the case(s) resized, delubricated and with the case mouth expanded and flared to taste, it comes time to install a fresh primer. If examination of the primer pocket shows a quantity of residue, fouling and suchlike, as noted, it's a good idea to remove that before proceeding. If you've made up a K-Spinner, it's just a second or so to push a primer pocket cleaner up into the pocket while it's whirring under power, as a finale to removing the sizing lube. Lacking a pocket cleaner, a small tuft of fine steel wool, twisted about the plain end of a spent kitchen match or short piece

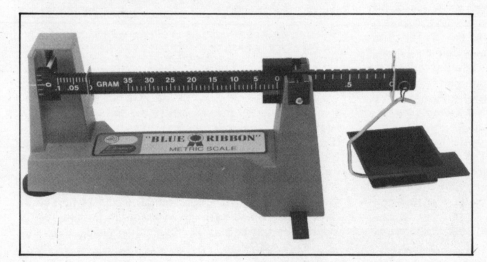

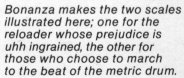

*Bonanza makes the two scales illustrated here; one for the reloader whose prejudice is uhh ingrained, the other for those who choose to march to the beat of the metric drum.*

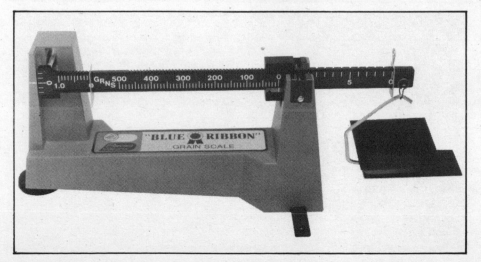

of wooden dowel in the appropriate diameter will do the same chore nicely.

Most contemporary designs of reloading presses incorporate a privoting primer arm, as illustrated in typical examples here. There are two diameters of primers in common use: .175-inch and .210-inch, termed small and large, respectively. Both diameters are available for pistol and rifle reloads. Thus, we have small pistol, large pistol, small rifle and large rifle primers.

As a usual rule, rifle-type primers have slightly greater amounts of priming compound, as well as a thicker, tougher cup. Some handguns may not be able to muster enough force on the firing pin to set off rifle-type primers reliably, causing some number of misfires as a direct result. The data for typical handgun cartridges was derived by using pistol-type primers. For that reason, even if rifle-type primers are set off dependably, their greater amount of priming compound may generate higher peak pressures.

When I'm reloading a cartridge case nominally intended as a rifle caliber — such as the .30-30, .35 Remington, .223 Remington and so on — it's my usual custom to use the appropriate diameter of rifle-type primers. Such loads usually are fired in guns such as the Thompson/Center Contender, having entirely ample amounts of firing pin force, and most if not all of the attendant load data was made up with the rifle primers.

We have a further class of primer types in the magnum primer and, for good measure, benchrest primers in the two basic rifle sizes. Magnum primers are available in some or all sizes and types, depending upon the maker. The priming compound used in magnum primers delivers a somewhat hotter spark as an aid in reliable ignition of the more reluctant powders such as ball or spherical types. The benchrest primers are of standard force for the given type, but are selected for superior uniformity and accuracy potential.

Primers should be seated firmly to the bottom of the priming pocket, but not with so much force as to deform the exposed primer cup visibly. The objective is to prestress the wafer of priming compound against the point of the primer anvil, as an aid toward uniform and positive ignition.

There have been devices intended to seat the primer

Grundgy, dirty cartridge cases often perform quite well but clean shiny ones certainly are nicer looking. Lyman Turbo tumblers do a splendiferous job of getting off the crud and verdigris in a quick quiet efficient manner.

some given slight distance below the surface of the case head, and primer micrometers to measure the seating depth. Such things would be much more useful if all cartridge cases were exactly uniform and identical to sixteen decimal places or so. As has been noted, cases vary to small but significant extents from one make/type to another. For that reason it's advantageous to sort your cases by headstamp, loading the given recipe into cases as nearly identical as may be feasible. Such reloads will usually dis-

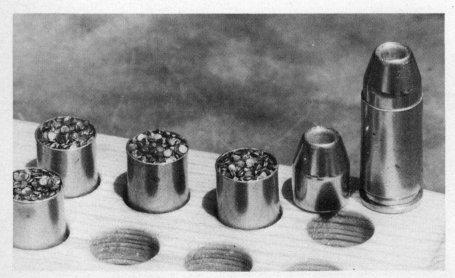

Every time I note that I regard reloading the 9mmP as faintly preferable to a root canal job, quadrillions of readers write to ask why (really, would I exaggerate?). This photo may help to shed a clue. This is a sub-max ration of Blue Dot for the 100-grain Speer and you can see the bullet seating rub.

*Above left is a shell holder balanced atop the ram and right is a shell holder installed in the slot and doing its accustomed thing. Holders from most makers fit presses from most other makers and yes we're glad.*

play accuracy that's usefully better than if made up in a randomly mixed lot of brass.

Various firms offer small primer seating presses for use as an alternative to the pivoting primer arm built into the press. Some of these priming presses have arrangements for feeding the primer into the top of the priming punch more or less automatically. Whether one approach is better than the other is largely a matter of individual preference. Personally, I prefer to seat the primers as a separate step, using an old press that was taken off the market nearly a quarter-century ago. It's obvious I can't recommend that as the way to go for others.

It should be noted that there are at least two basic approaches to reloading: You can perform all the steps in sequence on one case, taking it from spent hull to loaded round in one operation before going on to do the same with the next case. The other method is to perform each chore on a given quantity of cases before moving on to the next step in the procedure. Both have their advantages and the choice will depend upon the equipment in use, to some extent.

As I tend to put a high value upon quality control as an ongoing factor through the whole operation, I tend to favor the step-by-step technique over the load-all-at-once concept. Candidly, this is based upon a rueful awareness of a tendency to let my mind wander, with a distinct possibility of forgetting some vital step in the chain. Again, it's a matter of personal preference.

*Now and ever again it's nice to be able to pack your gear afield for resurrecting right on the spot. The Lee Precision turret is in use here with an RCBS Little Dandy doling out the charges. A skeet range gun rack has been pressed into duty as a loading bench and works quite well.*

*Resizing lube is a vital must unless you're using tungsten carbide resizing dies. Here are a couple examples with a pad for convenient application.*

Having reached the stage of the load-ready case, all sized, expanded, flared, degreased, primed and ready to get the powder charge and bullet, there remains the obvious step of determining the appropriate powder/bullet combination. As a customary thing, that is done by consulting a book of loading data. Most if not all such sources list a number of suitable powders, each at one or more charge weights suitable for use with a bullet of given weight for the cartridge under consideration.

There is an all-too-common inclination among reloaders to attempt making up the hottest loads possible. Such urges should be kept under taut rein. Most data sources carry frequent warnings to the effect that maximum loads must be used with caution or avoided. That is excellent advice, meriting your thoughtful consideration. If you need a further motive, beyond mere prudence, remind yourself that the most accurate loads are nearly always as charge weights below the maximum listings.

A good reloading scale, and the know-how to use it effectively, is an asset of great value. No matter how you measure out the powder charge, it should be weighed to make certain that it is within the listings given in the data books. It's also a good idea to check the weight of the bullet to be sure it's within the specified figures.

Powder measures come in several variants. There are rotary measures with adjustable measuring cavities, as well as rotary measures that employ sets of rotors having fixed cavities. Other measures slide back and forth — linear rather than rotary — some with cavities adjustable in size, others with bushing inserts to offer fixed cavities. In addition, there are dipper-type measures, exemplified by those supplied with the Lee kits.

Given a decent reloader's scale for use in calibrating the output, it's possible and not at all difficult to fabricate your own dipper-type measures. A spent cartridge serves as the dipper, with a couple inches of .125-inch brass welding rod for the stem and a short piece of hardwood dowel or .375-inch aluminum rod as the handle. The spent case can be

*A cordless drill carrying one of the super-handy K-Spinners is a sybaritic delight when reloading afield as it affords a zotz-quick means of getting the lube off the cases after they've been resized.*

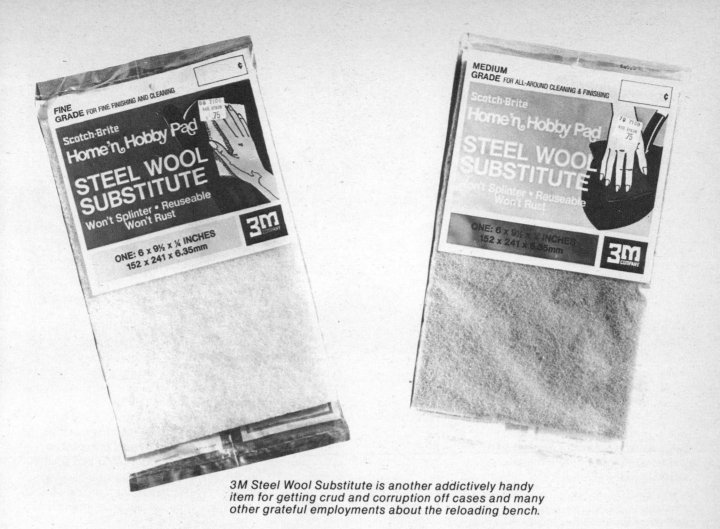

*3M Steel Wool Substitute is another addictively handy item for getting crud and corruption off cases and many other grateful employments about the reloading bench.*

*Happich's Simichrome, sold in most motorcycle shops or available from Brownell's, Inc., 210 South Mill, Montezuma, IA 50171 is the metal polish of all time. It costs a bit but one tube goes a long-long way!*

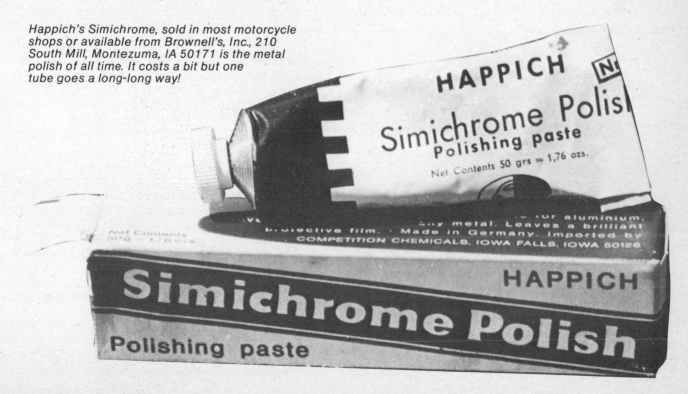

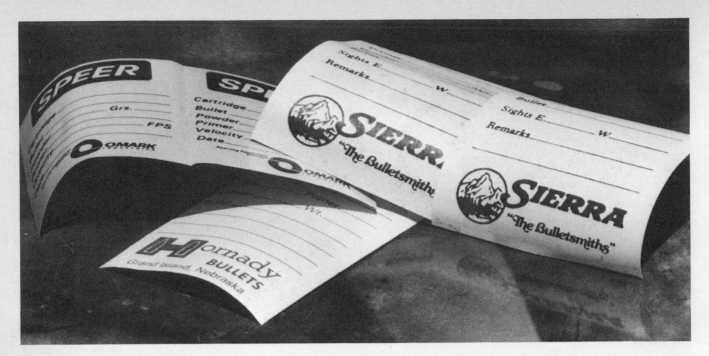

As discussed, don't lick bullet labels with your tongue lest you get painter's colic. Right, old Lyman #210 die bushed for use in cleaning up case-mouth dings. Below, my vote for the best of all chronographs goes to the Precisionics Speed-Meter II built by Robbin D. Riley in the cramped confines of Box 919 Silver City, NM 88061. Using one of these will spoil you for life on the lesser breeds!

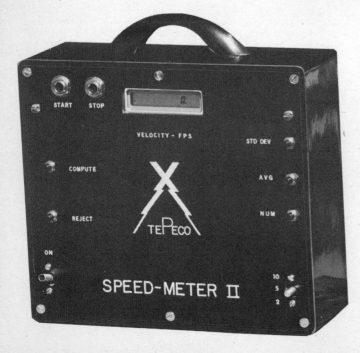

soldered to one end of the stem and a hole is drilled in one end of the handle to slip over the other end of the brass stem.

The small dipper in the nearby photograph uses a spent .25 ACP case, R-P headstamp, as its measuring cavity. Its capacity was verified by dipping ten charges of Hercules Bullseye, dumping all of them into the pan of the scale and weighing to obtain the total weight, which was 33.3 grains, out of that particular can of Bullseye. That averages out to 3.33 grains per dip. I note this with a couple of firm stipulations: If you decide to make up such a dipper, you must verify its drop on a good scale, from the can of powder you intend to use. Variations in powder density from lot to lot, as well as differences in dipping techniques, will affect the actual delivery. If it delivers 3.3 grains or so, that is a pretty useful charge for the .38 Special with bullets up to around 156 grains or so. Check the loading book of your choice to verify that.

If you feel impelled to make up maximum charges, as listed in the books, such charges should be weighed individually. They should neither be dipped nor dropped from any manner of measure. Maximum is maximum and any-

*A spent .25 ACP case, soldered to a suitable handle, will dip out hardly more than 3.4 grains of Hercules Bullseye to serve as a decent .38 Special charge using bullets no heavier than 158 grains. This one averages 3.33 grains. If made up and used, dippers must be checked on a powder scale.*

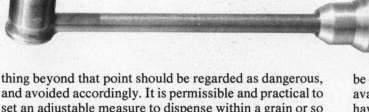

thing beyond that point should be regarded as dangerous, and avoided accordingly. It is permissible and practical to set an adjustable measure to dispense within a grain or so of the maximum weight, after which you pick up a pinch of powder and add a granule or so at a time until the scale beam hangs steady on the zero or witness line. They make powder tricklers for this chore, but I prefer doing it by hand.

If a good scale is a reloader's best friend — as it well may be — a cartridge loading block is not far behind. These are available commercially, more or less. If you happen to have access to a drill press — one of the handiest of all power tools, I think — it's so easy to make a loading block that the cost of a store-bought one is hard to justify. For most handgun calibers, just lay off the top surface in grids of five-eighths-inch each way and, at the intersections, drill one-half-inch holes to a suitable depth. That will serve for .38 Special and .45 ACP, as well as for most of the rest.

*Another handy homebuilt item. You could say that it represents a reinvention of the cigar box. The block holds four reloading dies and the rest of the space holds cases to be processed or cases that have been. A second plain box supplements it.*

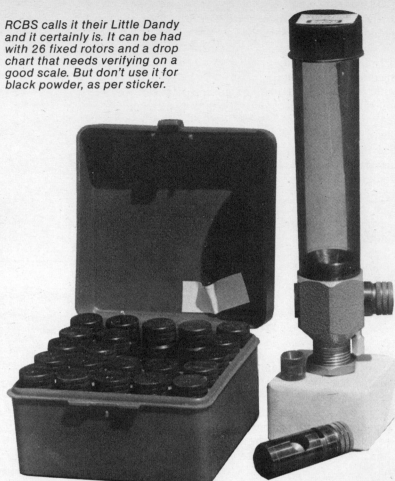

RCBS calls it their Little Dandy and it certainly is. It can be had with 26 fixed rotors and a drop chart that needs verifying on a good scale. But don't use it for black powder, as per sticker.

I've made up a bottoming cutter that will enlarge .5-inch holes to about .525-inch diameter, giving clearance for the .45 Auto Rim case and even for the belted-magnum rifle numbers.

Loading blocks can be made up to accommodate any desired number of cases. I usually make them up to hold fifty cases, but have several in other sizes. In use, load-ready cases are put into the holes and the powder charges are dispensed into each case in turn until each case is charged. Then, as a vital step in quality control, you take the block of charged cases under good light and take a keen look down into the neck of each case in turn, redundantly verifying that each has so much powder in it, but that no case has detectably more than any other. Having attended to that, you'll find that it adds usefully to your mental attitude when you go on to fire the resulting reloads.

Given load-ready cases that have been charged with powder by the procedures described, it remains but to seat and secure the bullet in the case necks. The basic procedure runs about as follows: Put a charged case in the shell holder atop the ram of the press and run it to the top of the stroke. Back off the seating stem of the bullet seating die and turn the die down into the top of the press until you feel it make first contact with the mouth of the upthrust case. Back the die off by a partial turn and lock it lightly in that setting with the locking ring on the outside of the die.

Now lower the ram and place one of the bullets lightly in the mouth of the case before running it back to the top of the ram stroke again. If the bullet nose does not meet the seating stem, turn the stem down until you feel it make contact. Back the ram down a bit, turn the stem down a bit, run the ram back up and start the bullet base into the mouth of the case. Bring the ram back down, examine the progress of the bullet seating, and turn the seating stem back down a trifle farther, as indicated.

Keep at this patient procedure until you have the bullet seated into the case mouth to a suitable depth. If the loads are for an autoloading pistol, the bullet must be seated so as to chamber easily; if for a revolver, seating must be such as to provide a suitable amount of clearance between the bullet tip and the front of the cylinder. For single-shots and the like, bullet seating must be sufficient to allow the action to close without undue effort.

With the bullet seated to appropriate depth, the flare at the case neck must be turned back in, lest it interfere with chambering the loaded round. Most bullet seating dies have a provision for turning the flared neck back in and many will perform a crimp at the neck when suitably adjusted.

The seating stem can be rotated upward by a turn or two at this point, whereupon the die body is turned down until it makes snug contact with the case mouth when the ram is at the top of its stroke. The ram is lowered slightly and the die body turned down perhaps an eighth of a turn. Run the ram to the top of its stroke, bring the ram back down and examine the condition of the case neck. If in doubt, try it in the chamber to be sure it will feed properly.

For several cartridges, it's possible to obtain taper crimping dies that do a good job of ironing the neck flare back in without a great deal of crimping. Such dies are used as the fourth die in the operation, since they have no seating stem. A taper-crimped case tends to deliver the bullet to the rifling in excellent condition at the instant of firing, whereas a heavily crimped mouth may retain some of its crimp, lacerating the sides of the bullet on the way out, particularly if the bullet is of soft lead alloy. If the crimp is still apparent in the mouth of the case after firing it is reasonable to assume that the load was over-crimped.

Many cast bullet designs provide a crimping groove at a suitable location and a lot of jacketed bullets have a knurled groove called a cannelure at the point where the case mouth ends up when suitably seated. If a jacketed bullet has no cannelure, you will not be able to crimp the case neck inward to any extent much beyond ironing the flare straight with the rest of the case wall.

As a rule, it is necessary that the bullet base be gripped securely by the case neck, so that the bullet will not be driven deeper into the case when fed through an autoloading pistol, likewise so that the bullet will not migrate forward under stress of recoil if it's one of the last rounds fired from a revolver. A crimped case neck is not too helpful in holding the bullet securely, even if executed fairly extravagantly. A taut grip of the case neck against the bullet base is much more effective and, given that, a heavy neck crimp is more or less superfluous and may degrade potential accuracy by gouging the sides of the bullet upon departure down the barrel.

The grip of the case neck against the bullet base is governed by the combination of bullet diameter and dimensions of the resizing die and expanding plug. The case neck should come out of the dies some few thousandths smaller in diameter than the bullet base, so that the bullet expands the case neck slightly during seating. Ideally, it should be possible to see a slight bulge in the case wall indicating the location of the lower end of the bullet.

You can verify the security of the bullet in the case by standing a loaded round on a bathroom scale, pressing downward on the tip of the bullet and noting the reading on the dial of the scale as it increases to the point at which the bullet moves. This may seem a bit primitive, but it is an effective way to determine the security of the seating. For a cartridge such as the .45 ACP, thirty pounds or more should be needed to move the bullet.

The importance of all this is that you must avoid loosely seated bullets that can be driven deeper into the case when going up the feed ramp and into the chamber of autoloading pistols. Even a modest amount of such deeper seating will have a strong effect upon peak pressures at the instant of firing, boosting them to a surprisingly great extent. In extreme examples, with all conditions at their worst, such a driven-back bullet can cause damage to the gun, shooter and/or bystanders.

In loads for revolvers, a loosely held bullet will not only move forward to hang up cylinder rotation — causing a fairly stubborn stoppage — but such a condition can also result in cartridges that will not fire properly. I became ruefully aware of that several years ago, having made up a quantity of .44 magnum reloads with a 240-grain cast bullet and a rather mild load of Hodgdon H110 powder. The powder level was well below the bullet base, leaving a considerable amount of empty space within the case. The case mouths were heavily crimped into the crimping groove of the bullet, but the grip of the case mouth against the bullet base was pretty casual. When fired in a Ruger Super Blackhawk, one or two loads in each cylinderful would merely go *ploof,* leaving the bullet lodged some few inches up the barrel. After driving enough of the stuck bullets back out with a length of .375-inch wooden dowel, I found it necessary to pull down the entire remains of the lot to salvage the cases and start over. Hodgdon H110 is one of those powders that responds well to the use of magnum primers — which were used on that dubious lot — and likewise performs best when the airspace within the cartridge is held to a minimum, commensurate with remaining below the maximum listings of load data.

As you're probably coming to suspect, bullet seating is an important and critical step in the reloading operation, with a decided effect upon the end performance of the ammunition. As with auto pistols and revolvers, single-shot pistols such as the Thompson/Center Contender have

*Light in weight, conveniently compact and remarkably competent, this is the C-H Junior CHampion currently retailing for about $114 for the press alone; a good one!*

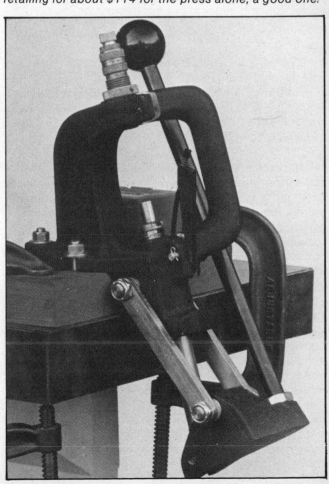

*From the makers of the Ransom Rest, the C'Arco Grand American is a progressive reloader with a feed platen that is actuated manually rather than by the lever.*

*Top, the step gauge of the vernier caliper used to measure rod protrusion with bullet held in contact with rifling leade; center, details of rod, collar and locking screw; lower, with chamber empty and rod pushed clear back, end of rod protrudes about half an inch from front face of the collar.*

their little foibles which the reloader is well advised to take into account and humor.

Accompanying photos show a simple device for checking the ideal seating depth for bullets used in Contender barrels. It consists of a small collar that can be moved along a piece of steel rod, with a locking screw on the side so that the collar can be locked in position as desired. The rod is cut from a length of cold-rolled steel and polished to prevent abrasion against the rifling in the bore. The length of the rod is about right if its front end protrudes about one-half-inch beyond the front face of the collar when the rear end of the rod is up against the standing breech in the empty chamber.

The exact amount of the rod's protrusion beyond the front surface of the collar can be measured to the nearest .001-inch by use of the step gauge on a vernier caliper. One end of the rod is faced off flat and the other is countersunk to provide a conical opening that gives a reliable location against the ogive of jacketed bullets. The seating gauge can be employed in a number of ways, all of them remarkably helpful. If you lack facilities for making up the lockable collar, pieces of white drafting tape can be used to mark the locations, at some sacrifice as to ultimate precision.

The seating gauge can be used to determine the maximum length over all (loa) for any given lot of bullets in the particular barrel at hand. In so doing, the flat end of the rod is run back to touch the standing breech with the action closed and the chamber empty. The collar is moved to touch the muzzle and is locked in place. The calipers are used to measure the amount of rod protrusion ahead of the front face of the collar and that dimension is noted for future reference.

The action is opened and a bullet alone — that is, a bullet not yet seated in a case — is inserted in the breech end of the barrel and pushed forward with a pencil, small piece of dowel, loaded round or whatever until it is felt to make snug contact with the commencement of the rifling, or *leade*. With the bullet held in that position, the gauge collar is loosened, the flat end of the rod is pushed against the bullet tip and the collar is held against the muzzle and locked in position again.

The amount of rod protrusion beyond the front collar face is measured with the vernier caliper, as before, and the distance is recorded. By subtracting the first distance, taken in the empty chamber, the remainder will be the loa

Left, RCBS Green Machine is easily capable of reloading fifty rounds every six minutes. Center, the $60 turret press from Lee Precision, here on a convenient base. Right, Ponsness-Warren P-200 Metal-Matic features a shell holder that moves from motionless die to die.

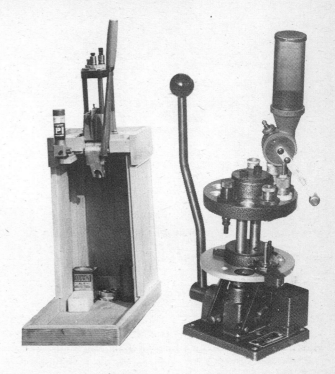

of a cartridge carrying that particular bullet that will put the ogive precisely in contact with the leade.

In actual practice, you will probably wish to seat the bullet a trifle deeper into the case to provide some amount of movement before being engraved by the lands of the rifling. In so doing, the peak pressures will be reduced, and the velocity likewise to a corresponding and proportional extent. A cartridge that puts the ogive tight up against the leade does not usually display better accuracy than one that allows a small amount of free jump to the leade.

The flat face of the rod was used in the procedure just described since the loa is measured with the vernier caliper between the case base and bullet tip. A further use for the gauge is to run the countersunk end down against the tip of a bullet on the chambered cartridge, locking the collar in contact with the muzzle. The cartridge is removed and used to push an unseated bullet up to touch the leade, whereupon the gauge is pushed down to touch the nose of

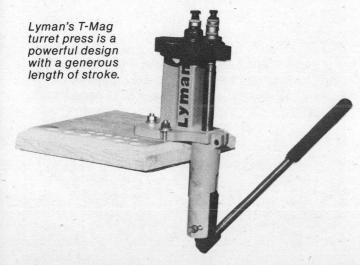

Lyman's T-Mag turret press is a powerful design with a generous length of stroke.

that bullet, with the collar still locked in its original setting. In so doing, you will be able to see some amount of gap between the rear face of the collar and the muzzle. That is the exact amount of free jump that the bullet will have at that seating depth. It is a trifle more accurate since it indexes to a point on the jacketed ogive, rather than against the bullet tip. On a soft-point bullet, variations of a few thousandths may exist from bullet to bullet, due to deformation of the soft tip in manufacture, shipping and handling.

Such a seating gauge finds many helpful applications in reloading, but I'd like to offer an urgent note of caution regarding its use in certain guns. In the Remington Model XP-100, for example, when working with a live round in the chamber, every possible safety precaution must be exercised to avoid the risk of firing the cartridge inadvertantly. Should that happen when the gauge rod is inserted in the bore, the consequences would be extremely undesirable, and that's an understatement! When working with the XP-100, it would be prudent to make up a dummy round, with no primer or powder, to check seating depth, pulling the bullet later to salvage it and the case. By the same token, when working with a pistol such as the Contender the hammer should not be cocked.

The foregoing are the general procedures and considerations that apply to making up reloaded cartridges. A further important point is the suitable packaging and identification as to the specifications of the reloads. Unless you possess and enjoy a memory vastly more eidetic than mine, you will have forgotten the details of the load in a matter of weeks, days or even hours. It is a gallingly frustrating thing to find yourself with a batch of reloads and no

This shows how the C-H Junior CHamp press was attached to its two-inch mounting plank by means of countersunk bolts and nuts to permit mounting it to any handy surface with the aid of C-clamps.

slightest recollection or clue as to what kind of powder they contain, or how much of it. The bullet may be more or less identifiable, and you may be able to pull the bullet so as to identify the powder by appearance — a dubious procedure, at best, and usually a hopeless challenge — weighing it, if it's identifiable.

It's ever so much shrewder and simpler to provide some manner of label at the time of reloading, to accompany the reloads until they are fired. Many bullet manufacturers provide a few gummed labels in each box of bullets as a helpful aid in keeping track of load data. *If you use such labels, do not lick the adhesive side with your tongue!* Consider that the gummed side will probably have picked up some amount of lead during the trip from the factory to your loading bench and licking the label is a sure way of taking the lead into your system, where it poses a serious hazard to health and well being.

There are several ways to keep track of the particulars of a batch of reloads. You can purchase a number of felt-tipped markers in assorted colors and make a small dab of color on the exposed face of the primer cup, with a suitable set of records to go with the various colors. After firing and upon further reloading, the primer is discarded, wiping out the data after it's no longer needed.

Obsolete calling cards can be used to record load data, or blank calling cards can be had from your printer. White drafting tape can be affixed to the cartridge container for marking down the details. It's better not to rely upon grease-pencilled notations on plastic cartridge boxes, since that can rub off in handling, leaving you back in the dark again.

We've mentioned pulling down reloaded ammo and the techniques for doing that warrant discussion. Several makers of reloading dies offer collet-type bullet pulling dies that can be installed in the top of the press in the same manner as a regular die. The cartridge is run up and the collet is

tightened around the bullet so that it's pulled free when the ram is run back down. That is the quickest and simplest approach, particularly if you have to pull down a quantity of loads. Likewise available are the inertia-type bullet pullers in which the cartridge head is secured in a collet to hold the load as the puller is struck several times against a solid surface to wrench the bullet loose. Either approach has its advantages and disadvantages, and having both types on hand is often a convenience, since deloading is sometimes an important part of reloading.

To the present, we've hardly more than mentioned loading presses in passing. They come in many forms, varying broadly as to cost, complexity, compactness and so on. There are a few pressless systems, such as the Lee kits that operate by percussion — tapping the cases in and out with a mallet — rather than leverage. There is the old Lyman #310 tong tool or "nutcracker," operating by simple leverage and a few similar examples.

Loading presses are designed to be fastened to a solid surface such as a loading bench. Most such devices require a mounting surface somewhat sturdier than ¾-inch plywood, and the nominal two-inch plank — actually about 1½ inches thick — is about the minimum that is apt to be satisfactory. It is possible to operate a reloading press

Lyman's Orange Crusher is one of the newest add-ons to their line. It has a long stroke to cope with the tallest cartridges such as the 8mm Rem mag along with a compound toggle leverage system and an option to switch from RH to LH configuration to suit taste.

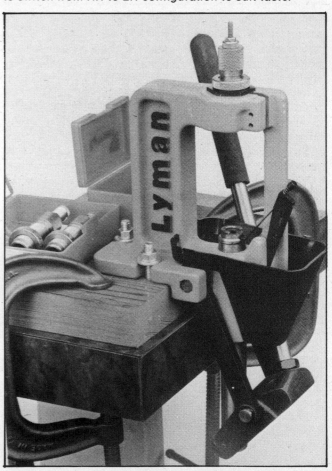

while seated, and some prefer to do so. I'd rather reload while standing. With most if not all presses, if used while standing, the ideal height above the floor for the upper bench surface is the distance from the upper edge of the reloader's belt to the floor. That gives good visibility and the best possible advantage from the standpoint of operating the press lever up and down. Improper arrangement and positioning, on a long reloading session, can leave you sore in places you didn't even know you had.

I have a few presses that are used so frequently that they are permanently bolted to the bench. One such is my RCBS Model A-2 that has been in use since 1959, with a tin can positioned beneath it to catch the spent primers as they fall down through the hollow ram. Not many presses made today offer that handy feature: The C-H Heavyweight CHampion is one of the few that comes to mind.

The standard thread size for reloading dies is ⅞-14. The small dies supplied for use with the Lyman #310 tong tool have ⅝-40 threads and Lyman can furnish bushing adapters for using such dies in the ⅞-14 presses. I have the #310 mouth-expander for the .45 ACP thus bushed and installed as the first die in the eight stations of my old Hollywood Senior turret press. I find it extremely handy for removing the mouth dents and dings that turn up frequently in cases that have been fired in the .45 auto pistols. By ironing the case necks to a nice round shape before they pass into the full-length resizing die, a lot of lost-case problems can be avoided.

Most if not all makers of reloading equipment have long since standardized upon the so-called universal shell holders, which is a state of affairs for which reloaders should feel appropriately grateful. The shell holders from most makers will fit the presses of other makers. Sadly, there is not much in the way of a standardized system of distinguishing the various shell holders by number. Several shell holders will accept more than one caliber of cartridge. A chart, clipped or photocopied from a manufacturer's catalog and posted on a nearby surface will offer a handy means of keeping track of the numbered shell holder needed for a given cartridge.

Storing the shell holders in the box with the loading die set is not the best approach, in view of the interchangeability of the holders, as noted. Upon needing a particular shell holder, you have to rummage through all the different die boxes in search of it. I prefer to store most of my shell holders on a piece of board drilled to accommodate the smaller diameter of the holder bases and labeled with most or all of the cartridges the given holder will handle. As far as I know, no enterprising maker of loading equipment has yet seen fit to offer such a shell holder storage rack commercially, so they have to be made up from hunks of scrap board.

Another approach I've come to favor for mounting presses is to bolt them to a small piece of two-inch plank, with the bolt holes counterbored from the underside to leave the lower plank surface flush. The base can then be secured to the bench top or any other suitably sturdy surface with a pair of C-clamps.

Since most reloading presses come with a few small accessory items, such as the two diameters of priming punch, I've made it a practice to fasten one of the snap-top plastic boxes to the top of the plank to aid in keeping track

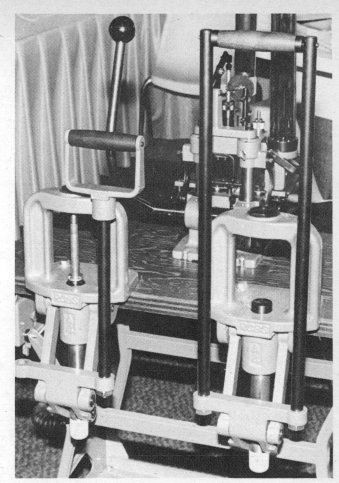

Newest entry to the RCBS line is the A-4, introduced early in 1982 and harking back to the legendary A-2 of reverant memory from 1959 or so. One has a choice between the spade-grip lever at left of the double-shafted variant at right. It has a shell holder to accept nearly all sizes and a configuration that is equally handy for northpaw, southpaw or anyone.

of such elusive little items. The plastic boxes currently used by Lyman for their bullet mould blocks work extremely well for such applications.

A further accessory meriting consideration is a receptacle of some sort to take along to the range or firing site for keeping track of the spent cases. In its simplest form, that can be a common paper bag. If you're working with several different cartridges, and toss all the empties into the same container, it can result in a time-wasting job of sorting them out later. A worthwhile alternative is to cut the tops off a suitable number of milk cartons, either the quart or half-gallon sizes, and make up a small carrying rack so that 9mm Luger cases can be segregated from the .380 auto size; .38 Specials from .357 magnums, and so on. A further possibility is to cut the tops from the unbreakable plastic soda bottles for use in sorting cases by caliber or — as may be necessary — by maker's headstamp within the same caliber.

It was noted earlier that cases differ from maker to maker. A salient example is the .22 Hornet — one of the best of the many cartridges in which the Thompson/Center Contender is offered. The .22 Hornet cases made by Rem-

RCBS has two primer seaters of which this is the somewhat flossier version. A later modification of the seater shown has an extension on the front of the lever to tip the primer feed forward automatically, thus speeding the operation.

ington — currently headstamped R-P — have considerably larger capacities than those from Winchester-Western with the W-W headstamp. If you load the two makes indiscriminately, the resulting sacrifice in uniformity and accuracy represents a serious handicap.

It's an easy, simple matter to determine relative case capacities between makes. Just adjust a rotary powder measure to drop enough of some fine-grained Ball-type powder to fill one case level full or nearly so. Then drop the same charge into another case and compare the levels visually. A further helpful check is to compare the weights

of the fired cases on the reloader's scales. You may find the variations rather surprising.

You may find it highly advantageous to work up the capability of taking your reloading operation afield, so that loads can be put up after firing in an effort to isolate those loads with the most desirable qualities. One of the more formidable problems of such an approach is to weigh the powder charges under outdoor conditions, with vagrant breezes to disturb the balance of the scale pan. If you're operating from a van or recreational vehicle, there's no problem at all, and a pretty sophisticated reloading setup can be fielded, needing only a level parking area.

Lacking such facilities, it is possible to construct a protected stand for the scale so that a hinged window can be lowered to defeat the wind, with the mounting surface capable of being leveled. Such a thing may prove objectionably bulky and bothersome. An alternative worth considering is to use the measures that employ fixed rotors or cavity bushings, such as the RCBS Little Dandy and one or more of the twenty-six rotors currently offered for it. Such measures need to be calibrated with the use of an accurate scale but, once that has been done and the figures recorded on a chart, such measures offer attractive advantages for field use. If you're planning to use several different powders, don't forget to include a small funnel for getting the surplus powder back into its proper can.

Bullet velocity can be measured with the aid of an instrument called a chronograph, and current patterns of those boast a lot of refinements over the models of earlier years. Not only are they compact and convenient, but several operate on batteries, with circuits that put no more than a modest drain on the pack. There was a time when nearly all chronographs operated on alternating-cycle house current, limiting operations to a radius equal to the length of the available extension cord. I thought I had the answer in the form of one of the small gasoline-powered generators, bought one, tried it out and it seemed to work okay. So I loaded the considerable bulk of the chronograph of that era, plus the generator and a ton or so of smaller needfuls and drove to Twin Falls, Idaho. Steve Herrett was then in the process of developing a number of wildcat cartridges for the Contender, working toward what would be finalized as his .30 and .357 Herrett rounds.

Sad to say, after making the long portage, setting up the chronograph and cranking up the little generator, we were quite unable to get a plausible reading out of it. Hauling it back to Southern California and trying it again, it worked just fine. My comments on the fiasco are best left to the imagination.

The chronograph I use today is the Speed-Meter II, made by Precisionics, Box 919, Silver City, NM 88062. A three-way switch on the readout box can be set for screen spacings of two, five or ten feet. I've made up a small portable screen holder, with the start and stop screens positioned two feet apart and the entire affair can be set up so as to clock bullets on the way to the target. Thus, if desired, it's a fairly simple matter to index any given hole in the paper as to its muzzle velocity. The readout box is mounted to a small table with detachable legs, so that it and the clipboard for recording data are convenient to the portable shooting bench.

A further useful aid for establishing the accuracy capabilities of a given handgun load is the Ransom Rest, made by C'Arco, Box 308, Highland, CA 92346. In use, the grips or stocks are removed and the receiver is clamped in one of the adapters available from C'Arco for nearly any reasonably popular handgun. The Ransom Rest needs to be attached to a solid support. I've made up such a rig so that it can be anchored by driving one of the wheels of the car onto its horizontal plank; a design concept worked out by my late good friend, Bill Corson.

An alternative approach, original as far as I know, is to mount the Ransom Rest to a small framework that has a scope sight mounted to its upper edge. The resulting rig, which I term the Robot Pistolero, is fired off a conventional shooting bench, using the scope reticle for aligning each shot in turn. That works surprisingly well with the guns and cartridges that are fairly modest as to recoil. At some point between the .38 Special and the .357 magnum, recoil hurls the framework about with more violence than you really want.

For the past several years, I've had a potentially handy accessory in the back of my head, awaiting the time and opportunity to make it up. It consists of a remotely actuated target carrier for use with the Ransom Rest. By pulling a length of nylon cord, string-loaded ratchet arrangements at the target would move a fresh section of a roll of shelf paper into position to catch the next group from the Ransom Rested test gun. The saving in time and effort seems attractive and, one of these times, I hope to get around to it. Never underestimate the creative ingenuity of the really lazy person, right?

*C-H 444-X press positions three loading dies plus their powder measure so that the cartridge can be completely reloaded by moving it through the four shell holders. This makes a convenient rig for typical hangun loads.*

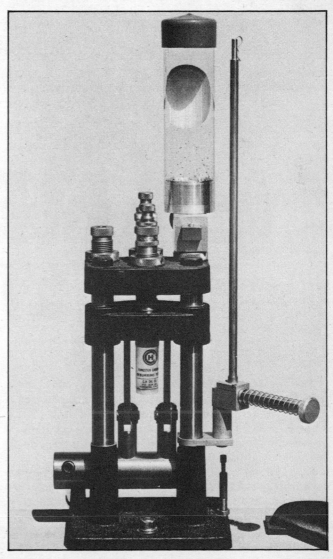

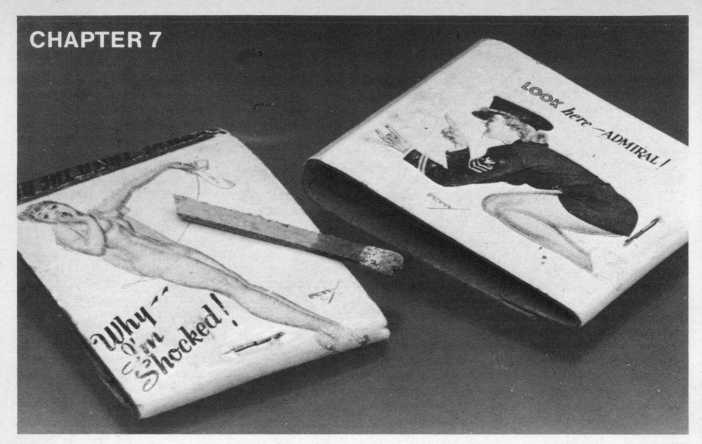

# CHAPTER 7

As noted here, a common paper match, after being ignited and waved out, weighs fairly close to one grain. This particular one from vintage circa 1950 folder turned out to weigh closer to 1.6 grains, but I decided to settle for it.

# HANDGUN BALLISTICS

THE FIELD of ballistics deals with several units of measurement not too often encountered elsewhere and it might be well to devote brief discussion to them. One potential source of confusion is the unit for small weight: the grain. That is not a single granule of powder but rather 1/7000 of an avoirdupois pound and those are the sort of pounds by which you buy groceries or read your weight on the bathroom scale. We use other weight systems such as the troy or apothecary, but a grain is a grain is a grain throughout all three. They diverge when it gets to ounces, but that needn't concern us here.

A common paper match weighs fairly close to one grain, if that helps to lend perspective. It's customary to quote powder charges by tenths of a grain and .1-grain is about the weight of a single sheet of gummed cigarette paper. A five-grain aspirin tablet will weigh somewhat more than 5.0 grains, presumably due to the presence of inactive ingredients. There are 437.5 grains in one ounce, so your reloaders scale can function as a pretty accurate postal scale in questions of whether you need one stamp or two.

Bullet velocity is given in feet per second and abbreviated as fps, sometimes FPS. The kinetic energy of a bullet is commonly quoted in foot-pounds of energy or fpe/FPE.

# Simple Math To Give You Handy Yardsticks For Measuring Cartridge Performance And Other Useful Data

Given the bullet weight in grains and its velocity in fps, it is a fairly simple matter to figure its energy in fpe. Most sources give you the classic textbook method with little further details and let it go at that. I propose to give you that, along with a bit of explanation as to just what we're doing and then go on to show you a handy shortcut or two that will give you the same answer without all that scutwork.

For purpose of illustration let us take the example of a 158-grain bullet at a velocity of 1250 fps and we'll say at the start that it has kinetic energy to the extent of slightly over 548 fpe. What we're going to do is find out how we get that 548.

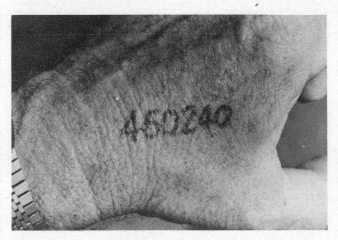

"...a number so useful to ballisticians that it's almost worth having it tattooed on the back of your hand for ready reference."

## BULLET ENERGY

Velocity squared, divided by 7000, divided by 64.32, times bullet weight, equals bullet energy. As I've a calculator here that runs up to nine decimals, I'm going to quote the complete answer in the early stages for purposes of illustration that will become apparent shortly.

Let's go through that step by step: Velocity squared means that you multiply the fps times fps, or 1250 times 1250, which gives us 1,562,500. We divided that by 7000, giving us 223.2142857. We divide that in turn by 64.32 and that gives us 3.470371357. We multiply that by the bullet weight in grains, 158 in this example, and that gives

us 548.3186744 fpe; the answer we wanted, a bit more accurately than we really needed, but the right answer to seven decimals.

## SECRET SHORTCUT #1

Dividing velocity squared by first one number and then by another number is all very well but, as it happens, if you multiply the second and third number and then divide the first number by the product of that multiplication, you get exactly the same answer, meanwhile saving the bother of one operation in division. Consider if you will:

96 divided by 4 divided by 2 is 12
4 times 2 is 8
96 divided by 8 is 12.

Before we take the obvious step, let's find out what we're doing when we divide by 7000 and then by 64.32: why are we doing that? As it turns out, 7000 is the number of grains in one avoirdupois pound (yes, we said that) and 64.32 is two times 32.16; but what's 32.16? Well, that's the figure given in most physics textbooks as the rate at which a falling body accelerates on its way to the surface of this particular planet when unsupported and in gravity's implacable grip. A falling body accelerates at the rate of 32.16 feet per second *per second,* or fpsps. If we assign the symbol G to 32.16 and T to the time of falling in seconds, a falling body attains a *final* velocity of G times T or an *average* velocity of ½ G×T. The distance fallen equals average velocity × T.

If an object — let's say a dropped golf ball — commences its fall with zero velocity, it will fall 16.08 feet in the first second, meanwhile acquiring a final velocity of 32.16 fps as of that instant. In the second second it accelerates from that to 64.32 fps and travels an additional 48.24 feet to reach a point 64.32 feet below the point of initial drop.

Our dropped golf ball will travel about 1024 feet in the first eight seconds of its plunge, assuming no retardation from atmospheric resistance. Its final velocity after eight seconds will be eight times G or 257.28 fps.

The foregoing figures were casually cribbed from my high school physics text, still in my possession though I had the devil's own time putting hands upon it. The value of G, I should note, is by no means a rock-solid constant, varying slightly in different parts of the world. Nor can I shed much light as to why we employ 2G as our second divisor; it puzzles me at least as much as it puzzles you, perhaps more. After an intent scan through the ancient textbook, I'm inclined to marvel that I ever got out of high school in the first place. I can only offer the word that this is the way it's done.

All of which is neither Damon nor yet Pythias from the standpoint of the discussion at hand. What really is pertinent is that we can multiply the 7000 times the 64.32 and that gives us the exceedingly convenvenient figure of 450,-240. It is a number so useful to ballisticians that it's almost worth having it tattooed on the back of your hand for ready reference. I call it the Foom-Factor and customarily abbreviate it as F. Make note of that please. If we toss in F in the ensuing discussion, you can take it to mean the number 450,240; a whole number whose decimal at the end is followed by an endless line of zeros.

## PROOF-TESTING THE PUDDING

Let's see if it works: 1250 times 1250 is still 1,562,500 and if we divide that by F we get 3.470371357 and that times 158 (bullet weight in grains) gives us 548.3186744 fpe. That's perzackly the same answer we got by the tedious, roundabout method in the first place and isn't that remarkable? Dead-on to the seventh decimal!

I could've fed you the Foom-Factor cold-turkey, but someone might ask you where the number came from and now you can hit them with the answer. Hence the roundaboutery, okay?

## FURTHER FESTIVE FANCIES & DEEP-DISH DELIGHTS

As it all happens to turn out, if we divide F (450,240, remember?) by any particular bullet weight in grains, it gives us an even handier shortcut for any and all future computations involving bullets of that weight.

F divided by 158 is 2849.620253 so let's see what happens if we just multiply 1250 times 1250 and then divide the resulting 1,562,500 by 2849.620253: As it turns out, the answer is 548.3186745 and we check back and find that, in comparison to the first two approaches given here, we are off to the extent of .0000001 fpe too much. Horrors, how gross! If you don't mind that much slop, you're welcome to the use of it, even so: Be my Guest, Edgar!

Here is a table of factors for the more popular bullet weights, derived by dividing 450,240 by the bullet weight in grains. To use, merely multiply velocity in fps times itself (that is, square the velocity) and divide by the factor shown here for the given bullet weight. The answer will be the energy in fpe. You're welcome to drop some of the decimals if you wish.

| BULLET WEIGHT (grains) | FACTOR | BULLET WEIGHT (grains) | FACTOR |
|---|---|---|---|
| 25 | 18009.6 | 158 | 2849.620253 |
| 30 | 15008 | 160 | 2814 |
| 35 | 12864 | 165 | 2728.727273 |
| 38 | 11848.42105 | 168 | 2680 |
| 40 | 11256 | 170 | 2648.470588 |
| 45 | 10005.33333 | 172 | 2617.674419 |
| 46 | 9787.826087 | 175 | 2572.8 |
| 50 | 9004.8 | 177 | 2543.728814 |
| 52 | 8658.461538 | 180 | 2501.333333 |
| 53 | 8495.09434 | 185 | 2433.72973 |
| 55 | 8186.181818 | 188 | 2394.893617 |
| 60 | 7504 | 190 | 2369.684211 |
| 63 | 7146.666667 | 192 | 2345 |
| 70 | 6432 | 196 | 2297.142857 |
| 75 | 6003.2 | 200 | 2251.2 |
| 80 | 5628 | 205 | 2196.292683 |
| 85 | 5296.941176 | 210 | 2144 |
| 88 | 5116.363636 | 215 | 2094.139535 |
| 90 | 5002.666667 | 220 | 2046.545455 |
| 95 | 4739.368421 | 225 | 2001.066667 |
| 100 | 4502.4 | 230 | 1957.565217 |
| 105 | 4288 | 235 | 1915.914894 |
| 110 | 4093.090909 | 238 | 1891.764706 |
| 115 | 3915.130435 | 240 | 1876 |
| 117 | 3848.205128 | 245 | 1837.714286 |
| 120 | 3752 | 250 | 1800.96 |
| 124 | 3630.967742 | 255 | 1765.647059 |
| 125 | 3601.92 | 260 | 1731.692308 |
| 130 | 3463.384615 | 265 | 1699.018868 |
| 135 | 3335.111111 | 270 | 1667.555556 |
| 136 | 3310.588235 | 275 | 1637.236364 |
| 140 | 3216 | 280 | 1608 |
| 142 | 3170.704225 | 285 | 1579.789474 |
| 146 | 3083.835616 | 290 | 1552.551724 |
| 148 | 3042.162162 | 295 | 1526.237288 |
| 150 | 3001.6 | 300 | 1500.8 |
| 152 | 2962.105263 | 310 | 1452.387097 |
| 154 | 2923.636364 | 320 | 1407 |
| 155 | 2904.774194 | 350 | 1286.4 |
| 156 | 2886.153846 | | |

## VICE VERSA & VERSE VISA

The foregoing is jim-dandy great if you know the velocity and projectile weight, but what if you have a final figure in mind for the energy and wish to find either the velocity or bullet weight, with the other figure as a starting point: What then, coach?

Well, it's almost as easy. For the sake of clarity, let's take to referring to velocity as V, weight as W, and energy as E. On that basis, the following apply:

The square root of (E divided by W times F) equals V.
E divided by (V times V divided by F) equals W.
V times V divided by F times W equals E.

The third and final one of those is the one we started out talking about, of course, but I tossed it back in for the sake of overall completeness and coherence. Anyone who wishes to convert those to classic algebraic equations is welcome to do so.

Let it be noted that we've gotten into parenthetical entries here and remember I said it wasn't quite as easy, okay? In the second example, we multiply 1250 times 1250 and then divide the resulting 1,562,500 by 450,240 to get 3.470371357 and, if our desired energy figure (E) was 548.3186744, when we divide that by the arrived-at number from the parentheses or 3.47..., we get 158 followed by seven nice round zeros. That is the applicable bullet weight for which we fared forth in quest, you'll recall, no? If you work it straight without parentheses, you get .000000001 as an answer or something just as silly.

I dealt with the second example first because the first is the worst in terms of intrinsic complexity, but still not much worse than a bad cold when all's said. Shall we have a go at finding the velocity (V), given the prerequisite bullet weight (W) and resulting energy in fpe (E)--?

A square root of a given number is another number that, multiplied times itself, gives the original number as the product of the multiplication. Thus the square root of four is two, the square root of nine is three, the square root of 69 is 8.306623863, and so on and so forth. We need to divide E by W, multiply that times F and then work the square root of the figure that results. Let's run through this one in terms of our illustrative example and see how it works, if it does:

The desired energy figure is of course 548.3186744 and that, when divided by the bullet weight of 158, gives us 3.470371357 and when we multiply that times 450,240 (or F), we get 1,562,500, which may sound familiar.

The square root of 1,562,500 is 1250.000000...

It is possible to work out square roots on paper, but it's a miserable chore. It is possible to buy calculators for down around eight bucks that perform the same operation with effortless ease. I regard that as a decent bargain and hope you feel the same.

## MOMENTUM VS. FPE

There are those who feel that a bullet's momentum is a vastly more relevant and pertinent figure than its kinetic energy as such. Momentum puts a lot more emphasis upon bullet weight than it does upon velocity. A heavy bullet moving comparatively slowly can and does pack a lot more momentum than a lighter bullet moving faster, even if both combinations work out to the same number of fpe. If anything, it's even easier to work out the momentum of a moving bullet than it is to dope its fpe. Let's take a look at the basic procedure:

Multiply the velocity times the weight and divide the product of that by 225,200; just that simple. In the well worn example we've been using, that would be 1250 times 158 divided by 225,200 and that come out to .876998224 and it seems quite defensible to round that to .877 for better maneuverability.

With the aid of the equations given previously, it's easy to find that a 305-grain bullet at 900 fps and a 76-grain bullet at 1800 fps both carry close to the 548 fpe figure.

The momentum of a 305-grain bullet at 900 fps would be 1.22 and for the 76-grain bullet at 1800 fps it would be .607 or so. Assuming a larger momentum figure is desirable, it favors heavier bullets for the obvious reason that the velocity goes in unsquared. Yes, you're quite correct: The 225,200 sounds suspiciously like one-half of our friendly Foom-Factor and one can't help but wonder if it shouldn't be 225,120 instead.

I would assume that more momentum would be useful in those combat matches where the load to be used must produce a given amount of movement on a ballistic pendulum in order to qualify. Its exact value in metallic silhouette shooting could be debated by reason of the fact a lighter bullet at higher velocity will carry more of its energy/momentum to the 200-meter mark than would a 305-grain bullet that starts at 900 fps. The trajectory of the latter would be objectionably curvaceous, one would think. Too, additional momentum would be obtained at the cost of more recoil to a fairly proportional extent since bullet weight is a major factor in recoil.

## BULLET SPIN

The purpose of the rifling in the bore is to impart a spinning motion to the bullet, thus giving it the same form of stability that enables a gyroscope top to balance on a length of string.

As you might assume, the exact rate of spin in revolutions per minute (rpm) or revolutions per second (rps) is a critical factor in determining bullet stability and resultant accuracy. Variations in length, weight and shape of the bullet would affect the exact rate of spin that would give optimum performance. Actually, the weight is only incidental insofar as it governs length. A long, pointed bullet needs to spin faster than a blunt-nosed slug of the same weight.

If a bullet spins too rapidly it is said to be overstabilized, and understabilized if the spin is too slow. Overstabilization is nearly as bad as understabilization in terms of optimum accuracy. A high rate of spin does affect the expansion of bullets that upset on impact, however. That is a fact often overlooked by those experimenters who load bullets to reduced velocities and fire them into test media to simulate expansion at extreme ranges.

Rotational speed, encountering but little resistance in the bullet's passage, falls off much more slowly than veloc-

*Bullet drop and velocity retention are affected by nose shape of the bullet, which governs the factor known as the ballistic coefficient. The round nose at left will lose velocity faster and drop farther than the spire point at right.*

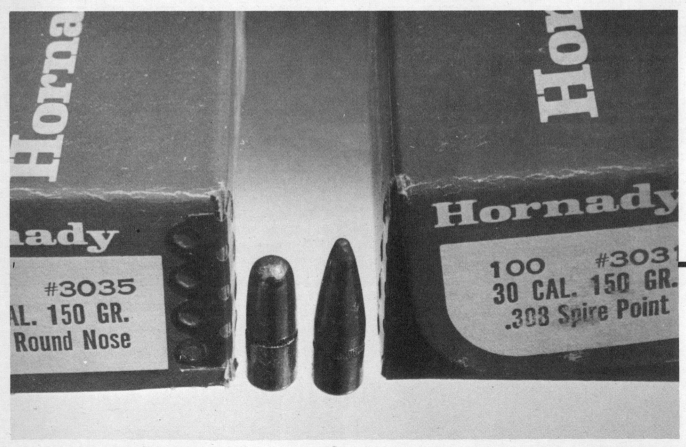

ity and that's why the sub-loaded expansion tests do not produce valid results.

With the rifling pitch and bullet velocity given, it's a simple matter to figure rotational speed. At a velocity of 1000 fps in a barrel with a pitch of one turn in twelve inches — or 1:12 as it's usually written — it's pretty obvious that the spin at the muzzle would be 1000 rps or 60,000 rpm. At the same velocity in a 1:9 barrel, mindful that nine inches is three-quarters of one foot, you'd divide the 1000 by .75 to get 1333 rps/80,000 rpm, and so on. A 1:14 barrel would mean dividing by 1.166 to get 857 rps/51,429 rpm and the corresponding figure for a 1:18.75 barrel would be 640/38,400.

For convenience, we'll drop the rpm figure and stay with the one for rps. If you've done much target work with wadcutter bullets in .38 Special revolvers it's probable you've noticed that a 148-grain wadcutter is marginally stable, if that, when fired at moderate velocities in a 1:18.75 barrel; the usual pitch used by Smith & Wesson in their .38 Special revolvers. That is indicated by the fact that some if not all of the holes in the paper are not perfectly circular, evidenced by holes that show the bullet was rubbing its side going through or keyholing to use the customary term. A barrel with 1:14 pitch tends to produce holes quite acceptably circular and usually a lot closer together.

Now it's entirely possible to increase bullet spin by upping the velocity. If we assume a 1:14 barrel stabilizes a 148-grain wadcutter nicely at 800 fps, what velocity do we need in a 1:18.75 barrel to achieve the same spin rate? The handy approach called a geometrical proportion provides the answer: first pitch divided by first velocity equals second pitch divided by second velocity or, more formally:

$$\frac{P^1}{V^1} = \frac{P^2}{V^2} \quad \text{or} \quad \frac{1.166}{800} = \frac{1.5625}{?}$$

The pitch figures are obtained by dividing 14 and 18.75 by 12. Pinning down the value of ? (or x, as we'd usually say) is simply a matter of multiplying $V^1$ times $P^2$ and dividing the product by $P^1$; cross-multiply and divide. When we multiply 800 times 1.5625 we get 1250 and that divided by 1.166 gives 1072 fps as the velocity needed to produce a spin rate of 686 rps in the 1:18.75 barrel to equal the spin imparted by the 1:14 barrel at 800 fps velocity.

## BULLET DROP

Since a bullet has no wings, it is unsupported once it clears the muzzle and it commences to drop at the same rate as any other falling body. It drops farther and farther, picking up downward speed, as it moves toward the target and meanwhile atmospheric resistance is applying the brakes to its velocity, all of which produces a bullet path somewhat resembling a parabola. As it makes its way along, cross winds may deflect it to the right or left to introduce further complications.

Most of today's handbooks carry extensive tables in which the various bullets are listed with a choice of several appropriate muzzle velocities, going on to provide the figures for remaining energy, velocity and net drop in inches at each of several realistic distances. Most such tables are for rifle bullets at rifle velocities. Until the recent interest in handgun silhouette shooting no one bothered much with handgun trajectories to two hundred meters or more.

There is an absolutely accurate, utterly valid and reliable technique by means of which you can find the drop for any bullet, any load, in any gun. It consists of setting up a target with a suitable aiming point at — for example — fifty yards, firing a five-shot group, moving out to mark the holes for prevention of future confusion and moving it to one hundred yards. At that point you fire a second five-round group, go forward and mark those holes and run the target to 150 yards for still another test group and so on.

An alternative you may prefer would be to set out a target at each of the test distances and fire five rounds apiece. That's an effective way to avoid getting your groups superimposed over each other.

There is a target specifically produced to assist and expedite such research. It's called the TRJ-123 target,

The Sharp Model EL-5100 calculator in unprogrammed mode displays the equation as above for a convenient final check before pressing the = key and, with that done, presents the answer as shown in the photo appearing below.

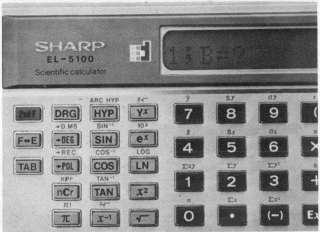

As an alternative and much faster approach, the equation can be programmed and when the COMP button (arrow) is pressed, it asks for the value of A, our velocity in this example. You enter 1250 or whatever on the number keyboard, press COMP again and it asks for B or bullet weight. So you enter 158 the same way, press COMP a third time and the answer appears. If you wish to use the same velocity or weight, merely press the COMP button twice and it uses the figure supplied previously.

made and sold by Rocky Mountain Target Company (Box 700, Black Hawk, SD 57718). The central aiming point is located fairly high in the large sheet of paper for the sake of catching groups from the longer distance on the lower part of the paper.

This is known as the empirical approach, or try it and find out. It produces the hardest kind of data to be had.

## MINUTE OF ANGLE

Elsewhere here a heavily decimaled figure is quoted for the divergence at one hundred yards for one minute of angle. It's a reasonably easy thing to determine, given a competent calculator. Visualize a circle with one hundred yards as its radius; two hundred yards as its diameter; using a figure of 3.141592654 as the value of pi, multiply that times the 200-yard diameter to obtain 628.3185307 yards as the circumference of the circle. Multiply that times 36 to convert the circumference to inches and it comes out to 22,619.46711 inches. Store that figure for a moment and reflect that there are 60 minutes of angle in

one degree and 360 degrees in a full circle; multiplying 60 times 360 gives 21,600 as the number of minutes in a full circle. Retrieve your circumference of 22,619.46711 inches and divide that by the 21,600 minutes and you get 1.047197551 inches as the spread for each minute of angle at that distance. With that established it's a simple matter to figure the spread of one moa at any other distance. Each minute of angle subdivides into sixty seconds of angle so you can divide by 60 to obtain .017453293-inch as the value of one second of angle (soa) at one hundred yards if you really crave something challenging to shoot for. Sorry, but I can't offer a simple technique for measuring group size to nine decimals.

## CALCULATORS

Some while back friend Dick Morgan touted me into buying a Sharp Model EL-5100 calculator and I've been grateful ever since. It costs a bit under $70, measures 2¾ by 6⅞ by about ⅜-inch in thickness, has ten memory keys running from A through J, shuts itself off in about seven

While it's nice to have a fancy programmable calculator, procedures covered here can be handled on a much less expensive unit such as this one, typically priced close to $10. Divide 450,240 by bullet weight in grains or look up the same figure on the accompanying chart. Enter that and press the M+ key to put it in Memory. Enter the velocity in fps; press X/=/÷/MR/= and the answer in fpe will appear on the screen, as here for our illustrative example. MR stands for Memory Recall in this instance.

minutes if you make no further entries, but retains the memories and so on when turned back on. It can be programmed with up to five equations, any of which can then be used in dialogic mode.

To amplify that: For convenience I use the A memory key for velocity, B for bullet weight and C for energy in fpe. With the suitable equation programmed, you press the COMP key and the screen reads "1;A=?," with the question mark flashing on and off. You tap your velocity in via the number keys, hit the COMP button again and the screen reads, "1;B=?," with the ? flashing on/off, so you feed it the bullet weight, press COMP one more time and the value of C in fpe comes back on the screen.

The real luxury comes in if you happen to be working the fpe for the same bullet weight at several different velocities. Once you've fed it the weight and entered the new velocity, when it wants to know the value of B again, you merely press the COMP key a second tme and it cheerfully works it out for the bullet weight presently in its data banks. All you have to do is feed it the velocities and copy down the answers.

Shift to STAT mode and it will gulp down figures and feed back averages or standard deviations at the tickle of a key. It will raise numbers to any power you fancy or give you the root to the sixth, seventeenth or whatever; tell you the number of five-card hands possible in a fifty-two-card deck and more other tricks than we've space to dwell upon here. Glory what I wouldn't've given for one of these thirty years ago, but I realize that if I'd had one in the early Fifties, once the batteries ran out, there were no fresh ones on the market. No problem now, as batteries were not only included, but it came with a spare set. Now that's really remarkable!

$$\text{MPH} \times 1.466 = \text{FPS}$$

$$\text{FPS} \times .682 = \text{MPH}$$

## DATA RECORDING

Browsing through Phil Sharpe's *Complete Guide To Handloading* recently I came upon a photo of Sharpe happily burbling into a Dictaphone he'd rigged to run off six-volt automobile batteries for the sake of getting down all the verbal details from shot to shot for later integration. I never had the privilege of making contact with Phil Sharpe

Portable sound recording equipment has seen a lot of progress since the days when the late Phil Sharpe enjoyed the use of his Dictaphone powered by his six-volt auto battery. The early ones recorded on cylinders that were bulky, relatively expensive and incapable of being recycled after the first use. Olympus X-01 puts an hour on each side.

although I owe the gent a great deal because his book took me by the hand and initiated me into the absorbing mysteries and goodly delights to be found about the loading bench.

For the same helpful assistance, I use an Olympus Pearlcorder Model X-01, smaller than the Sharp El-5100 although a trifle thicker. It operates on a pair of penlight batteries, records up to one hour on each side of the tiny cassettes, plays back with such fulsome fidelity that even my battered eardrums can understand it and recycles the cassettes when they're no longer needed. I got mine from Armament Systems and Procedures, Inc. (Box 356, Appleton, WI 54911).

## A MAJOR OMISSION

It seems a mandatory thing in discussions such as this to crank in a series of conversion factors for mutating familiar units into their equivalents in the metric system. I made a dutiful inclusion of all those in *ABC's Of Reloading, second edition.* I suspect that many a buyer of this book has eleventy-jillion sets of conversion tables for the metric ranged along sagging bookshelves. In the book at hand I propose to break tradition and leave them out. If this really hampers you, drop a line and I'll supply the needed magic numbers, okay?

## ERRATUM, ABC/R2

If you were one of this discerning readers who bought a copy of *ABC's Of Reloading* in the second edition please be advised that it bears a really atrocious booboo on the lower right hand corner of page 273. I don't know how many people proofed those pages with eyes like an emmetropic eagle peering through Zeiss binoculars, but one really shuddersome fluff eluded all of us. Ten lines up from the bottom of the RH column it reads 2870 (grains per square inch). Please cross out square and write cubic above that, won't you?

I would feel better if even one reader had pointed that error out to me but none have to date. Upon reflection, I find *that* pretty disquieting. Thus ends our math orgy for the work at hand. You may stand easy as there will be no quiz on it.

**CHAPTER 8**

As Dick Morgan fires a round from the Astra Model A-80, the 9mm spent case goes sailing skyward. At right, S&W's Model 547 handles the 9mmP cartridge also, and quite well.

# AUTOMATIC OR REVOLVER?

AS WE NOTED in chapter 1, there are two basic categories of repeating handguns — the revolver and the autoloading pistol — plus a few that do not fit comfortably into either family, such as the four-barreled COP and the Semmerling Model LK4 that is actuated manually to eject the spent case and chamber the next round.

Then of course there are the single-shots, such as the Thompson/Center Contender or the Merrill Sportsman, capable of enormous power and/or i-dotting accuracy — though not always simultaneously — but with some handicap as to rate of fire.

Nevertheless revolvers and autos represent a preponderant percentage of the handguns bought during any year and making your choice between one or the other can be a slightly maddening decision. I propose to examine the

strong and weak points of each, claiming no prejudice because I own, operate and enjoy the heck out of several of each. Which do I like best? Frankly, I've never managed to make up my mind.

As a generality that's pretty valid, autos hold more rounds than revolvers and can be carried with fully loaded spare magazines for a net gain in long-term rate of fire over revolvers, even when speedloaders are used to save time with the wheel-gun.

A revolver conserves its spent cases and delivers them neatly to the cupped palm of your free hand. The auto strews its brass blithely to the four winds that blow, loses some of the precious artifacts and gives you lower back pains as you police up the ones you manage to spot.

Pricewise, neither gun has any great edge over the other. It's rare these days to find either for less than $100, even in

## Both Have Assets And Liabilities, So It's No Easy Choice, But Here Are Some Of The Considerations.

used condition. Both go up and up from that level, with a few commanding over $2000 apiece and that's for a shooting gun, not a collector's treasure.

By reason of its indispensible cylinder, a revolver is greater in thickness than a comparable auto, thus presenting more difficulties as to concealability. Counterbalancing that flaw, the modern revolver of good design can be carried ready for instant action with minimal hazards from the standpoint of safety. With most — not necessarily all —auto designs, carrying the chambered round poses a threat that the safety catch might be nudged off and the trigger jostled, causing more adventure than anyone really needs or wants. Carrying an auto with a loaded magazine and empty chamber involves the delay of shucking the slide back to put it in readiness and that produces some

amount of noise which could be undesirable under certain circumstances.

Once an auto is brought into action with its first shot, some can chatter forth as many rounds as three loaded six-guns without pausing to catch breath. Offsetting that, speed in getting off the vital first round can make it unnecessary to fire many after that.

In the important aspect of reliability, most would award the decision to the revolver, although as we've noted they can be prey to occasional problems. A dud round in a revolver poses little difficulty because a second double-action pull will fire the next one — assuming it's functional. The big bad problem with either design is the cartridge with just enough spunk to get the bullet lodged in the bore. With an auto, it won't cycle the action so you've a clue that you

*The Semmerling Model LM-4 at left below fires the .45 ACP cartridge shown resting on it. For comparison, the Wilkinson Diane fires the .25 ACP cartridge, also lying on its respective gun. The Semmerling is a manually actuated repeater, while the Diane is an autoloader. It's interesting to compare size of guns and cartridges here.*

Right, the Merrill Sportsman single-shot from Rock Pistol here in .357/44 Bain & Davis, shown with gun. Below: This fifty-yard group from Colt .38 Super with Bar-Sto barrel measured 1-5/16 inches for five shots, Super Vel ammo.

have a problem, at least. With a revolver in rapid-fire mode it's treacherously easy to give the trigger a fast DA yank in such a situation and send a second bullet up to join the first, producing a certified, double-dip Excedrin headache!

In the area of accuracy it's just about a coin-flip between the two since they're about neck and neck from worst to best. As to deliverable foot-pounds per shot, it's much the same as with accuracy. I've seen autos that out-group most revolvers and revolvers that out-group most autos; own a

few of both, in fact. The better single-shots can trim the wicks of both kinds of repeaters, but that's admittedly beside the point.

Some would say the auto rules the roost in the area of rimfire chamberings since there's no need to worry about picking up the spent cases, for once. I'd even question that. Leaving fired hulls strewn about the landscape constitutes litterbugging and doing so in areas where cattle graze can kill a cow and leave her owner feeling understandably

Llama Omni .45 is a compact DA design that has the helpful feature of accepting the Colt Model 1911 magazines. The Omni is also made in 9mmP with semi-staggered magazine.

Federal's recently introduced #44SA load for the .44 Special carries a 200-grain lead semi-wadcutter hollow point that's butter-soft; it mushrooms impressively.

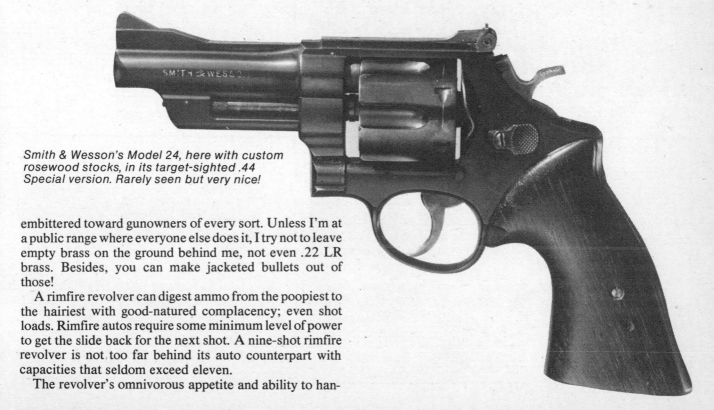

Smith & Wesson's Model 24, here with custom rosewood stocks, in its target-sighted .44 Special version. Rarely seen but very nice!

embittered toward gunowners of every sort. Unless I'm at a public range where everyone else does it, I try not to leave empty brass on the ground behind me, not even .22 LR brass. Besides, you can make jacketed bullets out of those!

A rimfire revolver can digest ammo from the poopiest to the hairiest with good-natured complacency; even shot loads. Rimfire autos require some minimum level of power to get the slide back for the next shot. A nine-shot rimfire revolver is not too far behind its auto counterpart with capacities that seldom exceed eleven.

The revolver's omnivorous appetite and ability to han-

dle loads across a broad range in power is certainly one of its outstanding virtues, regardless of caliber. In that area, we'd have to class most if not all autos as picky eaters that demand loads within a fairly narrow band between won't-work and Disasterville.

Disregarding capacity, does an auto fire faster? Don't cover that bet with money you can't spare! The intrinsic mechanism of the revolver is capable of cycling as fast as nearly any auto and somewhat faster than some of them. The revolver's sole tether as to rate of fire is the agility of the trigger finger and some nearly incredible bursts have been delivered by those with a lot of innate ability honed to

*Above, Colt's Super .38, here with target sights and combat stocks from Bullshooter Supply in fancy-grade bocote wood, carries nine potent rounds in its magazine. Left, the Llama Omni in 9mmP holds thirteen in its unusual looking magazine, with option to carry a fourteenth in the chamber.*

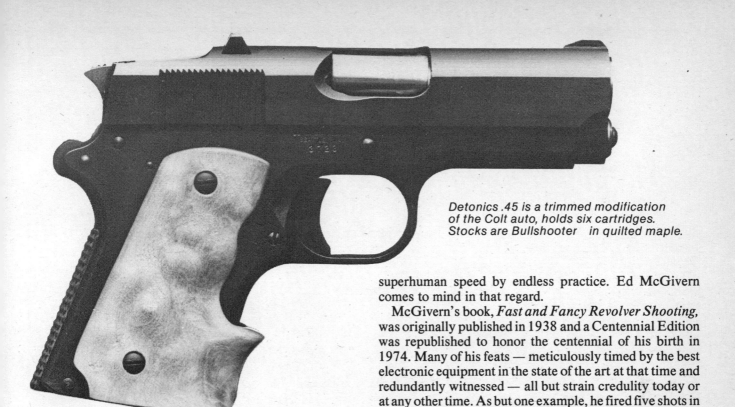

Detonics .45 is a trimmed modification of the Colt auto, holds six cartridges. Stocks are Bullshooter in quilted maple.

superhuman speed by endless practice. Ed McGivern comes to mind in that regard.

McGivern's book, *Fast and Fancy Revolver Shooting*, was originally published in 1938 and a Centennial Edition was republished to honor the centennial of his birth in 1974. Many of his feats — meticulously timed by the best electronic equipment in the state of the art at that time and redundantly witnessed — all but strain credulity today or at any other time. As but one example, he fired five shots in the space of two-fifths-second, all of which would have hit or nicked the edge of a regulation playing card. The exact

As discussed, rimfire revolvers such as this one from Charter Arms, can handle loads such as the CCI Maxi-Mag shotshells with no problems, whereas autoloaders probably won't function with them.

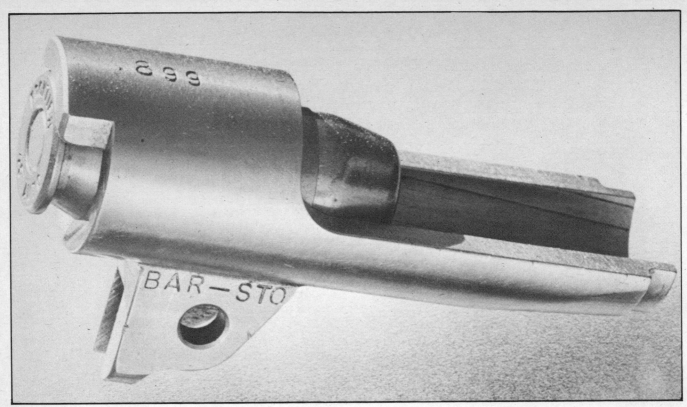

At one time, Bar-Sto made up convenient chamber gauges such as this one in .45 ACP from barrels that didn't quite meet inspection standards. No longer available, they offered an easy way to check loads for seating depth.

Here's the eminently popular .357 magnum round with one of its better cast bullets, from a Lyman #358156 mould. Although regarded as a round exclusively for revolvers, at least one autoloading pistol is being developed for it.

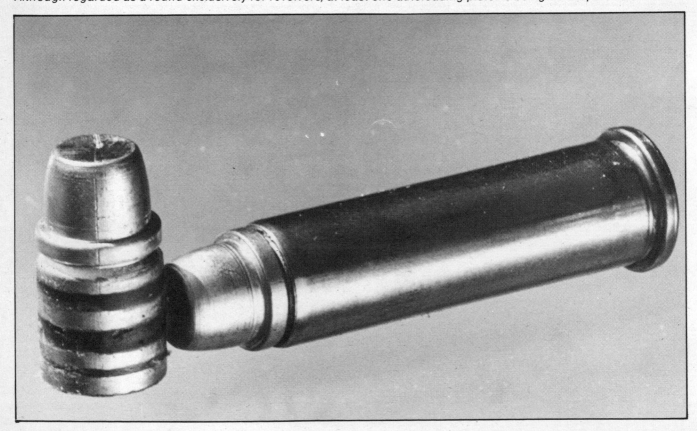

*There's little difference in size between these two in 9mmP: Llama Omni and Smith & Wesson 547, 3-inch round butt.*

distance to the target does not seem to be given but the accomplishment remains impressive, no matter the range involved.

In machine gun terminology that works out to about 750 rounds per minute for a quick burst. That is reasonably close to the pace of a caliber .50 Browning air-cooled machine gun, as used in WWII aerial combat. We sometimes see the sound of a machine gun written as *rat-a-tat-tat-tat.* They really do not sound like that at all. The caliber .50 sounded more like *booda-booda-booda.* The caliber .30 Browning of that era was considerably faster; about 1200 rpm or 20 rps and, if I may be forgiven in grossly paraphrasing the Bard, its sound could only be likened to that of a gargantuan bolt of canvas, from its weaver's loom untimely ripp'd. (*MacBeth,* Act V, Scene VIII and sorry about that, Bill!)

It is entirely possible for an ordinary mortal to fire either revolver or auto with remarkable rapidity: down to something like five shots in the space of about one second or so, give or take the odd nanosecond. It involves a slightly cheaty approach and after thoughtful cogitation I think it is best not to dwell upon the details of it. No, if you were about to ask, it does not involve use of the little hand-cranked trigger motor that came upon the market and faded back off of it after a brief interlude. All you need is two reasonably unarthritic hands and the know-how. Accuracy potential is in rough terms of all hits in the owie zone of a silhouette at six to ten feet. The major problem you see lies in controlling the recoil and the potential for getting

hurt during familiarization with the technique is unacceptably unattractive. If the remarkable McGivern had survived to these lawsuit-happy times, he might not have said some of the things he put in his book, either.

So the whole question of revolver versus autoloader sort of thickens down to a wrangle as to the intrinsic value of oranges over apples or vice versa. I have sometimes spun my mental wheels over the question of what gun I'd choose if I were put in the horrid position of being allowed to keep only one gun and let all the rest go. Shucks, even if I were allowed to keep one of each, it would still be a frightful decision to have to make. The head-count of utterly indispensible revolvers may be slightly higher than the corresponding figure for the autos, if that gives you any manner of helpful guidance, but a carefully winnowed assortment of both is by far and away the preferred alternative, imho: in my very tautly held if humble opinion.

On hand are a pair of thoughtful probes into the area of revolvers versus autoloaders, revolvers made up to handle ammunition nominally conceived for use in autos and allied topics from Claud S. Hamilton, more familiarly known as Red Laig to his intimates by reason of long and honorable service in the Field Artillery. I beg leave to give you a second opinion by appending his thoughts, but make no guarantees that it will help to solidify your mind on the matter, having never made pretense it was a simple choice. Without further ado, I relinquish the mike to the squire of South Staffordstrasse. Red Laig? You're on...

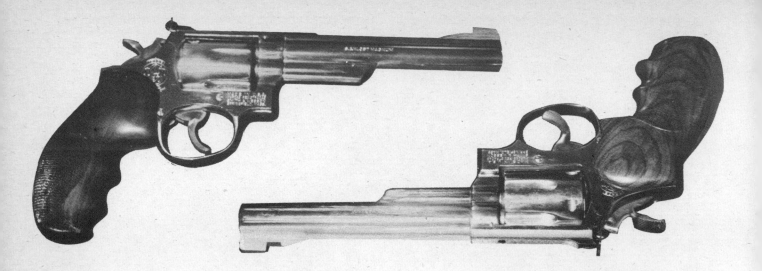

# Pistols Are Just Handguns — Revolvers Have Personality

*In checking out the potential of five different revolvers, it was discovered that this Python mounted in a Ransom Rest turned in overall best performance for accuracy.*

FOR YEARS I have listened to bird hunter friends tell tales of the performance of a new shotgun. To hear them tell it, shotguns are a law unto themselves and no two identical guns will ever handle the same lead in just the same way. Some pattern best with one size and weight shot, some with another. Deer hunters are just as bad on the subject of rifles. Last year I lent a fine new Safari Grade Browning .30/06 to a friend because his was temporarily out of action. Some days later I had it rather abruptly returned with the comment that it would not shoot to a minute of angle at one hundred yards and thus was useless.

Well, I have news for the long gun boys. Revolvers have personality, too. Not pistols, only revolvers. What's that?

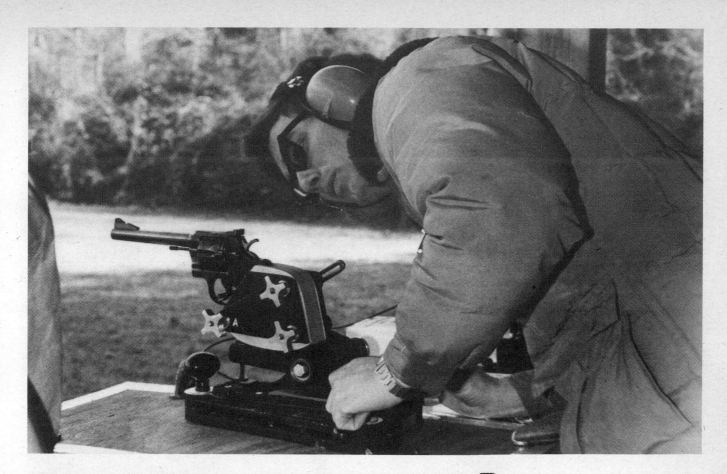

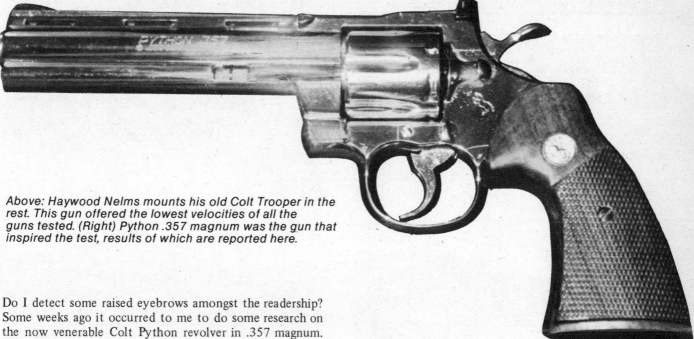

*Above: Haywood Nelms mounts his old Colt Trooper in the rest. This gun offered the lowest velocities of all the guns tested. (Right) Python .357 magnum was the gun that inspired the test, results of which are reported here.*

Do I detect some raised eyebrows amongst the readership? Some weeks ago it occurred to me to do some research on the now venerable Colt Python revolver in .357 magnum. Although I had not owned one until recently, some of my fondest memories are of a Python that had the smoothest trigger I have ever felt on a revolver. That gun belonged to friend and former great Army pistol shot George Snavely. It is the one with which I fired the best single shot I have ever fired offhand; a pinwheel ten dead in the middle of the black at twenty-five yards.

My new six-inch-barrel nickel Python has done some splendid work for me lately off the Ransom Rest using several powders and covering the span of bullet weights to give the Python a real workout. I selected handloads for two reasons. I can make them up for about half what factory ammunition costs and I can load them down a bit. I hate to strain any gun with maximum loads when they aren't really necessary.

For a control group I selected four other revolvers also with six-inch barrels: an older Trooper by Colt belonging to

Martha Penso marks the groups fired with the various revolvers on a test target. Note group differences. They were fired under the best controls that were available for this particular series of firing tests.

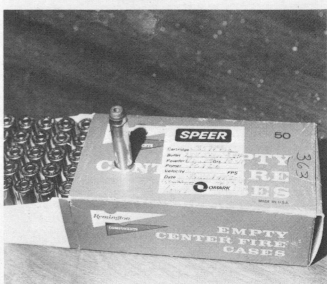

Above: This is load that was not used after the test staff found a lighter load of Blue Dot powder had shown definite pressure signs. (Left) Ten different combos of bullets and primers were utilized in testing revolvers.

Haywood Nelms, a new Ruger Security Six, and two nearly new S&W Model 19s.

Nelms' Trooper hasn't been fired much and is in super condition. Nelms is primarily a rifle man of the sort described earlier and he only uses the Trooper as a she bear defense gun when he hunts birds in certain remote areas.

The Security-Six is a nice, sturdy revolver. When fresh out of the box it had a rough breech face which tended to catch on the heads of cartridges in the cylinder preventing cylinder rotation. Nelms smoothed that up some for me before the shoot, however.

The two Model 19 S&Ws were thrown in mostly to see how two nearly identical revolvers might compare with the Python. They are built on lighter frames and both started life as round-butt snubbies. I sent them off to the factory for installation of six-inch barrels and had not fired more than a dozen rounds through either of them since their return.

Here is a listing of the ten handloads I put together. The last figure indicates the percent of the maximum loading Speer lists for that powder and bullet combination in their Number 9 Manual.

| LOAD NO. | BULLET | PRIMER | POWDER | PERCENT OF MAXIMUM |
|----------|--------|--------|--------|--------------------|
| 1 | Speer 125-gr JHP | CCI 350 | 18.0 gr H110 | 83 |
| 2 | Speer 140-gr JHP | FC 100 | 13.0 gr 630 ball | 87 |
| 3 | Speer 146-gr JHP | CCI 350 | 15.0 gr H110 | 81 |
| 4 | Speer 158-gr JHP | CCI 350 | 12.0 gr 630 ball | 86 |
| 5 | Speer 160-gr JSP | CCI 350 | 13.0 gr H110 | 76 |
| 6 | Speer 125-gr JHP | W-W 1½-108 | 11.0 gr AL-7 | 79 |
| 7 | Speer 140-gr JHP | R-P 2½ | 9.0 gr AL-7 | 69 |
| 8 | Speer 146-gr JHP | FC 100 | 10.5 gr Blue Dot | 84 |
| 9 | Speer 158-gr JHP | FC 100 | 11.0 gr Blue Dot | 90 |
| 10 | Speer 160-gr JSP | CCI 300 | 9.0 gr AL-7 | 82 |

*Nelms, who assisted throughout the series of revolver tests, aligns sky screens of SpeedMeter II chronograph.*

*Still retained in the Ransom Rest, the Colt Trooper is reloaded with a new batch of ammunition during the test.*

*One of the "control group" guns against which the Python was tested was the Ruger Security Six. This particular revolver fired the smallest group of all the guns tested.*

As things worked out, I did not use load number 9 at all. I am not familiar with Blue Dot powder and used it primarily on the recommendation of a friend who has had good luck with it. When the shooting progressed through load number 8, I picked up some clear signs of high pressure; hard extraction and badly flattened primers. This happened in all of the first three guns fired and that was enough for me. I scratched the number 9 load which contained both a heavier bullet and more Blue Dot than number 8. I wondered about this a bit because my number 8 load of Blue Dot was well below what Speer shows as a maximum load. Later I learned that Blue Dot has a reputation for erratic performance at temperatures near freezing, which it was during my shoot.

My plan had been to shoot four groups of each load through each gun. I quickly found that that would take too long and cut back to two each. At that it took more than 6½ hours. Martha Penso and Haywood Nelms helped me set up the rest and the chronograph at the Fairfax Rod & Gun Club range on a cold but sunny December day. By the time we called it quits we were all nearly frozen from the feet up.

How do you suppose the Python handled my test shoot? It came in dead last accuracy-wise, while turning in the highest velocities of the guns tested.

| | Average Velocity (fps) | Average Group (inches) |
|---|---|---|
| Python | 1241 | 2.4 |
| Trooper | 1186 | 1.9 |
| Security-Six | 1233 | 1.7 |
| Model 19/1 | 1207 | 1.2 |
| Model 19/2 | 1216 | 1.5 |

Most accurate loads were: Python, load 3; Trooper, load 1; Security-Six, load 5; Model 19/1, load 10; Model 19/2, load 2.

Now if that isn't a free-wheeling display of individualism I never saw one!

Nelms took turns with others in test crew in checking, recording the data from the chronograph for each gun.

Nelms takes care in repositioning the Trooper in rest. An effort was made throughout the tests to reduce as many as possible of variables that tend to crop up.

Ultimate proof of any gun test is in the groups that each of the firearms produces on paper. Nelms and another of the test staff carefully record the spread of the shots. The weather was cold for Virginia where tests were held.

The equipment used for the series of revolver tests was as simple as possible by design. The feeling of those conducting tests was that simplicity tends to retain project manageability.

It was obvious by this time that this wasn't going to turn out to be a basis for praising the Python! In all fairness, that fine revolver has done some splendid work for me with other ammunition and I am sure that it will do a lot more. What it does re-emphasize for me is the fact that one cannot speak of accurate or inaccurate handguns. You must consider the gun and ammunition combination as a team.

Nelms prepares one of the Model 19 Smith & Wessons for a round of shots with a particular load to determine the degree of accuracy and the correct load for specific gun.

My research uncovered some other facts about powders. While H110 is a fine, accurate powder, it is not well suited to light bullets. Load number 1 was a terrible roarer and gave an enormous muzzle flash while not generating all that much velocity. H110 and 630 Ball Powder shared honors for the best groups in all five guns and they covered the spread of weights from 125 to 160 grains.

I included the twin Model 19s primarily to see how two nearly identical revolvers might compare. They were close. I like the Model 19, despite its comparative light weight for the .357 cartridge and was pleased that the pair took top honors for accuracy. Their velocities were also amazingly close. Only in load number 10 did they differ by more than 30 feet per second, and with most loads it was much less. But there the similarity ended. They gave their best accuracy with entirely different loads and powders and bullets. Their best loads were the very ones that gave the poorest groups in the Python!

The only mechanical problem encountered all day was with the Security-Six which appears to need a little more breech face smoothing. Toward the end of its string it began to have the same old problem; cartridge case heads lodging back against the rough breech face and causing the cylinder to bind. I had to gently work the cylinder out, reposition the empty cases and close it again before I could continue firing.

To the outraged Python lovers I make no apologies for my chosen loads. They were good ones, carefully put together to give respectable groups, the three smallest being .919, .977 and .996-inch at twenty-five yards. It was not my fault that the Python refused to shoot anything smaller than 2.3 inches and shot one that measured 3.1 inches. I'll bet it does a heap better for me next time; especially if I consider its personality.

Smith & Wesson's Model 1917 Army revolver used half-moon clips to facilitate rapid extraction of spent .45 ACP cases. A ledge in the chamber supports the case mouth so that it can be fired without the clips, although at the expense of occasional broken fingernails. Canny way to extract such cases is work one loose and use its rim on rest.

## Three Oldies But Goodies — Of WWI Fame — Were The Primary Sidearm Of Earlier Days

TECHNOLOGY DEVELOPS in strange ways sometimes and this can lead to odd results. Have you ever carefully examined a modern double-action revolver, noted the skill, precision and mechanical know-how required to ream out six separate chambers about a single axis, then devise a mechanism to position each of them perfectly for its shot? No easy thing, certainly, and yet in 1917 when we found ourselves involved in a world war it was not revolvers but the comparatively simple Model 1911 pistol that caused a manufacturing bottleneck.

By 1917 only Colt and Springfield Armory had the experience and tooling necessary for production of the Model 1911, and their piecework production lines were hopelessly incapable of meeting the demand for sidearms created by mobilization. In those days handgun production was a far more serious military problem than it was in World War II or would be today. After the Indian Wars, Cavalry rode high in our military thinking. We were not wise enough to see that the machine gun and massed artillery fire had already made the horse soldier a part of history. To the horse soldier the pistol was as important as his rifle; when he faded from the scene it went with him as a serious war arm.

What seems strangest to us today is that in 1917 there was no commercial manufacturer willing or able to undertake large-scale manufacture of the Model 1911 pistol. Such was certainly not the case in World War II when Remington, Ithaca, and Union Switch & Signal pitched in and did the job.

In the event, Ordnance had to turn to Smith & Wesson and Colt to produce versions of their heavy-frame revolvers to take the .45 Automatic Colt Pistol cartridge. Fortunately, engineers at Smith & Wesson had been

Colt's Model 1917 was built on the New Service action that was introduced about 1904. Photo at lower left shows the regular .45 ACP round at left, with the .45 Auto Rim cartridge introduced by Remington in the Twenties. The .45 AR can be used in the S&W or Colt M'17 revolvers with no need for half-moon clips.

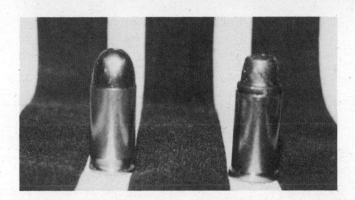

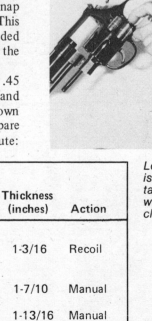

working quietly with the people at Springfield Armory where the new Government .45 cartridges were developed and had devised a stamped metal clip which would snap into the extractor grooves of three rimless cartridges. This little clip made it possible for the revolvers to be loaded quickly and easily with the rimless cartridges and for the spent cases to be easily extracted.

Colt converted their existing New Service revolver to .45 ACP and Smith & Wesson did the same with their .44 Hand Ejector Second Model. Both revolvers became known popularly as the 1917 Army. Here is how they compare physically to the pistol for which they were to substitute:

Loading with the half-moon clips is a zip-zip operation, but it takes some amount of time to wangle spent cases from the clips and replace with new ones.

| Gun | Weight, Loaded (ounces) | Overall Length (inches) | Height (inches) | Thickness (inches) | Action |
|---|---|---|---|---|---|
| Colt Model 1911 | 46 | 8½ | 5-3/8 | 1-3/16 | Recoil |
| Colt New Service | 47 | 10-5/16 | 5-7/16 | 1-7/10 | Manual |
| S&W | 45 | 10½ | 5-1/8 | 1-13/16 | Manual |

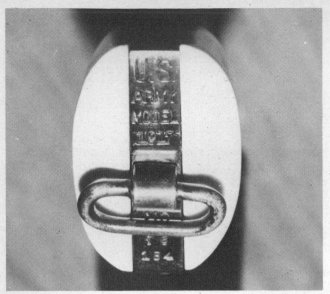

Above, both S&W and Colt revolvers carried service serial number on the butt. Colts also carried a different Colt number stamped on the yoke of the receiver.

Below, a recent commercial version of the Model 1911 auto in its Model 1911A1 modification of late Twenties.

Both revolvers have 5½-inch barrels measured from the origin of the rifling, as is customary, but this tends to conceal the fact that true bullet travel in the revolvers approximates 6¼ inches, while in the pistol bullet travel in the tube is a trifle more than four inches.

The two 1917 Army revolvers I examined were in virtually new condition due to the care and foresight of N.F. Strebe, dean of Maryland gunsmiths. Strebe accepted a contract to rebuild a number of these revolvers for the Army during the Korean War. Before the work was complete the revolvers were declared surplus and Strebe bought them and placed them in storage until 1976 when he put them on sale.

Both revolvers are tightly fitted and have barrel gaps of .002-inch. The barrels, slugged, measure .4525 and .452-inch, respectively. I have small hands and find that the Colt New Service is a large and clumsy revolver for me to use. Its trigger and action seem heavier and less smooth than those of the Smith & Wesson. These are war production revolvers and yet by today's standards they are beautifully made. Both came with the original plain walnut grips. I have replaced these with ivory on the S&W and stag on the Colt.

The main logistical problems generated by substitute standard arms have to do with ammunition. In this case the half-moon clip solved that. About the only logistical problems caused by the revolvers was the need to have armorers trained to repair all three handguns and to have the correct spare parts stocked. The revolvers did create a

Two 230-grain FMJ loads, by W-W and R-P, plus a 190-grain JHP from Super Vel were used by Hamilton in his tests reported here. A half-moon clip lies in Il Duce's path as he seems bent upon booting it for a field goal.

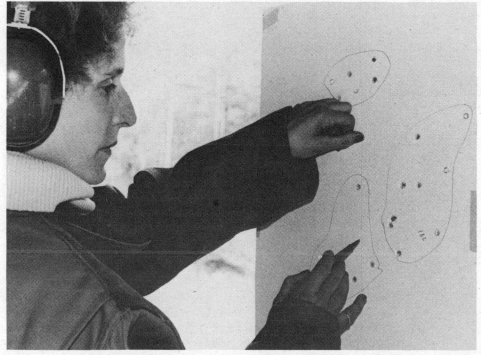

Martha Penso adds identifying data to some of the groups fired with M'17 revolvers.

The rather wide gap between rear of cylinder and recoil plate of the M'17 revolvers — S&W here — makes it difficult to impossible to rechamber to the .45 Colt.

Thin chamber walls and steels that were weak by most modern firearms standards make it unwise to fire heavy loads in the old revolvers made up in WWI emergency.

Indexing cut of the S&W is located over thinnest part of the chamber wall and it constitutes a definite weak point in design of that gun.

need for new holsters and a new ammunition pouch but these were minor compared to what we would have encountered with the adoption of another caliber as a substitute. Imagine the problems the Germans had in both world wars: They used several different pistols in each of three different calibers!

When it came to selection of a pistol, I could not locate an original Model 1911 and had to make do with a new Series 70/Mk IV Colt Government Model. All things considered, I don't think the comparison was unfair. Although the newer pistol does enjoy some engineering advantages, the quality of manufacture of the pre-World War I Colts and Springfield Armory guns was good indeed.

All three were made for the .45 ACP 230-grain full metal jacketed (FMJ) military cartridge. For a shooting comparison I used both Remington-Peters and Winchester-Western 230-grain FMJ loads, then decided to add some Super Vel 190-grain jacketed hollow points (JHP) just to see how the guns might handle this newer load.

Here are the four-group-average results of my twenty-five-yard shoot off the Ransom Rest:

| Gun | Load | Average Velocity (fps) | Average Group (inches) | Distance From Point of Aim (inches) |
|-----|------|------------------------|------------------------|-------------------------------------|
| S&W 1917 Army | W-W | 798 | 1.93 | 1 right, 1 high |
| | R-P | 817 | 1.77 | 2 right, 1 high |
| | SV | 1014 | 1.21 | 6 low |
| Colt 1917 Army | W-W | 783 | 2.05 | 8 right, 2 low |
| | R-P | 803 | 1.98 | 7 right, 2 low |
| | SV | 1004 | 1.45 | 7 right, 6 low |
| Colt Govt. Model | W-W | 775 | 1.80 | 1 right |
| | R-P | 794 | 2.10 | 1 high |
| | SV | 980 | 1.88 | 5 low |

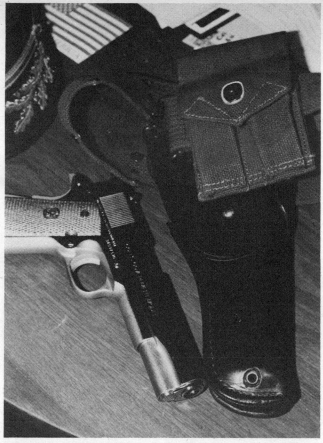

*The GI web belt, holster and magazine pouch for M1911.*

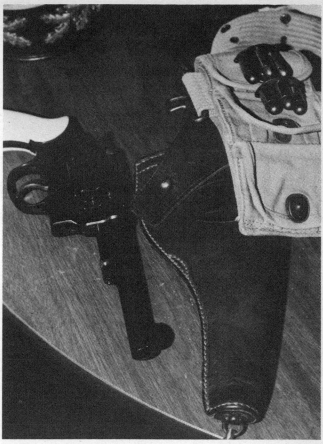

*Special holster and ammo pouch for M1917 revolvers.*

Based upon my recent experience shooting off the rest, these groups are all quite good coming from guns which have not been specially tuned for target work. Neither revolver shoots to point of aim as well as does the pistol. Some careful file work on the sights could probably correct that.

The 1917 Armys are fine revolvers if you find one in superb condition. Most of them I've seen have been put to rough use and are beyond practical repair. If you find a good one, there are things that must be kept in mind. To begin with, Smith & Wesson did not begin to heat treat all revolver cylinders until 1919. What this means with respect to the 1917 Armys I don't know; we have to assume that they were not so treated. I don't know the date for Colt

*In 1955 S&W introduced this Model 25 revolver in .45 ACP/AR with target sights, broad trigger and hammer spur. Similar Model 25s have since been offered for use with the .45 Colt round.*

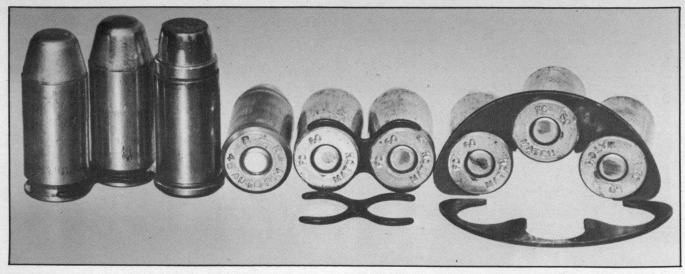

Ranch Products, Box 145, Malinta, OH 43535, makes these two-shot clips, called ⅓-moon clips for the M'17 .45 revolvers. A convenient feature is that they allow the clipped-together loads to be carried in ammo boxes.

but suspect it to be close to the same. The weak point on these big revolvers is their chamber walls. Smith & Wesson's heavy-frame revolver was a .44, actually .429-inch. Company engineers decided at the outset of the 1917 Army production to increase the outside diameter of the cylinder by .002-inch to better accommodate the larger .45 cartridge. The cylinder of my S&W 1917 measures 1.77 inches in diameter; the Colt cylinder measures 1.74 inches. The chamber walls for the S&W measure .067-inch while those of the Colt measure .054. But here there is a catch. The Smith & Wesson design locates the cylinder indexing cut right over the thinnest part of the chamber wall, and that point has a wall thickness on my gun of only

.031-inch! My Colt has the indexing cut somewhat offset but it also has a groove which decreases chamber wall thickness and forms a weak point. On the Colt the effective wall thickness at that point is .045-inch. Of course, the important point in all this discussion is not chamber wall thickness alone but the strength and temper of the steels used.

Strebe tells me that he has seen quite a few more surviving Colts than Smith & Wessons among the 1917 Army revolvers. This is certainly to be expected, I think, since about three times as many of them were made originally and delivered to the Ordnance. Smith & Wesson produced some 163,000 before the war ended.

Another look at the .45 ACP in its clip, with .45 Auto Rim. Latter is made only by R-P, but watch out for old cases that have balloon heads and cull those for deep-sixing!

*It's possible to run three ACP and three more AR in same load.*

Smith & Wesson made the 1917 Army in a commercial version beginning in 1920 and continuing until 1940. After the war two new target versions were made, the 1950 and 1955. The last became known as the Model 25 and is still offered today in both .45 ACP and .45 Colt calibers.

Most every owner of a 1917 Army sooner or later desires to convert it to .45 Colt. Believe me, it is not a good idea. In the first place it costs a great deal more than one might think. The excessively large headspace of the 1917 Army revolvers, necessary so that they might accommodate the half moon clip, makes it impractical to simply bore out the chambers for the longer .45 Colt; there would be excessive headspace and a bad job all around. What's required is a new cylinder chambered for .45 Colt, properly headspaced, and that costs money. The .45 ACP cartridge, and its rimmed version, the .45 ACP Rim, are more accurate and more efficient cartridges than the old Colt with today's powders, primers and bullets. They will, even at low 1917 Army pressures, deliver almost as good results as the .45 Colt. The .45 Colt is no magnum. If that's what you want, go to a .44 magnum and get the real thing!

Here are some good loads that I plan to try in my 1917 Army revolvers: •

One last word of caution: If you load your own ammunition, be extra careful with the .45 1917 Army. There are two kinds of .45 bullets available, one for the .45 ACP which measures .452-inch in diameter and the older version of the .45 Colt which measures .454-inch in diameter. Use of jacketed bullets of the .454 persuasion in the tighter .45 ACP barrel could cause excess pressures!

*If it wasn't sufficiently clear in the photo on a preceding page, here's a pencil pointing to the location of the indexing cut on the S&W cylinder at the thinnest point of the chamber wall. The Colt design offsets this to get a useful gain in chamber strength.*

| Bullet | Powder | Charge (grains) | Estimated Velocity (fps) | Remarks |
|---|---|---|---|---|
| Speer 200-gr JHP | Red Dot | 5.0 | 800 | |
| | | 5.3 | 850 | |
| | AL-5 | 8.3 | 840 | A clean burning powder |
| | | 8.1 | 800 | |
| | 700X | 4.2 | 750 | |
| Speer 225-gr JHP | 630 Ball | 11.0 | 825 | |
| | Herco | 7.0 | 820 | |
| | AL-7 | 8.6 | 825 | |
| | AL-5 | 8.0 | 780 | |
| Speer 250-gr Lead SWC | Herco | 6.4 | 850 | A hard, deep penetrator! |
| | 630 Ball | 10.7 | 830 | |
| | AL-7 | 7.5 | 760 | |
| | AL-5 | 7.5 | 780 | |

# CHAPTER 9

# VALUE TRENDS FOR COLLECTORS

## Handguns Increase In Value, Some More Than Others, And Here Are Some Valuable Guidelines!

*Presentation guns are often of interest to collectors and equally if not more so to the presentee. This Colt Series '70 Mark IV is in 9mm Luger and it has been rather extensively deflowered from its original unfired condition via the factory barrel and a pair of Bar-Sto stainless barrels in twists of 1:9 and 1:16. It's not for sale.*

IN GUN collecting by far the most activity and interest is in collecting of various handguns. This activity has kept the values of collectible handguns rising with such consistency that many handguns have an outstanding track record for appreciating in value. Like stocks, bonds, real estate and anything else of value some handguns have proven to be better choices than others.

As I rarely buy or sell handguns at retail levels, I'm a hopeless babe in the woods in regard to market values, collectability and similar vital matters. I've asked Charles W. Karwan to give us his thoughts on the matter, bowing to his vastly greater fund of expertise in the field.

"When making our handgun purchases few of us set out

consciously to pick handguns that will increase in value at a greater rate than others, but maybe we should," Karwan says. "Without getting into defining a handgun collector let me say it is smart for anybody contemplating the purchase of a handgun to consider purchasing a piece that has collector value or at least collector potential. You certainly don't have to be a collector to realize the financial advantages of such a purchase."

There are many circumstances when a handgun hunter, police officer, target shooter, or even plinker can purchase a pistol or revolver that will serve his purposes admirably yet increase in value at an accelerated rate as long as it is kept in good shape. For instance, a handgun hunter looking for a single-action .44 magnum would be smart to buy a

A pair of Webley revolvers, a Mark VI above a Mark V: These have increased in value from five to eight times their typical prices of about fifteen years ago and stand to maintain the trend as the years continue to march along.

The Mauser "Broomhandles," here in a M1980 commercial version, have had a tremendous record as investments. Presently they are legal with their original shoulder stock/holsters; a factor that adds greatly to their value.

discontinued Old Model Ruger Super Blackhawk rather than a new Ruger Super Blackhawk. It will shoot just as well as the new Ruger, but increases in value at a collector's rate, while the new Ruger will actually be worth less than he paid for it as soon as he takes it home. Likewise a police officer might choose a discontinued S&W M58 .41 magnum as a duty revolver and actually be better armed, in my opinion, than if he bought a new S&W M13 .357. At the same time the M58 has collector value, while the new M13 does not as yet. In the same way, a silhouette target shooter could pick an older Thompson/Center Contender that has collector value and not sacrifice anything to the shooter using the current model while keeping the financial upper edge.

The plinker might decide to perforate his tin cans with a long-discontinued High Standard Model HD which will never go down in value rather than a new .22 pistol that will. Of course in all the foregoing examples the better condition the gun is kept in, the more its value will increase. Likewise the original purchase price of the gun must be at or below the current market value for it to have *any* increase in value. Also, it is rarely a good idea to use a mint collectible specimen for anything other than collecting. Slightly used guns are something else altogether, as a careful user can maintain the gun's condition to at or near that which it had at purchase. In this way a handgun user can get many of the same financial rewards that the handgun collector has been enjoying all along.

"What kind of rewards are we talking about?" Karwan continues. " Some examples come to mind. About fifteen years ago I purchased a near-mint Remington-Rand M1911A1 in its original Remington-Rand shipping box from a gent who got it that way from the Director of Civilian Marksmanship only a few years earlier for $20. As I recall, the $65 I paid him at the time was high market value. That same pistol slipped from my grasp last year for $500. That's a 769% increase in value over fourteen years. Twelve years ago I purchased for $75 a somewhat beat-up but sound Ruger Flat Top .357 with a ten-inch

barrel. I had so much success with that long-barreled .357 on prairie dogs, gophers, and such that I started looking around for a similar Ruger Flat Top .44 magnum. Even then the Ruger collectors had driven the prices up to the point where I had to pay the awful price of $200 for the NRA VG Ruger ten-inch .44 that I eventually found a couple of years later.

"A new Super Blackhawk cost $125 then, so I was paying what I thought was a substantial premium. Last year I turned down $725 for the .44; a 363% increase in value in ten years. Interestingly my old trusty-dusty .357 would likely bring just as much or more because, I recently discovered, it turned out to be one of only about fifty ten-inch .357s that Ruger made with an eight-groove barrel. That's pushing a 1000% increase in value pretty close! Don't forget that is in spite of my having killed literally hundreds of varmints with it. Dean Grennell told me recently of seeing an S&W Model 24 1950 Target .44 Special with four-inch barrel sell for $900. Since that's 1200% more than the $75 he paid for his in March 1957, I could literally see his grin over the telephone."

Granted, those are the success stories and not a little luck entered into their coming about. However, back when Karwan was looking around for that ten-inch Ruger .44 he knew that no more were going to be made. The Flat Top series had bitten the dust several years earlier and the ten-

Contender at left is from the first thousand ever made, with scroll behind the puma, later omitted. Gun at right is of 1982 vintage with six-inch untapered barrel, both are in .22 long rifle. Six-inch factory Contender barrels are extremely rare with only about fifty ever produced.

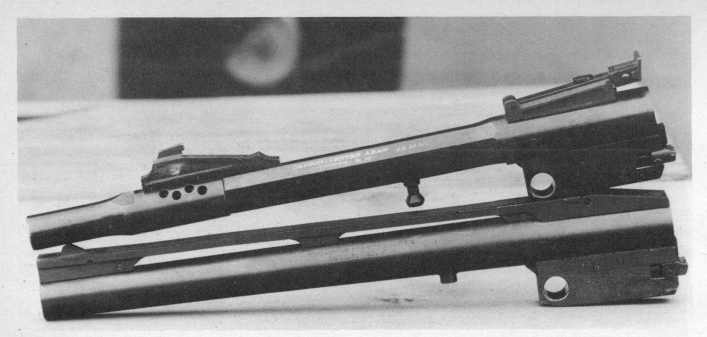

Above, the original version of the Contender Hot Shot barrel is positioned above a fairly current type. Both are in .44 magnum with removable choke tubes in the muzzle for use with the shot capsules from T/C. The chokes must be removed before firing solid-bullet loads. New version has a flip-up rear sight that's folded down here. Below, 8¾-inch barrels were offered by T/C at first but were dropped early because most of the orders were for the ten-inch. Thus factory barrels of this size are highly collectable; a .38 Special here.

inch version had been out of production at least eight years. Thus the supply was fixed. It took only an increase in interest in collecting Rugers to raise the demand. Given the economic law of supply and demand the value of my ten-inch Ruger had to go up. This law of supply and demand is the whole key to understanding why certain guns go up in value at a great rate while others just creep up a little if any.

Basically the law of supply and demand is simple enough. If the supply of any given item is less than the number of people who want that item the value of that item will go up. Conversely, if the supply of an item is greater than the number of people who want it the value goes down. Generally a handgun that is in production has a supply that about meets the demand so its value stays pretty stable.

"This is not always true," Karwan contends. "Only a few years back the *Dirty Harry* series of movies brought about such a demand for S&W M29 .44 magnums that the demand far exceeded the production of the factory. This drove the prices up at the marketplate to the point where many people were paying huge premiums over the factory retail price to buy an M29. Prior to *Dirty Harry* it was common to find M29s at gun shops that had fired less than a box of cartridges and had been traded in by the owner who didn't like the recoil. The price was usually a good bit under retail. My first M29 was just such a gun. Now that the fervor created by the movies has died down, it is easy to buy an M29 at retail price or even less. Many people who paid the huge premiums for their M29s would be lucky to break even and more likely would lose money if they had to sell their M29 on today's market, especially if inflation were to be figured into the equation."

The lesson from all this is never to pay more than retail price for a handgun that is in production and is not scheduled to be discontinued in the foreseeable future. It's an economic fact of life that if there is sufficient demand at the marketplace to raise prices over retail the folks who are in control of the supply will do their best to fill the demand. Eventually in most cases they will, and the price will drop. Even if the supply isn't increased, other factors such as competition from other suppliers will tend to drive down the demand and the price will again drop off.

As you can see, handgun models that are in current production do not have a great deal of potential for a value

*Down the years, T/C offered barrels for the Contender in a number of different chamberings including several for various caliber .17 cartridges, two of which appear above. All of the calibers illustrated above have since been dropped from production, as have others such as the 5mm Remington rimfire, thus are of interest to collectors. The rarest of such birds have no caliber designation, leaving little to photograph for illustration.*

*Most Contenders have an acid-etched engraving of a puma on both sides of the receiver, of which the one above is pretty typical of recent factory production.*

*Originally, the receiver etching included an area of scroll behind the puma, as here, but it was dropped about 1968. Contender serials started at 1000; gun above is 11##.*

*T/C added the feature of the cross-bolt safety in the side of the hammer at about serial 85000 and #11111 here was actually produced after that time; a state of affairs that could easily confound collectors of the remote future.*

increase because of the simple reason that there is usually sufficient supply to meet the demand. Discontinued models are an entirely different ball game. In this case the supply is fixed. Actually in a very real sense the supply of any given out-of-production model is actually dwindling. A certain number are constantly being lost to fire or other disasters and many of the surviving specimens are deteriorating as to condition due to rust, abuse, neglect, and use. Take this one step further and always pursue those models or model variations that were produced in the least quantities. Thus, given an equal demand, the more limited sup-

*This Tokagypt 9mm pistol was made in Hungary for export to the West — originally to Egypt, hence the name — and it's an extremely uncommon variation of the Tokarev pistol: a typical example of oddballs fetching high prices.*

ply of the less-common variation drives the value up. A good example of this is Dean Grennell's S&W Model 24 1950 Target .44 Special with four-inch barrel. Not a whole lot of S&W 1950 Target .44 Specials were made, just over five thousand. Of these the vast majority were six-inch-barreled models making the supply of four-inch specimens limited indeed. The four-inch variation commonly demands a substantial premium over the six-inch variation because of this.

Of the supply and demand equation that affects the value of a gun so much, in most cases the supply part is the easiest to put your hand on. Through the use of the many reference books available it is usually possible to get at least an approximate relative value on the rarity of a handgun. The demand side of the equation is a lot tougher and more fickle. As mentioned, exposure in the movies can

raise demand. Even a change in legislation can affect demand. A good example of this occurred a couple years back when the Bureau of Alcohol Tobacco and Firearms (BATF) ruled that certain handguns, because of their value and scarcity, when accompanied with an original shoulder stock would no longer be classified as short-barreled rifles. As a result they no longer had to be registered and a $200 transfer tax was no longer required for each change of hands. The BATF originally dropped these restrictions on a handful of rare Luger, Mauser, and similar pistol variations. Eventually it was expanded to include virtually all Mauser pistols cut for a shoulder stock and all long-barreled Lugers also cut for a shoulder stock. Also included were many other rare to uncommon variations of military pistols like the Browning Hi-Power, certain Nambus, etc. All of a sudden a virtually taboo area of collecting,

Colt Single-Action Army (top) and New Frontier .357 are to be dropped from production in 1982. A few may remain at modest prices but they are excellent bets for value climb.

Any Smith & Wesson Model 1950 Target revolver is an excellent investment, but examples such as this one with uncataloged factory five-inch barrel represents an exceptionally desirable find for the collector/shooter.

Despite the .45 Colt barrel rollmark, this Colt New Service is chambered for the .45 ACP cartridge; typical of the rare New Service variations with good potential that may be obtainable at comparatively moderate prices by shoppers.

that of pistols with shoulder stocks, was legally open, to a great extent. This drove demand way up and brought about huge overnight increases in value.

"I was lucky enough to have a Pre-WWII Browning 9mm cut for a shoulder stock as well as a commercial Mauser M1930 pistol that were both affected by the ruling," Karwan says. "The Browning jumped in value from $400 to $650 virtually overnight and is rising fast. Likewise the Mauser that I bought for $100 in 1967 would today — with an original shoulder stock, which I now have — bring $1500 to $1800. Yes folks, pistols can be a good investment! Again luck entered into this one, but even without the fickle finger of the BATF said Mauser would have been worth 1000% more than I paid for it."

Charles Karwan purchased this Colt Officers Model Heavy Barrel in 1973 for $75. A bargain at that time, its current value is approximately $375, partially due to being chambered for the less-common .32 S&W Long.

From top, pre-WWII S&W M&P Target .38 Special; pre-WWII .32-20 M&P; military-marked Victory Model .38 Special. Top two are good due to their scarcity; bottom because it crosses several areas of collector interest.

As mentioned, reference books can often supply information on the supply of certain models and variations. There is a peculiar phenomena that has recurred on numerous occasions where the release of a reference book on a given model will bring about increased interest and demand for certain models. This happened very clearly with the Luger pistols, S&W handguns, the Colt single-action, the Mauser pistols and possibly others. With the reference book, collectors could better identify what they had and establish its relative rarity. Some excellent recent books on post-WWII Colt Single-Actions and Rugers are having this effect right now. My crystal ball says that at least one book on the Browning Hi-Power pistols is in the wind. Also I can see a book on the Colt New Service revolver in the not too distant future. It definitely pays to keep track of the firearms reference books that are coming out. There is no doubt that they have a marked effect on demand.

Since we can't always have the BATF make a favorable ruling on our guns and we can't depend on some reference coming out and increasing demand, the best approach is to stick with the proven winners, at least in general.

Colt revolvers and pistols are among the first handguns collected by anybody. The world of handguns didn't really get very interesting until Sam Colt fielded the first practical repeating pistol. All the Colt models from the early Paterson through the Colt Single-Action Army revolver are in the blue-chip category of collectibles. Any out-of-production Colt in reasonably good condition has collector potential. At present there are several Colt models that are scheduled to be discontinued shortly. The foremost of these is the Colt Single-Action Army and New Frontier revolvers. If there was ever a case where a new gun had a guaranteed value increase built into it, this has to be it. Ironically many dealers overstocked these Colts when they heard of their upcoming discontinuance and are as a result discounting them. This makes them even better bargains. From the supply side, if you can, buy the variations that have been produced in the least quantities. These include any caliber other than .45 Colt and .357, nickel finish, and in the New Frontier any barrel length other than

Prior to GCA-1968, many matched sets of Browning auto pistols were imported from Belgium but the law stopped the supply of the two smaller ones, despite high demand.

7½ inches. Once all the single-action Colts dry up at the marketplace, which will likely take a year or so, the values will start rising. The lower production single-action variations are already getting substantial premiums.

Colt also announced that it would be replacing its Trooper Mark III series with a new improved Trooper Mark V. There have been quite a number of Trooper Mark III variations that have been produced in relatively small quantities that have a great deal of potential for value increases. These include all the eight-inch-barreled versions, particularly the .22 LR and .22 WMR and all the electroless nickel finished versions, particularly barrel lengths other than four-inch. The eight-inch-barreled Pythons chambered for .38 Special were also produced in a very small quantity and then discontinued. These can

*Any Luger in good shape at a reasonable price can be considered a worthwhile investment in Karwan's view.*

often be found at bargain prices in spite of their being one of the rarest variations of the Python.

"Amongst the older discontinued Colts," Karwan continues, " I think that the Colt New Service and the Double Action Army M1878 have some of the greatest potential for large increase in value. It is common to be able to buy many New Service variations that are relatively rare for under $500. An equally rare Colt Single-Action would bring over $1000. It's only a matter of time until these big old Colts catch on. Likewise with the DA Army. Since it was a historical contemporary of the famous single-action Colts and was produced in such small quantities they have tremendous possibilities.

"In the Colt automatics the models that have the most potential in my opinion are the Pocket .380s, the .25 ACPs, the pre-1911 Colt .38 ACP automatics, the less common Government Model variations, and the various Woodsman .22s.

"For many years Colt dominated the collectors interest in handguns. Since WWII, however, Smith & Wesson handguns have caught on and their values have skyrocketed. Like the various Colts any discontinued S&W in reasonably good shape has collector potential. The models in the greatest demand seem to be the large-framed big-bore variations such as the entire N Frame series, the Schofield model, the Russian model, and the other No. 3

variations. The models that have the greatest potential for a substantial increase in value, in my opinion, are the Pre-WWII target models, the discontinued Post-WWII K and N frame models, and the spur-trigger top-break single-actions. The smaller top-breaks across the board are relatively underpriced and have a lot of room for substantial increases.

"Probably because of the high prices demanded by Colts and Smith & Wessons on the collector market there has been a phenomenon that I don't think anyone could have predicted. That is the huge interest in collecting Rugers, particularly Ruger handguns. Unlike the relatively ancient Colt and S&W companies, Ruger has been around only since the late 1940s. Like their aforementioned brothers virtually any discontinued Ruger variation in good shape has collector potential. In the case of Rugers, more than Colts or S&Ws, the demand for collectible Rugers seems to be more evenly dispensed across the models. The Flat-Topped models do seem to draw the most attention, but otherwise the demand seems to be almost equally distributed across the models and variations.

"The result of this is that the value of collectible Rugers is more a function of their supply than of any particular demand. Thus, the rarer the model or variations, the higher the value. The Ruger company is such a dynamic company that they never seem to leave things in the status quo. Take

*The Browning Model 1935 9mm Hi-Power has an excellent track record for value appreciation and investment potential. Upper one here is exceptional: a pre-WWI tangent-sighted model cut for a shoulder stock. The other is an early post-WWI Browning commercial version. For the owner who wishes to use them, they are top-drawer shooters.*

for instance the Blackhawk .357 revolver. It started out as a 4⅝-inch Flat Top, then came 6½- and 10-inch barrels, then came a change in the grip frame and top strap now called the Old Model, a 9mm convertible was added to the line, then came the New Model with a transfer bar, next were stainless variations, and finally the current New Model with the warning on the barrel. In that transition period from Flat-Top to the current model there are virtually dozens of variations of Blackhawk .357s for the collector to pursue."

The whole key to collecting Rugers that have the greatest potential for value increases centers around knowing which variations are of the lowest production and hence in the shortest supply. One of the best references in this area is *Know Your Ruger Single Action Revolvers 1953-1963* which is available from the Ruger Collector's Association (RCA) Inc., P.O. Box 211, Trumball, CT 06611. The RCA has been instrumental in expanding the interest in collecting Rugers. They are at present the world's largest

specialty collectors association with a membership in excess of five thousand. For anyone interested in Rugers Karwan recommends they spend $17.50 to join the RCA.

With the rapid growth of interest in collecting Rugers the demand for discontinued Ruger variations is steadily rising across the board. The models with the greatest potential for value increase, in my opinion, are the Old Model Blackhawks, particularly the .30 carbine, the .41 magnum, and the center-fire convertibles; also the Old Model Super Blackhawk .44 magnum. One of the great appeals of Ruger is that the vast majority of the Rugers in circulation were purchased relatively recently by shooters. Very often they can be purchased from that shooter for little if any more than what a current variation would go for. Even if you are a shooter looking for a New Model Ruger to use, try to buy a New Model that has the two hundredth year inscription that Ruger put on its 1976 production or at least try to get a New Model without the warning on the barrel. Though these variations are subtle, they still put your purchase in the limited-supply category.

Not all the best handguns for appreciation of value are American made. A case in point is Lugers. Lugers increased in value so quickly from the period of 1965 to 1970 that many of us thought that the values would level off. My crystal ball was foggy on that one. Lugers have consistently increased at a rate that would make most stock portfolios envious. The number of distinct variations of Lugers runs into the hundreds. They have been made by DWM, Erfurt Arsenal, Simpson, Mauser Werke, and Krieghoff in Germany; Waffenfabrik Bern in Switzerland; and Vickers Limited in England. It is such a broad field that my best recommendation would be to buy only pieces in NRA Excellent minus condition or better and try to stay with the more odd-ball variations that were made in limited quantities. It can really pay off to research your piece thoroughly.

"I recently sold an artillery model Luger for $1400 that had a marking on it that signified its having been issued to the German Navy. That marking made about a $400 to $500 difference in the value of the piece in my favor. Knowledge is worth money in gun collecting and nowhere is that more true that in the field of Lugers. One way to increase the value of the piece if it is a variation that takes a shoulder stock is to find the correct stock for the piece. Invariably the value of the pistol and shoulder stock combination is greater than their separate respective values. This is not true with just Lugers, it also applies to any of the other pistols that are legal with a shoulder stock such as the Broomhandle Mauser.

The Mauser M1896 and its descendants commonly called Broomhandle Mausers in the U.S. constitute another pistol that has had a meteoric rise in value over the last fifteen years and there seems to be no end in sight. Like the Luger the Mauser is one of the most widely recognized pistols in the world that has become an all-time "classic." It is historically significant because it was the first truly successful semi-automatic pistol. "Also, like the Luger I would recommend buying pieces that are in near excellent condition or better and variations that are less common. Also always try to find the correct shoulder stock/holster for the piece. Other Mauser pistols are eagerly sought after by collectors, but none with the relish of the Broomhandles."

German Walthers, particularly the P38, the PP and the PPK have an excellent record for value increase in the U.S. As this is written a large number of Walther P38 and

*The Semmerling Model LM-4 .45 is a unique handful that may be one of the few production pistols good for investment.*

*The Walther Model PP (top) is being imported in large quantities due to a switch by German police to 9mmP guns. As such, they are an excellent value. The PPK on the bottom was effectively closed out from importation, making the supply of German-made PPKs in the U.S. a limited number. The PPK/S is being made in the U.S. at present.*

PPs have been imported into the U.S. at reasonable prices as a result of German police switching to more modern 9mm Parabellum handguns. Some of the most interesting of these are some French-made P38s and PPs that were purchased by the German police before Walther was able to get their German factory in production after WWII. Also to hit the country recently is a large quantity of German P38s made after WWII under French occupation. All of the aforementioned Walthers if in nice shape represent excellent values. Most of the advice given for the Lugers and Mausers also holds true for the Walthers: Basically know what you are doing.

The Browning Hi-Power 9mm pistols come in a myriad of variations that have attracted collectors in much the same way collectors were attracted to Lugers. The Browning HP has reached such wide distribution and recognition that it has achieved classic status. It is certainly one of the all-time best 9mm handguns to which more modern 9mms are constantly compared. Like the Luger it comes in hundreds of flavors. The variations that have had the best record for value increase are the Pre-WWII tangent-sighted specimens, the Inglis Canada-made pieces and virtually any piece that has markings connoting use by any army other than Belgium and Germany. An interesting variation that is on the market at very reasonable prices as this is written is the Argentine-made version. The ones imported are supposedly a police contract overrun. One can only speculate whether more will come into the U.S. in light of the problems over the Falkland Islands.

"I feel that the Browning HPs, be they Belgian-made, Canadian, Argentine-made, or even Indonesian-made, all have excellent potential for a fast increase in value. A good reference on the subject would help bring this about. The FN factory has announced that the single-action HP will be discontinued shortly to make way for a new double-action version, so I think even the currently available Brownings are a good bet. Other FN Browning pistols have done very well also. When the Gun Control Act of 1968 passed, the BATF ruled that the small Browning pocket .380s, .32s and .25s could no longer be imported. This effectively caused the supply of these handguns to be fixed. Demand has been sufficient to raise the price of these pocket autos severalfold. They still have a great deal of potential."

One area that has shown phenomenal growth in general is that of obsolete semi-automatic pistols. Some of the best have been the obsolete Astras, the less common Stars, the Japanese Nambu pistols, and many of the oddball pistols of European origin. It is not uncommon for many of these to sell for ten times or more what they did a short fifteen years ago.

For those who like revolvers the various Webley revolvers which sold so cheaply in the Sixties are now bringing good prices and these appear to be on the rise. Nazi-marked handguns receive a lot of attention. Just the mere presence of a Nazi acceptance stamp on a common model of Mab, Star, Astra, M1935A, or other substitute standard Nazi-issue piece can add greatly to the value. With all the talk of our military adopting a 9mm pistol to replace the venerable M1911A1 .45, there has been a resurgence of interest in the old war horse. Government Issue .45s are bringing high prices and nice specimens have a great potential for value increases.

If there was ever a handgun that was designed for shooters it has to be the Thompson/Center Contender. All the options of barrel configurations, sights, grips, and calibers presently available or available in the past would fill a book. In spite or maybe because of this, collector interest in the Contender variations is definitely on the rise. Many of the barrels that are no longer made will by themselves bring more than the price of a new Contender pistol. This is an area where a person can still get great buys. There is

This is the hard-to-find Browning Hi-Power as made in Canada. Karwan views these as an excellent investment.

This Nazi-marked Walther PPK has several features of interest to the collector/shooter. It crosses several areas of collector interest such as Walther, Nazi and martial. Likewise, no more can be imported due to GCA-1968 law.

even a growing Contender Collector's Association that can be contacted c/o Dr. Lenard Gammel, 205 Carrie, Star Route B, Lawton, OK 73501. Cost is $10 per year for which you get a quarterly newsletter.

"There is but one handgun that is presently in production and not scheduled for discontinuance that I can give an unqualified endorsement to as a collectible with tremendous possibility for value increases. That is the Semmerling Model LM-4 .45 ACP manually operated repeating pistol. This small handful is so unique that the demand for it has always greatly outstripped the meager supply of about two hundred produced per year. It holds the distinction of being the smallest repeating .45 in existence, the

only manually operated repeating pistol in production in the U.S., and functions by a truly unique system," Karwan says.

Commemorative handguns have quite an excellent record for holding values as a group though some individual runs were made in such great quantities that the supply greatly outstripped the demand making them a drug on the market. Commemoratives have a certain artificiality to them that doesn't appeal to me. If you decide to go into the field pay close attention to both the supply and demand factors. A pistol that commemorates the birth of Teddy Kennedy in a "limited" edition of 300,000 isn't a good buy at any price.

A similar field includes the "limited editions" put out by Mag-na-port and other specialty gunsmithing shops. These are usually good values at the original price offering, but do not expect the huge increases in value that some would like you to believe is the norm. In my experience it just is not there in the vast majority of cases.

Whatever handguns you decide to buy, try to get a specimen in the very best possible condition unless you plan to use it. Then a slightly used specimen would actually be preferable. Remember a mint in-the-box specimen can easily be worth double the value of an NRA Very Good condition example. Always keep the factory box that your handgun comes in even if it is a new in-production gun. To throw the box away is to throw money away at some future time.

There is a general trend that says the bigger the bore the higher the demand. This seems to hold particularly true for the Colt, S&W and Ruger revolvers, but even applies to the small automatics. The .380s will almost always bring more than the same model .32s. Handguns that cross over into several fields of interest invariably command premiums due to their higher demand. An example would be a U.S.-marked S&W Schofield .45. It would fit equally well in the collection of a S&W collector, a U.S. martial collector, or a Western period collector.

Even if you don't ever intend to sell the handgun you are buying it's nice to know that it's worth more than what you paid for it and its value is steadily increasing. For one thing, it gives you a justification for handgun purchases when your spouse complains.

*Hardly any handgun has mystique and charisma to excel that of the Colt Single-Action Army Model, here in an example of Colt's workmanship from the era immediately prior to the start of the Second World War.*

## Can A Collector Trophy Deliver Good Groups?
## Claud Hamilton Decided To Find The Answer!

Here's Col. Hamilton with his Mauser-built version of the Swiss Luger that he has described as the most accurate military auto pistol he's ever encountered — provided it's fired from the Ransom Rest, that is. Getting comparable group tightness when firing it handheld involves trying to cope with its really atrocious trigger pull; no mean feat!

**T**HE LUGER. There's a name to conjure by!
What is the strange fascination that this famous old pistol has evoked for more than seventy-five years? Why is it that collectors seek them out more than any other handgun and why do they pay such exorbitant prices just to add an unusual version to their collections?

Just before the turn of the century Georg Luger, an American engineer and inventor employed by Ludwig Loewe, worked with Hugo Borchardt on the manufacture of Borchardt's self-loading pistol. Borchardt, an American of German extraction, could find no interest in his pistol in his native land and had to go to Germany to find a company willing to invest in producing it for commercial sale. The Borchardt was a clumsy arm as it turned out, and no great success, but there is little doubt that its peculiar toggle lock breech design was what inspired Luger when he designed his own pistol a few years later. The toggle lock breech is a strong and expensive design to make.

Luger introduced his pistol in 1902 in 7.65mm Parabellum caliber. It was far from an instant success and this caused Luger and DWM Company to wage a years-long campaign both at home and abroad aimed at generating sales. Special markings and many minor variations were incorporated as a lure for potential buyers and these led to the tremendous number of variations available for collectors today. It took six years and a change to 9mm Parabellum before the German Army officially adopted the Luger pistol as the P-08.

By today's standards the Luger is considered to be unsafe and not worth serious consideration as a personal defense gun. It's a mixture of good and bad. The action is one of the best natural pointers ever designed. The workmanship of DWM, and later Mauser, is of highest quality. But for some of us, all the weight if concentrated at the rear making it a muzzle-light handgun to shoot. The trigger and sear system is a complicated design. The sear operates in the horizontal plane rather than vertically to

*Here's Hamilton's Luger in his Ransom Rest at the instant of firing, with toggles humping upward and the spent case just being kicked upward and out of the reciever (arrow).*

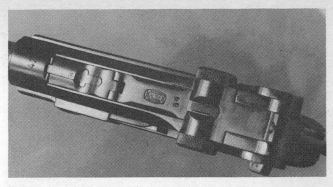

*Top of the receiver of #8264 with 42 indicating the year of manufacture, the Mauser trademark, another 64 stamp and view of its extremely rudimentary V-notch rear sight.*

release the striker. It is a loose-fitting arrangement prone to wiggling and makes trigger let-off nearly impossible to control. The safety is simply a plate of sheet metal that rises from the frame beside the sear to prevent it from moving outward to release the striker. The outside sear is a dangerous arrangement; the gun can be fired when the barrel and barrel extension have been dismounted from the frame if a cartridge has been carelessly left loaded in the chamber.

The sights on the Luger are a joke: thin, sharp blade front and tiny V-notch rear. Some say that the Luger's most endearing charm has to be its magazine. It is designed to hold its cartridges at a steep angle under tight control; necessary when you consider that the design of the gun requires the cartridge literally to jump a half-inch unsupported through the air as it feeds into the chamber! The magazine spring is so strong that a special tool is provided to depress it for loading.

Yet, with all its faults as a practical handgun, the Luger's popularity goes on. Perhaps it can be explained by the somewhat sinister appearance of the pistol and by its connection with Imperial Germany and two World Wars. Also, the magic of "no longer made" applies. Manufacture was terminated after the P-38 was adopted. Collectors competed for a finite number of existing guns and there was no such thing as a new, mint condition Luger. This changed, however, when Mauser and Interarms issued their

*In his comparison testing Hamilton also made use of an S&W Model 59 and a Browning Hi-Power, all chambered for the same 9mm Luger cartridge, also called Parabellum.*

*Here's a different Mauser-made Luger, #8264 to be exact, and you'll note how the final two digits of number appear upon most if not all parts; a match-numbered example.*

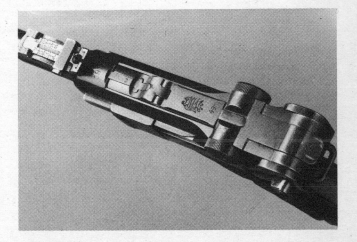

*Here's a DWM Luger in the long-barreled Artillery Model dating from 1917. Note the adjustable rear sight up front, which is graduated for use out to a range of 800 meters.*

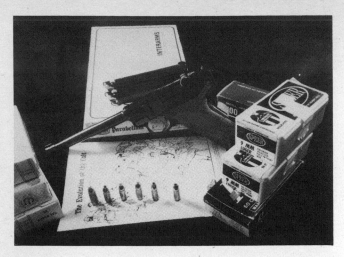

*The six-inch Luger with the ammunition used in the tests.*

joint announcement in 1971 to the effect that a limited number of new German Army P-06s would be made using the original tooling. Mauser had bought the Luger machinery when DWM was dissolved. Production has ceased and even these new guns are almost all gone from dealers' shelves by now and they do not seem to have depressed the prices demanded for Lugers at all. The new Swiss P-06 when originally introduced sold for $300 and the German P-08 for $400. I priced a new P-06 at Hunter's Haven in Alexandria, Virginia, in midsummer 1979 marked $665! That's an appreciation of 122 percent or fifteen-plus-percent a year. Not a bad inflation hedge.

"I am no great shakes as a marksman, but I have never been able to shoot a decent group with a Luger, new or old. It is reassuring to know that some really fine shots such as Dean Grennell and Jeff Cooper have the same trouble with that beastly trigger," Claud Hamilton reports.

"Some years ago a friend and veteran shooter told me that the Luger is the most accurate of all 9mm pistols when shot off a rest. I've always remembered his remark and wanted to see for myself. Recently, I've had my first access to a Ransom rest and an excellent pistol range where the rest could be solidly mounted. I finally had my chance to wring out one of the new Lugers without most of the human element.

"Ammunition for the 9mm Luger poses some unusual problems. Over recent years I've read occasional articles evaluating 9mm pistols in which the Luger often seems to get a low rating for reliability. To give the devil his due, this can be grossly unfair. It seems that a good number of shooters who ought to know better, still try to use American 9mm Parabellum ammunition in a Luger in good condition. Among its other quirks the Luger action is sensitive to recoil. Lugers simply won't operate reliably with ammunition loaded to American SAAMI standards. This all came about after World War I when Italian Glisenti pistols and some Spanish-made revolvers began to come into this country. These could fire the German 9mm cartridge but were too weak to handle it safely. American ammunition makers, for safety considerations, reduced the pressure levels for the 9mm Parabellum cartridge as loaded here."

W.H.B. Smith in his excellent work, *The Book of Pistols and Revolvers,* lists characteristics of some German loads tested after WWII by H.P. White Laboratories. All were German Government manufactured and full metal jacketed.

*Screwdriver tip indicates the sear of the Luger, mounted outside the frame and operating horizontally, rather than in the usual manner. Mentioned in chapter 2, it bears repeating here that the Luger can fire when disassembled!*

| DATE OF MANUFACTURE | WEIGHT (grains) | VELOCITY (fps) |
|---|---|---|
| 1918 | 123 | 1207 |
| 1941 | 124 | 1242 |
| 1941 | 99 | 1391 |
| 1943 | 98 | 1385 |
| 1944 | 91 | 1487 |

These last three loads were supposedly made up for use exclusively in submachine guns and it was originally claimed that they would fire with pressure too high to be safe in pistols. That is not true. Later ordnance tests have shown that they were actually loaded to lower pressures than older loads with heavier bullets. Their light bullets were made using sintered iron for the cores as a means of saving on scarce lead in wartime.

To give an idea of comparable U.S. loads, the accompanying chart lists four of the more common varieties available.

| BRAND/TYPE | VELOCITY (fps) |
|---|---|
| Speer 100-gr Jacketed Hollow Point | 1188 |
| Remington-Peters 115-gr JHP | 1192 |
| Smith & Wesson 115-gr JHP | 1193 |
| Remington-Peters 124-gr FMJ | 1084 |

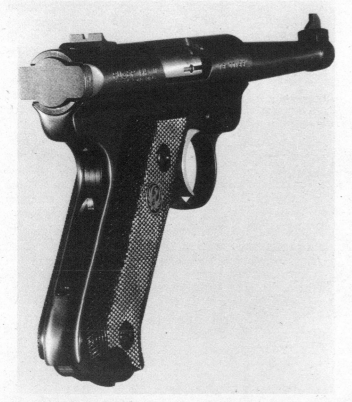

The Standard Model Ruger, as in this recent Mark II type, bears a strong resemblance to the Luger in balance and handling qualities, although its trigger pull is much better.

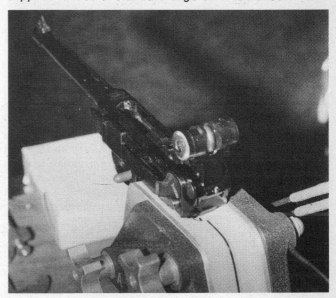

Hamilton encountered minor problems. His Luger has a grip safety, requiring cutting of clearances in adapter supplied for use of standard Lugers in the Ransom Rest.

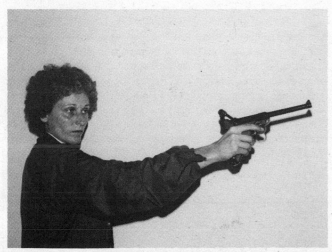

Many Americans find the Luger quite light in the muzzle. With the action locked open, Martha Penso checks it out.

They averaged some 160 feet per second slower. These will all fire in Lugers, but what usually happens is that they will not make the bolt travel back far enough to eject smartly, nor for the bolt to pick up a fresh cartridge. The empty case, often not ejected, is caught by the closing bolt in a classic stovepipe jam.

"For my shooting test of the new Luger I selected four brands of commercial loads and two others," Hamilton says.

Federal 115-gr JHP, lot 23A-7147
Super Vel 90-gr JHP, lot BE 141-99
Norma 115-gr JHP, lot 409728
Remington 115-gr JHP, lot LG20ED
Argentine Military Surplus 124-gr FMJ, lot unknown
  (loaded by Fabrica Militar de San Francisco)
Handload Hornady 115-gr JHP ahead of 7.0 grains
  Herco (Cases: Super Vel; Primers: R-P 1½)

*Above, removing stocks for installation in Ransom Rest. Left, Interarms distributed the Mauser-made Luger at the time it was still being produced, some few years ago.*

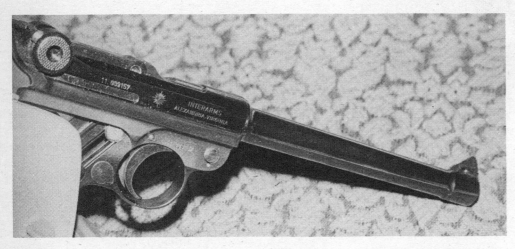

"The last two loads were included since they are Luger loads loaded nearly to the original German standards. My handload is above the maximum that Speer lists for this weight bullet in their Number 9 manual. From experience I have learned that any load of 6.9 grains or less of Herco is functionally marginal in my Luger. I needed something to shoot the Luger against for comparison purposes. I had a Smith & Wesson Model 59 in 9mm and Hunter's Haven was good enough to provide a Browning Hi-Power.

"I took the rest and the three guns out to the pistol range at the Fairfax Rod & Gun Club. Before setting up the rest I gave the Luger a final chance to shape up. I used a sandbag rest and two-hand hold, firing three groups of the Argentine military ammunition. This load is fun to shoot in Lugers:

it's a real sharp toggle-snapper. I've never had a jam or misfire with it. The best I could get was a cluster of three in under two inches and a pair of fliers.

"Turning to the Ransom rest, initially I had some trouble getting the Luger to fire when it was fastened tightly in the grip adapter. It turned out that the grip safety is activated by a flat sheet-metal strip which passes along the left side of the magazine well, then upward like an L to block the sear. This lever is exposed when the grips are removed. After a bit of tinkering I got the safety disengaged and the shooting went along well, except that I had to single load all of the U.S.-made ammunition, and frequently pick out the cases when they'd jam as the bolt closed. The groups, measured in inches between centers, turned out as listed in the chart.

| GUN | FED | NORMA | R-P | SUPER VEL | ARGENTINE MILITARY | HANDLOAD | AVERAGE |
|---|---|---|---|---|---|---|---|
| Luger | 1.38 | 1.20 | 1.10 | 2.70 | 1.25 | 1.05 | 1.44 |
| Browning Hi-Power | 2.25 | 1.85 | 1.95 | 2.25 | .99 | 1.25 | 1.75 |
| Model 59 | 2.10 | 2.80 | 1.99 | 2.20 | 2.50 | 2.40 | 2.33 |

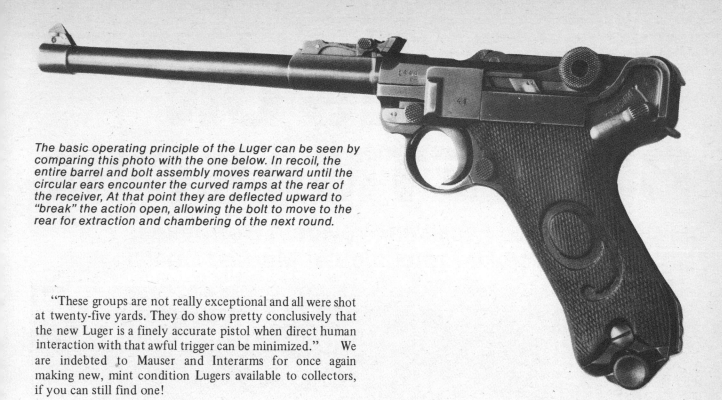

The basic operating principle of the Luger can be seen by comparing this photo with the one below. In recoil, the entire barrel and bolt assembly moves rearward until the circular ears encounter the curved ramps at the rear of the receiver, At that point they are deflected upward to "break" the action open, allowing the bolt to move to the rear for extraction and chambering of the next round.

"These groups are not really exceptional and all were shot at twenty-five yards. They do show pretty conclusively that the new Luger is a finely accurate pistol when direct human interaction with that awful trigger can be minimized." We are indebted to Mauser and Interarms for once again making new, mint condition Lugers available to collectors, if you can still find one!

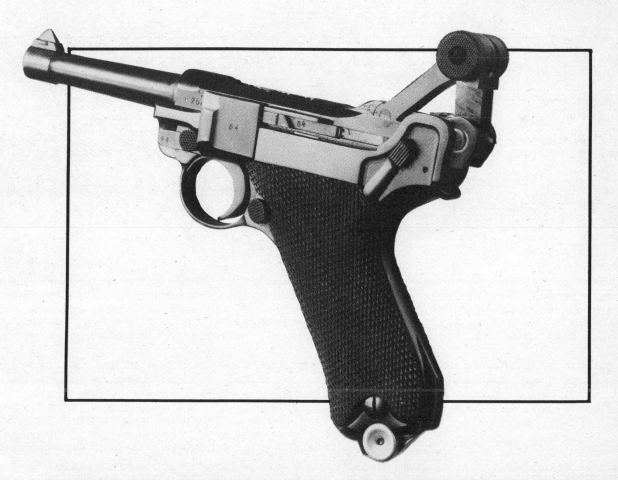

Upon firing of the last round, the action of the Luger locks in the open position, as in this photo. This view provides a readily apparent illustration of the "knee-action" design of the bolt and toggle portions. Action of the Luger is rigidly locked in closed position until well after the bullet has left the muzzle. The safety lever here is in firing position, thus covering the word, "Gesichert," German meaning approximately "secured," exposed when the safety is in its safe mode.

# CHAPTER 10

# NOTES ON BULLETMAKING

## *In-House Facilities Provide A Bottomless Source Of Projectiles At Modest Cost*

*Melting down a quantity of wheelweights for future use. The steel clips float to the surface to be skimmed off and discarded and small pieces of beeswax are stirred into the molten metal to aid in bringing dirt and other impurities. to the surface. Top of an old mess kit is used to make six-pound ingots. Proper eye protection is absolutely essential!*

ELSEWHERE HERE, Chuck Karwan discusses supply and demand as they affect the collectibility of handguns. The same relentless forces govern the availability of various variations of bullets you can buy as well as the necessary tooling for bullets you can make. Commercial producers of bullets and bulletmaking equipment are a practical group and those who aren't tend to drift out of business quickly. If there is not a demand for the product beyond some minimum level it's quite apt to be omitted from its maker's catalog for the coming year. It takes sales volume to keep any product obtainable and apathy on the part of the buy-ing public has sent more than one good idea to oblivion.

A set of bullet mould blocks starts out as a paired set of metal halves, with pins to assure precise alignment. Fastened into two sides of a special fixture, they are moved together against a rotating cutter of the desired contours to create the cavity that will form the bullet. The cutter is termed a cherry in the trade, presumably from the resemblance of the round ball cutters to that of fruit. Although ground from thoughtfully selected steel, the cutting edges of the cherry become blunted in the course of use so that resharpening is required. After about so many honings, enough metal is removed to render the tool unusable.

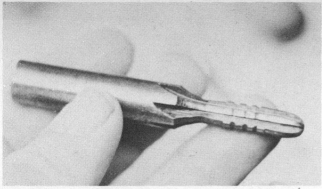

Here's an example of a cherry used at Lyman for cutting the cavity in a bullet mould. As discussed, these wear out in use and may not be replaced if sales did not warrant it.

Wheelweights are used for balancing auto wheels and may be available from garages and the like. Properly enriched with additives, this is an excellent source of bullet metal.

A four-cavity bullet mould from Hensley & Gibbs for their #264; a good design for 9mm, also fine for .38 Special use.

A replacement cherry is costly to produce. As a result, the mould maker is apt to take a long thoughtful look at the sales record for the given design in deciding whether to make up a new cherry or simply drop the mould design from the catalog. If you've ever wondered, that's the reason why a lot of mould designs are no longer available: They just didn't sell well enough to deserve listing. It's a pity because some of those were really good performers, but the word didn't get out clearly enough to sustain sag-

Taracorp markets Lawrence Brand bullet alloy and pure lead in bars such as these; a bit expensive but fine stuff!

ging sales, so off they went to bullet mould Valhalla, or wherever.

Reloading has achieved a level of popularity in this country such that the nation's reloaders turn out more rounds per year than do all of the large commercial cartridge companies combined. With the many attractive advantages of reloading, that's hardly surprising. Annual sales of primers serves as a pretty reliable barometer of reload production, but I doubt if it would be easy to find out what approximate percentage of those reloads are put up with homemade bullets; quite a large number, I'd suspect.

Of the various techniques suited for home bullet production, casting is the favorite by a massive majority. It requires a bullet mould, some suitable alloy, a means for melting and dispensing the alloy, and apparatus for sizing the cast bullet to exact and uniform diameter, meanwhile putting a suitable lubricant in the grooves around the bullet base.

Of the many mould designs, the wadcutter is probably the one that sees the widest use, followed by the semi-wadcutter and round-nose patterns. Moulds are available for turning out hollow-point bullets — usually in the semi-wadcutter or SWC format — but they operate by means of a small punch that has to be inserted in the mould before pouring, removed from the completed bullet and replaced for the next one: a somewhat tedious operation. Moulds have been offered to produce spire-point bullets in the .38 and .44 sizes, but acceptance of that shape was so limited

Brownells now list this lead thermometer in their catalog of gunsmith supplies. Immersion should be brief at the higher temperatures but it's a good way to check the temperature of the alloy and accuracy of the thermostat.

A Lyman mould for a .38 hollow point with cavity punch in place. Such moulds are made only in one-cavity mode.

that most if not all such designs have been dropped.

Moulds are also more or less available for casting hollow-base wadcutters or HBWC by use of a separate plug or punch in the mould similar to the ones for the hollow points. Again, the time-consuming aspect seems to limit its popularity. In factory bullets with the base cavity formed by swaging in high-speed automated presses, the HBWC bullet sells for a price comparable to that of the plain wadcutter and the inherent accuracy of the HBWC design makes it extremely popular as a commerical offering.

Various materials have been used in making up bullet mould blocks and most makers of moulds offer the sets of blocks as a separate item so the buyer can change them on the sets of handles, thereby saving the cost of an additional set of handles. The usual block material is cold-rolled steel, which works well but suffers from the age-old curse of ferrous artifacts: namely rust. At least two mould makers — Lee Precision and North East Industries — have shifted to aluminum mould blocks to bypass the rusting problem and those also work well, provided the cavities are thoroughly degreased before use.

Even the tiniest trace of oil or grease — hydrocarbons,

to use the chemical term — in mould cavities will react on contact with molten alloy to oxidize, thereby turning out imperfect bullets. As the alloy goes into the cavity it displaces the air that was in the otherwise empty cavity and that requires a judicious provision of air vents to allow the air to escape. If the vents are too small the alloy is apt to solidify before filling the mould cleanly. If the vents are too generous in size and area the alloy may flow into them before solidifying, producing a spiny effect on the finished bullet.

Molten alloy can be dipped with a ladle for pouring into the top of the mould or it can be dispensed by means of a lever-controlled valve from one of the bottom-delivery electric casting furnaces. The more elaborate of the electric lead-melters have thermostats to maintain the alloy at any desired temperature across a suitable range of temperatures. Alloy temperature has a decided effect upon cast bullet quality. Let us list the pertinent details on the three elemental metals commonly used in casting bullets:

| Name | Chemical Symbol | Melting Point F/C° | Specific Gravity |
|---|---|---|---|
| Lead | Pb | 621/327 | 11.4 |
| Tin | Sn | 450/232 | 7.3 |
| Antimony | Sb | 1166/631 | 6.62 |

Lead and tin in various ratios make up highly satisfactory casting alloys and it's usually accepted that one part of tin to ten parts of lead — a 10-1 mix as it's usually written — offers the maximum hardening effect with little or no benefit if the tin content is increased beyond that. Tin is a painfully expensive ingredient and the best source for it probably is 50-50 bar solder composed of equal parts tin and lead by weight. Leaner lead/tin alloys of 16-1 still work well and 20-1 is about as far as you can dilute the precious stuff with hope of decent results.

Introducing antimony to the mixture enables good hardness and grouping qualities at a saving in tin, but lead and

From left, H&G #264, Lyman #356402 and Saeco #377 bullets for use in 9mmP. If sized to .358, they often work well in .38 or .357 cases. Size to .356 for use in the 9mm.

Left, the Lyman #452460, with an H&G #68. These are my favorite cast bullet designs for the .45 ACP, .45 Auto Rim and .45 Colt. Highly accurate, they weigh about 190 grains.

The Saeco #377, left, is a cast version of Hornady's flat tip FMJ bullet developed by them at request of the USAF.

antimony alone make a poor alloy. Antimony, having a much higher melting point, solidifies into fairly pure crystals as the lead remains molten. That results in a composite of separated metals that is certain to present the fouling problems encountered with pure lead, regardless of the nominal hardness of the cast bullet.

Some minimum percentage of tin must be included with the lead and antimony for the sake of preserving the hardness and resistance to bore fouling of the lead as it solidifies.

Lyman favors a mixture they term #2 alloy composed of 90 Pb/5 Sn/5 Sb. Straight linotype metal runs about 86 Pb/3 Sn/11 Sb and it is somewhat harder than #2 alloy. Wheelweight metal is generally rated at 95.5 Pb/.5 Sn/4 Sb although it's my hunch that any tin that makes it into a wheelweight does so by pure fluke.

By way of enlightened self-interest, the bullet caster tends to develop contacts for obtaining any and all possible

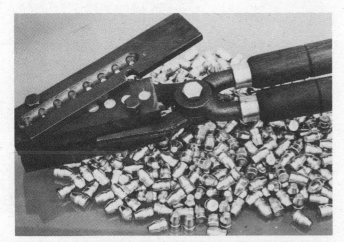

Gang moulds, such as this eight-cavity by Saeco, make speedy work of producing bullets in generous quantities.

quantities of just about any metal made up mostly of lead to serve as grist for the melting pot. Some authorities have condemned the humble wheelweight as unsuitable on grounds that it picks up road dirt during its original career and that gritty residue carries over into the bullet to abrade the bore. In point of actual fact, particles of dirt are so much lower in specific gravity that — if present — they will rise to the surface of the melted alloy during fluxing to be skimmed off and discarded with the rest of the dross.

Wheelweights offer a good economical source of raw material if you can obtain them at friendly cost, but they do need enriching with tin for satisfactory results. The operative attitude is try it and if it works, use it.

In the course of scrounging up castable metal, you may encounter occasional batches contaminated with some other impurity that makes it difficult to impossible to coax a decent bullet from the stuff, no matter how resolutely you turn up the thermostat on the furnace. Resist the impulse to attempt to salvage by putting more good alloy in with it. Instead, run it into a suitable ingot mould — the top half of an old stainless steel GI mess kit has long been my favorite

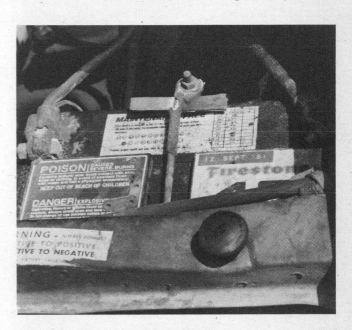

Auto battery plates should never be used as a metal for casting bullets! Battery makers recently have added metallic calcium to the lead. Calcium can combine with other bullet alloy metals to produce a highly toxic and dangerous gas. Better safe than sorry!

for that — and set them aside, suitably identified, for use as gluing weights or similar ballast.

The purpose of fluxing the alloy after it's melted is to coax the tin into combining uniformly with other ingredients, as well as getting the non-metallic impurities to the surface for skimming and discard. For fluxing, I've yet to find anything that works better than beeswax. I've tried other materials, some of which do the fluxing well, but seem to encourage rusting and corrosion in steel mould blocks.

Depending on the maker, mould blocks can he had with anywhere from one to ten or more cavities, with two and

Rust Free, from MJL Industries, Box 122, McHenry, IL 60050, does an effective job of rust removal without harm to the metal underneath. It works well for cleaning moulds.

The fastest shortcut to getting usable cast bullets from a cold start is to spray cavity surfaces and sprue cutter with RIG 3, followed by a blast from an air hose or can of Dust Off. Light warming with a propane torch is also helpful.

From RIG Products, Box 6874, Incline, NV 89450, RIG 2 makes a good rust preventive coating to preserve steel moulds after use while RIG 3 makes speedy work of taking all the oil off the surfaces in preparation for future casting.

Another highly effective rust preventive is Break Free, easily removed when desired. The set of #29244 Lyman blocks here has seen about twenty years of use but, with proper care, they're as good as the day they were new.

four cavities fairly common. A larger number of cavities tends to increase the production rate quite usefully over the output of the single-cavity blocks. As the cavities increase, the mould gets heavier and more fatiguing to manipulate. You can take a helpful lot of strain out of the operation by rigging some manner of guiding surface so the gang mould just slides along at the proper distance and alignment beneath the delivery spout. Some furnaces such as the RCBS Pro-Melt have an adjustable mould guide and a similar device can be had for the Lyman furnace. Lacking same, you can make one up of scrap plywood, perhaps topping it with sheet aluminum for durability — alloy won't stick to aluminum if it dribbles or spatters. At any rate such a guide/rest offers your aching wrist a welcome rest at each filling of the mould.

There are two basic approches to casting: the air-pour and pressure-pour techniques. In the air-pour, the sprue cutter of the mould is held perhaps half an inch or so beneath the delivery spout and the stream of molten alloy goes down into the opening and mounds up as the cavity fills. In the pressure-pour approach, the sprue cutter is held securely against the tapered snout of the delivery nozzle to prevent escape of the alloy, meanwhile delivering the alloy into the cavity at whatever head of pressure is available from the height of the alloy in the pot. Some favor one, some the other. Personally, I favor whichever method gives the best results in the given situation. If the air-pour gives bullets with corners that are rounded instead of cleanly filled, it's worth trying the pressure-pour, at least until the

SSK Industries, Route 1, Della Drive, Bloomingdale, OH 43910 markets a custom line of bullet moulds that are made for them by NEI but available solely from SSK. The designs include exceptionally heavy bullets for the .44 magnum and SSK can furnish load data to drive them to highly respectable velocities with good accuracy for silhouette firing.

mould blocks get nicely heated, at which point the air-pour may prove satisfactory.

When using the pressure-pour technique, take pains to crack the delivery valve open slowly at first. If you pop it open you're quite apt to find an air cavity in the bullet base that's more than ample cause to reject that bullet. Pressure pouring increases the likelihood of extruding alloy into the vent lines to produce bullets with a fishbone appearance. Those are readily removed with the wipe of a thumbnail after the bullet cools.

Any foreign matter that gets between the mould halves to keep them from closing tightly may result in a fin or two where the alloy seeps into the space and solidifies. If that happens examine the blocks and remove the impediment with a single-edged razor blade wielded with great care.

Rust spots in the critical cavity area respond fairly well to careful use of a pointed typewriter eraser and a drop or so of Rust Free may aid the removal. Rust Free is a useful fluid that loosens and dislodges rust, usually without affecting the surface finish of the metal. Unlike most rust removers, it has little or no effect upon blued gunmetal. If the rust has bitten deeply enough to leave a pit upon removal, the Rust Free can do nothing about that, but it's still by far the best way of dealing with small specks and flecks of the miserable stuff.

It's best to have two shallow cardboard trays to one side of the casting furnace; on the left if you're a northpaw. The

NEI mould blocks are made from a special alloy of aluminum in a wide variety of bullet designs and choice of number of cavities. The sprue cutter is of steel.

nearest one catches the sprues as you knock the cutter over and the next one catches the finished bullets as you tap the side of the handle tongs to dislodge them from one side of the blocks or the other. Never strike the blocks directly and never-*never* use the tip of a screwdriver or similar item to poke the bullets free.

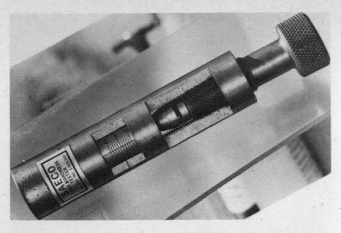

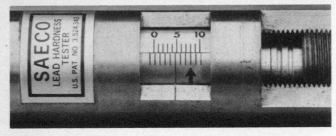

*Top, Saeco's lead hardness tester, partially tensioned. Center, pointed tip of test brale can be seen at the front of the Lyman #429348 bullet. Lower, tensioned by turning handle until the witness mark aligns with the center line, we note the #8 line (arrow) is precisely lined up with the line above it, indicating an arbitrary hardness figure of 8; fairly hard, since straight linotype metal usually tests at 9 with this instrument.*

A piece of hardwood dowel one inch in diameter and ten or twelve inches long serves well to knock the sprue cutter over. At one time in my casting career, I used a screwdriver with a plastic handle, but abandoned the practice abruptly one day when it slipped from my hand and lit in the melted alloy with spectacular pyrotechnic effects. Those were the days when I cast from an old frying pan atop the kitchen stove. That posed a number of hazards, meriting a fresh paragraph.

First of all, bullet casting is a somewhat malodorous operation that requires all the ventilation you can provide and perhaps a bit more. As you work with molten lead, some significant amount of infinitesimal lead particles become airborne and, if inhaled, pose a severe health hazard. Unless the present occupant has replaced the linoleum by now in that house back in Wisconsin, there's still a brown stain against the blue pattern, a souvenir of the night I picked up the old frying pan only to learn the wooden handle had worked loose. A good-sized gobbet of still-fluid alloy ended up inside the low-cut bedroom slip-

pers I was wearing at the time, getting every bit of my attention for a short while that seemed to last forever.

In an earlier chapter we discussed the vital need for eye protection while casting bullets or, for that matter, when performing any reloading operation whatsoever. The warning is repeated here for the sake of any reader who may have skimmed over it earlier. Some advocate wearing long sleeves and welder's gloves while casting and that certainly wouldn't hurt a thing unless the mercury is up in the nineties (F) in which case it could put you down from heat prostration. Along the way I've collected my rightful share of blisters and scabs at the casting couch — there's a small one at the base of my right thumb as I type this, in fact — and I regard that as a trifling inconvenience.

## TROUBLESHOOTING

As you grapple with the bullet-casting operation, remind yourself that no one ever claimed it was supposed to be simple and easy. If you can't produce an acceptable bullet, there are several factors that may be contributing to the problem. Some if not all of such problems may include:

Oil or other hydrocarbon on the surface of the cavity: The remedy is to flush the cavity halves with a pressurized degreasing agent such as RIG 2, illustrated.

Blocks not hot enough: Either continue casting and rejecting until they heat up properly or warm both halves judiciously with a propane torch.

Improper alloy or alloy too cool: Turn up the thermostat or heat source. If that doesn't help, pour the mix into an ingot mould and make up a fresh batch from the recipes suggested earlier here.

Bullets come out nicely filled but frosty in appearance: This is an indication that the alloy or blocks or both are too hot. Reduce the temperature slightly and take a bit more time before going back to the pot for a refill. If the sprues take overly long to frost up and solidify, use a down-blast small fan to cool that area between cycles. Never plunge the entire mould blocks into cold water, as some suggest. That can warp the blocks fatally or perhaps deliver a random droplet into the molten alloy to produce a steam-fired explosion. While it's nice to produce bullets that appear to have been turned from sterling silver on a jeweler's lathe, the fact is that some of the frosty-looking jobs turn out to shoot quite well. Nonetheless, excessive heat tends to burn off your tin content and you need that in your business.

After you've poured the alloy and mounded it up a bit on the sprue cutter, watch it carefully and you'll see it turn from bright to frosty in appearance as the sprue solidifies. If you tap the sprue lightly with the wooden handle of the casting mallet, you may find it dents easily and turns bright again. If so, wait a bit longer before knocking the cutter over. The sprue must be solidified completely before cutting. If it isn't, you'll build up a curving silvery smear along the top of the block where the cutter drags across it and that can cause rejectable bullets, too. In case of such a buildup, remove it with a single-edged razor blade and great care.

## SIZE/LUBING

Once cast to satisfactory standards, the bullet needs to be sized to uniformly accurate diameter, with a suitable lubricant put into its grooves. Failure to do so will foul up

*Here's an operator's-eye view of my setup for speedy and convenient sizing and lubing of cast bullets. Two C-clamps hold the a removable platform in front of the Saeco lube/sizer to save wasted motion in moving the bullets into and out of the sizing chamber, with a shallow cardboard tray to accept finished bullets and a handy table to receive the output.*

*My favorite bullet lubricant is red lithium-base type from Choate Machine & Tool Co., Box 218, Bald Knob, AR 72010. Performing well in all respects, its extremely high melting point keeps it from running at high temperatures.*

the bore so severely you're not apt to make the same mistake again.

There are several good and eminently satisfactory lube-sizers on the market, including the Lyman #450 and the unit from RCBS. A dozen years or so ago I came upon a Saeco lube sizer tabbed at $25 in a gun store, bought it and have come to know vast contentment in its use over the years since then. There are a number of good bullet lubricants on the market and many swear by mixtures of Alox and beeswax. For the past several years I've been using Choate red lithium lube with no slightest trace of disgruntlement. It delivers accurate results and — what I really appreciate — its melting point is way up there so that if you forget and leave some lubed bullets out in the blazing sunlight, the lube stays where it belongs and doesn't ooze out and away. I own no stock in any firm and am merely mentioning what I use and appreciate, hoping to save postage for both of us if you felt impelled to write and inquire, okay?

Goerg Enterprises, Box 521, Renton, WA 98055, makes this hollow-pointer and holding guide for use with .44 loaded rounds. Below, a plaster cast of the cavity in duct seal with pencil indicating where a fragment stopped. The #2 drill bit has a diameter of approximately .221-inch.

## SWAGED BULLETS

An alternative approach to casting is to cold-form the bullets by sheer pressure rather than melting and moulding. The process is called swaging and that rhymes with raging, not *swahh-jing*. It is a promising process with a lot of attractive advantages, but a few hangups remain in the works to the present. They are by no means hopelessly insurmountable, as we shall see.

A couple of decades ago the late Charles Heckman, then president of C-H, introduced his Swag-O-Matic bullet press; a simple device selling for modest price to make up swaged bullets with half-jackets that were available from several suppliers at the time. It was a neat system with a lot of good things going for it and with one flaw: The resulting bullets put some amount of bearing surface of raw, butter-soft lead into contact with the bore and it rubbed off something fierce. Just a few shots and you faced a long session with bronze bristle brushes and Hoppe's #9 bore-cleaner.

Heckman, a resourceful and innovative gent, might well have solved the problem, but the Fates did not give him the chance. With his loss, C-H changed hands a few times and finally settled down in Owen, Wisconsin. Once there, the new owners came up with what they termed their #101 swaging die sets that utilized the three-quarter-jacket instead of the original half-jacket to turn out a bullet that used a gilding-metal jacket that kept the soft lead from contact with the bore, totally avoiding the fouling problems.

The C-H #101 bullet swaging dies were designed to be used in conventional reloading presses, although not all presses are capable of handling them. In use, they impose quite a bit more stress on the top of the press ram than does conventional reloading so that the milled slot that holds the shell holder may become distorted in some presses. The C-H Heavyweight CHamp press is one of the best units for use with the #101 dies, having a fully hardened ram that is not detectably bothered by swaging stresses. I've also used my Pacific OO-7 press with the #101 dies with no apparent problems.

Some years earlier Ted Smith had designed a small but powerful bullet swaging press he called the Mity-Mite, intended solely for that operation and not capable of reloading operations. It accepted its own special sets of dies for the operation and generally performed quite well. After a time David and Richard Corbin made arrangements to make and market the Mity-Mite press and later on introduced a modification that increased the strength of the press greatly at some minor sacrifice of operating convenience. That consistsed of an integral upper bar added to the body casting to change the basic concept from a C-frame to the much stronger O-frame.

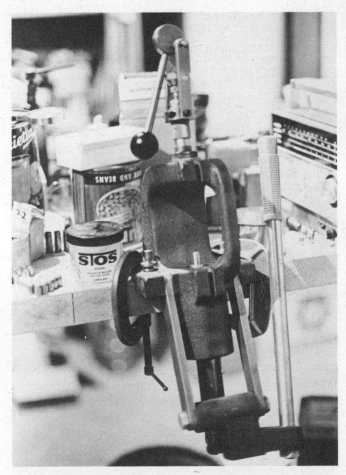

The C-H Heavyweight CHamp press set up for use with C-H bullet swaging dies to make bullets of the jacketed hollow point or jacketed soft point type, with ejector installed.

*Above and at lower right are steps in producing a jacketed bullet for the .41 magnum on the Corbin Bullet Press or Mity-Mite. The jackets must be drawn down from .44 size in a die furnished by Corbin for use in a reloading press. Cores are cast in pure lead, using a caliber .30 mould, Lyman #31141, then swaged to shape, seated in the jacket and finally put through the nose-forming die to bring the bullet to its completed shape. Hollow points can be made just as easily. The core-swaging die is in use above, with excess lead being extruded. Below left, a view of the Corbin Bullet Press.*

had to form a concave base in the jacketed bullet rather than the usual flat base. After the JHP bullet has been formed to conventional contours, it is a simple matter to adjust the dies, reverse the bullet and give it another pass through the press to "bump" its nose against the concave base punch. That results in a most interesting modification in which the basic hollow-point cavity is surrounded by part of a hemispheric concavity considerably greater in diameter than the usual frontal opening.

In plausible theory such a modification presents a much enlarged funnel effect to the point of impact, thereby amplifying the abruptness of energy transmission by a rather large and awesomely effective factor, In actual practice it performs in precise lines of expectation; perhaps even a bit more so. In .357 size at brisk velocity, expansion of such bullets in ballistic clay is to diameters of one inch or so.

As Dave Corbin likes to note, during the final portion of the stroke the leverage of the press approaches infinity, so that it is entirely capable of destroying itself if used incautiously. Apparently there were occasional problems of breakage in the earlier C-types. There has been in recent times a tendency for the Corbins to refer to their unit as the Corbin Bullet Press and such equipment is capable of turning out some remarkably professional-looking bullets in an infinite variety of forms and styles. It is no great challenge for the operator to duplicate the appearance and performance of most factory JSP or JHP bullets and, with further manipulation and passes through the press, the resulting bullets can be modified to designs not presently on the market.

For example, there is a dome-ended punch that can be

*Here's a step-by-step view of the .41 JSP bullet taking shape from cast lead core, jacket before and after drawing and assembly before and after seating, ending as at right.*

This was an exploration into making what I called a sort of quasi-Glaser bullet. Shot was compressed in the jacket held in place by a reversed gas check after nose-forming.

The quasi-Glasers weighed about 86 grains loaded in .357 mag cases ahead of 17.0 grains of Blue Dot.

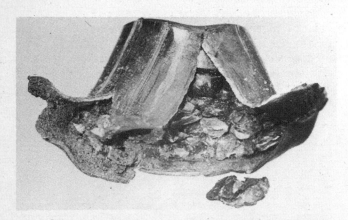

The quasi-Glaser would keyhole scant inches out of the muzzle and did not disintegrate completely upon impact. Here's the bullet recovered after hitting the 4½-inch cube of duct seal. It retained a fair portion of its starting weight.

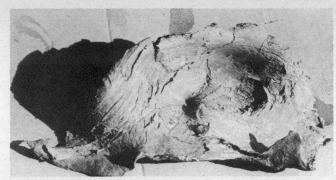

And here is how a 4½-inch cube of duct seal looked after being hit from the far side with the quasi-Glaser, lower left photo. Duct seal is a fairly tough medium, otherwise the effects would have been considerably more violent.

Here are some variants of the .38 Mourning Glory design, including some before and after applying the distinctive domed nasal concavity. The concave base is optional.

Three Mourning Glory .38s with three more that were fired into damp clay. Note the extravagant expansion and the remarkable retention of the original core and jacket. These were fired in the Merrill Sportsman .357-44 B&D at a bit over 1800 fps and penetrated about 3½ inches.

Here are two of what I call the Parajax — thus named because they are guaranteed to open — with the domed punch of the Corbin die set in the background. Made up as fairly conventional JHP bullets, the noses are bumped against domed punch to recontour the noses to the funneled shape that can be seen here. It seems to amplify expansion usefully.

My private term for such bullets is *Mourning Glory*, and a slight modification of the design is known as the *Parajax*, because it's guaranteed to open. Dreaming up catchy designations is at least half the fun of experimental research in bullet design.

The jacketed bullet probably represents the upper limits of capability in expanding bullets to the present, due to the ability of the jacket to fairly well maintain projectile integrity through the impact phase. Despite that, the jacketed bullet has one notable disadvantage, whether you buy them or build them: I refer to the cost of the jacket itself. The doggoned little things cost around three or four cents apiece and making them is an operation requiring complicated, sophisticated, *expensive* machinery, even given an access to strips of gilding metal to serve as raw material. Making bullet jackets is a long way from the status of cottage industry in the current and foreseeable state of the art.

As far as I know, this is the only hand tool on the market today for applying a cannelure to bullets, either cast or jacketed. It's made by C-H Tool & Die Corporation.

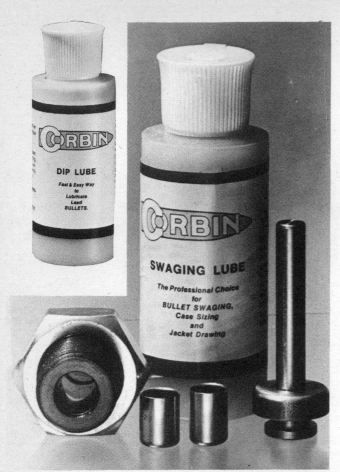

Here are some TMJ types, meaning totally jacketed bullet. A gas check encloses and protects the base.

Corbin swaging lube is applied to the .44 jackets before they are drawn down to .41 size with punch and die set shown here. Inset: Corbin dip lube protects lead alloy bullets at moderate velocities, not for high-velocity use.

Back in the Fifties Jim Harvey of Lakeville Arms came up with what he called the *Jugular Bullet*. Its distinctive feature was a small washer of pure zinc, of full bullet diameter, securely attached to the bullet base by means of a rivet-like extrusion of bullet metal through the central hole of the washer. The idea was that in firing the zinc washer sort of gathered up the fouling as it was deposited to blow it on out the muzzle, meanwhile depositing a light coating of zinc in the bore.

The principle seemed to work, I'm told. I never had the opportunity of working with the zinc-base bullets, but those who did reported that even bullets of pure lead could be driven to impressive velocities without encountering bore-fouling problems. Harvey's approach involved casting them in special moulds made by Lyman at the time, with a tiny slot into which the zinc washer was hand-inserted before pouring the alloy or molten lead. As you may imagine, that was a delicate operation and rather time-consuming. Probably as a more or less direct result

Here are two of the Spelunkers — thus named because when they hit they go "Spelunk!" — in .41 magnum size, with the tip of the homemade forming punch visible at left. Note the inward-sloping outer rim that serves somewhat the same function as the pilot chute on a parachute in initiating expansion at the instant of primary impact. These are made up from wadcutters cast in a Hensley & Gibbs #255 mould at a weight of about 175 grains; size-lubed before final swaging.

A lube/sized #68 H&G .45 bullet has been put through Swag-O-Matic with Spelunker punch adjusted to make a limited cavity, leaving a nose that functions in the auto.

An overall and closer view of the C-H Swag-O-Matic swaging press with nose-forming punch for the .38 Spelunker installed. Ejection of the finished bullet is handled automatically on downstroke of the handle.

Here, in .44 Special, are a few of the tentative designs that were worked up and tested in developing Spelunker to its final versions; fourth from left worked quite well.

Alberts Bullets markets this 146-grain HS bullet, coated with a lubricant resisting leading to fairly high velocities.

The cup point nose punch of original Swag-O-Matic die set, here in .452-inch diameter, with a half-jacketed bullet. Note the exposed lead surrounding the cavity.

Spelunker punches are made up of 1½-inch sections cut from a length of 5/8-inch cold-rolled steel bar, as noted.

Bullets used by Cols. Thompson and La Garde in their tests against cadavers and
live animals in 1904. The bullets are arranged by caliber, and their relative stopping
power was found to be about in the same order.
1. .30 cal. Luger, jacketed. Weight 92.5 gr., 1420 f. s., 415 ft. lbs.
2. 9 mm Luger, jacketed. 123.5 grains, 1048 f. s., 301 ft. lbs.
3. .38 Long Colt, Lead. 148 gr., 723 f. s., 191 ft. lbs.
4. .38 A. C. P., jacketed. 130 gr., 1107 f. s., 354 ft. lbs.
5. .38 A. C. P. soft point. 120 gr., 1048 f. s., 293 ft. lbs.
6. .45 Colt, lead. 250 gr., 720 f. s., 288 ft. lbs.
7. .45 Colt, hollow point. 220 gr., 700 f. s., 239 ft. lbs.
8. .455 man-stopper. 218.5 grains, 801 f. s., 288 ft. lbs.
9. .476 lead. 288 gr., 729 f. s., 340 ft. lbs.

*British .455 man-stopper bullet, #8 above, was illustrated in Hatcher's Textbook of Pistols and Revolvers, published in 1935. Presumably, it was developed quite a bit earlier. Text discusses its similarity to the Spelunker.*

*With its fairly sharp front edge, the Spelunker cuts a very neat hole, even in the tough plastic of this 12-ga shotshell! Mirror is arranged to show both entrance and exit holes done by a 125-grain from a six-inch .38 Special barrel. Made by swaging a lube/sized Saeco #377 bullet.*

the zinc-base bullet drifted into disuse and might have joined a host of other such concepts of interest solely to reloading historians.

In quite recent times, however, A.F. "Tony" Sailer — now executive vice-president of C-H Tool & Die Corp. — addressed himself to the problem of working up an economical alternative to the gilding metal jacket and focused his attention upon the zinc washer, once again. Since C-H has worked extensively with the swaging approach, Sailer developed dies for swaging bullets of pure lead with the zinc washer securely riveted to the base and reports that the performance is highly satisfactory, likewise impressive. To the present moment I've not had an opportunity to work with this system personally, but I report it here as an avenue that appears to show a great deal of promise for future development. The cost of the zinc washers is far below that of the gilding metal jackets with their high percentage of always-critical copper.

## THE SWAST BULLET

Like Sailer, I've been interested in working up a bullet for handgun use that bypasses the need for a jacket, meanwhile offering the outermost maximum in ability to expand upon impact, even at relatively modest velocities. The basic concept of the bullets from the C-H Swag-O-Matic press has had a lot of appeal to me since I first encountered

A .38 and .44 Spelunker; latter uses a #429384 Lyman wadcutter as its starting point after being lube/sized.

The .38 Spelunker at right was fired into duct seal ahead of 2.7 grains of Bullseye from a three-inch barrel at a velocity of about 700 fps; expansion was to .55-inch size. This illustrates the effect of the primary cone, both before and after impact. Penetration was about three inches here.

it back in the early Sixties. As originally conceived, such bullets used a half-jacket: a small cup of caliber diameter about .25-inch in length to enclose the bullet base. The remainder of the bullet ahead of the half-jacket was of full bullet diameter and the major drawback was that such bullets would foul the bore in a thoroughly miserable and unacceptable manner, even if the lead portion was alloyed judiciously to harden it.

Bullets of conventional cast design with suitable lubricant in the grooves could be driven to respectable velocities without serious fouling problems, being clearly superior to the half-jacketed type in that respect. The Swag-O-Matic came with half a dozen or so different nose punches in each diameter, including the cup point pattern that made a hemispherical cavity in the nose of nearly full bullet diameter. Early tests demonstrated conclusively that the cup point bullet would expand like no-tomorrow in just about any target medium it encountered: a great concept if only one could skirt around that bore-fouling bugaboo...

Early in 1964 I hit upon the approach that seems pretty obvious in latter-day retrospect. I simply took a cast wadcutter — one of the shorter of the two versions from the Lyman #35887 mould — that had been size/lubed to put grease in its grooves and gave it a pass through the Swag-O-Matic with the cup point punch installed. The grease

remained in the grooves, having no place to go and being quite incompressible. The bullet came out of the Swag-O-Matic with the hemispherical cavity in all its formidable glory.

Tests at that time showed good accuracy, no fouling problems at all, and quite impressive expanding ability. The production procedure took some amount of time of course, but it required no costly ingredients beyond regular bullet alloy and lube. I called it the swast bullet as they were SWaged after being cAST.

Quite a lot of years oozed through the glass, hour by hour, until I found myself up in the early Eighties in possession of one of Dave Corbin's metal lathes; a 10x24-inch Jet brand which I dubbed Mister Atkins in honor of Chet Atkins, my favorite guitar-picker. The old Swag-O-Matic press and its box of tooling had accompanied me and one day I happened upon it and noted that Heckman had supplied it with a few blank nose punches in case I felt inclined to form them up to some custom contour of the momentary fancy. Gradually the idea seeped through the layers of mental limestone that — a generation later — I now had the easy capability for doing something interesting and constructive with those blank nose punches.

The dies and lower punches of the Swag-O-Matic set were of impressively hardened steel, but the nose-punch blanks were of some alloy soft enough to cut in the lathe like warm Velveeta cheese, only more neatly. I used up the entire modest supply of the original blank punches in designs that left something to be desired, ardently. By that time it was a simple matter to determine that I had access to an endless supply of punch blanks simply by sawing 1.5-inch sections from a .625-inch length of cold-rolled steel bar stock, economically available from the local hardware store by the yard. You true up the top end, make a small counterbore, drill it with a letter I bit for a .272-inch starting hole and thread that 5/16-24 to suitable depth. That takes care of the hole for attaching it to the upper punch holder of the Swag-O-Matic.

Following that, you reverse the workpiece in the lathe chuck and proceed to dress it down to desired diameter making frequent checks with the micrometer and, that done, you can sculpture the cavity punch to any contour your imagination can dream up and your clumsy hands can capture in steel.

Early on I learned that the profile for the punch that

Three zinc-base .38 Spelunkers made by S&S Precision Bullets in slightly hardened lead. Note how the alloy is extruded through washer to anchor it firmly to the base.

*Two views of recontouring a .45 round with H&G #92 bullet to the 7° nose form of French Arcane cartridge. Compound rest is set at 35° and operation of lathe is in reverse at low speed to prevent heat buildup in the bullet.*

forms the inner cavity must not have parallel lines, because if it does the swaged bullet will cling to it quite tenaciously. If you maintain a reasonable amount of downward taper you can forget that problem.

I hate to say it, but I needed something like eight or ten experimental prototypes to get the format of the inner cavity reasonably close to being perfected. That bugs me because once I hit upon it, it seemed as if I should have been able to go there no later than the third try.

The original Swag-O-Matic bottom dies have a bleed hole of about .0925-inch for escape of surplus metal in ordinary use. For recontouring bullet noses you don't need that, nor do you want it. There is a small size of brazing rod that mikes the aforementioned .0925-inch — a tad under 3/32-inch — and I discovered that a short section of that cut off with the jeweler's saw, deburred and carefully inserted into the bleed hole of the lower die solved that problem in a highly satisfactory manner. In use, it builds up pressure against the outer casing and makes it a challenge to get the lower die out when you change calibers, but that's a minor problem.

The original Swag-O-Matic handle is rather short and if it ever had a handle grip, I lost that years back. With the lathe at hand — O blissful delight! — it was a simple matter to make a wooden handle extension with a neat aluminum ferrule around the hole to keep it from splitting under stress.

The basic principle of seating a HBWC bullet into the case neck with cavity to the fore is older than most hills. I suspect that at least half the people who ever dabbled in reloading have discovered the possibility with radiant joy; I know I did.

The trouble with the reversed HBWC — or Bass-A round, as I tend to think of it — is that the skirts are a bit thinner than would be ideal if that were the envisioned final purpose of the bullet. At rather moderate velocities in media such as duct seal, the skirts shear off the Bass-A bullet early on, leaving the solid base to penetrate as well as it can manage. Obviously it would be better if the skirts were sturdy enough so as to parachute to maximum diameter and continue pushing and rearranging the target material.

Lyman had a HBWC mould in .410-inch diameter, their #41027, though I'm not certain if it remains in their offering of moulds still available; they've dropped so many useful numbers. Alberts recently added a HBWC for the .32 S&W Long and, apart from the ubiquitous .38 Special diameter, that seems to be about the crop so far as HBWC designs are concerned: none for the .44 or .45 sizes, as far as I know.

Given bottom dies and lower punches for the Swag-O-Matic, it is hardly any trouble at all — even for a machinist with eleven left thumbs such as humble self — to whomp forth top punches capable of maximizing expansion quite effectively for the diameter in question.

Familiar as you must be by this time with my fondness for tacking weird names onto otherwise prosaic artifacts, I trust it will come as no painful shock to note that I refer to this general category of swast bullets as the *Spelunker*. The rationale being that when they hit they tend to go *spelunk!*

Just how well do they perform? Thought you'd never ask! The 125-grain version for the .38 Special, shoved by a picayune 2.7 grains of Bullseye from the three-inch barrel of Li'l Montgomery goes into duct seal and spreads to caliber .55 as measured on the recovered bullet. With the same load from the six-inch barrel of the BK-38, it picks up enough additional velocity to mushroom to about caliber .65-inch.

*As discussed, Lee Precision offers this .38 semi-wadcutter design in weights of 105 and 140 grains; both work exceptionally well in the .38 Special or .357 magnum*

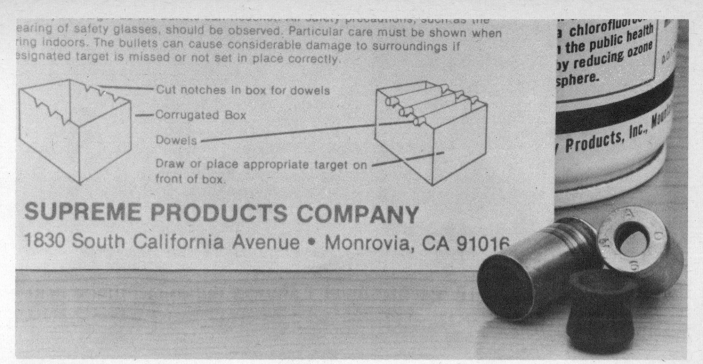

earing of safety glasses, should be observed. Particular care must be shown when ring indoors. The bullets can cause considerable damage to surroundings if esignated target is missed or not set in place correctly.

— Cut notches in box for dowels

— Corrugated Box

— Dowels

Draw or place appropriate target on front of box.

## SUPREME PRODUCTS COMPANY

### 1830 South California Avenue • Monrovia, CA 91016

*Discussed at greater length in the later chapter on Indoor Artillery, here are the Supreme rubber bullets in the .45 size, also usable in .44 size. The primer provides the sole power source and flash holes have been enlarged with a #25 drill bit to .1495-inch diameter to avoid primer setback and the cases have been marked in red for identification.*

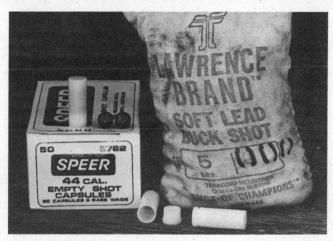

*An interesting possibility is to put two of the Lawrence Brand 000 buck shot in .44 Speer capsule to double the number of holes at a single loading. The dispersion is not too abrupt and short-range accuracy is quite good.*

The same bullet ahead of 5.4 grains of W-W 231 powder represents a level just below maximum in the +P category for the .38 Special and those come out of the three-inch barrel at 1048 fps, out of the six-inch barrel at 1210 fps; respective energies are 305 and 406 fpe. The resulting impact commotion of the load from the three-inch barrel was depicted graphically in a couple of photos back in the chapter on handgun diameter and a plaster cast of the entire cavity resembles a lavishly fertilized rutabaga in general size and contours.

What about accuracy? It's by no means as shoddy as you might expect. From twenty-five yards the BK-38 made four solid hits out of five in a 1.25-inch aiming paster with the fifth spreading the center-to-center span to about 1.75 inches. The good four went into about 11/16-inch. At the same distance, Li'l Montgomery put four into a clump

you could hide with a playing card and the fifth blew it to nearly seven inches. Both groups were well centered about the point of aim and, superimposed upon a lifesized silhouette target — recalling the rutabaga-sized cavity cast — it's clearly apparent that you'd have one sorely-besmote silhouette, even from the little three-incher.

Let there be no pretense nor misimpression that the concept is new or even close to it. Hatcher's 1935 edition of *Textbook Of Pistols And Revolvers* included a line drawing of the cross-section of a British bullet he designated as the .455 man-stopper; illustration #8 on page 419. The design, we can logically assume, predates 1935 by some indeterminate number of years and it is conceptual kin to the Spelunker with one minor exception.

The Spelunker, as presently refined, has a biangular nasal crater. In designs for use in revolvers, the primary cone starts at dead maximum bullet diameter, shelving inward at an included angle of typically 132 degrees for about the first .090-inch thickness of skirt wall, in the example of the .38 size, at which point it reangles downward at an included angle of forty to sixty degrees, depending somewhat upon caliber and modification. The secondary cone puts its apex fairly close to the bullet base; within .125-inch or so in the later versions.

The function of the broad primary angle is to initiate expansion with all possible alacrity upon initial contact with the target medium. The outer edge of the primary cone is substantially equal to full bullet diameter. As the upset commences it is accelerated by the fact that the bullet at that instant still carries the greater part of its arriving velocity plus rapid rotation. In effect, the primary cone fills much the same function as the pilot chute of a parachute so that the secondary cone can snap to full-open mode with all possible dispatch.

Abruptness of energy transmission is the key aspect. If

This one is called "Dermolition Debbie," made in a .38 half-jacket from Corbin with a #0 buck shot swaged to shape. It can be driven to high velocities and expansion is quite good, even at modest pace of the one on right.

This gives a closer look and the larger buck shot pellets used with the domed punch of Corbin Bullet Press leave the front shaped as shown. Refer to top left, next page.

it's spread over even a modest time span, energy can be absorbed and tolerated with little serious discomfort. If it's all delivered right-now, it has a great deal more useful effect. Picture if you will an enormous door for a bank vault, perhaps six feet in diameter and weighing a ton or so. It's standing open so you walk up and deliver an all-out roundhouse swing with clenched fist and all you have behind it. You'll walk away nursing some number of shattered knuckles and it's unlikely the vault door even quivered.

But if you were to walk up to the same door, extend the tip of a forefinger and exert a steady push, the chances are you'd be able to move the door and even edge it into closed position.

The basic principles apply: Energy transferred over a lengthy time span raises little or no fuss. Equivalent energy applied over the space of just a few microseconds is something else entirely.

Every now and again, when hot news flashes are in short supply, the papers will run a tired old retread story. They raise a terrible fuss over the fact that the police department of this or that city is carrying hollow-point bullets as their duty load. It's fairly customary to refer to such projectiles as dum dums. The term, if you didn't know, stems from India's Dum-dum Arsenal where expanding-bullet cartridges were made up at one time. Such newspaper philippics usually beat their breast and bleat over the fact that bullets of that type are "outlawed by the Geneva Convention!"

In point of cold fact, the Geneva Convention had nothing whatsoever to do with expanding bullets. The gathering at which the signatory powers agreed to refrain from using expanding bullets in smallarms was held at The Hague; in 1907 as I recall, or along about that time. The USA was not a signatory to the pact. Despite that, we've employed spitzer-point FMJ rifle bullets in the major conflicts since that time, and round-nose FMJ bullets in handgun loads.

A year or so ago there was a brief flurry in the firearms press over a new handgun load developed in France called the Arcane. Such cartridges carried bullets turned from electrolytically pure copper, with noses that carried a straight taper to a sharp point. The intent was to enhance capability for penetration in hard targets and reports indicated they achieved a good deal of success in that area. At the same time, when fired into yielding materials such as duct seal, the cavitation was quite impressive.

I never managed to get hands upon any of the actual Arcane loads, but managed to synthesize what I called ersatz Arcanes by turning some conventional lead alloy bullets down to pointed contours closely similar to those shown in photos of the French ammo. Firing them into duct seal produced remarkably large entrance openings with .45 ACP bullets having an included angle of seventy degrees at the nose. It suggested that FMJ bullets could be made with points tapering at about the same angle that would perform quite a bit better than the usual round-nose shape, meanwhile complying with all the rules of international warfare.

What we might term blunt spire-point handgun bullets, including the Arcane and similar types, make effective use of a basic principle that I think of as the snowplow effect. At the bullet velocity the angle displaces target material violently in all directions perpendicular to the bullet path, imparting moving inertia to the impact medium that tends to make it push surrounding medium out of its path. With the tapered conical nose such effects are much more apparent than with the round-nose bullet design. The difference is easy to test and evaluate by firing into a suitably plastic medium such as duct seal, perhaps going on to make casts of resulting cavities for side-by-side comparison.

Incidentally, speaking of the Arcane loads, should any of those find their way into your hands, it would be wise to refrain from firing them since the reports on them noted that they generated peak pressures well in excess of the maximum figures specified by our Sporting Arms & Ammunition Manufacturers Institute, or SAAMI.

As comments here tend to suggest, handgun ammunition performance can be upgraded usefully by means of thoughtful projectile design, without need to exceed maximum pressure figures specified by SAAMI. We've brought up a few interesting possibilities and others may still be awaiting discovery. Down the years there seems to have been a certain detectable reluctance on the part of ammunition manufacturers to offer handguns with outstanding potential for expansion. Lee Jurras made the preliminary breaks in the log jam in the early Sixties with his Super Vel loads and, once it was proved to the major makers that there was an interesting market for such ammo, a great many of them lost little time in adding comparable entries to their lines.

Today you can buy several versions of factory loads in JHP bullet designs and most if not all of them will expand in suitable media at the velocities they attain. About the only attempt at maximum-effort cartridges is the .38 Spe-

*Two of the Dermolition Debbie bullets can be seated in a .38 Special load or three in a .357 case, using a powder charge suitable for the combined weight for multiple use.*

*Entrance openings of .45 ACP test loads in duct seal with 90° and 70° points, compared to that of the conventional round nose military load. The difference is substantial!*

cial Scorpion Hydra-Shok and if it's offered in any other calibers, I've not heard of it. Alberts Bullets markets a bullet highly similar to the one used in the Hydra-Shok load for use by reloaders. Apart from that, HBWC bullets can be purchased in .32 S&W Long size and .38 Special size. Those who work with the .41 and .44 magnums, the .45 ACP and Auto Rim or the .45 Colt can buy a few decent JHP designs and that's about the size of it.

Whether or not there is a market for a maximum-expansion bullet such as the Spelunker in other diameters as well as .38 is a good question. A nearby bulletmaker believes there may be and plans to put them into production for sale to law-enforcement agencies, both as the bullet alone and loaded rounds. That is not my project, but interested parties can direct inquiries to S&S Precision Bullets, Box 1133, San Juan Capistrano, CA 92693. Present plans of the firm envision commencing production in late 1982 and self-addressed, stamped envelopes included with inquiries will be appreciated.

Another area that offers interesting exploration for the do-it-yourself bulletmaker is the lighter designs in a given diameter. Among the advantages of such bullets, you get more bullets per pound of alloy; the recoil is milder; the accuracy is often exceptional and the higher velocity obtainable beneath the specified maximum pressures tends to flatten the trajectory to useful extents. In the .38 Special

sizes, I've had extremely satisfactory results with a little semi-wadcutter design in a mould from Lee Precision that casts at a nominal weight of 105 grains. If a bullet is seated into the case mouth beyond the customary depth, the resulting peak pressures will increase quite perceptibly. With that cautionary note kept firmly in mind, I've had gratifying gains in accuracy by seating the 105-grain Lee SWC into the case necks of .38 Specials with its front shoulder as much as .10 to .20 inch below the mouth. Powder charges for such loads are intentionally held to low levels, such as 2.7 grains of Bullseye. The case mouths on such loads are taper-crimped rather than roll-crimped. Lee Precision has a similar design for the .38 or .357 with the identical nose profile at a typical weight of 140 grains; likewise an easy-caster and a promising grouper with appropriate powder charges. While the 105-grain is at its best out to about twenty-five yards, the 140-grain version holds good groups to fifty yards and beyond.

A good lightwight design for the .44 Special or magnum is Lyman's #429348 at about 180 grains and my second favorite for that diameter is Lyman's #429215, a SWC with gas check at about 215 grains.

For the .45 ACP, the Hensley & Gibbs #68 SWC at about 190 to 200 grains is hard to beat. Most of the bullets from moulds intended for use in the 9mmP cartridge come out large enough to permit accurate sizing to .358-inch for experimental trials in .38 or .357 revolvers and some of those perform quite well with right powder charge. It must always be borne in mind — as Claud Hamilton pointed out earlier — that the bullet and charge must be custom tailored to the specific gun for optimum results and even two nominally identical guns are apt to show different preferences in loads.

Given the capability for producing your own bullets offers access to an infinite number of additional bullets to try behind countless different charges in the eternal quest for the one magic combination that drives them all through the same hole. More, if you ever find it or come pretty close, you can roll out an endless supply of duplicates made up to the same recipe until you become bored with such perfection and channel your interests to other areas.

It would be wise not to attempt holding your breath until you reach that point, however.

*H&G #292, left, duplicates Hornady's USAF design. The same load was recontoured to a nose angle of 70° to produce the "ersatz Arcane" loads appearing here.*

# CHAPTER 11

# HANDGUN POWDERS AND PRIMERS

## Information On The Items That Put The Fire In Firearms

*A cross-sectioned view of a Boxer-type primer after firing in a .357 magnum case. Parts are not quite in original location, but they are close. The wafer of priming compound lies just beneath the inner surface of the primer cup and the tip of the firing pin dents the primer cup inward, crushing and igniting the priming mixture to send hot gases down through the flash hole.*

**W**HILE A LIVELY interest remains in the original type of propellants commonly termed black powder or gunpowder, and in those sporting arms designed solely for its use, the scope of the book at hand is fairly well centered upon the so-called smokeless powders or, more precisely, nitro powders.

The principal difference between the two types is that black powder is a mechanical mixture of three primary ingredients — charcoal, sulfur and saltpeter — in which the last named supplies the oxygen for combustion of the first two components. In nitro powders the oxygen necessary for combustion is contained within the molecule of the material(s), thereby improving its burning qualities quite sharply.

Guncotton or nitrocellulose was discovered by Schoenbein in 1845, nitroglycerin by Sobrero in 1846. Traditionally a lot of major scientific discoveries are made by accident and I seem to recall hearing that Schoenbein inadvertantly dropped his handkerchief in some concentrated nitric acid, plucked it out with a set of tongs, rinsed it off thoroughly and did not discover its notable new properties until his wife, after laundering it, essayed to iron it, whereupon the hanky burst into a pyrotechnic display that thoroughly demoralized the innocent lady. That may be pure folklore and I only note that I seem to recall having heard it,

Above, popular handgun powders from Hercules; not shown is their Reloder-7 that finds occasional use in bottlenecked cases. Left, Du Pont powders suitable for reloading cartridges for handguns.

Winchester-Western powders tend to come and go; The 630 shown here is no longer on the market, and the exact fate of some of the others is slightly uncertain at press time.

Here are some but by no means all of the Hodgdon powders suitable for use in handgun reloading.

I think. It is to be hoped that Signora Sobrero did not participate in her spouse's discovery of nitroglycerin in the same way, as that is remarkly nasty material, once it goes into its act.

The earliest forerunner of the modern nitro explosives was picric acid, discovered by J.R. Glauber at some no-longer-recorded point in his lifespan (1604-1668). Produced by treating wood with strong nitric acid, it saw use as a yellow dye until its explosive properties were discovered, rather belatedly, in 1805. Even so, it was not until 1871 when Sprengel discovered that picric acid could be detonated if it was in proximity to exploding fulminate of mercury. By that time nitrocellulose and nitroglycerin were

fully upon the scene. Scientific progress made much shorter strides in those days.

Application of new discoveries moved rather sluggishly, too. The American War Between The States made little or no use of nitro explosives, meanwhile consuming black powder in prodigious quantities, creating a severe problem for the Confederacy in obtaining sufficient supplies of saltpeter.

Once nitro explosives were discovered, a lot of technical details remained to be worked out before they became attractively practical. Early efforts tended to erupt in spectacular explosions and profound loss of further interest. It was not until 1865 when Frederich Abel, working for the British Government, discovered that the objectionably hysterical properties of guncotton were due to the difficulty of removing the last traces of the acids used in its initial manufacture. As it turned out, that was an important discovery that led directly to the nitro powders we use today, if not always with appropriate gratitude to those researchers of earlier days.

Apart from the fission and fusion effects that made their debut in 1945, nearly all modern propellants and explosives are highly dependent upon the singular properties of the element nitrogen; a remarkably commonplace material that constitutes about four-fifths of the air we breathe, among other things. Nitrogen is flighty stuff, entering into chemical combinations reluctantly and severing its connections with brusque enthusiasm, given no more than moderate excuse. There are other gaseous elements that are much less gregarious than nitrogen — helium, neon, argon, krypton, xenon and perhaps radon — and it's a bit

*Left, three similar but different W-W powders in the order of their appearance from about 1961 to the present. Below, 295 HP appeared in the early Sixties, was withdrawn and the similar 296 came along later. The 630 P data should never be used in loading with 630 powder; both are discontinued.*

bemusing to speculate upon the properties of the explosives that could be concocted from them, could they but be coaxed into combination with various other elements.

A quick sidenote you're welcome to skip if you're in a hurry: About three decades ago I made my first assault on the world of letters against the field of science fiction and even got a few stories published and, some years later, even collected a small amount of money for them. By the time the cash came neaping in — all $80 of it — I'd had the good luck to blunder into writing about firearms and the rest is history; not especially natural, but history, withal. During one of those primal space-opera efforts concerning a sort of futuristic paratrooper, I made note that the landing area had been softened by a liberal lacing of a monstrously powerful explosive known as tulium argate. That was based upon the tacit assumption that tulium will be discovered at some point in the years up ahead. I should note the story in question carried the Ar̶ ̶sley byline as I had another under my natural name in ̶ ̶same issue.

The first military smokeless powder was developed in 1886 by the French engineer Vielle, who christened it Poudre B in honor of General Boulanger — French for baker. Vielle was employed in the French government laboratories at the time. In 1888 the Swedish chemist Nobel introduced Ballistite and, later the same year, the British introduced Cordite.

One of the most relentlessly reoccurring phrases in mystery stories, even to modern times, is, "...the acrid stench of burnt Cordite." Presumably, in most instances, this implies a propellant for pistols and, in point of plain fact, damned few handgun cartridges are apt to be encountered with Cordite as the driving charge, but who cares? The words roll so trippingly out of the typewriter, *n'est-ce pas?*

Cordite was made by gelatinizing insoluble nitrocotton of high nitration with nitroglycerin and acetone. That was the approach for the early version, at least. By the time of WWI, the original composition had been modified to fifty-

*Importing powders is so complex and costly as to discourage the practice. Both Norma and Alcan powders were made in Sweden but neither are readily available in today's domestic market.*

The powders appearing above are among the slowest in burning rate suitable for handgun reloading and then largely in high-energy rounds such as the 7mm T/CU for Contenders.

These are typical of the medium powders, ranked as to burning rates, suited to magnum handgun cartridges having straight-sided cases. That's H4198 atop the can of Blue Dot, also H110 above the can of H4227 if they're hard to decipher in the final printed copy.

Powders below are typical of the fastest in burning rates, finding their major uses in moderate-velocity target loads or in cases inherently incapable of handling top pressures.

*Two cans of Du Pont IMR-4198 powder that probably date from some indeterminate point prior to WWII. Although the labels show severe wear, the contents remain in fine shape!*

eight percent nitroglycerin, thirty-seven percent guncotton and five percent mineral jelly. Despite the cooling properties of the mineral jelly, the combustion temperature was so high that bore erosion was insufferable. Accordingly, the formula was revised to thirty percent nitroglycerin, sixty-five percent guncotton and five percent mineral jelly. The guncotton used in Cordite was a relatively high level of nitration; about thirteen percent, so as to be only about eighty-five percent insoluble in blends of ether and alcohol.

In manufacture, Cordite was extruded in long strands, giving rise to its name. Once chopped into suitable lengths, it took sixty to ninety days to dry it properly, depending upon strand diameter. That Cordite was employed as the propellant for handgun cartridges at some receding point in time is attested by the fact that the rather unlikely Webley-Fosbery Automatic Revolver was rollmarked on the LH side of its receiver with the ultimatum, ".455 Cordite only."

If it helps to shore up your faith in the fitness of things, I can confide that I have a small quantity of cartridges in .303 British caliber (calibre?) on hand that are in fact loaded with veritable Cordite in long, stringy strands. I pulled one down and, goaded by scientific curiosity, took one strand out away from flammable materials, held it in a pair of tweezers, lit one end with the pocket Zippo and can soberly testify that the odor is about as acrid as I could possibly imagine and I think my imagination is fairly well developed. As with a candle flame, the stench is likewise reminiscent of scorched nostril hairs...

The bulk of the domestic offerings of nitro powders are made up by nitrating the shortest of the cotton fibers, those unsuited for routine use in textiles, including the linters that cling to the cotton seed after passage through the cotton gin. In times of severe stress it has been found possible and practical to eke out the cotton with some amount of wood pulp, up to twenty-five percent or a bit better. Nitrated wood, technically, becomes nitrolignin and other materials have been nitrated along the way; starch, for but one more example, to form nitrostarch. A Du Pont shotgun powder of the Thirties — MX — was termed a multi-base powder, containing various nitrated materials although its exact composition was not specified in the work that discusses it: *Smokeless Shotgun Powders* by Wallace H. Coxe, published by Du Pont in 1933.

The problem of acid residue remains with us, well over a century after Abel identified it. Powders vary from lot to lot — an observation that can trigger heated debate in some quarters — and some may carry slightly higher traces of acid content than others; a fact that has a significant effect

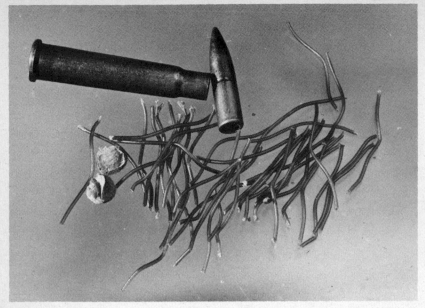

Here's some of the actual Cordite, as salvaged from a round of .303 British military rifle ammo and yes, its stench is acrid! Below, reproduced from a 1935 Stoeger's Shooter's Bible, the Webley Fosbery automatic revolver was rollmarked, "455 Cordite Only."

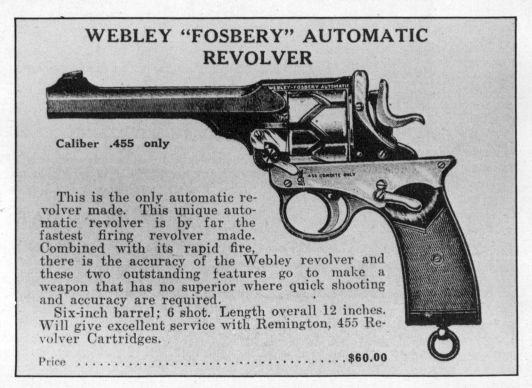

## WEBLEY "FOSBERY" AUTOMATIC REVOLVER

Caliber .455 only

This is the only automatic revolver made. This unique automatic revolver is by far the fastest firing revolver made. Combined with its rapid fire, there is the accuracy of the Webley revolver and these two outstanding features go to make a weapon that has no superior where quick shooting and accuracy are required.

Six-inch barrel; 6 shot. Length overall 12 inches. Will give excellent service with Remington, 455 Revolver Cartridges.

Price ........................................$60.00

upon their long-term keeping properties. Bruce Hodgdon tells me the quantity of the powder has a decided effect upon the likelihood that a powder may deteriorate, given a tendency to do that in the first place. All other conditions being equal, a one-pound container of powder will resist spoilage much better than a one-hundred-pound drum of the identical powder.

I have a couple of canisters of Du Pont IMR-4198 that probably predate WWII by some unguessable number of years and, despite the ravages of time being clearly apparent on the labeling, the contents remain as fresh and lively as the distant day they left Wilmington. Every decade or so I make up a few suitable loads from these vintage lots to verify their innate pizzazz remains untarnished.

I have samples of Hercules Bullseye spanning across about thirty years and I find it diverting to lot against lot occasionally. A curious thing: the charge weight from a volume-type measure may vary moderately, but thus dispensed the resulting velocities across the chronograph remain about as close as if all the cartridges were loaded from the same can. I find that rather impressive. Much the same applies for my collection of Hercules 2400 lots and I think it speaks well for the quality control personnel at the Hercules plant.

All the foregoing notwithstanding, if you make a practice of giving cans of powder a good home for decade after decade, it behooves you urgently to make periodic checks on how well each can is surviving the timeflow. A really bad batch in its final throes is capable of spontaneous ignition. What that could do to other cans of powder stored nearby is not a comforting thing to contemplate.

Routine inspection of powder stores is just one seductively helluva good idea. One of the first concernable symptoms is if it shows signs of attacking the tin-plated steel portions of the container, as indicated by a reddish haze in the air if you pour some into a pan, prior to funneling it back into the can again. Unless you're plagued with anosmia — the condition describable as smell-blindness — you can sniff at the neck of the uncapped can and ascertain quite a bit of useful data on its condition. The residual solvent scents of ether, alcohol, acetone and whatnot are no cause for alarm; a fragrance gunners come to recognize and savor. What should trigger your alarm circuits into flaring coalescence is any sharp tang of acid odor which, once encountered, tends to brand itself indelibly into the mental/olfactory circuits. It is forty-some years since I last scented nitric or sulfuric acids in their free and pure state, but the nasal memory is as permanent as for the treacherous geranium fragrance of phosgene gas.

Powder with an acid smell needs to be disposed of quickly and safely. You may save the picturesque container as a souvenir if you wish, but get rid of the powder, *right-damn-now!* Safe disposal techniques vary in choice from person to person. You can flush it down the toilet — Britons read water-closet — or you can strew it widespread across the lawn in hopes that, in decomposing, its nitrogen will enrich the soil. If you're plagued with burrowing rodents you can decant modest quantities into the holes, drop in a cigarette butt and retire briskly. You can pour it out onto concrete to be ignited with suitable precautions or, if you've a better idea, employ it at your own risk and discretion.

One of the perks of a job such as I have is that all manner of people seem to regard you as the logical disposal site for unwanted items vaguely ballistic in nature. That is not an entirely unalloyed blessing, but it brings up a couple of points that need discussion. Once, a dozen or so years

*Hercules Bullseye powder is one of the oldest and certainly one of the most popular handgun powders of all time. The cardboard package, upper, was in use for some time after WWII, being replaced by the metal can at left below, then the one in the center and finally back to the cylindrical cardboard canister of the present.*

back, a benefactor — identity long forgotten — laid off the better part of a one-pound coffee can of some pale-gray flakes with the cryptic information that it was Hercules Hi-Temp. A more intrepid researcher might have essayed to work up suitable loads for the stuff, but mercifully I didn't. Later, on quizzing some of the folks from Hercules, I learned that Hi-Temp was made up for "shooting" oil wells. It carries a percentage of RDX, a fairly sophisticated right-now explosive, making it monstrously unsuitable as a propellant. I've used some for discouraging the indigenous gopher population to pretty good effect and retain the remnants, albeit quite cautiously.

The other great hairy no-no-NO!, powderwise, is the stuff they load into blank cartridges so the local American Legion post can do a respectful fusillade over the grave of a departed comrade. Occasionally such blank loads find their way into the hands of reloaders to cause vast complexities and problems if attempts are made to salvage and reuse the powder for propelling projectiles. The powder used in blanks, *mes enfants,* is designed to detonate with all possible brisance to create decibels, not to drive bullets. Put it behind even a lightweight bullet and you'll convert your pet hunk of hardware to deadly shrapnel. Consider yourself duly warned, no? Likewise, pass the friendly word along to your buddies who didn't happen to buy a copy of this book.

If Schoenbein and Sobrero helped to put us in the cushy spot we enjoy these latter days, the efforts of a Scottish pastor, the Reverend Doctor Alexander John Forsyth, merit at least equal recognition. Forsyth, who died in 1843, contributed percussion ignition to the shooting activities. The detonating properties of the various metallic fulminates had been discovered at least as early as 1663, but it took Dr. Forsyth's intrepid pioneering to harness

Below are three different packages used for Hercules 2400 powder over the past thirty years or so and, at left, a can of the Hodgdon H240, discontinued several years ago that was comparable to 2400 in performance and properties.

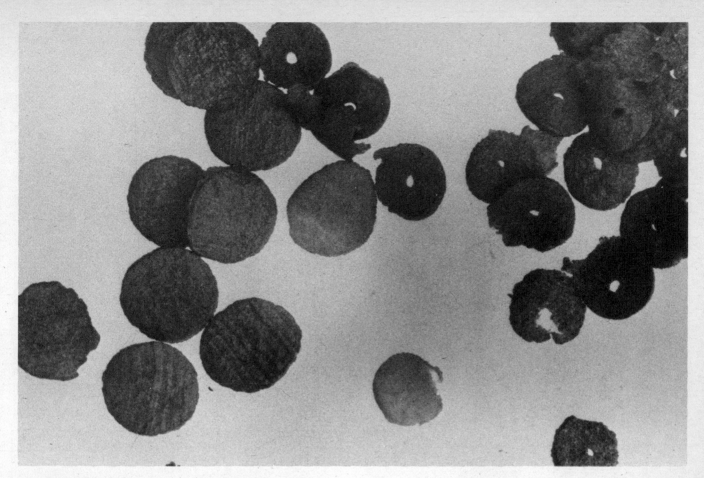

*New powders come along rather seldom and Du Pont's
800-X shows great promise for use in magnum cases
for handguns. In photo above, 800-X flakes are larger
(left) than the 700-X flakes at right and, unlike the
700-X, flakes of the 800-X do not have perforations.*

them usefully. First there had been the matchlock, with its
bit of cord that had been saturated in a solution of saltpeter,
then dried to be applied to torch off the charge of powder.
That was followed by the flintlock in which a scrap of flint
was slammed against a steel frizzen to produce a shower of
sparks directed toward a priming charge of black powder
that fed flame to the igniting/driving charge.

Forsyth's work compressed all that duration into the
snap of a cap that flashed the powder charge to send the
bullet down with minimal delay. To really appreciate his
contribution to the sport we all love, you need to have fired
at least one round from a flintlock to savor the oppor-
tunities it affords for developing flinch. A shot from a
matchlock isn't really necessary.

As with most powders, the modern primer tends to
maintain its efficiency over an extended period of storage

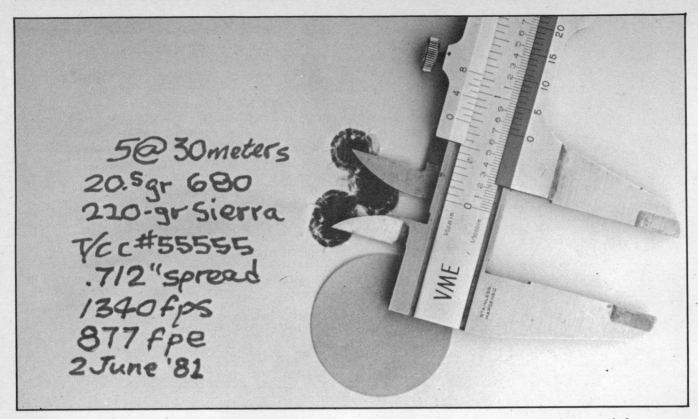

5@ 30 meters
20.5gr 680
220-gr Sierra
T/cc#55555
.712"spread
1340fps
877 fpe
2June '81

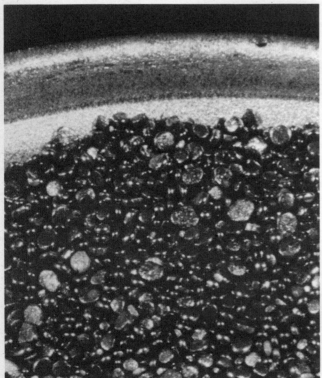

W-W 680 powder sees little listing in manuals for use in handguns to date. The #10 Speer manual has loads for it in the .45 Winchester magnum. Group above was fired in a T/C Contender with ten-inch bull barrel and M8-2X Leupold scope with 20.5 grains of 680 behind the 220-grain Sierra Silhouette bullet in .41 magnum for a .712-inch spread at thirty meters: hard to fault accuracy like that! Granules of 680 are at left, greatly magnified.

priming compound for sporting and/or military ammo. Its combustion residue tended to attack and embrittle the brass cartridge cases. The next priming compound after that contained amounts of potassium chlorate and it worked well, but had the serious fault of leaving residues of potassium chloride after firing. Being similar to common table salt — sodium chloride — it was hygroscopic, which is to say it gathered moisture from the air and caused severe problems from rust and corrosion unless followed by prompt and thorough cleaning. Corrosive chlorate primers were used in most military small arms ammo up through about 1952 although commercial ammunition shifted to the non-corrosive priming compounds several years earlier. Most military ammunition carries headstamps that more or less specify the year of its manufacture rather than the caliber designation, making it reasonably possible to decide whether an unfired round has a corrosive primer or not. If there is any reason to doubt, cleaning should be prompt and meticulous after firing and, even with modern primers, it's still a good idea and hurts nothing.

Modern smokeless powders vary from each other chiefly in their burning characteristics and in the pressure curve they generate in burning. Burning takes place quite rapidly, but by no means instantaneously, and the burning

quite successfully. They should be stored under conditions of moderate temperature and humidity; not subjected to extremes of either. It is not good policy, for example, to store them in hermetically sealed containers with packets of silica gel since the priming compound has and needs a modest moisture content to function properly.

Mercuric fulminate was abandoned many years ago as a

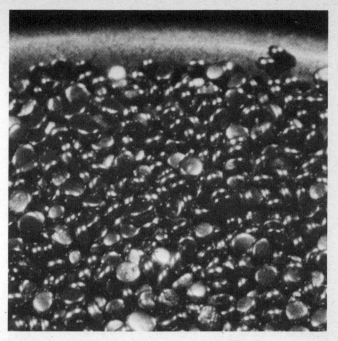

Here and at right are macrophotos of two Hodgdon powders that work well in the 7mm T/CU. Above is H322, an extruded type with tiny perforations.

Hodgdon H335 is of the type Hodgdon terms Spherical, resembling bridge-mix candy at this fairly high rate of magnification; roughly 15X.

Du Pont marketed their Hi-Skor pistol powder for a brief time about 1964, then dropped it in favor of the 700-X that remains in production. Their P-5066 was somewhat similar to Bullseye in burning rate and was mourned by a lot of handgunners when it was dropped. The others shown here remain in production down to the present.

*A number of reloaders have come to some amount of grief down the yars through confusing the two Hercules powders here. At this level of magnification, it's obvious the Bullseye flakes at left are thinner than the 2400 flakes at right but the difference isn't nearly that apparent to the unaided eye. If the fast-burning Bullseye is loaded to weights appropriate for the slow-burning 2400, all hell is out for noon and damage to gun and/or shooter is quite probable. Using 2400 by mistake for Bullseye results in loads that fire poopily, if at all. Both are magnificent powders when used as directed but this points up the need for positive identification!*

occurs at the surface of the powder granule. In the example of a flake or cylindrical granule, as burning takes place the amount of surface area is reduced, thereby slowing the combustion. Many types of powder have a perforation running lengthwise through the granule to serve the useful purpose of maintaining combustion vigor for a brief interval after ignition. As burning progresses the surface in the perforation increases and provides a considerable increase in granule area.

As the pressure increases, the rate of burning accelerates more or less proportionally and the actual response to those conditions is what gives the various powders their unique and distinctive characteristics or personalities. Some powders require a fairly high pressure level in order to burn properly. In other examples a comparable pressure level accelerates the burning rate so violently as to cause faster burning and still higher pressures which, in turn produce further increases. The trick in harnessing a given powder for maximum efficiency lies in using the charge weight that is optimum for the particular cartridge and bullet.

If a fast-burning powder is dispensed too generously behind a bullet so heavy as to offer excessive inertial resistance, the peak pressures will exceed safe levels and damage to the gun and/or injury to the shooter and nearby personnel is quite apt to occur. If a slower-burning powder is loaded to produce peak pressures that are too low, its

combustion will be incomplete and quantities of unburned granules will be left in the barrel, chamber and receiver area.

Determining the proper amount of a particular powder for a given set of conditions is a project that needs to be handled by experienced technicians and it is by no manner of means an area of endeavor for the amateur experimenter. Even lab workers with years of experience can encounter the occasional surprise, as one of my acquaintances did in fairly recent times. He intended to make up a load with Hercules 2400 powder for use in the .357 magnum and, in reaching for the familiar blue can of powder, happened to pick up a can of Hercules Red Dot instead. The latter is also put up in cans with labels of approximately the same shade of blue.

The two Hercules powders are sufficiently different in appearance that a close look should have triggered alarmed awareness of the incipient problem, but for some reason the lab worker went ahead and made up the loads with the Red Dot at a charge weight suitable for 2400. That the gun did not blow up is a tribute to the dedication of Sturm, Ruger & Co., its manufacturer. Nevertheless, after firing the first round, it became urgently apparent that there was a problem and the spent case showed a marked reluctance toward extraction.

After hearing his rueful account of the near-mishap, I took the precaution of applying some day-glo red circular

W-W 231 is a fast-burning type favored for target work and often capable of exceptional accuracy. A Ball Powder, its granules are flattened by rolling.

Hercules Blue Dot includes a few flakes that are blue in color — not apparent here — along with others of a shade ranging more toward greenish in general hue.

Du Pont IMR-4198 is typical of their Improved Military Rifle series, with central perforations. It resembles automatic pencil lead broken in short bits.

Extremely flexible and versatile, Hercules Unique is of medium burning rate and it frequently delivers excellent accuracy in straight-sided handgun cases.

Du Pont SR-4756 flakes are usually unperforated but you may find a few, as here, that carry perforations.

Fastest of Du Pont's IMR series, IMR-4227 granules are considerably shorter in length than the IMR-4198.

Hercules Red Dot has occasional flakes that are red in color, granules are sliced quite thin, tend to curl.

Hodgdon H110 was developed for .30 GI carbine and is a good one for the hotter loads in magnum cases.

W-W 296 is a fine-grained Ball Powder that meters well in rotary measures; a good one for magnums.

Du Pont SR-7625 granules are perforated quite uniformly and slightly thicker than their SR-4756.

pasters to my cans of Red Dot liberally enough to make certain at least one would be visible from any angle. It is not a bad idea and, in any event, when you pick up a can of powder to dispense some, it is an even better idea to get into the habit of taking a long and thoughtful look at its label to verify it's the powder you really had in mind.

The practice of using a labeled powder can to contain powder other than its original contents is a poor one that should be avoided. Even if relabeled, confusion is all too treacherously possible. When using powder in a rotary measure, it's a good idea to affix an identifying label to the reservoir; a hand-lettered strip of white draftsman's tape works quite well. The unused powder should be returned to its container after the last charges have been dispensed and

any remnants of powder not clearly labeled should be discarded in the coldest of blood; safely, of course.

Earlier in the book here Claud Hamilton makes reference to encountering high-pressure responses in an out-of-the-book load of Hercles Blue Dot powder on an extremely cold day. That is a problem I've never run into, although I've had a few examples of loads that developed too much pressure when fired at extremely high ambient temperatures.

We hear occasional accounts of damaging pressures ostensibly rising from a notably mild load. In most such reported instances it involves 148-grain wadcutters put up in .357 magnum cases ahead of 2.7 grains of Hercules Bullseye, although one writer claimed it was possible in the

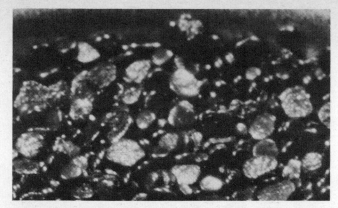

Hodgdon HS7 is a fairly slow Spherical number that shows up well for such cases as the .38 Colt Super.

W-W 748 is a slightly flattened Ball Powder that's a great favorite in small to medium bottleneck cases.

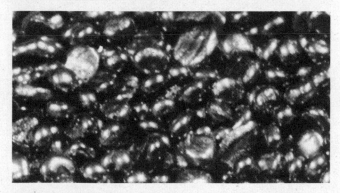

This is the discontinued and keenly mourned W-W 630 that was capable of remarkably high velocities.

Hercules Reloder-7 carries a sprinkling of granules that are colored red, blue and yellow, also dark gray.

.38 Special case, as well. The latter did not report any specific instance from personal knowledge, but merely indulged in some amount of semi-hysterical hand-wringing.

In high probability such loads contain double charges — by no means impossible to produce when using progressive loaders — coupled with bullets seated slightly beyond the customary depth by reason of accumulations of bullet lubricant in the seating die. A double charge — 5.4 grains of Bullseye — under a deep-seated bullet can produce pressures that are hazardous, and *will* produce them. Personnel at the Hercules labs have spent a lot of time and effort in attempting to duplicate the so-called "detonation load" and have concluded that it's a complete impossibility if the charge is held to 2.7 grains of Bullseye at the customary bullet seating depth for the 148-grain wadcutter bullet, either in .38 or .357 cases. I mention this primarily because it's a matter that accounts for a number of inquiries from readers so, having read the foregoing comments, you now know at least as much about it as I do, perhaps even more.

The choice of which powder to use of the several listed in the tables of the loading manuals is not a simple one. What seems to work the best is to make up some loads with each of a few different powders, fire the test loads under conditions that minimize human error and let the gun indicate its own preference. Needless to say, it is an extremely good idea not to start at the maximum manual listings, but at some point below them. Even nominally identical guns can, will and do respond differently to a given load and if the gun at hand is a picky eater it's far better to find out in a painless manner.

The handgun reloaders of this country have lost access to a number of longtime favorite powders that include such examples as the Swedish powders from Norma and Bofors — the latter having been sold under the Alcan name — and a number of good performers from makers such as Winchester-Western. Powders tend to appear less frequently than they are discontinued and one of the few new powders in recent times is Du Pont's Hi-Skor 800-X, a slower-burning powder than the same maker's 700-X.

The preliminary work I've done with 800-X indicates it to be a most promising powder for use in the larger magnum cases. It's a bit bulky so that performance is limited in small-capacity cases such as the 9mmP. With lightweight bullets in the .41 magnum nothing else comes even close to it, although it produces a stunning muzzle blast in the shortest barrels.

It's a good idea to retain your older editions of the handbooks and manuals since such works tend to drop listings of discontinued powders promptly and the day may come when it's quite handy to be able to look up load data for a powder no longer made.

Unless afflicted with the acid residue problem discussed earlier, powders tend to bear up well in extended storage. I've cans here that date back prior to WWII and the powder seems to work as well as the same number fresh off the shelf. Much the same is true of primers if they are left in the original packages — as they certainly should be! — and stored in conditions of moderate temperature and humidity.

# CHAPTER 12

# INDOOR ARTILLERY

*This Daisy Model 717 is my favorite fly-swatter: an operation customarily pursued without use of pellets. Once cocked, the side lever is given one fast flick and the muzzle is slowly and patiently moved to within an inch or two of the intended client. A touch of the trigger at that point disintegrates the insect by the force of the air blast alone. It is most gratifyingly effective against cockroaches who fancy themselves safe in a remote corner.*

I**T IS ENTIRELY** logical and predictable that the more ardent handgunners, locked in by inclement weather or other uncontrollable factors, may yearn to ply their craft at suitably reduced levels of energy. To this end, quite a lot of ingenuity has been expended down the years and I tend to doubt if the end is in sight.

Daisy at one time produced a small pistol they called the Targeteer, faintly resembling a long-barreled Colt Woodsman, made up of nickel-plated steel stampings. It was cocked for firing by pulling the slide/barrel assembly rearward and the projectiles were tiny spheres. During the brief heyday of the Targeteer, special ammo was marketed for it, but in point of fact common #6 shot works acceptably well. Its report is nearly inaudible, with accuracy a little dubious and the power of the tiny pellets is hardly sufficient to puncture a small toy balloon.

In the years before WWII the Stoeger catalog listed a tiny pistol powered by rubber bands that also propelled a small pellet about the size of a #6 to respectable levels of

## Can A Dedicated Handgunner Find Interest And Happiness In Delivering Energy A Fraction Of A Foot-Pound At A Time? Anything Is Possible!

Above, Daisy's long-extinct Targeteer resembled a Colt Woodsman in general lines and shot #6 shotgun pellets. Below, the .45 size of Supreme rubber bullets, as loaded into .45 ACP brass. Flash holes have been opened to .1495-inch with a #25 drill bit to avoid primer backup and the modified cases are striped with a red felt-tip marker for identification.

accuracy. They were said to be capable of potting flies most of the time at short range. I never encountered one of those, although I've always felt the concept held a lot of interest. We'll get back to mechanical flyswatting in a bit.

The typical handgunner who owns and has become fairly competent with things such as .44 magnum revolvers has an understandable tendency to view pygmy-powered pistols with amused contempt. That is an attitude that can lead to some pretty rude awakenings and rueful reassessments. You have my sincere word on that score.

I just looked and yup, it's still there: a small scar on the palm of my left hand, half an inch down from the juncture between the second and third finger, shaped much like a single parenthesis and with a radius pretty close to .110-inch. There was no need to employ measuring devices to verify that. It's all on mental tape; on the permanent iridium tape that is not in the least apt to fade.

That particular scar commemorates the exact moment at which I acquired vast and utterly indelible respect for fast-moving objects, never mind at all how ridiculously minute and impalpable the weight of such things might be.

The year was 1948, or perhaps early in 1949. I had stumbled upon a Benjamin caliber .22 pneumatic pistol that was for sale at about $7.50 and, quite miraculously, had been able to pony up the price to assume the light bur-

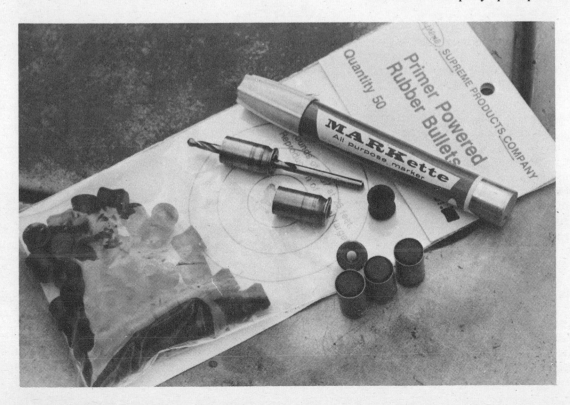

CCI's current rimfire line includes .22 Mini Caps in short cases (left) and long cases (right). The latter is termed *zimmer patrone,* German for "room cartridge." Both are modest in report, recoil and penetration. The longer case avoids a lot of fouling problems in guns normally used for the .22 long rifle cartridge.

den of its ownership. Then as now I was insensately beguiled by maverick concepts and that all ended up in a small research quest that established that #0 empty gelatin capsules, to be had at modest cost from the local pharmacy, were a delightfully precise fit in the bore of a .22 air pistol.

On the purchasing safari to the druggist, I'd taken along a small pocket caliper to check dimensions rather than the actual Benjamin, by way of allaying the concern of the pharmacist; a notably flighty soul whose name was and perhaps still is Karl Dobyns. I had reasons. On an earlier occasion I'd needed a small amount of potassium nitrate for making up a photographic print toner whose formula I'd come upon in a magazine. I'd tried to buy an ounce of the stuff and Dobyns had explained he couldn't sell me that particular chemical because, "...if you were to add certain other chemicals, you could use it to make *gunpowder!"* It carried no weight when I assured him I already had gunpowder and I only wanted the saltpeter for making up print toner.

At any rate, I'd gotten back home with a few dozen of the zero-size capsules and it appeared the calipers had not lied. They fitted into the chamber of the Benjamin quite nicely and it only remained to verify that they would go down the bore and emerge. Meditatively, mind on other matters, I gave the pump a couple of strokes, cupped left palm over the muzzle to catch the capsule for further use, and snapped the trigger.

I caught the capsule, right enough! The hemispherical nose sheared off on impact and the sides drilled through a heavy callous I had there at the time and on down through the dermal layers to a depth of nearly .25-inch. I plucked the remains free and proceeded to bleed like a stuck hog for a lengthy while, meanwhile making comments grossly inappropriate for quoting in the well-mannered tome at hand.

I don't have one on hand to toss onto the scale but I'd guess an empty #0 capsule might weigh about .2 grain at the outside, probably less. What its muzzle velocity might be on two pumps from a now-vintage Benjamin pneumatic pistol is anyone's guess and yours would be at least as valid as mine. The point to bear thoughtfully in mind is that even the most ephemeral artifact packs a lot of pizzazz when it's moving fast.

A decade and a bit went past and the folks up at CCI came out with a practice projectile they called the Red-Jet, made of wax dyed red in an assortment of diameters from .30 to .45 or so. They sent me samples, along with helpful instruction sheets on how to construct a suitable backstop by draping bits of rug over wooden dowels supported

rdest Shooting, Safest,
Economical Air Pistol
Target Practice and
or three pumps give
verage use.   Patridge

As illustrated in a 1935 edition of Stoeger's Shooter's Bible, here is an early version of the Benjamin air pistol that shot an empty #0 gelatin capsule into my left palm. After I'd healed a bit, the capsules were filled with artist's oil pigments in assorted vivid shades for an impromptu investigation into varmint-branding.

horizontally. The Red-Jets were powered solely by the force of a primer in the given case and they didn't weigh much.

Gripped by zeal to try out the new gizmos, I quested about the basement for bits of scrap carpet and, finding none, made use of some towels that were in the laundry hamper in lieu thereof. After firing several rounds to good effect it occurred to me to see how the towels were faring. Thus it came to pass that I had to explain to my wife by my first marriage how it had come to pass that some of her recently purchased bath towels had caliber .45 moth holes in them, despite being woven of cotton and moth-safe by usual expectations. The same lady and I remain in precarious wedded bliss down to the present moment which, in my book, gives her useful credentials toward sainthood.

The CCI Red-Jets have long since drifted over into the Twilight Zone and onward into status as collector items, I guess. You can achieve much the same effect by pressing a primed case down into a cake of paraffin wax. If the wax is moderately warm, it cuts more easily.

It is generally true of sub-squib loads such as these, with power furnished solely by the primer, that the point of impact will be somewhat lower than with conventional loads. The usual explanation is that recoil is much lower and the upward impetus to the barrel does not "throw" the lightweight bullet as high as it would a heavier one.

A further problem is that sub-squib loads usually show a considerable amount of primer set-back; sometimes enough to interfere with cylinder rotation. The remedy for that is to enlarge the flash hole in the case head and that in turn necessitates marking such modified cases in a manner distinctive enough to prevent their future use in making up conventional loads. I usually stuff the cases onto the K-Spinner mandrel and apply ink from a felt-tipped marker or a dab or Prussian blue oil paint, allowing the latter to dry thoroughly before further use.

After extensive firing of indoor practice loads, it is an exceptionally good idea to clean the chambers and bore thoroughly before going on to fire conventional ammo.

Speer still markets plastic cases and plastic bullets for use in .38/.357 and in .44 Special/magnum guns as well as plastic bullets for use in .45 ACP/Auto Rim. With a good backstop — best not to use bath towels! — these are almost infinitely reusable. Both sizes of the cases have primer pockets dimensioned to accept the large pistol primer size and the magnum type is customarily employed although any temptation to enrich performance with just a tiny squinch of powder should be uhh personally resisted.

Given practice on a fanatically dedicated level, some really goshawful expertise can be honed up with such loads. Bill Jordan uses — or at least used to use — wax bullets in his eminently memorable exhibitions and would work his relentless way from pie plates down to saccharine tablets, firing at distances of six or eight feet, always from the hip. The silver-tongued devil would beguile some comely young damsel up from the audience to hold the aluminum pie plate, which would be drilled awesomely by the wax bullet, upon which *Le Maestro* would assure the pop-eyed lass, "Yo' showed real courage theah...po' judgment, but *real courage!*" If he ever missed a shot on any of his countless performances when he served as roving ambassador of good will for the National Rifle Association, the word of it never reached my ears. I note all that, not so much for the sake of Jordan's ego as for reassurance that

*Is the .22 Hornet an indoor cartridge? Well, under suitable conditions, yes it is. The .22 size of air gun pellets can be reverse-seated in the mouths of primed cases for use in .22 Hornet Contender barrels with decent short-range accuracy.*

such efforts have a practical and useful amount of potential value.

Steve Herrett uses wax bullet loads extensively in working up designs for some of his custom handgun stocks. His procedure is to tack or tape a common playing card to the wall, stand off at a suitable distance and make instinctive stab-shots at it, noting the resulting point of impact. When he hits upon a stock contoured so as to dump the coal right down the chute by that approach he figures he has a good design there and I tend to agree he's probably correct in so assuming. If you'd ever wondered why Herrett stocks perform so well, now you know.

If leaky memory can be relied upon — and sometimes it cannot! — I believe I cranked in a photo earlier of the primer-powered rubber bullets currently being marketed by Supreme Products Company (1830 South California Avenue, Monrovia, CA 91016). They are put up in fifty-packs in two sizes; one for the .38/.357 and the other for dual employment in .44 or .45 sizes in their various permutations. These perform extremely well and the resilient projectiles are virtually indestructible although by no manners of means unloseable.

The Supreme folks sent me some samples to try out and I put some up in .45 ACP cases for use in the .45 Combat Masterpiece — my term for the considerably modified S&W Model 1917 cut down to four inches in the barrel, illustrated elsewhere here. It makes a really great load in that gun and, after preliminary shakedown tests, I ambled across the street to show it to my neighbor, a retired Gyrene jet-jockey. He was duly impressed and intrigued, as I knew he'd be. Pointing to one of the nauseous indigenous land snails that was millimetering its turgid way across his

driveway, he asked if it could put one of those away. I said there was one way to find out and cut down on the critter, double-action from the hip and splattered it to slimy smithereens in a fan-shaped fallout pattern. Jordan Himself couldn't've done much better. The only small flaw in the ointment was that the joyously rebounding projectile ricocheted off the drive into my neighbor's garage. He has the second-messiest garage on our small street. He has assured me that, if he ever comes across it, he'll return it to its rightful place in the first-messiest garage...

I really like these little rubber bullets. As with most such affairs, they benefit from having the flash holes enlarged. Penetration is about 1.5 inches in styrofoam plastic, urgently suggesting/demanding that they be used with all cautious care. The accuracy potential is excellent, although at the usual lowered point of impact. The instructions say each bullet is good for, "...in excess of 500 firings." I can believe that with no strain, so long as you don't lose it along the way.

Warren Center tells me that the .22 Hornet barrel has been one of the most popular chamberings for the T/C Contender, ever since it was launched in 1967 and down to the present. I can certainly see why and I'm glad because it has given that spunky little cartridge a badly needed further lease on life and it's a round *par excellence* in the Contender. With the right loads and a decent scope atop the barrel half-inch groups at fifty yards are reasonable expectations. I should qualify that by noting it's in reference to the ten-inch bull barrel.

Given a Contender with a barrel for .22 Hornet, you can have other innocent merriment, as well. It can be used for firing pellets nominally manufactured for and intended for

*One of the old, ultra-short CB cap cases was used to make this homemade dipper. With that much Bullseye powder, reversed pellet blew hole in board.*

use in air guns, with one important qualification: If you seat such pellets with the hollow skirt to the rear, you're quite apt to blow the little noses clean off, leaving the rest of the pellet lodged at some point downbore to pose a serious threat in firing the next shot. The easier, simpler, much more practical approach is to seat the air gun pellet in the .22 Hornet case mouth with skirts to the fore. When thus done, it goes up the barrel and out the muzzle with few if any problems. Visual checks of the bore after firing are sensible precautions.

In this application a tiny-tiny amount of powder can prove useful. Specifically, somewhere between .25-grain and .5-grain of Bullseye and yes, you're right: That can be a bit of a challenge to dispense uniformly. If in doubt, stay with the primer alone. The flash hole will need little or no enlargement and, if enlarged, the case should be branded with obvious identification as discussed earlier.

The air gun pellets that have worked the best for me in such maverick applications have been the .22 size by Benjamin. Short-range accuracy can be downright mind-boggling and what is even more so is the eerie silence of the report. Admittedly my ears are dreadfully lo-fi but, even so, the loudest noise produced in firing these is usually the sound of the reversed projectile striking something. Even powered by a small rifle primer alone, these are apt to penetrate the .25-inch lumber of an old apple crate if you have one of those antique collectibles around — I have several. If you get the chance and manage to pink a house mouse successfully with one of these, you will have little left to take to your neighborhood taxidermist. A reversed air gun pellet can be regarded for all intents and purposes as a sort of teeny-bopper Spelunker, particularly if launched at respectable velocities.

Earlier in the chapter I vowed we'd take up power fly-swatting and I've not forgotten that. In all fairness, however, I must issue a warning: Once mastered, the practice tends to become intensely addictive. It is by no means restricted to the common house-fly and it is at least equally applicable to sow-bugs, cockroaches, mosquitoes, tent caterpillars and so on, *ad infinitum.*

In Chuck Karwan's guest chapter I noted I seldom buy or shop for guns at the retail level. I do make exceptions, however. At least twice in the recent decade I went that far

and yes, anyone who'd go that far wouldn't stop there, probably. One example was the Daisy Model 717. I wanted one of those so badly I could taste it and my contacts at the Daisy works are somewhat short of doodley-zilch. So I shelled forth fifty-odd bucks and got one and hardly had it unpacked from the shipping container when a scion grabbed it, dropped it, and caused a dire trauma to its rear sight. I got it back to functioning condition, albeit a bit woggled-about in appearance. Even so, it is a pretty nice short-range target pistol, tautly curtailed in power but gratifying in accuracy.

I'd guess I've shot the Daisy M717 upward of fifty times empty for every time I've triggered it with a pellet in the chamber. It is of the pneumatic rather than spring-piston design which means it causes no harm if you shoot it sans pellet. Doing so unleashes a pretty savage blast of released air from its muzzle; more than sufficient to discorporate a fly or other small bug to component atoms, or at least molecules, within a distance of one inch or so.

If you really hanker to disintegrate an offending insect to its primal protons and electrons, there's nothing else around that functions one-nineteenth so well as a stoutly-pumped Sheridan air rifle, but that takes some amount of effort and, unless we feel sharp and urgent need of exercise for its own therapeutic sake, well...

The M717 Daisy needs but a cock of the bolt sleeve and a single easy stroke of the side-cocking lever and it's ready to go for the next few minutes. Pressure tends to bleed off fairly quicky if your intended quarry takes alarm and flies away. If that happens, another quick flick of the pump lever readies it to deal with a client coming along later.

Power fly-swatting knows no open season, nor closed season. There is no bag limit. You needn't worry if the target is cock or hen. You need no license. In parts of the world such as the one in which I reside, the sport is wide-open the year around, if not longer. The cost out of pocket is non-existent, once you've acquired the gun in the first place. Your projectile is, quite literally, as free as the air you breathe. There is, as you might expect, one small amount of bad news and I'll try to break that to you as gently as I can manage: You can write off hopes of achieving immortality in the Boone & Crockett record books, for the good and sufficient reason that your trophy tends to self-destruct at the instant of harvesting.

Sorry about that...

*Primer alone mushrooms pellet to shape shown and with the tiny amount of Bullseye, you get the larger lower crater with 1½-inch penetration in duct seal.*

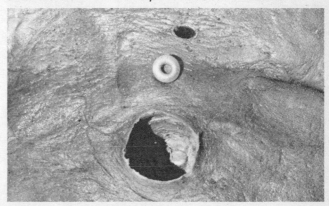

# CHAPTER 13

# RIMFIRE HANDGUNS

## You Can't Reload The Spent Cases, But The Loaded Ammo Is Priced Fairly Painlessly

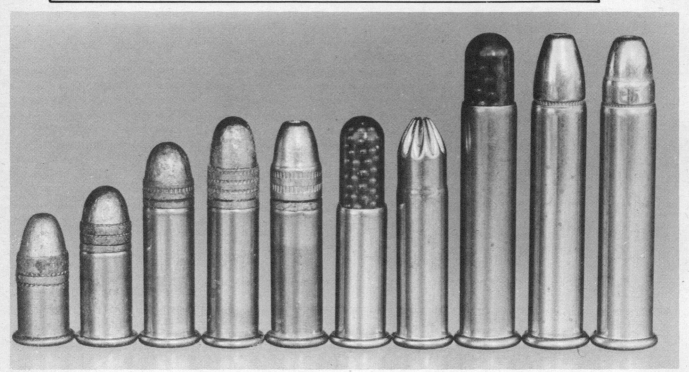

*A representative sampling of typical rimfire ammunition includes (1) a CB cap in the old extra-short case; a .22 short; a .22 long; a .22 long rifle with solid bullet; a .22 long rifle hollow point; a CCI .22 LR shot load with plastic capsule; a .22 shot load with crimped case mouth; a CCI .22 WMRF shot load; a CCI .22 Winchester magnum rimfire with hollow-point bullet and a CCI .22 WMRF carrying a solid bullet.*

**M**OST RIMFIRE handguns of the present fire caliber .22 bullets with varying amounts of velocity and force. It was not always so. In the Nineteenth Century and the early part of this one, larger rimfire cartridges saw considerable use. A recent edition of Barnes' *Cartridges of the World* lists no less than twenty-five different American rimfire cartridges in caliber .25 up to caliber .56 sizes.

The several types, sizes and varieties of .22s seem to have inherited the rimfire world, in rifles as well as handguns. The influencing factor was probably a matter of sheer logistics. No dealer cares to stock a cartridge unless he can count upon a reasonable traffic in it. Gunmakers are not inclined to produce a model for which ammo is difficult to obtain for the simple reason that such guns would sell poorly, if at all.

The rimfire handguns offer a lot of attractive advantages, as a group. With some exceptions, the guns are relatively inexpensive, as is the ammunition. Their reports and recoil are modest to moderate, making them superbly suited for the beginner or the occasional shooter. Their capability as to accuracy usually ranges from decent and acceptable up through eye-popping incredibility. If the intended game is target shooting, a .22 will leave its mark in the paper as nicely as a .38, with the stipulation that a larger bullet diameter may come a trifle closer to cutting the line to count as a higher score.

The .22 BB and CB caps stand at the bottom of the peck-order in this group. Originally put up in cases measuring about .270-inch from base to mouth, the bullet for the BB cap was a stubby, lightweight affair while the CB carried a bullet more or less the size, weight and shape of the more

Really too pretty to fire, Ruger made a limited run of 5000 stainless steel versions of their Standard Model auto in mid-1982 at the time it was phased out and replaced by the Mark II model.

A Mark II Ruger, left, with the earlier Mark I bull barrel, shows how the medallion changed sides along the way and shifted from black-on-silver to silver-on-black. Note slide lock added to Mark II.

Ruger's Single-Six .22 rimfire revolver, here in the New Model, can be changed back and forth between .22 LR and .22 WMRF by the simple operation of switching factory-fitted cylinders.

familiar .22 short. In recent years the BB cap has been phased out and the CB cap is now loaded in cases about .410-inch in length, the same as used for the .22 short. CCI loads the same bullet, at a roughly comparable power level, into cases about .605-inch in length, the same size used for the .22 long and .22 long rifle.

CCI designates that load as their Index #0038 Long CB (Zimmer Patrone). The last is German, roughly translating to room cartridge. The concept makes excellent sense and I suspect that CCI has been pleased but puzzled by the demand for it. A friend who'd probably prefer to remain unidentified uses these in goodly quantity for informal target work at a sturdy backstop in his urban garage and the occasional muted snap of their report goes unnoticed by his neighbors amid the general noise pollution that abounds these days.

Loads put up in the .270-inch or .410-inch cases, if fired in any quantity from a chamber cut for use with the .605-inch cases, will leave a hard ring of powder and primer residue at the mouth within the chamber that resists removal fairly stubbornly. That poses a problem when you go to fire a load in the .605-inch case, since it may prove quite difficult to chamber it until the fouling has been removed. By offering the Long CB, CCI makes it possible to skirt neatly around the whole problem, assuming you wish to operate at lower levels of noise and velocity.

The .22 short remains alive and well, a reliable seller on the lists of ammo makers everywhere, in standard-velocity and high-velocity loadings, with solid or hollow-point bullets. There are a few autoloading pistols chambered for exclusive use of the .22 short, usually intended for Olympic rapid-fire competition or practice.

The .22 long survives down to the present, albeit rather precariously. It carries the lighter bullet used in the .22 short — typically about 29 grains — put up in the .605-inch case and driven by a fairly generous charge of powder to velocities well beyond those of the .22 short, even in its high-velocity versions.

One might assume that such a load would be popular with rimfire handgunners, but in this instance one would be incorrect. With few exceptions, .22 longs will not function through autoloaders, although they'll perform quite nicely in revolvers.

The .22 long rifle is probably King of the Mountain, as

Early in 1978 Colt reintroduced their .22 Service Model Ace, with target-sighted slide similar to that of their Gold Cup .45 models. To the present, this is the only .22 LR auto remaining in the Colt catalog. The stocks are a homemade set in Hawaiian koa.

far as rimfire cartridges are concerned. Put up in the .605-inch case, its solid bullet runs about 40 grains, its hollow point more like 37 or 38 grains. Under ideal conditions the .22 LR cartridge is one of the most accurate short-range cartridges in the world and its group-sprawl at the greater distances isn't all that disgraceful.

It is a fact not as widely known as it should be, but one should never try to pull bullets from rimfire cartridges by means of inertia-type bullet pullers, since there is a severe risk that the cartridge may be set off by transmitted impact. If you must remove a bullet from a rimfire load, drill a hole in a piece of hardwood about the thickness of the case length using a #2 drill bit. Insert the cartridge in the hole, fasten the wood in a vise and apply a pair of pliers to the exposed bullet, using patient care and — by all means! — wear a good pair of safety glasses. Bullets thus pulled and put on the scales may register weights a few grains away from manufacturer's specifications.

A recent sub-group of the .22 LR is what we might term the super-speedy types. First of these on the scene was CCC's Stinger, making its debut as 1976 faded into 1977. On a recent project involving pull-downs of several such loads, the Stinger bullet turned out to weigh 30.8 grains.

Winchester-Western brought forth a comparable entry they called the Xpediter with a bullet that, when pulled, weighs 30.0 grains; specified at 29.0 grains in their catalog.

Remington, not to be outdone, brought forth first the Yellow Jacket with hollow-point bullets weighing 32.5 grains on my scales, followed by a solid-bullet version called the Viper. Along the way Federal produced some .22 LR loads that carried bullets of about 38.3 grains, making hardly any fuss over them. In the 1.75-inch barrel of the

Freedom Arms Model FA-L minivolver (if I may coin the term), the Federal #514 load with its 38.3-grain bullet hit 867 feet per second (fps) for a five-shot average, good for 64 foot-pounds of energy (fpe); it shaded all the rest, tallies for which ran as follows:

W-W Xpediter, 30.0 grains, 970 fps/63 fpe;
Remington Yellow Jacket, 32.5 grains, 905/59;
CCI Stinger, 30.8 grains, 923/58;
CCI Long CB, 30.6 grains, 453/14.

As barrels get longer, the Stinger comes into its own and outdistances the pack. On a later wring-out session for the recently introduced Mark II Standard Model Ruger .22 auto, with its 4.75-inch barrel, five-shot averages ran like this:

Remington Yellow Jacket, 1209 fps/106 fpe;
Remington Viper, 1171/110;
W-W Xpediter, 1170/91;
CCI Stinger, 1449/144;
Federal #510 Lightning, 1120/107;
Federal #514 Power-Flite, 1106/104;
Remington High-Velocity, 1119/111.

At the same session I had a prototype Super-14 Contender barrel chambered for the .22 LR and it delivered the Stingers at an average pace of 1643 fps. Taking its bullet weight as 30.8 grains, that works out to 184.6 fpe; considerably more than marginally impressive in my book!

A final variant of the .22 LR is the shot loads made up for use in such chambers. CCI does these with a plastic capsule while most other makers merely put a fold-crimp in an

This is the floating chamber that's used in the Service Model Ace to develop sufficient backthrust to work the action. Chamber is installed at the rear of its travel.

extra-length case to encapsulate a modest pinch of #12-size shot pellets. The latter will lead up the rifling pretty severely. The CCI capsules avoid that problem. In either example, net results tend to be disappointing. Few if any of the wee pellets will even get through the paper-thin walls of an aluminum beverage can at point-blank distance.

That is not always a total liability. Several years ago, while off on a shooting safari, friend Tom Hayden and I stopped our vehicles and knocked off a can apiece of cola beverage. With the cans empty I began tossing them skyward and potting at the airborne containers with my Colt Woodsman. After just a bit of such joyous pursuits a green genie materialized amid tendrils of curling fumes. It was a game warden with all the due and valid credentials and he was intent to nail my hide to the nearest wall for endangering anyone and everyone within a one-mile radius with my irresponsible pistolry.

With some minor difficulty I broke into his impassioned diatribe and begged that he merely take a thoughtful look at one of the cans that'd served as targets. Reluctantly he did so and ground to a halt like a run-down, crank-wound phonograph. The cans showed innumerable tiny dings from the shambling mini-pellets. I displayed the unfired remains of the box and at length he took his grudging leave and let us live.

If you were about to ask, my shooting buddy Tom Hayden has never even met any of Henry Fonda's children.

Over and beyond the .22 LR in its many forms, we have the .22 WMRF or .22 magnum cartridge with its case about 1.050 inches in length, available with solid or hollow-point bullets. The .22 mag can and does muster an impressive amount of ker-zopp. It operates through bore dimensions identical to those favored by the .22 LR, so that gunmakers such as Sturm, Ruger & Co. can offer their Single-Six with auxiliary cylinders to permit optional use of .22 LR or .22 WMRF out of the same basic chassis by means of a simple switch of cylinders.

In the matter of handguns for rimfire rounds, I've worked with several down the years and can offer my impressions for such value as you may choose to put upon them. In revolvers, Colt makes their Diamondback with a six-inch barrel that is just a joy and a delight. It is pretty close to a scaled-down version of their Python and, fed the load it likes, it will hold every hit on a dime-sized circle at twenty yards, with contemptuous ease.

Smith & Wesson makes their K-22 Masterpiece with its six-inch barrel and a four-inch version they call the .22 Combat Masterpiece. Both are fine pistols by any standard; accurate and reliably trouble-free. To the present Ruger does not make a double-action revolver in .22 rimfire, but they have the single-action Single-Six, as noted. The Model 904 Harrington & Richardson has a heavy barrel and a nine-shot cylinder. I find it does fine with high-velocity .22 LR ammo, but tends to keyhole with standard-velocity loads. Accuracy with the high-velocity loads in the M504 is decently acceptable.

Ruger's great success with their .22 autoloaders may be the reason they've never gone to a .22 DA revolver. Quite recently they updated the Standard Model .22 auto that's been a best-seller since its debut in 1949. The magazine capacity is increased by one round, from nine to ten and they've added a lock-open feature to hold the bolt back after firing the last round. A pair of shallow scallops on each side at the rear of the receiver give a better grip on the cocking ears of the bolt. As a final salute to the original version, five thousand guns were produced in stainless steel, bearing William B. Ruger's signature and carrying a red eagle emblem on the stock medallion, much in the manner of the originals prior to the death of Alexander Sturm, about 1951. At that time Bill Ruger changed the color to black in somewhat the same vein as the color shift from red to black for Rolls-Royce nameplates at the time of Royce's death.

Initially Ruger Standard Model autos carried their single medallion on the LH stock and it was a colored bird — eagle? hawk? arguments run either way — against a silver background. Later, that was changed to a silver bird against a colored field and the medallion shifted to the RH stock. Whether all the shifts occurred simultaneously, I can't say.

There are other fine .22 LR handguns and the one High Standard called The Victor is one of the best I've encountered. It is extremely accurate and, as I believe I've noted elsewhere, it's capable of holding groups to about one inch at fifty yards with the right load.

There can be a world of difference, accuracywise, in what you put through any .22 rimfire, be it handgun or rifle. A bit of comparison testing will usually disclose the one the given gun likes best and it probably will be a different load from the favorite of some other gun. It is most definitely a test worth running.

This shows the floating chamber removed from the barrel, together with the ejector of the Service Model Ace. Powder residue tends to build up in the mating surfaces to produce stoppages, but use of Break Free, as discussed, minimizes the problem.

# CHAPTER 14

*Dan Wesson Arms revolvers, such as this .357 magnum, offer vast versatility by easy changes to barrels of assorted lengths and, for good measure, it's just as easy to shift to the quick-change stock of choice.*

# SWAPPABLE BARREL SYSTEMS

**T**HERE ARE several avenues available whereby a gun of a given nominal chambering can be rigged up to fire cartridges other than the one originally intended. The concept dates back for so many years I wouldn't even try to pinpoint its origin. Conversion kits from the various O-frame Colts — of which the Model 1911/A1 is the most familiar example — have been in the state of the art since some time before I acquired my first handgun. There have been kits for firing the .22 LR cartridge in the .45 ACP guns and, as I recall, other kits to convert some if not all of the Colt Ace guns — a .22 LR on the O-frame — to fire .45 ACP or perhaps even the Colt .38 Super cartridge.

As a general rule it takes quite a bit of complex doing to switch between the .45 ACP and the .38 Super or 9mm Luger models. That is due to a change in the location of the ejector more than anything else. I believe it can be done. I think I've read that it has been done. It is my impression that it's not done easily.

Before WWII Colt had an O-frame they called the Colt Ace that fired the .22 LR cartridge from a barrel with integral chamber. Not many of those were made and I never happened to own one, but a friend had one in the early Fifties and I used to shoot it occasionally with great enjoyment. It was capable of respectably decent accuracy, comparing favorably with nearly any other handgun handling the .22 LR cartridge.

Along about that time — the late Thirties — the concept

# A Look At Several Approaches For Firing
# Several Different Cartridges From One Gun

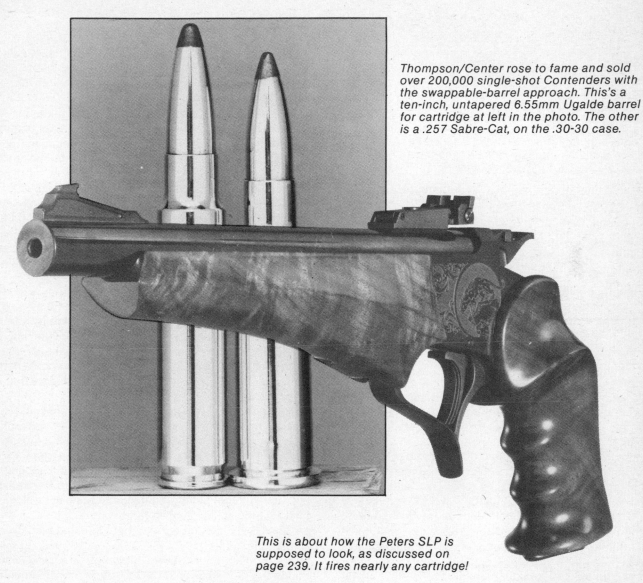

Thompson/Center rose to fame and sold over 200,000 single-shot Contenders with the swappable-barrel approach. This's a ten-inch, untapered 6.55mm Ugalde barrel for cartridge at left in the photo. The other is a .257 Sabre-Cat, on the .30-30 case.

This is about how the Peters SLP is supposed to look, as discussed on page 239. It fires nearly any cartridge!

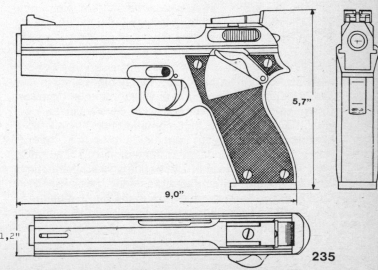

of the floating chamber produced the Colt Service Ace .22, simultaneously siring the latterday conversion kits for transmuting the .45 ACP into a .22 LR auto. In recent years Colt reintroduced the .22 Service Ace, complete with a slide that fairly well duplicates the slide from their .45 Gold Cup target models. As with all of the Service Ace guns and the recent .22 LR conversion kits, this embodies the floating chamber. With the pensioning off of the Woodsman line a decade or so ago, the Service Ace is the only .22 LR auto remaining in the Colt line at present.

The principle of the floating chamber is that high-pressure powder gasses get down into the crevice between the front of the chamber and the rear of the barrel proper to give the floating chamber a lusty boot to the rear which is arrested by an integral lug. As a result the rearward impe-

*Above left, the National Match bushing and, right, the collet-type bushing, as used on O-frame Colts. Below, my .38 Super with Bar-Sto .38S barrel in place, original factory barrel on top and the 1:10 Bar-Sto 9mm barrel with collet bushing in front.*

tus is amplified vastly, assuring that the slide will go back all the way and, meanwhile, generating a subjectively felt recoil that is not too much less than you'd get when firing .45 ACP loads.

Therefore, the .45 handgunner who can't resurrect his spent brass can fire at moderate cost in reasonable simulation of the sensations of using .45 ACP. Even today a well-connected and resourceful reloader can come surprisingly close to making up .45 ACP reloads at not much over the retail cost of .22 LR, provided no allowance is included for person-hours expended, power for the melting pot and so on.

A well-tuned and lovingly maintained .45 ACP, working with the loads that pamper its individual prejudices, will probably turn in tighter groups than the Service Ace or any other O-frame carrying one of the conversion units with the floating chamber. I hate to say it, but honest candor permits no choice: It tends to crud up and stop working in the course of firing a comparatively modest number of rounds of .22 LR. There is a remedy for that problem that works fairly well and that consists of cleaning all the mating surfaces carefully, then gooping them liberally with Break Free, allowing the medication to age and work its way into the pores of the metal for a day or so, if possible. That does not help the accuracy greatly, but it does tend to keep the system firing through a usefully larger number of rounds. If you were about to mourn the fact that the original, solid-chamber .22 Ace is no longer readily to be had in the marketplace, I couldn't agree more fulsomely. While

we're at it, I wish Colt would bring back one or more of the Woodsman models.

There is at least one firm that has carved out a substantial business in producing drop-in barrels for the O-frame Colts and other guns. I refer to Bar-Sto Precision Machine, operating until recently out of beautiful downtown Burbank and currently situated at 73377 Sullivan Road, Twentynine Palms, CA 92277. Bar-Sto barrels have earned an impressive amount of legendary charisma, every bit of it fully justified, in my personal experience. The barrels are crafted out of an exotic alloy of stainless steel that can and usually does group like no-tomorrow. Not all stainless barrels possess this engaging trait, but Bar-Sto barrels surely do.

Part of the secret of the success of the Bar-Sto barrels lies in the fact that Irv Stone makes use of the ledge at the front of the chamber to aid in supporting the chambered cartridge. That distinction is particularly telling in the example of the .38 Colt Super cartridge. How much difference does it make? In checking out the Bar-Sto barrel for my .38 Super, I put it on a Ransom Rest and ran five rounds of Super Vel factory loads through it, carrying the 112-grain JSP bullets. The resulting group at fifty yards spanned just 1-5/16 inches between centers. Reinstalling the original barrel, firing the same load off the Ransom Rest, the group spanned a trifle over eighteen inches.

Stone started out fitting his Bar-Sto barrels with the collet-type bushing introduced in the Colt MK IV Series '70 guns and even went on to provide collet bushings on barrels for Commander-length barrels, oblivious of the fact that Colt said that was impossible. Apparently a long succession of dunderheaded customers insisted upon banging the collet bushings free of the barrels, breaking fingers off in the process — collet fingers, that is. Finally Stone sighed wearily and recognized the innate stupidity of some handgunners and switched back to exclusive use of the National Match-type bushing. That marked a mournful day on the calendar for the rest of us, but so it goes, no?

Even with the NM bushings, the Bar-Sto barrels do not perform all that dreadfully. I have one in 9mmP chambering with the NM bushing that recently came quite close to matching the colleted barrel for the .38 Super in a shoot-off, and I don't know about you, but I find that notably impressive.

While it is a considerable challenge — or practically impossible — to convert a .45 O-frame to .38 Super or 9mmP, and vice versa, it usually presents little or no difficulty to switch an O-frame from .38 Super to 9mmP or vice versa. Not long after I got my .38 Super stainless steel barrel from Bar-Sto I got another in 9mmP. Like the .38 Super, the 9mm barrel had the earlier collet-type bushing basically identical to that introduced by Colt in their MK IV Series '70 guns. The 9mm barrel was rifled at a pitch of one turn in ten inches or 1:10 as it's usually written.

Installed in the basic .38 Super gun, the 9mm barrel did not feed and function with the reliability I'd hoped for when using the original .38 Super magazine, but when I managed to obtain a 9mm magazine the performance in that area improved sharply. The 9mm magazine has a small filler strip at the rear to compensate for the difference in length between the 9mm and .38 Super. This seems to be most helpful in assuring trouble-free functioning.

Bar-Sto can furnish barrels longer than the usual five inches of the Government Model. The added length merely projects ahead of the barrel bushing and it offers some modest gain in velocity. As an optional feature, recoil control slots can be milled in the upper surface of the longer barrels ahead of the bushing. I've never worked with one of those, but my friend the late Bill Corson did and he reported, with considerable puzzlement, that the slotted barrel seemed capable of detectably higher velocities than an identical unslotted barrel of equal length. He was unable to explain that — as I am also — but he said the difference was demonstrably repeatable, time after time; one of the baffling enigmas that ballisticians encounter now and again.

Bar-Sto likewise offers barrels chambered for the .38-45 Clerke cartridge for installation in .45 ACP O-frames. The cartridge was designed and developed by John A. "Bo" Clerke (pronounced *Clark*) several years ago; a wildcat number created by necking the .45 ACP case to accept bullets of .355-inch diameter. Since the head dimensions of the cartridge are unchanged, it works out of the original magazines used with the .45 ACP and the ejector remains functional. Conversion is a simple matter of disassembling the .45 auto and replacing its barrel with one of the .38-45 Clerke.

Sad to say, that's about the only thing that's simple in working with the .38-45 wildcat. It is tethered to the peak

*Left, one of the Texas Contender carbine conversions for the T/C Contender, here in .218 Bee. Revolver is a former Model 28 S&W, converted to .41 mag and treated to Leon Smith's barrel-change idea.*

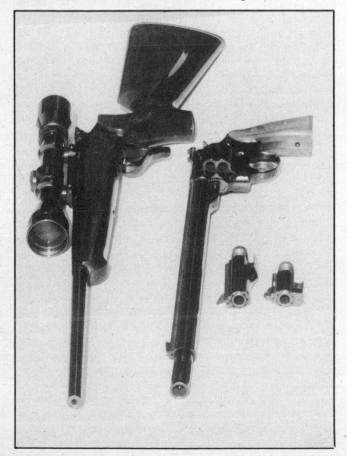

pressure limitations of its parent .45 ACP case, usually taken to be about 19,900 pounds per square inch (psi). If anyone has ever worked with a .38-45 pressure barrel, I've not heard of it. I've endeavored to hold pressures at about that level by judicious interpolation of load data for the .38 Special at levels below the +P listings in the manuals. I'm not sure if that keeps the pressures under the red line when transferred to the .38-45 case, but I'm reasonably sure of one thing: Loads at that careful and sensible level function poorly if at all in the O-frame guns with .38-45 barrel installed.

There is a good and logical reason for holding pressures down in the .38-45 and that is due to the area of case head that hangs unsupported over the feed ramp. At that point there is nothing but a small thickness of brass between ten tons of ravening pressure and the outside air. If the brass gives way, it jets a dreadful blast down into the magazine with consequences that are painfully interesting. I've had that experience exactly once and, fortunately, there was no magazine in place so that the gases had a reasonable amount of avenue for escape. Even so, they cracked both sides of a sturdy set of Jay Scott stocks and left me with a right palm that didn't stop tingling for a week or so. I note that in hopes of sparing someone else the same experience, or a worse one.

I happen to have a ten-inch bull barrel for the T/C Contender that has the bore of a .357 magnum, but it's chambered for the .38-45 Clerke case. Since its head is fully supported, it bypasses the sharp need to keep peak pressures at the 20,000 psi level. Since its groove diameter is .357-inch or so, one can make use of all the bullets for the .38 or .357 and — oddly enough — it groups extremely well with bullets in the .355-inch diameter nominally intended for use in the 9mmP. I have a Leupold M8-2X scope on that barrel in Conetrol mounts and it was my hopeful intent that it would serve as the great test vehicle of all time for checking out the .38-45 cartridge. It did serve extremely well. It's a lovely barrel and it can drive the bullets in the weight range of 80 to 90 grains forth at velocities somewhat over 2000 feet per second (fps). Groups down around one inch or even tighter are fairly common at a distance of twenty-five yards. That's all quite fine, but (sigh!) it doesn't contribute much by way of data that can be used for five-inch barrels in the O-frame autos.

I have two five-inch barrels for the .38-45 to be used in O-frame Colts, one is a Bar-Sto and the older one was made up by Bo Clerke and fitted to my M1911 (ol' Loudmouf) by Armand Swenson. They differ in headspace dimensions by a matter of about .023-inch so that cases have to be tailored for one or the other. The original Clerke barrel takes the longer headspace while the shorter loads function in either the Bar-Sto or T/CC barrel quite nicely.

The Clerke barrel is throated to accept wadcutter bullets seated to leave not too great an amount of full-diameter bullet protruding ahead of the case mouth. The Bar-Sto barrel has zilch by way of clearance for such things and the T/CC barrel not much more. In the two autos there are any number of load combos that function as manual pumpactions. That is, you shoot and then strip the slide back by hand to eject the spent case and chamber a fresh one. That's rather to the good since it avoids the problem of los-

*The Smith & Wesson Model 539 is a steel-frame version of their Model 39, likewise fitted with guarded and fully adjustable rear sight. Bar-Sto can furnish stainless 1:16 pitch barrels for this and/or the Model 59 — they're interchangeable — which will group about one inch at twenty-five yards off a rest.*

ing the painfully hand-formed cases. It sort of defeats the basic intent of the autoloading pistol, however.

I've been grappling with the .38-45 round in grim earnest since about the start of 1967, off and on in intermittent fitful sessions. I've gotten some pretty fine groups out of the T/C Contender barrel. I have yet to get a group out of either of the auto barrels that I'd feel greatly inclined to claim as my own. I've probably channeled more thin-lipped person-hours into the .38-45 project than into any other that comes to mind and have gotten back less by way of productive results, with the specific exception of the Contender barrel, for it. If you're inclined to waive the stipulation that it has to be held below the 19,900 psi peaks, I can make the cartridge self-load in either barrel. In fact, along the way I've gotten velocities and energies out of the cartridge that bleach my mane a few more shades lighter every time I happen to think about it.

In all this galling frustration, I do not seem to be alone and that is some minor consolation, certainly. I've not heard of anyone who's succeeded in taming the .38-45 into a tackdriving pussycat purring placidly at the hearth. I regard that as a small consolation; a damned small consolation.

It all distills down to this fractious fraction: If you've clean run out of reloading worlds to conquer, the .38-45 Clerke will keep you out of mischief and safe from boredom for a remarkably long and indeterminate while.

There is at least one uncharted corridor still awaiting intensive exploration. The folks up Seattle way who make the .45 Detonics have worked up a wildcat round they call the .451 Detonics magnum, based upon a case with the head dimensions of the .45 ACP, but just a bit longer. The

brass for this is produced heavier and tougher about the head so that they say the maximum working pressure is substantially higher. Presumably, such cases could be used for making up dreadnought .38-45 brass for further furious assaults on that particular battlement. I've not gone down that particular trail to the present. Right now, I'd like to just sort of lick my wounds and mutter darkly.

Case forming dies and reloading dies for the .38-45 Clerke remain available from RCBS and the easy access is via Huntington Die Specialties, Box 991, Oroville, CA 95965. As preferred, your nearby dealer can place orders through his RCBS jobber.

Bar-Sto also makes stainless barrels for the Model 1935 Browning Hi-Power and recently has developed one that fits either the Model 39 or 59 Smith & Wesson. All of these are rifled 1:16, with relatively narrow lands and wide grooves rather than the equal-width lands and grooves used by S&W. Irv Stone reports machine-rest groups with the Bar-Sto barrel in an S&W Model 59 that span one inch or less between centers. Claud Hamilton has one of these barrels in his Model 59 and has taken to sending burn-copies of one-hole groups gotten with it off the Ransom Rest. I don't kow about you, but I find that impressive.

Sterling Arms has a single-shot pistol they call the X-Caliber that is vaguely similar in appearance to the Thompson/Center Contender. We had one briefly for photographing with the firm stipulation that it should not be fired. That's the only one I've seen to date. It's said to be available in .22 LR, .22 WMRF, .357 magnum and .44 magnum and interchangeable barrels are made in lengths of eight and ten inches.

Jim Rock owns and runs Rock Pistol Manufacturing Co. at 704 East Commonwealth, Fullerton, CA 92631, producing the Merrill Sportsman single-shot pistol with barrel lengths of 9, 10¾ or 14 inches in about fourteen different calibers. The fourteen-inch is not made in .22 LR. I have one of these in .357/44 Bain & Davis, a wildcat case based on the .44 magnum, and it is capable of really outstanding accuracy and power. My barrel measures twelve inches and the load it likes is 20.0 grains of W-W 296 behind the 180-grain Speer JSP rifle bullet at .358-inch diameter. That load moves out at an average of 1760 fps/1238 fpe and groups right about one inch at fifty yards, handheld off the sandbag rest with a Leupold M8-4X scope mounted on the barrel by means of its integral tip-off grooves. That's the only barrel I've ever used in the Merrill, but I'd rate it highly satisfactory on that basis.

Leon Smith, Box 773, Redding, CA 96001 operates TLS Gunsmithing and performs a remarkable conversion on the heavy N-frame Smith & Wesson revolvers, fitting them with barrel shrouds as used with the .357 model of Dan Wesson Arms revolvers and chambering the cylinder for just about any reasonable cartridge, with interchangeable barrels in any practical length. I have one that started life as a Model 28 S&W Highway Patrolman in .357 magnum and ended up as a .41 magnum with barrels of 2¾, 4 and 16-plus inches, Mindful of Leon's surname and the source of the shrouds, I refer to this one informally as the SS&WW .41 mag and like it very much.

Early in 1982 I had a letter from Patrick J. Shanahan, president of H. Geisser, Inc., 378 West Main Street, Waukesha, WI 53186. It concerned the Peters SLP Model 02 which, as he noted, was soon to be commercially available in the United States. Made in West Germany, the self-loading pisol (SLP) is gas-operated and kits consisting of slide/barrel assemblies and magazines are planned to be made available to handle a mind-boggling variety of cartridges: 7.63mm Mauser, .30 Luger, 9mm Luger, .38 Colt Super, 9mm Winchester magnum, .44 Auto Mag, .45 ACP, .45 Winchester magnum, .22 LR, .22 Jet, .38 Special, .41 magnum and .44 magnum. Prices of the gun in various grades, fitted for one cartridge, ranged from $1445 to $1895; subject to change without notice, of course. Magazine capacity with the .45 Win mag is listed as fifteen rounds.

Another local gunsmith called from somewhere in Utah to say he had kits for firing all manner of cartridges in the .45 O-frame Colt including the 7.63mm Mauser and a cast of thousands. He said he was sending literature, but none ever arrived. To date there has been no further word on the Peters SLP either, but I'll try to include the line drawing to give you an idea of its appearance.

Needless to say, the king of swappable-barrel handguns is the Thompson/Center Contender. Serial numbers on the T/CC receivers are now running in the 200,000 brackets and Warren Center tells me they figure there are about five barrels out for each receiver. At ten inches for the average barrel, that's about 158 miles of Contender barrels, or enough to stretch from Los Angeles to San Luis Obispo or so. Correct me if I'm wrong, but I don't think any other single-shot pistol in history has sold as many units or dollar's worth, not by a monstrous margin. Quite recently, Center tells me, they've decided to offer the Super-14 barrel in .22 LR. I've worked with a prototype of that and find it extremely accurate and the CCI Stinger loads move out of it at well over 1600 fps. I've recently been working up loads for two wildcat Contender barrels: a ten-inch in 6.5mm Ugalde and a fourteen-inch in .257 Sabre-Cat. Respectively, they're made on .223 Rem and .30-30 Win cases. Case capacities are similar — typical charges come to within about 1/16-inch to the mouth of a .44 magnum case — and energy figures are running in the upper 1300 fpe brackets. As singles go, it's a tough gun to contend with.

*A product of Warren Center's notable ingenuity, here's a close look at how the T/C Contender shifts to use either rimfire or center-fire ammo. Click-detented circular insert on the hammer face can be turned half a turn — for rimfire here — to strike one but not the other of the two firing pins seen in the other photo.*

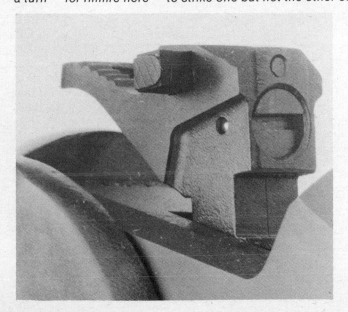
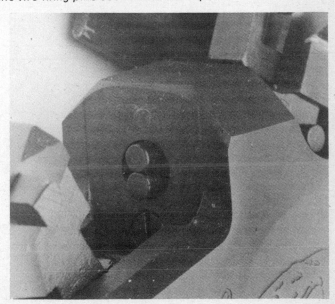

# THOUGHTS & NOTES ON HANDGUN TRAINING

## *Properly Done, A Lot Of Learning Can Be Passed Along In A Short Time*

## CHAPTER 15

*Kelly Morgan tries her first shot with a .22 long CB out of the six-inch Contender, under close supervision. Tom Ferguson comments, "Inexperienced woman students are easier to instruct because they do as told and don't think they know better." Amen!*

**O**NE OF THE more stimulating, rewarding and adventurous activities in which a reasonably adept pistolperson can indulge is the patch-cording of acquired expertise along to those whose experience in such pursuits is limited or nonexistent.

Along the way, once you acquire a useful knack for the pursuit, there is the slightly galling reflection that you can bring a totally green student, in the course of perhaps one brief afternoon, to a level of competence higher than the instructor managed to scale over the course of a number of self-taught years. Like the photographer who shoots every-

thing in color plus black-and-white, you tend to view that with mixed emulsions.

It is pertinent to the discussion to comment briefly on my own first encounters with two highly unrelated activities: chess and flying. I'd always assumed chess was terribly complicated and difficult to understand and learn. Not so said my friend of that era, a dentist named Gerry Kincannon. He gave me a fast cram course on how the pieces move and made it seem so easy I beat him on the third game we played. After that, he put his guard clear up and it didn't happen again for a whole lot of games.

For my first airplane ride, I had the bad luck to ride a

*Her first five shots on the target were a little low but fairly close together at twenty-five yards.*

North American AT-6 behind a stone-bonkers RAF flight instructor who — treacherous devil — assured me he only intended to go up, fly about a bit and come back down; no aerobatics or crazy stuff like that. The takeoff was great. I'd been daft on aircraft nearly all my life and was really relishing the new experience when the guy up front began turning it every which-way but loose, all in staccato tempo. Quickly stripped of my first enchantment, by the time I got back down my view of flying was so totally jaundiced that some of the attitude remains, almost exactly forty years later.

The obvious connection to our topic is the desirability of making shooting seem much simpler than the student expected and to avoid turning them clean off at the very start. For example, don't start them with a planet-wrecker load in the .44 magnum!

Dick Morgan and Magali Akle are a team who work at photography, screenwriting and anything else that seems apt to pay. They got in touch as a result of reading a few things I'd done for the magazine and Morgan said they were trying to settle upon a suitable small handgun for recreational shooting and to have in the event of sudden dire need. We got together and I let them try several items from my personal armory. Morgan had done a bit of shooting, long ago; Akle had never done any at all. Morgan has a heavy enthrallment for auto pistols and can't seem to shake it. Akle formed a thick rapport with the Chuck Wardized S&W Model 10 (Li'l Montgomery) practically from the instant of first encounter and well before the first session ground to its end she was shooting it to better effect than its owner usually does. I regard that with mixed emotions, as noted earlier.

It was purely a matter of doing a few demonstrations which she picked up in high fidelity and improved upon. "Inside of seven yards or so," I informed her, "only stupes and sissies use the sights." She considered that, nodded thoughtfully and filed it away with a click clearly audible to my blast-worn ears. Within half a dozen cylinderfuls she cinched down the useful ability of merely looking at something, twitching the trigger and seeing a hole materialize

*As the student's first repeater, the six-inch .22 LR Colt Diamondback is excellent. The CCI long CBs were used for the first six, shifting to standard-velocity long rifles for the rest of the rimfires.*

right *there.* Like riding a bicycle, once acquired, this seems to be a knack one does not lose easily.

Within the past week Morgan called up to advise he has a daughter named Kelly, aged 21, and he yenned to put her through the Grennell Academy of Applied Pistolcraft for Refined Young Ladies, from which Ms. Akle had matriculated so resoundingly a bit earlier. I said sure, why not? The details were arranged.

My initial impression of Kelly Morgan was that she would benefit greatly from an easy and gradual immersion into the noisy joys of handgunning. She did not seem to have the degree of case-hardened realism that Ms. Akle possesses; few have, as I stop to think about it.

With that consideration in mind, I started Kelly out with a T/C Contender carrying a .22 LR barrel and loaded it with the long CB load by CCI. I let her watch me fire a few shots with it, then gave it to her empty so she could get used to its light trigger pull in dry-fire mode. Early in the game surprises are the last thing you want, especially including rounds that fire unexpectedly.

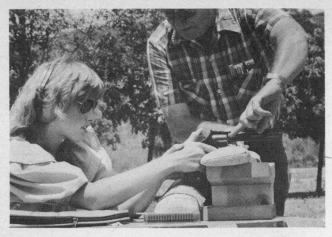

Here I'm pointing out the extreme hazards of getting an incautious finger in line with the gap between the barrel and cylinder, due to leaking hot gases there.

The student tried the .22 Diamondback off the bench in both SA mode — as here — and DA, with no need to worry about the distracting lurches and wobbles.

Left, my son Bill is giving Kelly a brief lecture on operation of the MK II Ruger .22 auto, with its slide locked back. Above, student is getting acquainted with loading .22 LRs into magazine.

Morgan drew some diagrams to show her the proper arrangement of front and rear sights with the target and we let her try a five-round group on the target off the bench. She kept them on the paper, fairly well clustered although a bit off the point of aim.

With that, I brought out the six-inch .22 LR Colt Diamondback, loading the chambers with standard-velocity long rifles and fired six rounds with it, with explanations on how the firing could be done in either SA or DA mode and the advantages of each. Again, I let her dry-fire it both ways before loading it for her first few shots.

She commented that the cartridges felt stronger than what she'd been shooting and I agreed that they were, but only slightly so; it was no big thing. After six or a dozen rounds of that, I scrounged up an empty can, set it on the ground before a good backstop and fired six shots at it by way of demonstration, using a two-handed hold from about waist level. I explained the principle of walking them into the target by observing where it hit and correcting for it slightly. This works incredibly well if you're standing on solid ground, but it doesn't work at all if you happen to be standing up in a small boat since the motion underfoot louses up your built-in computer.

Returning to the bench, she prepared to fire at the target and cupped her left hand just beneath the barrel. I pointed out the hazard of doing that, explaining that considerable quantities of hot gas and small particles blast to each side from the gap between cylinder and barrel. She accepted that. If she hadn't, I could have held a piece of paper beside the gun and fired it to demonstrate what happens; it's impressive.

Further coaching on the proper hold was followed by another group on the paper. Most beginners tend to grasp the handle area too low and you need to keep reminding them to take a higher hold. Having gotten reasonably familiar with the Diamondback, we moved forward and she tried a few six-round bursts on the can, firing with the two-handed hold from waist level. By the second or third try, she was punching the can every few shots, knocking it to the rear. The immediate visible effects in can-rolling are an effective factor in learning reinforcement and help to sustain interest, too.

Left, firing DA with the .45 S&W, the stance is impressively cool and businesslike. Below, I'm showing her how to check the .45 auto for empty condition.

In the upper shot below, she's strafing heck out of a can with the Diamondback and, lower, the look on her face says it all. Note the cylinder is open!

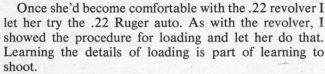

It takes repeated patient reminders and hands-on demonstrations to make a correct grasp of the gun a matter of unthinking habit. You're right in noting my left hand is in the hazard zone, and I knew it!

Once she'd become comfortable with the .22 revolver I let her try the .22 Ruger auto. As with the revolver, I showed the procedure for loading and let her do that. Learning the details of loading is part of learning to shoot.

By the same easy stages, we took her up through the larger guns and cartridges. First I'd shoot it as she watched, then she'd dry-fire to try out the trigger pull before going on to live ammo.

Without being obvious about it, the instructor must stay close and keenly vigilant, ready to control any unexpected situation that may turn up. We had an example of the need for that when the Model 39 ejected a spent 9mm case unerringly into the student's neckline. Those cases come out searing-hot and it is a distraction few veteran shooters could ignore. Being nearby and alert, it was a simple matter to relieve her of the still-loaded auto as she coped with the calamity. I note this by way of underscoring the urgent need for instructing beginners one on one, always ready for the improbable situations that can and do turn up.

By the time Kelly had progressed to the .45, she was holding and firing it as if she'd been doing it for half a

By way of assuring proper regard for safety, I let her blop a hunk of duct seal with a .38 Spelunker. Right, by the time she'd progressed to the .45 auto with mid-range loads, she said, "poopy!"

lifetime or better. First I let her try the cut-down Model 1917 S&W revolver and then shifted to the Model 1911 auto after she'd gotten used to the six-shooter. All of the larger ammo consisted of reloads at moderate target levels and after emptying the M1911 her comment was that it seemed like a nice gun but it felt a little poopy going off. I chose to accept that as a compliment to the instructing technique, but didn't say so.

The approach was so effective in fact that Kelly began clamoring for bigger and even bigger guns to try. She got to the point of firing full-pack loads in the Model 57 S&W with its six-inch barrel. Each shot would move her a foot or so back, meanwhile producing an expression of dreamy zest on her lightly freckled features. She announced that she was ready to try a .44 magnum and I had to admit in all embarrassment that I'd neglected to bring one along.

I had the distinct impression at the start that the gunnery training was much more Dick's idea than Kelly's. Somewhere early in the process — about the time she got the first holes in the can, I think — it reached the "Hey, this is *fun!*"

point and there was no further need for urging or coaxing. Hardly to anyone's surprise, she became highly adept at rolling the can without reference to the sights with either Li'l Montgomery or the cut-down Model 1917 .45, favoring the latter slightly because it tended to knock the cans farther.

As the Morgans took their departure, she was asking if they could do that again, some time soon and I couldn't avoid the rueful contemplation that she'd become a better handgunner in an afternoon than I'd been after some few years of self-taught questing about; gratifying from an instructor's viewpoint, but a bit galling when regarded as a fellow handgunner...

Here, she's belting forth factory 9mm loads in the S&W Model 539 and the text discusses why a scarf or bandanna about the neck would have been a good idea. All of the photos here are by Dick Morgan. I had more pressing things to do!

# CHAPTER 16

# HANDGUN CONSERVATION

## You've Invested, You Have It, And Now You Want To Enjoy It Through The Years: Here Are Some Thoughts On That!

**W**ITH A BIT of luck, plus some reasonably sensible procedures, a good handgun can be expected to deliver excellent service over a long span of years, thereby helping to offset and justify its fairly considerable cost and running value. The Model 24 Smith & Wesson .44 Special Target Model I bought in March of 1957 for a scraped-up $75 is nearly as good a gun today as it was when I acquired it second-hand in the days of the Eisenhower administration. The Model 1911 Colt is a considerably better gun today than when I peeled off $25 for it at some point in the latter Fifties or early Sixties.

Part of that lies in a modest amount of routine maintenance — which we'll be discussing here — and the happy fact that I still have both also hinges upon good luck in that I never let them get in the wrong place at the wrong time so

Identification data can be shot on 35mm film and stored in a safe deposit box for later printing in time of sharp need. Camera is zeroed on serial, as seen in box.

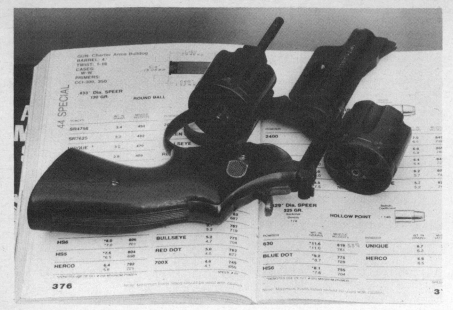

It was a "Black Day At Bad Rock" when this favorite Model 24 S&W became a candidate for a cylinder transplant. Adherence to sensible load data, such as the Speer Manual (background) could have kept the gorgeous original cylinder in perfect shape forever.

that some scurvy scut had a chance to relieve me of their ownership. We'll discuss that, too, albeit with certain reservations, as will be specified.

The Model 24 S&W currently has a different cylinder than the one that came on it. The original cylinder carries the serial number of the gun — standard S&W practice at the time — but there came the bleak moment, galling to recall in retrospect, when I decided to try an unsanctioned charge of powder in the Model 24 with the result that I jugged at least two of its chambers so badly that moderate loads would leave cases resisting extraction. I sent it back to the factory for cylinder replacement, which was but a modest $18 at the time — about 1964 — and asked for the return of the original cylinder, which was done. The new cylinder works pretty good, but it does not seem to have quite the same level of heartwarming accuracy as did the original.

So that brings us to the first basic law of handgun conservation: Take great care never to over-tax the gun with doodle-eyed reload recipes. Stay with loads given in the manuals and, better yet, with loads from such sources below listed maximums.

If you get a pretty good gun, hang on to it and don't swap it off until or unless you are utterly certain you have a closely comparable gun that is considerably better. Then swap off the first and hang on to the second with all possible tenacity. Law II reads, "Good guns are for keeping."

The M1911 Colt fooled me for years into thinking it was a Remington-Rand simply because it carried an R-R slide. Checking a list of serial numbers in Hofschmidt's excellent book on the .45 auto showed that it was actually made by Colt in 1918, making it one of the few guns I own that are older than I am. The Model 1917 Smith & Wesson is one of the others. I bought that from Gil Hebard in the summer of 1965 for his asking price of $35. Years later I bumped into Hebard at a show, mentioned I still had the M'17 and he rather wistfully asked if I'd care to sell it back, at double the purchase price.

In 1976 I went to Germany as a guest of Carl Zeiss Optical Company and along the way they passed out gorgeous little 10X Zeiss binoculars to all of the touring journalists. There was a distraction about then and one of the party laid down his new binoculars to make a run for the telephoto lens for his camera — our hosts having thoughtfully provided a distant spectacle of exceptional interest to afford the new owners a chance to try out their glasses. By the time he got back with the telephoto lens, some unknown other member of the party had doubled his/her supply of Zeiss binoculars, just that snake-tongue speedily.

My binoculars stayed with me for a few years and I loved them dearly. I used to pack them in my shooting kit on range runs for checking holes in targets, for which they were superbly suitable. One time too often I left them lying exposed in the shooting kit when I went forward to change targets and some bystander presumably recognized their excellence and relieved me of them. Moshe Dayan is said to have lost the sight of his eye when a bullet hit a pair of binoculars through which he was peering. I've often hoped the current possessor of those fine hunks of Zeiss glassware might suffer an identical fate. Yes, that's an unfriendly attitude, but it happens to be how I feel on the subject.

Rule III: Never leave a gun or other valued item unguarded in a situation where you'd hesitate to leave an unchaperoned twenty-dollar bill, for exactly the same reason! Even if you miss it instantly — which I did not — your chances of recovery are less than zilch.

Maxim #4 (Be consistent!) — Well, no, but all seriousness aside — make and keep a carefully detailed list or record of all guns, with full descriptions including serial numbers. Update the list occasionally, taking great pains to record the dope on all new purchases as they are acquired. Keep such lists and records in the safest place you can think of, well removed from the actual items so that a thoughtful thief can't rip off your records at the same time as purloining the actual artifacts.

In point of fact, I also maintain a photo record of all such hardware, including a sharp close-up snap of the serial number together with an overall view of the gun showing any special equipment it carries. If you don't have the innate capability to do that, having a friendly photographer do it for you could end up being worth much more than the modest cost. Keep records of what you paid for each gun or other serial-numbered item, retaining the sales slip and/or cancelled check, if at all possible. Maintain a warranty file, with dates of purchase carefully recorded. In case of loss, such things can be valuable beyond price in dealing with insurance adjusters.

Law V: Carry adequate insurance and, if you depend upon a homeowner's policy, cross-examine your insurance agent rigorously to find out just where you stand on the agreed-upon value of the guns, whether they're covered if stolen from a car, and similar pertinent details. If you wish, tape record the conversation and file the dated tape with the other records. Tape with the agent's knowledge and consent, of course.

Law VI: Disperse your valuable items in a number of unlikely places to minimize the risk of losing them all in one raid.

Law VII: Don't forget the hiding places. Make a record if your memory is like mine and then don't lose the record.

I could list several crafty strategems for cutting the risk of loss to burglars, but I'm not going to do so, mindful that the sticky-fingered nerds might steal a copy of this book and read this chapter with bright-eyed interest. All I can suggest is that you try to see your house or gun storage area from the eyes of a potential burglar. Where would be the first place you'd look, or the second and so on? Where could a gun or other valuable be hidden where no one would ever dream of looking? Most homeowners follow typical patterns in storing such things and most burglars are intimately familiar with the more likely possibilities.

Law VIII: The burglar might turn up with a metal detector and/or a cutting torch. The latter can nullify the security of the sturdiest vault in a bit of time, meanwhile leaving a frightful mess on the carpet! Consider burglar alarms, watchdogs and so on, but do not pin total faith on any of them. We've a neighborhood watch arrangement in our immediate neighborhood. Cars that belong in the area are well known. Others have the license number and description of car and occupant(s) recorded together with time, date and other pertinent comments. Such records are kept indefinitely and duplicate entries are made up and passed along to police officers residing in the immediate area if any particular suspicion attaches to the given incident. To get away with much loot the thief needs some manner of vehicle, and if you can identify the vehicle that's a step in identifying the thief.

Law IX: Encourage your neighbors to be snoopy; you be the same way.

When/if you sell a gun to someone else, retain your own record of it indefinitely, meanwhile making note of the sale. I've lost track of the number of times such a buyer has called up, wistfully wanting to know if I could supply the serial number. I've been able to do so every time, except one long-ago occasion that was the episode that started me in the practice. A few times now, having the number has enabled the loser to get it back, but the odds aren't good.

Law X: Never give a lousy burglar an even break! Make it tough for the miserable so-and-sos, before, during and after the crime.

The preceding comments apply in general to other items including but not limited to photographic equipment, office equipment such as typewriters, vehicles, stereo and video equipment, microwave ovens, silverware and — put it this way — anything a creep could lift and carry away that could be liquidated for even a few dollars.

Consider suitably insured and secured remote storage

*It says in the text not to leave a gun or similar item lying unattended where you'd feel queasy about parking a nice, crisp $20 bill. In point of fact, a gun such as this merits the same concern as about fifteen $20 bills but, in point of further fact, I had to borrow this one from a neighbor lady for the photo: It was all she had!*

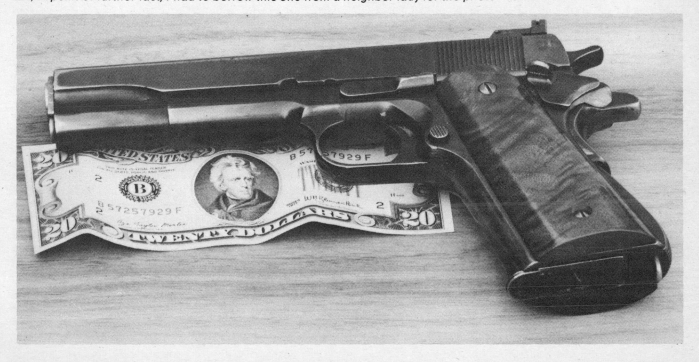

facilities for such equipment that is used seasonally or rarely.

Law XI: Neglect not thy maintenance. A gun ruined by rust or other careless neglect is as hopelessly gone as if it had been spirited from the premises, never to return. Depending upon local conditions, wipe the metal surfaces with a reliable rust preventive. My own preference is for Break Free or Triflon. Wipe down and reapply at suitable intervals. Always clean the bore promptly if there is any reason to suspect the ammunition fired have been corrosive in any way. After cleaning avoid storing the gun so that cleaning fluids or lubes can run into the wooden parts.

Law XII: Avoid detail stripping unless you're certain you know what you're doing and how to get it back together again! That should be repeated about three more times, but I'll spare you the exposure if you promise to remember, okay?

Law XIII: It's bad luck to be superstitious.

Law XIV: Get to know state and local firearms laws and regulations of your place of residence intimately and well. Observe all such laws scrupulously and be keenly mindful of the consequences if you don't. For example, some jurisdictions regard carrying a loaded magazine or revolver speedloader as tantamount to actually carrying a loaded gun and being caught with such a combination in your vehicle can get the gun confiscated plus possible other penalties so that you could end up wishing it'd gotten stolen instead.

A national magazine ran a discussion some while ago by a writer who said he had taken to carrying a Smith & Wesson Model 39 9mm auto about his local neighborhood for self-protection. He related an incident in which he'd been accosted by a man with a knife, bent upon lifting his billfold. As the assailant approached, the writer hauled out the Model 39 and blammed a slug into the knife-artist's thigh. While it was not spelled out specifically, the implication was that he went on about his affairs, leaving the wounded robber mouthing scatalogical commentary.

Massad F. Ayoob has authored an excellent and exhaustive book on the complexities of defensive shooting. The title is *In The Gravest Extreme,* and I recommend it

Depending upon the laws in your place of residence, it could be illegal to carry a loaded magazine or speedloader in the car. Know the laws and obey them, to avoid confiscation and kindred woes.

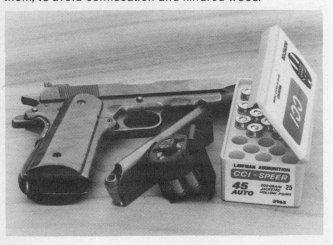

A sensible amount of cleaning and maintenance is an immense help in conserving the utility and value of handguns. Products such as these work well for such purposes and help them shoot better.

without reservation to anyone who envisions any remote chance of having to engage in a shoot-out. Ayoob gives cogent reasons for avoiding the use of a gun if at all possible. Even if the law finds your shooting justified and releases you free and clear, he observes, the surviving target or his/her survivors can be expected to bring civil suit against you. They are quite apt to win, regardless of the provocation.

Meanwhile, I'd like to leave you with a bit of information of which you may not be aware. The ejected empty case from an auto pistol can be identified as having been fired from the given gun by any reasonably competent ballistics expert and, what's more, it's quite common to leave a remarkably clear fingerprint on the case when loading the magazine. Should an emergency situation arise that leaves no alternative to firing, a revolver full of shot loads has obvious tactical virtues. The person who shoots and runs is apt to be regarded by the law as being on a rough par with a hit-and-run automobile driver. Clearly, if time permits, the reluctant user of an auto pistol would find it shrewd procedure to police up the spent brass. At least, that was the ironic reflection that went through my mind after reading the account of the foiled knifester. The episode certainly made absorbing copy, but the wisdom of revealing the details — if factual — seemed quite dubious. If the incident was purely fictitious, little or nothing could be done to the writer, but if it inspired others to run through the same plot-frame, the consequences to them could be pretty traumatic. Whether the constitutional guarantees against self-incrimination would hold water in such a situation is an interestingly moot point. These were other thoughts that occurred as I walked around the account, kicking its tires meditatively and thinking about it.

The foregoing represents a chosen selection from a much larger body of considerations relevant to enjoying the ongoing ownership of firearms in general and handguns in particular. It is up to the given reader to trace each thread of conjecture to its primal roots so as to exploit thoughtful precautions to the fullest. As for me, I'm still ruminating over the matter myself and I surely wish you much success in your own efforts. Handgun conservation is a way of life; one of several.

**CHAPTER 17**

# THE LAST
# BLAST

*A Valiant Effort To Tie Up All
Loose Ends In Sight*

One great gun.
DAN WESSON'S .22 LR.

FIRST OF ALL, if you've skipped forward as suggested earlier to pick up further details on the Invicta cartridge, it pains me to announce that no more information has turned up on it as the final pages go down. With any decent sort of luck I may be able to tell you more about it than you really cared to know when/if the fourth edition of PARD appears. In the meantime, Robert Olsen can perhaps supply information on the current status of the quo as he's the inventor/developer of the ingenious concept. He can be reached by mail at 307 Conestoga Way, #37, Eagleville, PA 19403 and I'm sure he'd appreciate a self-addressed, stamped envelope (SASE) with such inquiries. The revolver for the Invicta cartridge will be an especially modified Dan Wesson Arms revolver and, although DWA guns are made in Monson, Massachusetts, inquiries about them should be directed to the attention of Duane Small, DWA, Inc., Box 168, Union Lake, MI 48085.

I have a few late-breaking items to update the otherwise admirably exhaustive coverage of the handgun field presented in our catalog section that starts when this chapter ends. Smith & Wesson now has their Model 539 in production and I have an example of it here. It has the protected, fully-adjustable rear sight and the receiver is of steel rather than high-tensile aluminum alloy. I've recently completed a comparison test between the M539 and the earlier Model 39-2 and can report that the 539 seems to throw a tighter group than its alloy frame counterpart, but not by a broad margin because the alloy-frame job did remarkably well. Both guns chewed their way through an extensive assortment of factory ammo and reloads — including several cast bullet reloads — with absolutely perfect track records in feeding and functioning: not a single jam or even

*Robert Olsen holds an early prototype of a Dan Wesson Arms revolver made up to handle the .357 Invicta cartridge that was discussed earlier here.*

*Production version of the .45 ACP Hard Cap shot load will use the round-nosed cups illustrated here.*

a momentary hesitation. It is none too common to encounter so happy a state of affairs and thus it's always a pleasure to be able to report it.

In a recent phone conversation with old friend Warren Center I told him that I'd had fantastically fine results with a custom-built Super-14 Contender barrel in .22 long rifle and he confided that Thompson/Center plans to make that cartridge a standard offering in the Super-14 barrels. It's not listed in the catalog section, but it's to be hoped you'll be able to order them through your dealer by the time this book comes off the press. With the right scope it's a tackdriver and the CCI Stinger loads come out of it at well over 1600 feet per second (fps).

Earlier in the book there is a photo of the Hard Cap load for the .45 ACP; a shot load that feeds and functions through the magazine in semiauto mode. A nearby photo shows the round-nosed cups that will be used in the production of the .45 Hard Cap, rather than the flat-tipped cups illustrated earlier.

A footnote to the discussion on making your own .45 stocks: The hole-spacing gauge that was shown has never delivered the pinpoint precision that I wistfully had in mind. In recent weeks I dreamed up and built the adjustable hole-spacing tool shown here. It's on a length of ⅜-inch cold-rolled steel rod and the sliding/locking collar is much the same as utilized on the bullet-seating depth gauge illustrated and discussed earlier, with the addition of a hardened steel pin fastened into a hole in the lower surface with Stud 'N Bearing grade Loctite. A second pin is held in the end of the rod by means of a 10-32 hex-head set screw that goes in from the end of the rod, barely visible in the photo.

The pins are made from short sections of the hardened nails intended for use in concrete and they are harder than the proverbial pawnbroker's heart. Dremel makes a thin grinding wheel to go in a small mandrel for the Dremel Moto-Tool and that works fine for cutting off and shaping the points of the sections of concrete nails, with the short piece chucked in the drill press and turning at medium high speed as the Dremel grinder is applied to it.

I made a preliminary setting at the requisite 3.074-inch spacing with the aid of the vernier caliper, tried it out with the brad-pointed letter B drill bit ground to shape by Ron Perry and found to my delight that the system turns out utterly perfect hole-spacing with monotonous regularity.

With uncharacteristic foresight I used it to make a pair of small punchmarks in a scrap piece of hard maple, identified the setting guage and filed it away for a fast and simple aid in resetting the points to the 3.074 distance at times of future need. That freed the tool for other applications and it has proven extremely convenient for a host of shop operations that are real tooth-gritters if you don't have something comparable to use on them. With that done, my son Andy expressed a yen for a similar gizmo to hold an Xacto knife for cutting circles and it proved a simple project to knock that out. The little pens branded Le Pen have the same diameter as the Xacto knife handle — a letter O drill bit as I recall — so that the circle cutter can become a compass with a choice of several ink colors, just as easily.

John S. Clark of Clark Manufacturing (14810 Wagon Trail Road, Box 250, Pearland, TX 77581), has developed and is marketing a cartridge case transfer gauge that strikes me as diabolically ingenious. The front knob rides a stem that slides through the outer body, with spring tension to require about twenty pounds of force to make it move. In use, the knob and stem are pulled forward far enough so that, inserted into the chamber, the knob and stem are pushed back into the outer body as the action is closed. Upon opening the action the gauge is removed, having picked up the vital headspace dimension for that individual chamber.

All you need do at that point is to remove the decapping stem from your full-length resizing die, run the ram of the press to the top of its stroke, holding the gauge against the

*Left, one of the Clark transfer gauges adjusted to duplicate the headspace of this .300 Winchester mag case. Gauges are available for most cartridges.*

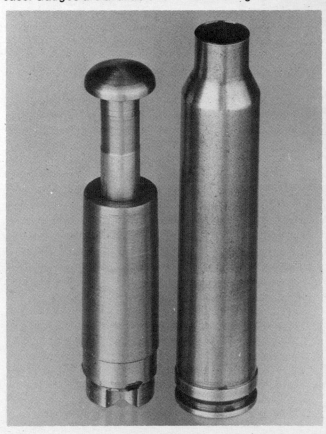

shell holder as you turn the resizing die body downward until it makes contact with the top of the gauge. Tighten the die locking collar to hold it in place, lower the press ram, put away the gauge, replace the decapping stem with its mouth-expanding collar and you are ready to size the cases to an utterly precise fit in the given chamber. Clark makes such gauges in several sizes and types for use with any cartridge that would benefit from such a device and the retail price at press time is $25, postpaid; Texas residents add sales tax on that amount. Inquiries should be accompanied by a SASE.

Armament Systems and Procedures, Inc. (Box 356, Appleton, WI 54911) performs a remarkable conversion on the Ruger Speed-Six revolvers, boring out and rerifling the barrel and fitting a five-shot unfluted cylinder so as to handle the .44 Special cartridge. They also perform extensive customizing on the Smith & Wesson Model 39, modifying it to an extremely compact but efficient small pistol they call the Asp. To the present the Ruger conversion to .44 Special has no official name, although I tend to think of it as the Fast-Five. The Ruger modification runs about $400 when performed on the customer's gun and I believe the cost of the Asp conversion is comparable to that.

*Discussed on the previous page, this adjustable guide for hole spacing performs magnificently in laying out .45 stocks and has countless other uses about the shop.*

*A prototype of the Ruger Speed-Six converted to use .44 Special ammo, with an unfluted five-round cylinder, radioluminous sights and rosewood stocks.*

Inquiries for further details can be directed to the firm's president Kevin Parsons, PhD, at the address given.

In chapter 14 I mentioned the problem of the .38-45 with its pressure limitations. Two firms are at work presently with extra-strength modifications of the .45 ACP case. Detonics .45 Associates, 2500 Seattle Tower, Seattle, WA 98101 has a slightly longer version for the .451 Detonics magnum and SSK Industries, Route 1, Della Drive, Bloomingdale, OH 43910 trims .45 Winchester magnum cases for their .41 Avenger, similar to the .38-45, but operating with .410-inch-diameter bullets.

Chuck Ward of C. Ward Conversions — creator of the modified S&W Model 10 (Li'l Montgomery) mentioned here rather frequently — can be reached at Box 610, Raymore, MO 64083.

Austin F. Behlert, who made up what I call my BK-38, is head of Behlert Custom Guns, Inc., currently at Route 1

North, Box 227, Monmouth Junction, NJ 08852. Some listings will have the firm at Union, New Jersey, from which it moved over a year ago.

A photo of the Texas Contenders carbine conversion of the T/C Contender appears in chapter 14 and it's a remarkably nice modification that results in a delightful small rifle. Frank Kendrick heads up Texas Contender Firearms, 4127 Weslow, Houston, TX 77087. At the same address there's an organization called the Texas Contender's Gun Club, with dues of $15 per year, which includes membership in the National Rifle Association. Members of TCGC rate a five percent discount on all Contender merchandise and may occasionally receive bulletins from TCF announcing special sale prices or new Contender merchandise in stock as well as details on collectible variants of the Contender. A brochure describing all this and more is free on request at the address given. In a phone call to Kendrick to check details on that, he noted that their newest wrinkle is to add a non-removable muzzle brake to the Super-14 Contender barrels, making them slightly over sixteen inches in length and thus legal to use with the shoulder stocks as supplied for making up the Texas Contender carbines.

I already have twenty-two-inch barrels for the TC carbine in .218 Bee, .30 Herrett and .357 Herrett and placed an order with Kendrick for one of the brake-fitted S-14 barrels in .41 magnum. As he noted, the modified barrels would be usable with the original handgun stocks or with the shoulder stocks, at the owner's option. They can also supply an eighteen-inch smoothbore barrel in .410-bore that, with their shoulder stock, converts the Contender into a sweet little break-action shotgun or back to the usual handgun format in a few minutes of simple parts changing.

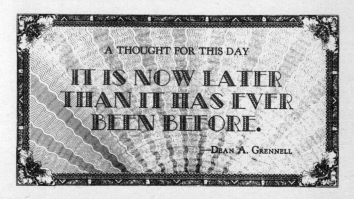

A THOUGHT FOR THIS DAY

IT IS NOW LATER THAN IT HAS EVER BEEN BEFORE.

— Dean A. Grennell

# TODAY'S HANDGUNS

## COMPETITION HANDGUNS

**BERNARDELLI MODEL 100 PISTOL**
**Caliber:** 22 LR only, 10-shot magazine.
**Barrel:** 5.9".
**Weight:** 37¾ oz. **Length:** 9" over-all.
**Stocks:** Checkered walnut with thumbrest.
**Sights:** Fixed front, rear adj. for w. and e.
**Features:** Target barrel weight included. Heavy sighting rib with interchangeable front sight. Accessories include cleaning equipment and assembly tools, case. Imported from Italy by Interarms.

**BERETTA MODEL 76 PISTOL**
**Caliber:** 22 LR, 10-shot magazine.
**Barrel:** 6".
**Weight:** 33 ozs. (empty). **Length:** 8.8" over-all.
**Stocks:** Checkered plastic.
**Sights:** Interchangeable blade front (3 widths), rear is fully adj. for w. and e.
**Features:** Built-in, fixed counterweight, raised, matted slide rib, factory adjusted trigger pull from 3 lbs. 5 ozs. to 3 lbs. 12 ozs. Thumb safety. Blue-black finish. Wood grips available at extra cost. Introduced 1977. Imported from Italy by Beretta Arms Co.

**BRITARMS 2000 MK.2 TARGET PISTOL**
**Caliber:** 22 LR, 5-shot magazine.
**Barrel:** 5⅞".
**Weight:** 48 oz. **Length:** 11" over-all.
**Stocks:** Stippled walnut, anatomically designed wrap-around type with adjustable palm shelf.
**Sights:** Target front and rear. Interchangeable front blades of 3.2mm, 3.6mm or 4.0mm; fully adjustable rear.
**Features:** Offset anatomical and adjustable trigger, top loading magazine. Satin blue-black finish, satin hard chrome frame and trigger. Introduced 1982. Imported from England by Action Arms Ltd.

**COLT GOLD CUP NAT'L MATCH MK IV Series 70**
**Caliber:** 45 ACP, 7-shot magazine.
**Barrel:** 5", with new design bushing.
**Weight:** 38½ oz. **Length:** 8⅜"
**Stocks:** Checkered walnut, gold plated medallion.
**Sights:** Ramp-style front, Colt-Eliason rear adj. for w. and e., sight radius 6¾".
**Features:** Arched or flat housing; wide, grooved trigger with adj. stop; ribbed-top slide, hand fitted, with improved ejection port.

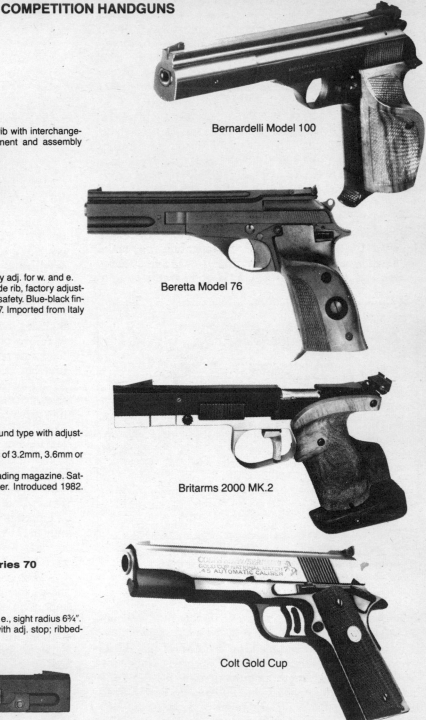

Bernardelli Model 100

Beretta Model 76

Britarms 2000 MK.2

Colt Gold Cup

Domino Model SP-602

**Domino O.P. 601 Match Pistol**
Similar to SP 602 except has different match stocks with adj. palm, shelf, 22 Short only, weighs 40 oz., 5.6" bbl., has gas ports through top of barrel and slide to reduce recoil, slightly different trigger and sear mechanisms.

**DOMINO MODEL SP-602 MATCH PISTOL**
**Caliber:** 22 LR, 5-shot.
**Barrel:** 5.5".
**Weight:** 41 oz. **Length:** 11.02" over-all.
**Stocks:** Full target stocks; adjustable, one-piece. Left hand style avail.
**Sights:** Match. Blade front, open notch rear fully adj. for w. and e. Sight radius is 8.66".
**Features:** Line of sight is only ¹¹⁄₃₂" above centerline of bore; magazine is inserted from top; adjustable and removable trigger mechanism; single lever takedown. Full 5 year warranty. Imported from Italy by Mandall Shooting Supplies.

# COMPETITION HANDGUNS

## HAMMERLI STANDARD, MODELS 208 & 211
**Caliber:** 22 LR.
**Barrel:** 5.9", 6-groove.
**Weight:** 37.6 oz. (45 oz. with extra heavy barrel weight). **Length:** 10".
**Stocks:** Walnut. Adj. palm rest (208), 211 has thumbrest grip.
**Sights:** Match sights, fully adj. for w. and e. (click adj.). Interchangeable front and rear blades.
**Features:** Semi-automatic, recoil operated. 8-shot clip. Slide stop. Fully adj. trigger (2¼-lbs. and 3 lbs.). Extra barrel weight available. Imported from Switzerland by Mandall Shooting Supplies.

Hammerli Standard Models 208 & 211

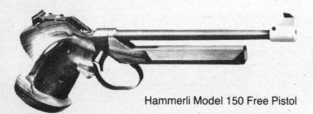

Hammerli Model 150 Free Pistol

## HAMMERLI MODEL 150 FREE PISTOL
**Caliber:** 22 LR. Single shot.
**Barrel:** 11.3"
**Weight:** 43 ozs. **Length:** 15.35" over-all.
**Stocks:** Walnut with adjustable palm shelf.
**Sights:** Sight radius of 14.6". Micro rear sight adj. for w. and e.
**Features:** Single shot Martini action. Cocking lever on left side of action with vertical operation. Set trigger adjustable for length and angle. Trigger pull weight adjustable between 5 and 100 grams. Guaranteed accuracy of .78", 10 shots from machine rest. Imported from Switzerland by Mandall Shooting Supplies.

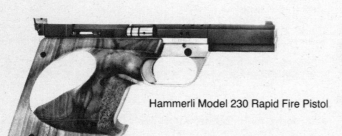

Hammerli Model 230 Rapid Fire Pistol

## HAMMERLI MODEL 230 RAPID FIRE PISTOL
**Caliber:** 22 Short.
**Barrel:** 6.3", 6-groove.
**Weight:** 43.8 oz. **Length:** 11.6".
**Stocks:** Walnut.
**Sights:** Match type sights. Sight radius 9.9". Micro rear, click adj. Interchangeable front sight blade.
**Features:** Semi-automatic. Recoil-operated, 6-shot clip. Gas escape in front of chamber to eliminate muzzle jump. Fully adj. trigger from 5¼ oz. to 10½ oz. with three different lengths available. Designed for International 25 meter Silhouette Program. Imported from Switzerland by Mandall Shooting Supplies.

## HAMMERLI MODEL 120-1 FREE PISTOL
**Caliber:** 22 LR.
**Barrel:** 9.9".
**Weight:** 44 oz. **Length:** 14¾" over-all.
**Stocks:** Contoured right-hand (only) thumbrest.
**Sights:** Fully adjustable rear, blade front. Choice of 14.56" or 9.84" sight radius.
**Features:** Trigger adjustable for single- or two-stage pull from 1.8 to 12 oz. Adjustable for length of pull. Guaranteed accuracy of .98", 10 shots at 50 meters. Imported from Switzerland by Mandall Shooting Supplies.

High Standard X Series Custom 10-X

## HIGH STANDARD X SERIES CUSTOM 10-X
**Caliber:** 22 LR, 10-shot magazine.
**Barrel:** 5½" bull.
**Weight:** 44½ oz. **Length:** 9¾" over-all.
**Stocks:** Checkered walnut.
**Sights:** Undercut ramp front; frame mounted fully adj. rear.
**Features:** Completely custom made and fitted for best performance. Fully adjustable target trigger, stippled front- and backstraps, slide lock, non-reflective blue finish. Comes with two extra magazines. Unique service policy. Each gun signed by maker.

# COMPETITION HANDGUNS

**HIGH STANDARD SUPERMATIC CITATION MILITARY**
**Caliber:** 22 LR, 10-shot magazine.
**Barrel:** 5½" bull, 7¼" fluted.
**Weight:** 46 oz. **Length:** 9¾" (5½" bbl.)
**Stocks:** Checkered walnut with thumbrest.
**Sights:** Undercut ramp front; frame mounted rear, click adj.
**Features:** Adjustable trigger pull; over-travel trigger adjustment; double acting safety; rebounding firing pin; military style grip; stippled front- and backstraps; positive magazine latch.

High Standard Supermatic Citation Military

**HIGH STANDARD SUPERMATIC TROPHY MILITARY**
**Caliber:** 22 LR, 10-shot magazine.
**Barrel:** 5½" bull, 7¼" fluted.
**Weight:** 44½ oz. **Length:** 9¾" (5½" bbl.)
**Stocks:** Checkered walnut with thumbrest.
**Sights:** Undercut ramp front; frame mounted rear, click adj.
**Features:** Grip duplicates feel of military 45; positive action mag. latch; front- and backstraps stippled. Trigger adj. for pull, over-travel

**HIGH STANDARD VICTOR**
**Caliber:** 22 LR, 10-shot magazine.
**Barrel:** 5½".
**Weight:** 47 oz. **Length:** 9⅝" over-all.
**Stocks:** Checkered walnut with thumb rest.
**Sights:** Undercut ramp front, rib mounted click adj. rear.
**Features:** Vent. rib, interchangeable barrel, 2 - 2¼ lb. trigger pull, blue finish, back and front straps stippled.

**M-S SAFARI ARMS MATCHMASTER PISTOL**
**Caliber:** 45 ACP, 7-shot magazine.
**Barrel:** 5".
**Weight:** 45 oz. **Length:** 8.7" overall.
**Stocks:** Combat rubber or checkered walnut.
**Sights:** Combat adjustable.
**Features:** Beavertail grip safety, ambidextrous extended safety, extended slide release, combat hammer, threaded barrel bushing; throated, ported, tuned. Finishes: blue, Armaloy, Parkerize, electroless nickel. Also available in a lightweight version (30 oz.) and stainless steel. Made by M-S Safari Arms.

M-S Safari Arms Matchmaster Pistol

**M-S Safari Arms Model 81NM Pistol**
Similar to the Matchmaster except weighs 28 oz., is 8.2" over-all, has Ron Power match sights. Meets all requirements for National Match Service Pistols. Throated, ported, tuned and has threaded barrel bushing. Available in blue, Armaloy, Parkerize, stainless steel and electroless nickel. From M-S Safari Arms.

**M-S Safari Arms Model 81 Pistol**
Similar to Matchmaster except chambered for 45 or 38 Spec. mid-range wadcutter; available with fixed or adjustable walnut target match grips; Aristocrat rib with extended front sight is optional. Other features are the same. From M-S Safari Arms.

M-S Safari Arms Model 81 Pistol

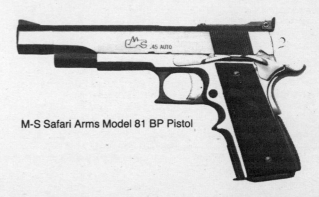

M-S Safari Arms Model 81 BP Pistol

**M-S Safari Arms Model 81BP**
Similar to the Matchmaster except designed for shooting the bowling pin matches. Extended slide gives 6" sight radius but also fast slide cycle time. Combat adjustable sights, magazine chute, plus same features as Matchmaster.

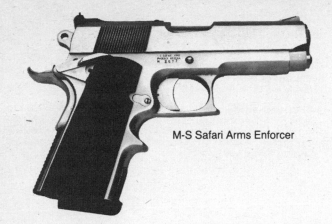

M-S Safari Arms Enforcer

**M-S Safari Arms Enforcer Pistol**
Shortened version of the Matchmaster. Has 3.8" barrel, over-all length of 7.7", and weighs 40 oz. (standard weight), 27 oz. in lightweight version. Other features are the same. From M-S Safari Arms.

M-S Safari Unlimited Silhouette

**M-S SAFARI ARMS UNLIMITED SILHOUETTE PISTOL**
**Caliber:** Any caliber with 308 head size or smaller.
**Barrel:** 14¹⁵⁄₁₆" tapered
**Weight:** 72 oz. **Length:** 21½" over-all.
**Stocks:** Fiberglass, custom painted to customer specs.
**Sights:** Open iron.
**Features:** Electronic trigger, bolt action single shot. Made by M-S Safari Arms.

Navy Grand Prix Silhouette

**NAVY GRAND PRIX SILHOUETTE PISTOL**
**Caliber:** 44 Mag., 30-30, 7mm Spacial, 45-70; single shot.
**Barrel:** 13¾".
**Weight:** 4 lbs.
**Stocks:** Walnut fore-end and thumb-rest grip.
**Sights:** Adjustable target-type.
**Features:** Uses rolling block action. Has adjustable aluminum barrel rib; matte blue finish. Made in U.S. by Navy Arms.

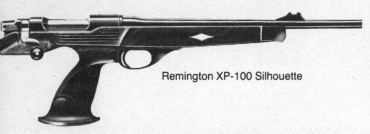

Remington XP-100 Silhouette

**REMINGTON XP-100 SILHOUETTE PISTOL**
**Caliber:** 7mm BR Remington, single-shot.
**Barrel:** 14¾".
**Weight:** 4⅛ lbs. **Length:** 21¼" over-all.
**Stocks:** Brown nylon, one piece, checkered grip.
**Sights:** None furnished. Drilled and tapped for scope mounts.
**Features:** Universal grip fits right or left hand; match-type grooved trigger, two-position thumb safety.

**RUGER MARK II TARGET MODEL AUTO PISTOL**
**Caliber:** 22 LR only, 10-shot magazine.
**Barrel:** 6⅞" or 5½" bull barrel (6-groove, 14" twist).
**Weight:** 42 oz. with 6⅞" bbl. **Length:** 10⅞" (6⅞" bbl.)
**Stocks:** Checkered hard rubber.
**Sights:** ⅛" blade front, micro click rear, adjustable for w. and e. Sight radius 9⅜" (with 6⅞" bbl.).

Ruger Mark II Target Model

**SEVILLE "SILHOUETTE" SINGLE ACTION**
**Caliber:** 357, 41, 44, 45 Win. Mag.
**Barrel:** 10½".
**Weight:** About 55 oz.
**Stocks:** Smooth walnut thumbrest, or Pachmayr.
**Sights:** Undercut Patridge-style front, adjustable rear.
**Features:** Available only in stainless steel. Six-shot cylinder. From United Sporting Arms of Arizona, Inc.

SIG/Hammerli P-240

## SIG/HAMMERLI P-240 TARGET PISTOL
**Caliber:** 32 S&W Long.
**Barrel:** 6".
**Weight:** 34¼ oz. **Length:** 10" over-all.
**Stocks:** Walnut, target style, unfinished.
**Sights:** Match sights; ⅛" undercut front, ⅛" notch micro rear click adj. for w. and e.
**Features:** Semi-automatic, recoil operated; meets I.S.U. and N.R.A. specs for Center Fire Pistol competition; double pull trigger adj. from 2 lbs., 15 ozs. to 3 lbs., 9 ozs.; trigger stop. Comes with extra magazine, special screwdriver, carrying case. Imported from Switzerland by Mandall Shooting Supplies and Waidmanns Guns International.

## SMITH & WESSON 22 AUTO PISTOL Model 41
**Caliber:** 22 LR, 10-shot clip.
**Barrel:** 7⅜", sight radius 9⁵⁄₁₆".
**Weight:** 43½ oz. **Length:** 12" over-all.
**Stocks:** Checkered walnut with thumbrest, usable with either hand.
**Sights:** Front, ⅛" Patridge undercut; micro click rear adj. for w. and e.
**Features:** ⅜" wide, grooved trigger with adj. stop; wgts. available to make pistol up to 59 oz.

Smith & Wesson Model 41

## SMITH & WESSON 22 MATCH HEAVY BARREL M-41
**Caliber:** 22 LR, 10-shot clip.
**Barrel:** 5½" heavy. Sight radius, 8".
**Weight:** 44½ oz. **Length:** 9".
**Stocks:** Checkered walnut with modified thumbrest, usable with either hand.
**Sights:** ⅛" Patridge on ramp base. S&W micro click rear, adj. for w. and e.
**Features:** ⅜" wide, grooved trigger; adj. trigger stop.

## SMITH & WESSON K-38 S.A. M-14
**Caliber:** 38 Spec., 6-shot.
**Barrel:** 6".
**Weight:** 38½ oz. **Length:** 11⅛" over-all.
**Stocks:** Checkered walnut, service type.
**Sights:** ⅛" Patridge front, micro click rear adj. for w. and e.
**Features:** Same as Model 14 except single action only, target hammer and trigger.

Smith & Wesson K-38 S.A. M-14

## SMITH & WESSON 38 MASTER Model 52 AUTO
**Caliber:** 38 Special (for Mid-range W.C. with flush-seated bullet only). 5-shot magazine.
**Barrel:** 5".
**Weight:** 41 oz. with empty magazine. **Length:** 8⅝"
**Stocks:** Checkered walnut.
**Sights:** ⅛" Patridge front, S&W micro click rear adj. for w. and e.
**Features:** Top sighting surfaces matte finished. Locked breech, moving barrel system; checked for 10-ring groups at 50 yards. Coin-adj. sight screws. Dry firing permissible if manual safety on.

Smith & Wesson Model 52

## SMITH & WESSON 1955 Model 25, 45 TARGET
**Caliber:** 45 ACP and 45 AR, 6 shot.
**Barrel:** 6" (heavy target type).
**Weight:** 45 oz. **Length:** 11⅞".
**Stocks:** Checkered walnut target.
**Sights:** ⅛" Patridge front, micro click rear, adjustable for w. and e.
**Features:** Tangs and trigger grooved; target trigger and hammer standard, checkered target hammer. Swing-out cylinder revolver. Price includes presentation case.

## TAURUS MODEL 86 MASTER REVOLVER
**Caliber:** 38 Spec., 6-shot.
**Barrel:** 6″ only.
**Weight:** 41 oz. **Length:** 11¼″ over-all.
**Stocks:** Over size target-type, checkered Brazilian walnut.
**Sights:** Patridge front, micro. click rear adj. for w. and e.
**Features:** Blue finish with non-reflective finish on barrel. Imported from Brazil by International Distributors.

Taurus Model 86 Master

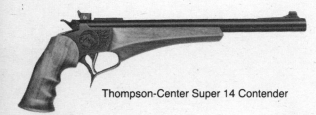

Thompson-Center Super 14 Contender

## THOMPSON-CENTER SUPER 14 CONTENDER
**Caliber:** 222 Rem., 223 Rem., 7mm TCU, 30 Herrett, 357 Herrett, 30-30 Win., 35 Rem., 41 and 44 Mag., 45 Win. Mag. Single shot.
**Barrel:** 14″.
**Weight:** 45 oz. **Length:** 17¼″ over-all.
**Stocks:** Select walnut grip and fore-end.
**Sights:** Fully adjustable target-type.
**Features:** Break-open action with auto safety. Interchangeable barrels for both rimfire and centerfire calibers. Introduced 1978.

Unique D.E.S. 69

## UNIQUE D.E.S. 69 TARGET PISTOL
**Caliber:** 22 LR.
**Barrel:** 5.91″.
**Weight:** Approx. 35 oz. **Length:** 10.63″ over-all.
**Stocks:** French walnut target style with thumbrest and adjustable shelf; hand checkered panels.
**Sights:** Ramp front, micro. adj. rear mounted on frame; 8.66″ sight radius.
**Features:** Meets U.I.T. standards. Comes in a fitted hard case with spare magazine, barrel weight, cleaning rod, tools, proof certificate, test target and two year guarantee. Fully adjustable trigger; dry firing safety device. Imported from France by Solersport.

Unique D.E.S. VO 79

## UNIQUE D.E.S. VO 79 TARGET PISTOL
**Caliber:** 22 Short.
**Barrel:** 5.85″, Four gas escape ports, one threaded with plug.
**Weight:** 44 oz.
**Stocks:** French walnut, target style with thumbrest and adj. palm shelf. Hand stippled.
**Sights:** Low, .12″ front, fully adj. rear.
**Features:** Meets all UIT standards; virtually recoil free. Four-way adj. trigger, dry-firing device, all aluminum frame. Cleaning rod, tools, extra magazine, proof certificate and fitted case. Imported from France by Solersport.

## WALTHER FREE PISTOL
**Caliber:** 22 LR, single shot.
**Barrel:** 11.7″.
**Weight:** 48 ozs. **Length:** 17.2″ over-all.
**Stocks:** Walnut, special hand-fitting design.
**Sights:** Fully adjustable match sights.
**Features:** Special electronic trigger. Matte finish blue. Introduced 1980. Imported from Germany by Interarms.

## WALTHER GSP MATCH PISTOL
**Caliber:** 22 LR, 32 S&W wadcutter (GSP-C), 5-shot.
**Barrel:** 5¾".
**Weight:** 44.8 oz. (22 LR), 49.4 oz. (32). **Length:** 11.8" over-all.
**Stocks:** Walnut, special hand-fitting design.
**Sights:** Fixed front, rear adj. for w. & e.
**Features:** Available with either 2.2 lb. (1000 gm) or 3 lb. (1360 gm) trigger. Spare mag., bbl. weight, tools supplied in Match Pistol Kit. Imported from Germany by Interarms.

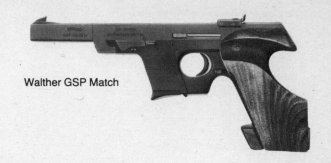

Walther GSP Match

## Walther OSP Rapid-Fire Pistol
Similar to Model GSP except 22 Short only, stock has adj. free-style hand rest.

## WICHITA MK-40 SILHOUETTE PISTOL
**Caliber:** 7mm IHMSA, 308 Win. F.L. Other calibers available on special order. Single shot.
**Barrel:** 13", non-glare blue; .700" dia. muzzle.
**Weight:** 4½ lbs. **Length:** 19⅜" over-all.
**Stocks:** Metallic gray fiberthane glass.
**Sights:** Wichita Multi-Range sighting system.
**Features:** Aluminum receiver with steel insert locking lugs, measures 1.360" O.D.; 3 locking lug bolts, 3 gas ports; flat bolt handle; completely adjustable Wichita trigger. Introduced 1981. From Wichita Arms.

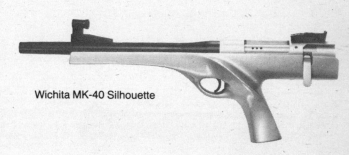

Wichita MK-40 Silhouette

## WICHITA SILHOUETTE PISTOL
**Caliber:** 7mm IHMSA, 308, 7mm x 308. Other calibers available on special order. Single shot.
**Barrel:** 14¹⁵⁄₁₆" or 10¾".
**Weight:** 4½ lbs. **Length:** 21⅜" over-all.
**Stocks:** American walnut with oil finish, or fiberglass (yellow or black). Glass bedded.
**Sights:** Wichita Multi-Range sight system.
**Features:** Comes with either right- or left-hand action with right-hand grip. Fluted bolt, flat bolt handle. Action drilled and tapped for Burris scope mounts. Non-glare satin blue finish. Wichita adjustable trigger. Introduced 1979. From Wichita Arms.

Wichita Silhouette Pistol

## WICHITA CLASSIC PISTOL
**Caliber:** Any, up to and including 308 Win.
**Barrel:** 11¼", octagon.
**Weight:** About 5 lbs.
**Stock:** Exhibition grade American black walnut. Checkered 20 lpi. Other woods available on special order.
**Sights:** Micro open sights standard. Receiver drilled and tapped for scope mount.
**Features:** Receiver and barrel octagonally shaped, finished in non-glare blue. Bolt has three locking lugs and three gas escape ports. Completely adjustable Wichita trigger. Introduced 1980. From Wichita Arms.

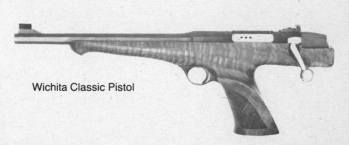

Wichita Classic Pistol

American Arms TP-70

## AMERICAN ARMS TP-70
**Caliber:** 22 LR, 25 ACP
**Barrel:** 2.6"
**Weight:** 12.6 oz. **Length:** 4.72" over-all.
**Stocks:** Checkered, composition.
**Sights:** Open, fixed
**Features:** Double action, stainless steel. Exposed hammer. Manual and magazine safeties. From M & N Distributors.

## AMT 45 ACP HARDBALLER LONG SLIDE
**Caliber:** 45 ACP.
**Barrel:** 7".
**Length:** 10½" over-all.
**Stocks:** Checkered walnut.
**Sights:** Fully adjustable Micro rear sight.
**Features:** Slide and barrel are 2" longer than the standard 45, giving less recoil, added velocity, longer sight radius. Has extended combat safety, serrated matte rib, loaded chamber indicator, wide adjustable trigger, custom fitted barrel bushing. From AMT.

## AMT "BACKUP" AUTO PISTOL
**Caliber:** 22 LR, 8-shot magazine; 380 ACP, 5-shot magazine
**Barrel:** 2½"
**Weight:** 17 oz. **Length:** 5" over-all.
**Stocks:** Smooth wood.
**Sights:** Fixed, open, recessed.
**Features:** Concealed hammer, blowback operation; manual and grip safeties. All stainless steel construction. Smallest domestically-produced pistol in 380. From AMT.

## AMT 45 ACP HARDBALLER
**Caliber:** 45 ACP.
**Barrel:** 5"
**Weight:** 39 oz. **Length:** 8½" over-all.
**Stocks:** Checkered walnut.
**Sights:** Adjustable combat-type.
**Features:** Extended combat safety, serrated matte slide rib, loaded chamber indicator, long grip safety, beveled magazine well, grooved front and back straps, adjustable target trigger, custom-fitted barrel bushing. All stainless steel. From AMT.

## AMERICAN DERRINGER 25 AUTO
**Caliber:** 25 ACP or 250 Magnum; 7-shot magazine.
**Barrel:** 2.1".
**Weight:** 15½ oz. **Length:** 4.4" over-all.
**Stocks:** Smooth rosewood.
**Sights:** Fixed.
**Features:** Stainless or ordnance steel. Magazines have finger extension. Introduced 1982. From American Derringer Corp.

American Derringer 25 Auto

Arminex Trifire Pistol

## ARMINEX TRIFIRE AUTO PISTOL
**Caliber:** 9mm. Para. (9-shot), 38 Super. (9-shot), 45 ACP (7-shot).
**Barrel:** 5".
**Weight:** 38 oz. **Length:** 8" over-all.
**Stocks:** Contoured smooth walnut.
**Sights:** Interchangeable post front on rib, rear adjustable for windage and elevation.
**Features:** Single action. Slide mounted firing pin block safety. Specially contoured one-piece backstrap. Convertible by changing barrel, magazine, recoil spring. Introduced 1982. Made in U.S. by Arminex Ltd.

### ASTRA CONSTABLE AUTO PISTOL
**Caliber:** 22 LR, 10-shot, 380 ACP, 7-shot.
**Barrel:** 3½″
**Weight:** 26 oz.
**Stocks:** Moulded plastic
**Sights:** Adj. rear.
**Features:** Double action, quick no-tool takedown, non-glare rib on slide. 380 available in blue or chrome finish. Imported from Spain by Interarms.

Astra Constable

### BAUER AUTOMATIC PISTOL
**Caliber:** 25 ACP, 6-shot.
**Barrel:** 2⅛″.
**Weight:** 10 oz. **Length:** 4″ over-all.
**Stocks:** Plastic pearl or checkered walnut.
**Sights:** Recessed, fixed.
**Features:** Stainless steel construction. Has positive manual safety as well as magazine safety.

Bauer Stainless Auto

### BERNARDELLI MODEL 80 AUTO PISTOL
**Caliber:** 22 LR (10-shot); 380 ACP (7-shot).
**Barrel:** 3½″.
**Weight:** 26½ oz. **Length:** 6½″ over-all.
**Stocks:** Checkered plastic with thumbrest.
**Sights:** Ramp front, white outline rear adj. for w. & e
**Features:** Hammer block slide safety; loaded chamber indicator; dual recoil buffer springs; serrated trigger; inertia type firing pin. Imported from Italy by Interarms.

Bernardelli Model 80

### BERETTA JETFIRE AUTO PISTOL
**Caliber:** 25 ACP
**Barrel:** 2½″.
**Weight:** 8 oz. **Length:** 4½″ over-all.
**Stocks:** Checkered black plastic.
**Sights:** Fixed.
**Features:** Thumb safety and half-cock safety; barrel hinged at front to pop up for single loading or cleaning. Made in U.S., available from J. L. Galef.

Beretta Minx Pistol

### Beretta Minx M2 Auto Pistol
Same basic gun as Jetfire except in 22 Short, weighs 10 oz. 6 shots.

### BERETTA MODEL 81/84 DA PISTOLS
**Caliber:** 32 ACP (12-shot magazine), 380 ACP (13-shot magazine).
**Barrel:** 3¾″
**Weight:** About 23 oz. **Length:** 6½″ over-all.
**Stocks:** Smooth black plastic (wood optional at extra cost).
**Sights:** Fixed front and rear.
**Features:** Double action, quick take-down, convenient magazine release. Introduced 1977. Imported from Italy by Beretta USA.

Beretta Model 81

## BERETTA MODEL 92 SB, 92 SB COMPACT
**Caliber:** 9mm Parabellum (15-shot magazine, 14-shot on Compact).
**Barrel:** 4.92".
**Weight:** 33½ oz. **Length:** 8.54" over-all.
**Stocks:** Smooth black plastic; wood optional at extra cost.
**Sights:** Blade front, rear adj. for w.
**Features:** Double-action. Extractor acts as chamber loaded indicator, inertia firing pin. Finished in blue-black. Introduced 1977. Imported from Italy by Beretta USA.

## BERETTA MODEL 70S PISTOL
**Caliber:** 22 LR, 380 ACP.
**Barrel:** 3.5".
**Weight:** 23 oz. (Steel) **Length:** 6.5" over-all.
**Stocks:** Checkered black plastic.
**Sights:** Fixed front and rear.
**Features:** Steel frame in 380, light alloy in 22 (wgt. 18 oz.). Safety lever blocks hammer. Slide lever indicates empty magazine. Magazine capacity is 8 rounds (22). 7 rounds in 380. Introduced 1977. Imported from Italy by Beretta USA.

## BERSA MODEL 644 AUTO PISTOL
**Caliber:** 22 Long Rifle, 10-shot magazine.
**Barrel:** 3½".
**Weight:** 26½ oz. **Length:** 6½" over-all.
**Stocks:** Contoured black nylon.
**Sights:** Blade front, rear drift-adj. for windage.
**Features:** Has three safety devices; firing pin safety, hammer safety and magazine safety. Button release magazine with finger rest. Introduced 1980. Imported from Argentina by Interarms.

## BROWNING BDA-380 D/A AUTO PISTOL
**Caliber:** 380 ACP, 13-shot magazine.
**Barrel:** 3¹³/₁₆".
**Weight:** 23 oz. **Length:** 6¾" over-all.
**Stocks:** Smooth walnut with inset Browning medallion.
**Sights:** Blade front, rear drift-adj. for w.
**Features:** Combination safety and de-cocking lever will automatically lower a cocked hammer to half-cock and can be operated by right or left-hand shooters. Inertia firing pin. Introduced 1978. Imported from Italy by Browning.

## BROWNING HI-POWER 9mm AUTOMATIC PISTOL
**Caliber:** 9mm Parabellum (Luger), 13-shot magazine.
**Barrel:** 4²¹/₃₂".
**Weight:** 32 oz. **Length:** 7¾" over-all.
**Stocks:** Walnut, hand checkered.
**Sights:** ⅛" blade front; rear screw-adj. for w. and e. Also available with fixed rear (drift-adj for w.).
**Features:** External hammer with half-cock and thumb safeties. A blow on the hammer cannot discharge a cartridge; cannot be fired with magazine removed. Fixed rear sight model available. Imported from Belgium by Browning.

Browning Louis XVI Hi-Power

### Browning Louis XVI Hi-Power 9mm Auto
Same as Browning Hi-Power 9mm Auto except: fully engraved, silver-gray frame and slide, gold plated trigger, finely checkered walnut grips, with deluxe walnut case.

### High Power 88 Auto Pistol II
Similar to the standard Browning High Power except available only with fixed rear sight, military parkerized finish, black checkered polyamid grips. Comes with extra magazine. Introduced 1982. Imported from Belgium by Howco Distributors, Inc.

Browning Challenger II Pistol

### BROWNING CHALLENGER II AUTO PISTOL
**Caliber:** 22 LR, 10-shot magazine.
**Barrel:** 6¾".
**Weight:** 38 oz. **Length:** 10⅞" over-all.
**Stocks:** Smooth impregnated hardwood.
**Sights:** ⅛" blade front on ramp, rear screw adj. for e., drift adj. for w.
**Features:** All steel, blue finish. Wedge locking system prevents action from loosening. Wide gold-plated trigger; action hold-open. Standard grade only. Made in U.S. From Browning.

Browning Challenger III Pistol

### Browning Challenger III Auto Pistol
Similar to the Challenger II except has a 5½" heavy bull barrel, new lightweight alloy frame and new sights. Over-all length is 9½", weight is 34 oz. Introduced 1982.

### BUSHMASTER AUTO PISTOL
**Caliber:** 223; 30-shot magazine.
**Barrel:** 11½".
**Weight:** 5¼ lbs. **Length:** 20½" over-all.
**Stocks:** Synthetic rotating grip swivel assembly.
**Sights:** Post front, adjustable open "y" rear
**Features:** Steel alloy upper receiver with welded barrel assembly, AK-47-type gas system, aluminum lower receiver, one-piece welded steel alloy bolt carrier assembly. From Bushmaster Firearms.

Bushmaster Auto Pistol

### CHARTER EXPLORER S II PISTOL
**Caliber:** 22 LR, 8-shot magazine.
**Barrel:** 8".
**Weight:** 28 oz. **Length:** 15½" over-all.
**Stocks:** Serrated simulated walnut.
**Sights:** Blade front, open rear adj. for elevation.
**Features:** Action adapted from the semi-auto Explorer carbine. Introduced 1980. From Charter Arms.

Charter Explorer S II Pistol

Colt Service Model Ace

**COLT SERVICE MODEL ACE**
**Caliber:** 22 LR, 10-shot magazine.
**Barrel:** 5″
**Weight:** 42 oz. **Length:** 8⅜″ over-all.
**Stocks:** Checkered walnut.
**Sights:** Blade front, fully adjustable rear.
**Features:** The 22-cal. version of the Government Model auto. Based on the Service Model Ace last produced in 1945. Patented floating chamber. Original Ace Markings rolled on left side of slide. Introduced 1978.

Colt Government Model

**COLT GOV'T MODEL MK IV/SERIES 70**
**Caliber:** 9mm, 38 Super, 45 ACP, 7-shot.
**Barrel:** 5″.
**Weight:** 40 oz. **Length:** 8⅜″ over-all.
**Stocks:** Sandblasted walnut panels.
**Sights:** Ramp front, fixed square notch rear.
**Features:** Grip and thumb safeties, grooved trigger. Accurizor barrel and bushing. Blue finish or nickel in 45 only.

**Colt Conversion Unit**
Permits the 45 and 38 Super Automatic pistols to use the economical 22 LR cartridge. No tools needed. Adjustable rear sight; 10-shot magazine. Designed to give recoil effect of the larger calibers. Not adaptable to Commander models. Blue finish.

Colt Combat Commander

**COLT COMBAT COMMANDER AUTO PISTOL**
**Caliber:** 45 ACP, 7-shot; 38 Super Auto, 9-shot; 9mm Luger, 9-shot.
**Barrel:** 4¼″.
**Weight:** 36 oz. **Length:** 8″ over-all.
**Stocks:** Sandblasted walnut.
**Sights:** Fixed, glare-proofed blade front, square notch rear.
**Features:** Grooved trigger and hammer spur; arched housing; grip and thumb safeties.

**Colt Lightweight Commander**
Same as Commander except high strength aluminum alloy frame, wood panel grips, weight 27 oz. 45 ACP only.

Detonics Auto Pistol

**DETONICS 45 PISTOL**
**Caliber:** 45 ACP, 6-shot clip; 9mm Para., 8-shot clip.
**Barrel:** 3¼″ (2½″ of which is rifled).
**Weight:** 29 oz. (empty); MK VII is 26 oz. **Length:** 6¾″ over-all, 4½″ high.
**Stocks:** Checkered walnut.
**Sights:** Combat type, fixed; adj. sights avail.
**Features:** Has a self-adjusting cone barrel centering system, beveled magazine inlet, "full clip" indicator in base of magazine; standard 7-shot (or more) clip can be used in the 45. Throated barrel and polished feed ramp. Mark V, VI, VII available in 9mm. Introduced 1977. From Detonics.

## EAGLE 357 MAGNUM PISTOL
**Caliber:** 357 Magnum, 9-shot clip.
**Barrel:** 6″, 8″, 10″, 14″ interchangeable.
**Weight:** 52 oz. **Length:** 10¼″ over-all (6″ bbl.).
**Stocks:** Wrap-around soft rubber.
**Sights:** Blade on ramp front, adjustable combat-style rear.
**Features:** Rotating six lug bolt, ambidextrous safety, combat-style trigger guard and adjustable trigger. Military epoxy finish. Announced 1982. Imported from Israel by Magnum Research Inc.

## ERMA KGP22 AUTO PISTOL
**Caliber:** 22 LR, 8-shot magazine.
**Barrel:** 4″.
**Weight:** 29 oz. **Length:** 7¾″ over-all.
**Stocks:** Checkered plastic.
**Sights:** Fixed.
**Features:** Has toggle action similar to original "Luger" pistol. Slide stays open after last shot. Imported from West Germany by Excam. Introduced 1978.

## F.I.E. "SUPER TITAN II" PISTOLS
**Caliber:** 32 ACP, 380 ACP.
**Barrel:** 3⅞″.
**Weight:** 28 oz. **Length:** 6¾″ over-all.
**Stocks:** Smooth, polished walnut.
**Sights:** Adjustable.
**Features:** Blue finish only. 12 shot (32 ACP), 11 shot (360 ACP). Introduced 1981. From F.I.E. Corp. (32 cal. made in Italy, 380 made in U.S.).

## F.I.E. "TITAN 25" PISTOL
**Caliber:** 25 ACP, 6-shot magazine.
**Barrel:** 2⁷⁄₁₆″.
**Weight:** 12 oz. **Length:** 4⅝″ over-all.
**Stocks:** Checkered nylon; checkered walnut optional.
**Sights:** Fixed.
**Features:** External hammer; fast simple takedown. Made in U.S.A. by F.I.E. Corp.

## F.I.E. TITAN II PISTOLS
**Caliber:** 32 ACP, 380 ACP, 6-shot magazine; 22 LR, 10-shot magazine.
**Barrel:** 3⅞″.
**Weight:** 25¾ oz. **Length:** 6¾″ over-all.
**Stocks:** Checkered nylon, thumbrest-type; checkered walnut optional.
**Sights:** Adjustable.
**Features:** Magazine disconnector, firing pin block. Standard slide safety. Available in blue or chrome. Introduced 1978. From F.I.E. Corp. (32 cal. made in Italy, 380 made in U.S.).

## ERMA KGP32, KGP38 AUTO PISTOLS
**Caliber:** 32 ACP (6-shot), 380 ACP (5-shot).
**Barrel:** 4″.
**Weight:** 22½ oz. **Length:** 7⅜″ over-all.
**Stocks:** Checkered plastic. Wood optional.
**Sights:** Rear adjustable for windage.
**Features:** Toggle action similar to original "Luger" pistol. Slide stays open after last shot. Has magazine and sear disconnect safety systems. Imported from West Germany by Excam. Introduced 1978.

Erma KGP22 Pistol

## ERMA-EXCAM RX 22 AUTO PISTOL
**Caliber:** 22 LR, 8-shot magazine.
**Barrel:** 3¼″.
**Weight:** 21 oz. **Length:** 5.58″ over-all.
**Stocks:** Plastic wrap-around.
**Sights:** Fixed
**Features:** Polished blue finish. Double action. Patented ignition safety system. Thumb safety. Assembled in U.S. Introduced 1980. From Excam.

## F.I.E. "THE BEST" A27B PISTOL
**Caliber:** 25 ACP, 6-shot magazine.
**Barrel:** 2½″.
**Weight:** 13 oz. **Length:** 4⅜″ over-all.
**Stocks:** Checkered walnut.
**Sights:** Fixed.
**Features:** All steel construction. Has thumb and magazine safeties, exposed hammer. Blue finish only. Introduced 1978. Made in U.S. by F.I.E. Corp.

F.I.E. Titan II Pistol

## FTL 22 AUTO NINE PISTOL
**Caliber:** 22 LR, 8-shot magazine.
**Barrel:** 2¼", 6-groove rifling.
**Weight:** 8¼ oz. **Length:** 4⅜" over-all.
**Stocks:** Checkered plastic.
**Sights:** U-notch in slide.
**Features:** Alloy frame, rest is ordnance steel. Has barrel support sleeve bushing for better accuracy. Finish is matte hard chrome. Introduced 1978. Made in U.S. From FTL Marketing.

FTL·Auto Nine Pistol

## GUARDIAN-SS AUTO PISTOL
**Caliber:** 380 ACP, 6-shot magazine.
**Barrel:** 3.25"
**Weight:** 20 oz. **Length:** 6" over-all.
**Stocks:** Checkered walnut.
**Sights:** Ramp front, combat-type rear adjustable for windage.
**Features:** Double action, made of stainless steel. Custom Guardian has narrow polished trigger, Pachmayr grips, blue slide, hand-fitted barrel, polished feed ramp, funneled magazine well. Introduced 1982. From Michigan Armament, Inc.

Guardian-SS Stainless Pistol

## HECKLER & KOCH P9S DOUBLE ACTION AUTO
**Caliber:** 9mm Para., 9-shot magazine; 45 ACP, 7-shot magazine.
**Barrel:** 4".
**Weight:** 31 oz. **Length:** 7.6" over-all.
**Stocks:** Checkered black plastic.
**Sights:** Open combat type.
**Features:** Double action; polygonal rifling; sliding roller lock action with stationary barrel. Loaded chamber and cocking indicators; un-cocking lever relaxes springs. Imported from West Germany by Heckler & Koch, Inc.

Heckler & Koch P9S Pistol

## HECKLER & KOCH HK-4 DOUBLE ACTION PISTOL
**Caliber:** 22 LR, 25 ACP, 32 ACP, 380 ACP, 8-shot magazine (7 in 380).
**Barrel:** 3¹¹⁄₃₂".
**Weight:** 16½ oz. **Length:** 6³⁄₁₆" over-all.
**Stocks:** Black checkered plastic.
**Sights:** Fixed blade front, rear notched drift-adj. for w.
**Features:** Gun comes with all parts to shoot above four calibers; polygonal (hexagon) rifling; matte black finish. Imported from West Germany by Heckler & Koch, Inc.

## HECKLER & KOCH P7 (PSP) AUTO PISTOL
**Caliber:** 9mm Parabellum, 8-shot magazine.
**Barrel:** 4.13".
**Weight:** 29 oz. **Length:** 6.54" over-all.
**Stocks:** Stippled black plastic.
**Sights:** Fixed, combat-type.
**Features:** Unique "squeeze cocker" in front strap cocks the action. Squared combat-type trigger guard. Blue finish. Compact size. Imported from West Germany by Heckler & Koch, Inc.

Heckler & Kock P7 (PSP) Pistol

## HECKLER & KOCH VP 70Z DOUBLE ACTION AUTO
**Caliber:** 9mm Para., 18-shot magazine.
**Barrel:** 4½".
**Weight:** 32½ oz. **Length:** 8" over-all.
**Stocks:** Black stippled plastic.
**Sights:** Ramp front, channeled slide rear.
**Features:** Recoil operated, double action. Only 4 moving parts. Double column
magazine. Imported from West Germany by Heckler & Koch, Inc.

Heckler & Koch VP 70S Pistol

Helwan Auto Pistol

## HELWAN 9mm AUTO PISTOL
**Caliber:** 9mm Parabellum, 8-shot magazine.
**Barrel:** 4½".
**Weight:** 33 oz. **Length:** 8¼" over-all.
**Stocks:** Grooved black plastic.
**Sights:** Blade front, rear drift-adjustable for windage.
**Features:** Updated version of the Beretta Model 951. Made by the Maadi Co.
for Engineering Industries of Egypt. Introduced to U.S. market 1982. Import-
ed from Egypt by Steyr Daimler Puch of America.

## HIGH STANDARD SHARPSHOOTER AUTO PISTOL
**Caliber:** 22 LR, 10-shot magazine.
**Barrel:** 5½".
**Weight:** 42 oz. **Length:** 10¼" over-all.
**Stocks:** Checkered walnut.
**Sights:** Ramp front, square notch rear adj. for w. & e.
**Features:** Military frame. Wide, scored trigger; new hammer-sear design. Slide
lock, push-button take down.

High Standard Sharpshooter

### High Standard Survival Pack
Includes the High Standard Sharpshooter pistol finished in electroless nickel,
extra magazine, and a padded canvas carrying case with three interior pockets for carrying the extra magazine, knife, compass, etc. Introduced 1982.

## HIGH STANDARD SPORT-KING AUTO PISTOL
**Caliber:** 22 LR, 10-shot.
**Barrel:** 4½" or 6¾".
**Weight:** 39 oz. (4½" bbl.). **Length:** 9" over-all (4½" bbl.).
**Stocks:** Checkered walnut.
**Sights:** Blade front, fixed rear.
**Features:** Takedown barrel. Blue only. Military frame.

## INGRAM M-10, M-11 SEMI-AUTO PISTOLS
**Caliber:** 9mm, 45 ACP(M-10), 380 ACP (M-11)
**Barrel:** 5.75" (M-10), 5.06" (M-11).
**Weight:** 6¼ lbs. (M-10). **Length:** 10.5" over-all (M-10).
**Stocks:** High impact plastic.
**Sights:** Protected post front, aperture rear fixed for 100 meters.
**Features:** Semi-auto versions of the selective-fire submachine guns. 45 and
380 have 16-round magazines, 9mm is 32 rounds. Made in U.S. by R.P.B.
Industries.

Interdynamic KG-9 Pistol

## INTERDYNAMIC KG-9 PISTOL
**Caliber:** 9mm Parabellum; 32 shot magazine.
**Barrel:** 5".
**Weight:** 46 oz. **Length:** 12½" over-all.
**Stocks:** High-impact plastic.
**Sights:** Blade front; fixed, open rear.
**Features:** Semi-auto only. Straight blowback action fires from an open bolt.
Entire frame is high-impact black plastic. Introduced 1982. From F.I.E. Corp.

### JENNINGS J-22 AUTO PISTOL
**Caliber:** 22 LR, 6-shot magazine.
**Barrel:** 2½".
**Weight:** 13 oz. **Length:** 4¹⁵⁄₁₆" over-all.
**Stocks:** Checkered walnut.
**Sights:** Fixed.
**Features:** Satin chrome finish. Introduced 1981. From Jennings Firearms.

Jennings J-22 Pistol

### IVER JOHNSON MODEL X300 PONY
**Caliber:** 380 ACP, 6-shot magazine.
**Barrel:** 3".
**Weight:** 20 oz. **Length:** 6" over-all.
**Stocks:** Checkered walnut.
**Sights:** Blade front, rear adj. for w.
**Features:** Loaded chamber indicator, all steel construction. Inertia firing pin. Thumb safety locks hammer. No magazine safety. Lanyard ring. Made in U.S., available from Iver Johnson's.

### IVER JOHNSON PP22 AUTO PISTOL
**Caliber:** 22 LR, 25 ACP.
**Barrel:** 2.85".
**Weight:** 14½ oz. **Length:** 5.39" over-all.
**Stocks:** Black checkered plastic.
**Sights:** Fixed.
**Features:** Double action; 7-shot magazine. Introduced 1981. From Iver Johnson's.

### IVER JOHNSON PP30 "SUPER ENFORCER" PISTOL
**Caliber:** 30 U.S. Carbine.
**Barrel:** 9".
**Weight:** 4 lbs. **Length:** 17" over-all.
**Stocks:** American walnut.
**Sights:** Blade front; click adjustable peep rear.
**Features:** Shortened version of the M1 Carbine. Uses 15 or 30-shot magazines. From Iver Johnson's.

Llama Omni D.A. Pistol

### LLAMA OMNI DOUBLE-ACTION AUTO
**Caliber:** 9mm (13-shot), 45 ACP (7-shot).
**Barrel:** 4¼".
**Weight:** 40 oz. **Length:** 9mm—8", 45—7¾" over-all.
**Stocks:** Checkered plastic.
**Sights:** Ramped blade front, rear adjustable for windage and elevation (45), drift-adjustable for windage (9mm).
**Features:** New DA pistol has ball-bearing action, double sear bars, articulated firing pin, buttressed locking lug and low-friction rifling. Introduced 1982. Imported from Spain by Stoeger Industries.

Llama Large Frame Auto

Llama Small Frame Auto

### LLAMA LARGE FRAME AUTO PISTOLS
**Caliber:** 38 Super, 45 ACP.
**Barrel:** 5".
**Weight:** 30 oz. **Length:** 8½" over-all.
**Stocks:** Checkered walnut.
**Sights:** Fixed.
**Features:** Grip and manual safeties, ventilated rib. Engraved, chrome engraved or gold damascened finish available at extra cost. Imported from Spain by Stoeger Industries.

### LLAMA SMALL FRAME AUTO PISTOLS
**Caliber:** 22 LR, 32 ACP and 380.
**Barrel:** 3¹¹⁄₁₆".
**Weight:** 23 oz. **Length:** 6½" over-all.
**Stocks:** Checkered plastic, thumb rest.
**Sights:** Fixed front, adj. notch rear.
**Features:** Ventilated rib, manual and grip safeties. Model XV is 22 LR, Model XA is 32 ACP, and Model IIIA is 380. Models XA and IIIA have loaded indicator; IIIA is locked breech. Imported from Spain by Stoeger Industries.

## MAB MODEL P-15 AUTO PISTOL
**Caliber:** 9mm Para., 15-shot magazine.
**Barrel:** 4½".
**Weight:** 41 oz. **Length:** 8⅛" over-all.
**Stocks:** Checkered black plastic.
**Sights:** Fixed.
**Features:** Rotating barrel-type locking system; thumb safety, magazine disconnector. Blue finish. Introduced 1982. Imported from France by Howco Distr., Inc.

Turkish MKE Pistol

## LLAMA 9mm LARGE FRAME AUTO PISTOL
**Caliber:** 9mm Para.
**Barrel:** 5".
**Weight:** 38 oz. **Length:** 8½" over-all.
**Stocks:** Moulded plastic.
**Sights:** Fixed Front, adj. rear.
**Features:** Also available with engraved, chrome engraved or gold damascened finish at extra cost. Imported from Spain by Stoeger Industries.

## MKE AUTO PISTOL
**Caliber:** 380 ACP; 7-shot magazine.
**Barrel:** 4".
**Weight:** 23 oz. **Length:** 6½" over-all.
**Stocks:** Hard rubber.
**Sights:** Fixed front, rear adjustable for windage.
**Features:** Double action with exposed hammer; chamber loaded indicator. Imported from Turkey by Mandall Shooting Supplies.

## N.A.M. 45 WIN MAG+
**Caliber:** 9mm, Win. Mag. (7-shot magazine.).
**Barrel:** 5⅜".
**Weight:** 51 oz. **Length:** 9¼" over-all.
**Stocks:** Checkered rubber combat-type.
**Sights:** Ramped blade front, rear adjustable for windage and elevation.
**Features:** Stainless steel slide and frame, non-corrosive alloy steel for other parts. Polished feed ramp, throated barrel. Precision-fitted barrel bushing, hand-honed action. **Announced** 1982. From North American Mfg. Corp.

O.D.I. Viking D.A. Pistol

## O.D.I. VIKING D.A. AUTO PISTOL
**Caliber:** 9mm Para. or 45 ACP.
**Barrel:** 5".
**Weight:** 39 oz.
**Stocks:** Smooth teakwood standard; other materials available.
**Sights:** Fixed. Blade front, notched rear.
**Features:** Made entirely of stainless steel, brushed satin, natural finish. Features the Seecamp double action system. Spur-type hammer. Magazine holds 9 rounds in 9mm, 7 rounds in 45 ACP. Made in U.S.A. From O.D.I.

## O.D.I. Viking Combat Model D.A. Pistol
Same construction and design as Viking model except has 4¼" barrel, ring-type hammer, and weighs 36 oz. Made in U.S.A. by O.D.I.

## RAVEN P-25 AUTO PISTOL
**Caliber:** 25 ACP, 6-shot magazine.
**Barrel:** 2⁷⁄₁₆".
**Weight:** 15 oz. **Length:** 4¾" over-all.
**Stocks:** Smooth walnut.
**Sights:** Ramped front, fixed rear.
**Features:** Available in blue, nickel or chrome finish. Made in U.S., available from EMF Co.

## RG 26 AUTO PISTOL
**Caliber:** 25 ACP, 6-shot magazine.
**Barrel:** 2½".
**Weight:** 12 oz. **Length:** 4¾" over-all.
**Stocks:** Checkered plastic.
**Sights:** Fixed.
**Features:** Blue finish. Thumb safety. Imported by RG Industries.

Raven P-25 Pistol

Ruger Mark II Auto

## RUGER MARK II STANDARD AUTO PISTOL
**Caliber:** 22 LR, 10-shot magazine.
**Barrel:** 4¾" or 6".
**Weight:** 36 oz. (4¾" bbl.). **Length:** 8¾ (4¾" bbl.).
**Stocks:** Checkered hard rubber.
**Sights:** Fixed, wide blade front, square notch rear adj. for w.
**Features:** Updated design of the original Standard Auto. Has new bolt hold-open device, 10-shot magazine, magazine catch, safety, trigger and new receiver contours. Introduced 1982.

SIG P-210-1 Pistol

## SIG P-210-1 AUTO PISTOL
**Caliber:** 7.65mm or 9mm Para., 8-shot magazine.
**Barrel:** 4¾".
**Weight:** 31¾ oz. (9mm) **Length:** 8½" over-all.
**Stocks:** Checkered walnut.
**Sights:** Blade front, rear adjustable for windage.
**Features:** Lanyard loop; polished finish. Conversion unit for 22 LR available. Imported from Switzerland by Mandall Shooting Supplies and Waidmanns Guns International.

## SIG P-210-6 AUTO PISTOL
**Caliber:** 9mm Para., 8-shot magazine.
**Barrel:** 4¾".
**Weight:** 37 oz. **Length:** 8½" over-all.
**Stocks:** Checkered black plastic.
**Sights:** Blade front, micro. adj. rear for w. & e.
**Features:** Adjustable trigger stop; ribbed front stap; sandblasted finish. Conversion unit for 22 LR consists of barrel, recoil spring, slide and magazine. Imported from Switzerland by Mandall Shooting Supplies and Waidmanns Guns International.

SIG-Sauer P-220 Pistol

## SIG-SAUER P-220 D.A. AUTO PISTOL
**Caliber:** 9mm, 38 Super; 45 ACP. (9-shot in 9mm and 38 Super, 7 in 45).
**Barrel:** 4⅜".
**Weight:** 28¼ oz. (9mm). **Length:** 7¾" over-all.
**Stocks:** Checkered walnut.
**Sights:** Blade front, drift adj. rear for w.
**Features:** Double action. De-cocking lever permits lowering hammer onto locked firing pin. Squared combat-type trigger guard. Slide stays open after last shot. Imported from West Germany by Interarms.

SIG-Sauer P-225 Pistol

## SIG-SAUER P-225 D.A. AUTO PISTOL
**Caliber:** 9mm Parabellum, 8-shot magazine.
**Barrel:** 3.8".
**Weight:** 26 oz. **Length:** 7³⁄₃₂" over-all.
**Stocks:** Checkered black plastic.
**Sights:** Blade front, rear adjustable for windage.
**Features:** Double action; decocking lever permits lowering hammer onto locked firing pin. Squared combat-type trigger guard. Shortened, lightened version of P-220. Imported from West Germany by Interarms.

SIG-Sauer P-230 D.A. Pistol

## SIG-SAUER P-230 D.A. AUTO PISTOL
**Caliber:** 380 ACP (7 shot).
**Barrel:** 3¾".
**Weight:** 16 oz. **Length:** 6½" over-all.
**Stocks:** One piece black plastic.
**Sights:** Blade front, rear adj. for w.
**Features:** Double action. Same basic design as P-220. Blowback operation, stationary barrel. Introduced 1977. Imported from West Germany by Interarms.

## SILE-SEECAMP II STAINLESS DA AUTO
**Caliber:** 25 ACP, 8-shot magazine.
**Barrel:** 2", integral with frame.
**Weight:** About 10 oz. **Length:** 4⅛" over-all.
**Stocks:** Black plastic.
**Sights:** Smooth, no-snag, contoured slide and barrel top.
**Features:** Aircraft quality 17-4 PH stainless steel. Inertia operated firing pin. Hammer fired double action only. Hammer automatically follows slide down to safety rest position after each shot—no manual safety needed. Magazine safety disconnector. Introduced 1980. From Sile Distributors.

Sile-Benelli Model B76 Pistol

## SILE-BENELLI B76 DA AUTO PISTOL
**Caliber:** 9mm Para., 8-shot magazine.
**Barrel:** 4¼", 6-groove. Chrome-lined bore.
**Weight:** 34 oz. (empty). **Length:** 8¹/₁₆" over-all.
**Stocks:** Walnut with cut checkering and high gloss finish.
**Sights:** Blade front with white face, rear adjustable for windage with white bars for increased visibility.
**Features:** Fixed barrel, locked breech. Exposed hammer can be locked in non-firing mode in either single or double action. Stainless steel inertia firing pin and loaded chamber indicator. All external parts blued, internal parts hard-chrome plated. All steel construction. Introduced 1979. From Sile Dist.

## SMITH & WESSON MODEL 59 DOUBLE ACTION
**Caliber:** 9mm Luger, 14-shot clip.
**Barrel:** 4".
**Weight:** 27½ oz., without clip. **Length:** 7⁷/₁₆" over-all.
**Stocks:** Checkered high impact moulded nylon.
**Sights:** ⅛" serrated ramp front, square notch rear adj. for w.
**Features:** Double action automatic. Furnished with two magazines. Blue finish.

Smith & Wesson Model 59

## SMITH & WESSON 9mm MODEL 39 AUTO PISTOL
**Caliber:** 9mm Luger, 8-shot clip.
**Barrel:** 4".
**Weight:** 26½ oz., without magazine. **Length:** 7⁷/₁₆" over-all.
**Stocks:** Checkered walnut.
**Sights:** ⅛" serrated ramp front, adjustable rear.
**Features:** Magazine disconnector, positive firing pin lock and hammer-release safety; alloy frame with lanyard loop; locked-breech, short-recoil double action; slide locks open on last shot.

Smith & Wesson Model 439

## SMITH & WESSON MODEL 439 DOUBLE ACTION
**Caliber:** 9mm Luger, 8-shot clip.
**Barrel:** 4".
**Weight:** 27 oz. **Length:** 7⁷/₁₆" over-all.
**Stocks:** Checkered walnut.
**Sights:** ⅛" square serrated ramp front, square notch rear is fully adj. for w. & e.
**Features:** Rear sight has protective shields on both sides of the sight blade. Frame is alloy. New trigger actuated firing pin lock in addition to the regular rotating safety. Magazine disconnector. New extractor design. Comes with two magazines. Introduced 1980.

## SMITH & WESSON MODEL 459 DOUBLE ACTION
**Caliber:** 9mm Luger, 14-shot clip.
**Barrel:** 4".
**Weight:** 28 oz. **Length:** 7⁷/₁₆" over-all.
**Stocks:** Checkered high-impact nylon.
**Sights:** ⅛" square serrated ramp front, square notch rear is fully adj. for w. & e.
**Features:** Alloy frame. Rear sight has protective shields on both sides of blade. New trigger actuated firing pin lock in addition to the regular safety. Magazine disconnector; new extractor design. Comes with two magazines. Introduced 1980.

## STAR MODEL PD AUTO PISTOL
**Caliber:** 45 ACP, 7-shot magazine.
**Barrel:** 3.94".
**Weight:** 28 oz. **Length:** 7⁷⁄₁₆" over-all.
**Stocks:** Checkered walnut.
**Sights:** Ramp front, fully adjustable rear.
**Features:** Rear sight milled into slide; thumb safety; grooved non-slip front strap; nylon recoil buffer; inertia firing pin; no grip or magazine safeties. Imported from Spain by Interarms.

Star Model PD Pistol

## STAR BM, BKM AUTO PISTOLS
**Caliber:** 9mm Para., 8-shot magazine.
**Barrel:** 3.9".
**Weight:** 25 oz.
**Stocks:** Checkered walnut.
**Sights:** Fixed.
**Features:** Blue or chrome finish. Magazine and manual safeties, external hammer. Imported from Spain by Interarms.

Star Model BM, BKM Pistol

## STERLING MODEL 300
**Caliber:** 25 ACP, 6-shot.
**Barrel:** 2½".
**Weight:** 13 oz. **Length:** 4½" over-all.
**Stocks:** Black Cycolac.
**Sights:** Fixed.
**Features:** All steel construction.

Sterling Model 400 MK. II D.A.

## STERLING MODEL 302
**Caliber:** 22 LR, 6-shot.
**Barrel:** 2½".
**Weight:** 13 oz. **Length:** 4½" over-all.
**Stocks:** Black Cycolac.
**Sights:** Fixed.
**Features:** All steel construction.

## STERLING MODEL 400 MK II DOUBLE ACTION
**Caliber:** 32, 380 ACP, 7-shot.
**Barrel:** 3¾".
**Weight:** 18 oz. **Length:** 6½" over-all.
**Stocks:** Checkered walnut.
**Sights:** Low profile, adj.
**Features:** All steel construction. Double action.

Sterling Model 300 Pistol

Steyr GB D.A. Pistol

## STEYR GB DOUBLE ACTION AUTO PISTOL
**Caliber:** 9mm Parabellum; 18-shot magazine.
**Barrel:** 5.39".
**Weight:** 33 oz. **Length:** 8.4" over-all.
**Stocks:** Checkered walnut.
**Sights:** Post front, fixed rear.
**Features:** Gas-operated, delayed blowback action. Measures 5.7" high, 1.3" wide. Introduced 1981. Imported by Steyr Daimler Puch.

## STOEGER LUGER 22 AUTO PISTOL
**Caliber:** 22 LR, 10-shot.
**Barrel:** 4½".
**Weight:** 30 oz. **Length:** 8⅞" over-all.
**Stocks:** Checkered walnut.
**Sights:** Fixed.
**Features:** Action remains open after last shot and as magazine is removed. Grip and balance identical to P-08.

Stoeger Luger 22 Auto

## TARGA MODELS GT32, GT380 AUTO PISTOLS
**Caliber:** 32 ACP or 380 ACP, 6-shot magazine.
**Barrel:** 4⅞".
**Weight:** 26 oz. **Length:** 7⅜" over-all.
**Stocks:** Checkered nylon with thumb rest. Walnut optional.
**Sights:** Fixed blade front; rear drift-adj. for w.
**Features:** Chrome or blue finish; magazine, thumb, and firing pin safeties; external hammer; safety lever take-down. Imported from Italy by Excam, Inc.

## TARGA GT380XE GT32XE PISTOLS
**Caliber:** 32 ACP or 380 ACP, 12-shot magazine.
**Barrel:** 3.88".
**Weight:** 28 oz. **Length:** 7.38" over-all.
**Stocks:** Smooth hardwood.
**Sights:** Adj. for windage.
**Features:** Blue or satin nickel. Ordnance steel. Magazine disconnector, firing pin and thumb safeties. Introduced 1980. Imported by Excam.

## TARGA MODEL GT27 AUTO PISTOL
**Caliber:** 25 ACP, 6-shot magazine.
**Barrel:** 2⁷⁄₁₆".
**Weight:** 12 oz. **Length:** 4⅝" over-all.
**Stocks:** Checkered nylon.
**Sights:** Fixed.
**Features:** Safety lever take-down; external hammer with half-cock. Assembled in U.S. by Excam, Inc.

Taurus PT-92 Auto Pistol

## TAURUS MODEL PT92 AUTO PISTOL
**Caliber:** 9mm P., 15-shot magazine.
**Barrel:** 4.92".
**Weight:** 34 oz. **Length:** 8.54" over-all.
**Stocks:** Black plastic.
**Sights:** Fixed notch rear.
**Features:** Double action, exposed hammer, chamber loaded indicator. Inertia firing pin. Blue finish.

Thompson 1911A1 Auto Pistol

## THOMPSON 1911A1 AUTOMATIC PISTOL
**Caliber:** 45 ACP, 7-shot magazine.
**Barrel:** 5".
**Weight:** 39 oz. **Length:** 8½" over-all.
**Stocks:** Checkered plastic with medallion.
**Sights:** Blade front, rear adj. for windage.
**Features:** Same specs as 1911A1 military guns—parts interchangeable. Frame and slide blued; each radius has non-glare finish. Made in U.S. by Auto-Ordnance Corp.

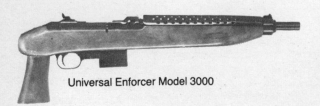

Universal Enforcer Model 3000

## UNIVERSAL ENFORCER MODEL 3000 AUTO
**Caliber:** 30 M1 Carbine, 5-shot magazine.
**Barrel:** 10¼" with 12-groove rifling.
**Weight:** 4½ lbs. **Length:** 17¾" over-all.
**Stocks:** American walnut with handguard
**Sights:** Gold bead ramp front. Peep rear.
**Features:** Accepts 15 or 30-shot magazines. 4½-6 lb. trigger pull.
**Price:** Blue finish . . . . . . . . . . . . . . . . . . . . . . . . . . . . . . . . . . . . . . . . **$279.00**

## VEGA STAINLESS 45 AUTO
**Caliber:** 45 ACP, 7-shot.
**Barrel:** 5".
**Weight:** 40 oz. **Length:** 8⅜" over-all.
**Stocks:** Checkered walnut, diamond pattern.
**Sights:** Choice of fixed high combat-type or adjustable rear.
**Features:** Made completely of stainless steel and matches the original 1911A1 Colt almost exactly. Has both grip and thumb safeties. Slide and frame flats are polished, rest sand blasted. From Pacific International Merchandising Corp.

## WALTHER PP AUTO PISTOL
**Caliber:** 22 LR, 8-shot; 32 ACP, 380 ACP, 7-shot.
**Barrel:** 3.86".
**Weight:** 23½ oz. **Length:** 6.7" over-all.
**Stocks:** Checkered plastic.
**Sights:** Fixed, white markings.
**Features:** Double action, manual safety blocks firing pin and drops hammer, chamber loaded indicator on 32 and 380, extra finger rest magazine provided. Imported from Germany by Interarms.

## Walther American PPK/S Auto Pistol
Similar to Walther PP except made entirely in the United States. Has 3.27" barrel with 6.1" length over-all.

## WALTHER P-38 AUTO PISTOL
**Caliber:** 22 LR, 30 Luger or 9mm Luger, 8-shot.
**Barrel:** 4¹⁵⁄₁₆" (9mm and 30), 5¹⁄₁₆" (22 LR).
**Weight:** 28 oz. **Length:** 8½" over-all.
**Stocks:** Checkered plastic.
**Sights:** Fixed.
**Features:** Double action, safety blocks firing pin and drops hammer, chamber loaded indicator. Matte finish standard, polished blue, engraving and/or plating available. Imported from Germany by Interarms.

## VIKING SEMI-AUTO MINI PISTOL
**Caliber:** 9mm Para., 36-shot magazine.
**Barrel:** 7½".
**Weight:** About 5½ lbs. **Length:** 14" over-all.
**Stocks:** Retractable wire. Pistol grip and fore-end of high impact plastic.
**Sights:** Post front, L-type flip rear for 100 and 200 meters.
**Features:** Blow-back action, manual and grip safeties. Finished in matte olive green color Introduced in 1982. From W.S.I.

Walther PP Auto Pistol

Walther P-38 Auto Pistol

## Walther P-38IV Auto Pistol
Same as P-38 except has longer barrel (4½"); over-all length is 8", weight is 29 oz. Sights are non-adjustable. Introduced 1977. Imported by Interarms.

## Walther P-5 Auto Pistol
Latest Walther design that uses the basic P-38 double-action mechanism. Caliber 9mm Luger, barrel length 3½"; weight 28 oz., over-all length 7".

## WILDEY AUTO PISTOL
**Caliber:** 9mm Win. Mag. (14 shots), 45 Win. Mag. (8 shots).
**Barrel:** 5", 6", 7", 8", or 10"; vent. rib.
**Weight:** About 51 oz. (6" bbl.).
**Stock:** Select hardwood, target style optional.
**Sights:** Adjustable for windage and elevation; red or white inserts optional.
**Features:** Patented gas operation; selective single or autoloading capability; 5-lug rotary bolt; fixed barrel; stainless steel construction; double-action trigger mechanism. Has positive hammer block and magazine safety. From Wildey Firearms.

Wilkinson "Linda" Auto Pistol

## WILKINSON "LINDA" PISTOL
**Caliber:** 9mm Para., 31-shot magazine.
**Barrel:** 8⁵⁄₁₆".
**Weight:** 4 lbs., 13 oz. **Length:** 12¼" over-all.
**Stocks:** Checkered black plastic pistol grip, maple fore-end.
**Sights:** Protected blade front, Williams adjustable rear.
**Features:** Fires from closed bolt. Semi-auto only. Straight blowback action. Cross-bolt safety. Removeable barrel. From Wilkinson Arms.

## ARMINIUS REVOLVERS
**Caliber:** 38 Special, 357 Mag., 32 S&W (6-shot); 22 Magnum, 22 LR (8-shot).
**Barrel:** 4" (38 Spec., 357 Mag., 32 S&W, 22 LR); 6" (38 Spec., 22 LR/22 Mag., 357 Mag.); 8⅜" (357 Mag.).
**Weight:** 35 oz. (6" bbl.). **Length:** 11" (6" bbl. 38).
**Stocks:** Checkered plastic; walnut optional for $14.95.
**Sights:** Ramp front, fixed rear on standard models, w. & e. adj. on target models.
**Features:** Thumb-release, swing-out cylinder. Ventilated rib, solid frame, swing-out cylinder. Interchangeable 22 Mag. cylinder available with 22 cal. versions. Also available in 357 Mag. 3", 4", 6" barrel, adj. sights. Imported from West Germany by F.I.E. Corp.

## ASTRA 357 MAGNUM REVOLVER
**Caliber:** 357 Magnum, 6-shot.
**Barrel:** 3", 4", 6", 8½".
**Weight:** 40 oz. (6" bbl.). **Length:** 11¼" (6" bbl.).
**Stocks:** Checkered walnut.
**Sights:** Fixed front, rear adj. for w. and e.
**Features:** Swing-out cylinder with countersunk chambers, floating firing pin. Target-type hammer and trigger. Imported from Spain by Interarms.

### Astra Model 41, 44, 45 Double Action Revolver
Similar to the 357 Mag. except chambered for the 41 Mag., 44 Mag. or 45 Colt. Barrel length of 6" only, giving over-all length of 11⅜". Weight is 2¾ lbs. Introduced 1980.

Charter Arms Bulldog

## CHARTER ARMS BULLDOG
**Caliber:** 44 Special, 5-shot.
**Barrel:** 3".
**Weight:** 19 oz. **Length:** 7¾" over-all.
**Stocks:** Checkered walnut, Bulldog.
**Sights:** Patridge-type front, square-notch rear.
**Features:** Wide trigger and hammer; beryllium copper firing pin.

### Charter Arms Bulldog Tracker
Similar to the standard Bulldog except has adjustable rear sight, 4" or 6" bull barrel, ramp front sight, square butt checkered walnut grips. Available in blue finish only.

Charter Arms Target Bulldog

## CHARTER TARGET BULLDOG
**Caliber:** 357 Mag., 44 Spec., 5-shot.
**Barrel:** 4".
**Weight:** 20½ oz. **Length:** 8½" over-all.
**Stocks:** Checkered American walnut, square butt.
**Sights:** Full-length ramp front, fully adj., milled channel, square notch rear.
**Features:** Blue finish only. Enclosed ejector rod, full length ejection of fired cases.

Charter Arms Police Bulldog

## CHARTER ARMS POLICE BULLDOG
**Caliber:** 38 Special, 6-shot.
**Barrel:** 2", 4", 4" straight taper bull.
**Weight:** 21 oz. **Length:** 9" over-all.
**Stocks:** Hand checkered American walnut; square butt.
**Sights:** Patridge-type ramp front, notched rear.
**Features:** Accepts both regular and high velocity ammunition; enclosed ejector rod; full length ejection of fired cases.

## CHARTER ARMS UNDERCOVER REVOLVER
**Caliber:** 38 Special, 5 shot; 32 S & W Long, 6 shot.
**Barrel:** 2", 3".
**Weight:** 16 oz. (2"). **Length:** 6¼" (2").
**Stocks:** Smooth walnut or checkered square butt.
**Sights:** Patridge-type ramp front, notched rear.
**Features:** Wide trigger and hammer spur. Steel frame.

Charter Arms Undercover

### Charter Arms Pathfinder

Same as Undercover but in 22 LR caliber, and has 3" or 6" bbl. Fitted with adjustable rear sight, ramp front. Weight 18½ oz.

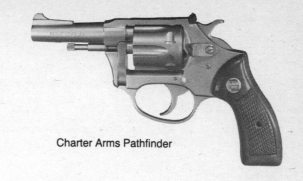

Charter Arms Pathfinder

### COLT PYTHON REVOLVER

**Caliber:** 357 Magnum (handles all 38 Spec.), 6 shot.
**Barrel:** 2½", 4", 6" or 8", with ventilated rib.
**Weight:** 38 oz. (4" bbl.). **Length:** 9¼" (4" bbl.).
**Stocks:** Checkered walnut, target type.
**Sights:** ⅛" ramp front, adj. notch rear.
**Features:** Ventilated rib; grooved, crisp trigger; swing-out cylinder; target hammer.

Colt Python 357

### COLT TROOPER MK III REVOLVER

**Caliber:** 22 LR, 22 WMR, 38 Spec., 357 Magnum, 6-shot.
**Barrel:** 4", 6" or 8".
**Weight:** 39 oz. (4" bbl.), 42 oz., (6" bbl.). **Length:** 9½" (4" bbl.).
**Stocks:** Checkered walnut, square butt.
**Sights:** Fixed ramp front with ⅛" blade, adj. notch rear.

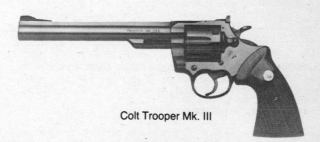

Colt Trooper Mk. III

### Colt Lawman/Trooper Mark V Revolvers

Modified versions of the Lawman MK III and Trooper MK III revolvers. Internal lockwork has been redesigned to reduce trigger pull in double action and give faster lock time. Grip has been redesigned for more comfort. MK V Trooper has adjustable rear sight, and red insert front sight, vent rib 4", 6", 8" barrel; MK V Lawman has 2" or 4" barrel, fixed sight and solid rib. Introduced 1982.

Colt Detective Special

### COLT DETECTIVE SPECIAL

**Caliber:** 38 Special, 6 shot.
**Barrel:** 2".
**Weight:** 22 oz. **Length:** 6⅝" over-all.
**Stocks:** Full, checkered walnut, round butt.
**Sights:** Fixed, ramp front, square notch rear.
**Features:** Glare-proofed sights, smooth trigger. Nickel finish, hammer shroud available as options.

### COLT LAWMAN MK III REVOLVER

**Caliber:** 357 Mag., 6 shot.
**Barrel:** 2" or 4", heavy.
**Weight:** 33 oz. **Length:** 9⅜".
**Stocks:** Checkered walnut, service style.
**Sights:** Fixed, glare-proofed ramp front, square notch rear.

Colt Lawman Mk. III

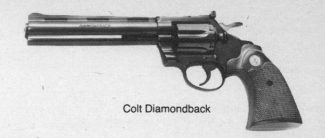

Colt Diamondback

## COLT DIAMONDBACK REVOLVER

**Caliber:** 22 LR or 38 Special, 6 shot.
**Barrel:** 4" or 6" with ventilated rib.
**Weight:** 24 oz. (2½" bbl.). 28½ oz. (4" bbl.). **Length:** 9" (4" bbl.)
**Stocks:** Checkered walnut, target type, square butt.
**Sights:** Ramp front, adj. notch rear.
**Features:** Ventilated rib: grooved, crisp trigger; swing-out cylinder; wide hammer spur.

## F.I.E. MODEL N38 "Titan Tiger" REVOLVER

**Caliber:** 38 Special.
**Barrel:** 2" or 4".
**Weight:** 27 oz. **Length:** 6¼" over-all. (2" bbl.)
**Stocks:** Checkered plastic, Bulldog style. Walnut optional ($15.95).
**Sights:** Fixed.
**Features:** Thumb-release swing-out cylinder, one stroke ejection. Made in U.S.A. by F.I.E. Corp.

## HARRINGTON & RICHARDSON M686 REVOLVER

**Caliber:** 22 LR/22 WMRF, 6-shot.
**Barrel:** 4½", 5½", 7½", 10" or 12".
**Weight:** 31 oz. (4½"), 41 oz. (12").
**Stocks:** Two piece, smooth walnut-finished hardwood.
**Sights:** Western type blade front, adj. rear.
**Features:** Blue barrel and cylinder, "antique" color case-hardened frame, ejector tube and trigger. Comes with extra cylinder.

## Harrington & Richardson Model 649 Revolver

Similar to model 686 except has 5½" or 7½" barrel, one piece wrap around walnut-finished hardwood grips, western-type blade front sight, adjustable rear. Loads and ejects from side. Weighs 32 oz.

H&R Model 649

## HARRINGTON & RICHARDSON M622 REVOLVER

**Caliber:** 22 S, L or LR, 22 WMR, 6 shot.
**Barrel:** 2½", 4", round bbl.
**Weight:** 20 oz. (2½" bbl.).
**Stocks:** Checkered black Cycolac.
**Sights:** Fixed, blade front, square notch rear.
**Features:** Solid steel, Bantamweight frame; patented safety rim cylinder; nonglare finish on frame; coil springs.

H&R Model 622

## HARRINGTON & RICHARDSON M732

**Caliber:** 32 S&W or 32 S&W Long, 6 shot.
**Barrel:** 2½" or 4" round barrel.
**Weight:** 23½ oz. (2½" bbl.), 26 oz. (4" bbl.).
**Stocks:** Checkered, black Cycolac or walnut.
**Sights:** Blade front; adjustable rear on 4" model.
**Features:** Swing-out cylinder with auto. extractor return. Pat. safety rim cylinder. Grooved trigger.

H&R Model 732

## HARRINGTON & RICHARDSON M929

**Caliber:** 22 S, L or LR, 9 shot.
**Barrel:** 2½", 4" or 6".
**Weight:** 26 oz. (4" bbl.).
**Stocks:** Checkered, black Cycolac or walnut.
**Sights:** Blade front; adjustable rear on 4" and 6" models.
**Features:** Swing-out cylinder with auto. extractor return. Pat. safety rim cylinder. Grooved trigger. Round-grip frame.

H&R Model 929

## HARRINGTON & RICHARDSON M949
**Caliber:** 22 S, L or LR, 9 shot.
**Barrel:** 5½" round with ejector rod.
**Weight:** 31 oz.
**Stocks:** One-piece, smooth frontier style wrap-around, walnut-finished hardwood.
**Sights:** Western-type blade front, rear adj. for w.
**Features:** Contoured loading gate; wide hammer spur; single and double action. Western type ejector-housing.

H&R Model 950

## H&R SPORTSMAN MODEL 999 REVOLVER
**Caliber:** 22 S, L or LR, 9 shot.
**Barrel:** 4", 6" top-break (16" twist), integral fluted vent. rib.
**Weight:** 34 oz. (6"). **Length:** 10½".
**Stocks:** Checkered walnut-finished hardwood.
**Sights:** Front adjustable for elevation, rear for windage.
**Features:** Simultaneous automatic ejection, trigger guard extension. H&R Crown Lustre Blue.

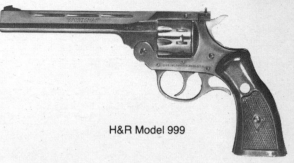

H&R Model 999

## HARRINGTON & RICHARDSON MODELS 604, 904, 905
**Caliber:** 22 LR, 9-shot (M904, 905), 22 WMR, 6-shot (M604)
**Barrel:** 4" (M904 only), 6" target bull.
**Weight:** 32 oz.
**Stocks:** Smooth walnut.
**Sights:** Blade front, fully adjustable "Wind-Elv" rear.
**Features:** Swing-out cylinder design with coil spring construction. Single stroke ejection. Target-style bull barrel has raised solid rib giving a 7¼" sight radius.

H&R Model 905

## Harrington & Richardson Models 603, 903
Similar to 604-904 except has flat-sided barrel.

## HIGH STANDARD SENTINEL
**Caliber:** 22 LR and 22 Mag. with extra cylinder.
**Barrel:** 2" or 4".
**Weight:** 22 oz. (2" barrel). **Length:** 7⅛" over-all (2" barrel).
**Stocks:** Checkered walnut.
**Sights:** ⅛" serrated ramp front, square notched rear.
**Features:** Double action, dual swing-out cylinders; steel frame; blue finish; combat-style grips. From High Standard.

High Standard Sentinel

## HIGH STANDARD DOUBLE-NINE CONVERTIBLE
**Caliber:** 22 S, L or LR, 9-shot (22 Mag. with extra cylinder).
**Barrel:** 5½", dummy ejector rod fitted.
**Weight:** 32 oz. **Length:** 11" over-all.
**Stocks:** Smooth walnut, frontier style.
**Sights:** Fixed blade front, rear adj. for w. & e.
**Features:** Double-action, Western styling, rebounding hammer with auto safety block; spring-loaded ejection. Swing-out cylinder.

High Standard Camp Gun

## High Standard Long Horn Convertible
Same as the Double-Nine convertible but with a 9½" bbl., adjustable sights, blued only. Weight: 38 oz.

## HIGH STANDARD CAMP GUN
**Caliber:** 22 LR and 22 Mag., 9-shot.
**Barrel:** 6".
**Weight:** 28 oz. **Length:** 11⅛" over-all.
**Stocks:** Checkered walnut.
**Sights:** ⅛" serrated ramp front, rear adjustable for windage and elevation.
**Features:** Double-action; comes with two cylinders; blue finish; combat-style wrap around grips. From High Standard.

## HIGH STANDARD CRUSADER COMMEMORATIVE REVOLVER
**Caliber:** 44 Mag., 45 Long Colt.
**Barrel:** 6½", 8⅜".
**Weight:** 48 oz. (6½").
**Stocks:** Smooth Zebrawood.
**Sights:** Blade front on ramp, fully adj. rear.
**Features:** Unique gear-segment mechanism. Smooth, light double-action trigger pull. First production devoted to the commemorative; later guns will be of plain, standard configuration.

## LLAMA COMANCHE REVOLVERS
**Caliber:** 22 LR, 38 Special, 357 Mag.
**Barrel:** 6", 4" (except 22 LR, 6" only).
**Weight:** 22 LR 24 oz., 38 Special 31 oz. **Length:** 9¼" (4" bbl.).
**Stocks:** Checkered walnut.
**Sights:** Fixed blade front, rear adj. for w. & e.
**Features:** Ventilated rib, wide spur hammer. Chrome plating, engraved finishes available. Imported from Spain by Stoeger Industries.

## Llama Super Comanche Revolver
Similar to the Comanche except; large frame, 357 or 44 Mag., 4", 6" or 8½" barrel only; 6-shot cylinder; smooth, extra wide trigger; wide spur hammer; over-size walnut, target-style grips. Weight is 3 lbs., 2 ozs., over-all length is 11¾". Blue finish only.

## RG 14 REVOLVER
**Caliber:** 22 LR, 6-shot.
**Barrel:** 1¾" or 3".
**Weight:** 15 oz. (1¾" bbl.) **Length:** 5½" over-all.
**Stocks:** Checkered plastic.
**Sights:** Fixed.
**Features:** Blue finish. Cylinder swings out when pin is removed. Imported by RG Industries.

## RG 31 REVOLVER
**Caliber:** 32 S & W (6-shot), 38 Spec. (5-shot).
**Barrel:** 2".
**Weight:** 24 oz. **Length:** 6¾" over-all.
**Stocks:** Checkered plastic.
**Sights:** Fixed.
**Features:** Cylinder swings out when pin is removed. Blue finish. Imported by RG Industries.

## RG 40 REVOLVER
**Caliber:** 38 Spec., 6-shot.
**Barrel:** 2".
**Weight:** 29 oz. **Length:** 7¼" over-all.
**Stocks:** Checkered plastic.
**Sights:** Fixed.
**Features:** Swing-out cylinder with spring ejector. Imported by RG Industries.

## HIGH STANDARD HIGH SIERRA DOUBLE ACTION
**Caliber:** 22 LR and 22 LR/22 Mag., 9-shot.
**Barrel:** 7" octagonal.
**Weight:** 36 oz. **Length:** 12½" over-all.
**Stocks:** Smooth walnut.
**Sights:** Blade front, adj. rear.
**Features:** Gold plated backstrap and trigger guard. Swing-out cylinder.

Llama Comanche

Llama Super Comanche

## RG MODEL 74 REVOLVER
**Caliber:** 22 LR, 6-shot.
**Barrel:** 3".
**Weight:** 21½ oz. **Length:** 7¾" over-all.
**Stocks:** Checkered plastic.
**Sights:** Fixed.
**Features:** Swing-out cylinder with spring ejector. Introduced 1980. Imported from Germany by RG Industries.

## RG MODEL 39 REVOLVER
**Caliber:** 32 S&W, 38 Spec., 6-shot.
**Barrel:** 2".
**Weight:** 21 oz. **Length:** 7" over-all.
**Stocks:** Checkered plastic.
**Sights:** Fixed.
**Features:** Swing-out cylinder with spring ejector. Introduced 1980. Imported from Germany by RG Industries.

## RG 38S REVOLVER
**Caliber:** 38 Special, 6-shot.
**Barrel:** 3" and 4".
**Weight:** 3", 31 oz.; 4", 34 oz. **Length:** 3", 8½", 4", 9¼".
**Stocks:** Checkered plastic.
**Sights:** Fixed front, rear adj. for w.
**Features:** Swing out cylinder with spring ejector. Imported from Germany by RG Industries.

## ROSSI MODELS 68, 69 & 70 DA REVOLVERS
**Caliber:** 22 LR (M 70), 32 S & W (M 69), 38 Spec. (M 68).
**Barrel:** 3".
**Weight:** 22 oz.
**Stocks:** Checkered wood.
**Sights:** Ramp front, low profile adj. rear.
**Features:** All-steel frame. Thumb latch operated swing-out cylinder. Introduced 1978. Imported from Brazil by Interarms.

Rossi Model 68

## RUGER SECURITY-SIX Model 117
**Caliber:** 357 Mag. (also fires 38 Spec.), 6-shot.
**Barrel:** 2¾", 4" or 6", or 4" heavy barrel.
**Weight:** 33½ oz. (4" bbl.) **Length:** 9¼" (4" bbl.) over-all.
**Stocks:** Hand checkered American walnut, semi-target style.
**Sights:** Patridge-type front on ramp, white outline rear adj. for w. and e.
**Features:** Music wire coil springs throughout. Hardened steel construction. Integral ejector rod shroud and sighting rib. Can be disassembled using only a coin.

Ruger Security-Six

## RUGER POLICE SERVICE-SIX Models 107, 108, 109
**Caliber:** 357 (Model 107), 38 Spec. (Model 108), 9mm (Model 109), 6-shot.
**Barrel:** 2¾" or 4" and 4" heavy barrel.
**Weight:** 33½ oz. (4" bbl.). **Length:** 9¼" (4 bbl.) over-all.
**Stocks:** Checkered American walnut, semi-target style.
**Sights:** Patridge-type front, square notch rear.
**Features:** Solid frame with barrel, rib and ejector rod housing combined in one unit. All steel construction Field strips without tools.

Ruger Police Service-Six

## RUGER SPEED-SIX Models 207, 208, 209
**Caliber:** 357 (Model 207), 38 Spec. (Model 208), 9mm P (Model 209) 6-shot.
**Barrel:** 2¾" or 4".
**Weight:** 31 oz. (2¾" bbl.). **Length:** 7¾" over-all (2¾" bbl.).
**Stocks:** Round butt design, diamond pattern checkered American walnut.
**Sights:** Patridge-type front, square-notch rear.
**Features:** Same basic mechanism as Security-Six. Hammer without spur available on special order. All steel construction. Music wire coil springs used throughout.

## RUGER STAINLESS SECURITY-SIX Model 717
**Caliber:** 357 Mag. (also fires 38 Spec.), 6-shot.
**Barrel:** 2¾", 4" or 6".
**Weight:** 33 oz. (4 bbl.). **Length:** 9¼" (4" bbl.) over-all.
**Stocks:** Hand checkered American walnut.
**Sights:** Patridge-type front, fully adj. rear.
**Features:** All metal parts except sights made of stainless steel. Sights are black alloy for maximum visibility. Same mechanism and features found in regular Security-Six.

## RUGER REDHAWK
**Caliber:** 44 Rem. Mag., 6-shot.
**Barrel:** 7½".
**Weight:** About 3¼ lbs. **Length:** 13" over-all.
**Stocks:** Square butt. American walnut.
**Sights:** Patridge-type front, rear adj. for w. & e.
**Features:** Stainless steel, brushed satin finish. Has a 9½" sight radius. Introduced 1979.

Ruger Redhawk

### SMITH & WESSON M&P Model 10 REVOLVER
**Caliber:** 38 Special, 6 shot.
**Barrel:** 2″, 4″, 5″ or 6″.
**Weight:** 30½ oz. (4″ bbl.). **Length:** 9¼″ (4″ bbl.).
**Stocks:** Checkered walnut, Magna. Round or square butt.
**Sights:** Fixed, ⅛″ ramp front, square notch rear.

S&W Model 10-H.B.

### SMITH & WESSON 38 M&P AIRWEIGHT Model 12
**Caliber:** 38 Special, 6 shot.
**Barrel:** 2″ or 4″.
**Weight:** 18 oz. (2″ bbl.). **Length:** 6⅞″ over-all.
**Stocks:** Checkered walnut, Magna. Round or square butt.
**Sights:** Fixed, ⅛″ serrated ramp front, square notch rear.

### Smith & Wesson 38 M&P Heavy Barrel Model 10
Same as regular M&P except: 4″ ribbed bbl. with ⅛″ ramp front sight, square rear, square butt, wgt. 34 oz.

### SMITH & WESSON Model 13 H.B. M&P
**Caliber:** 357 and 38 Special, 6 shot.
**Barrel:** 3″ or 4″.
**Weight:** 34 oz. **Length:** 9¼″ over-all (4″ bbl.).
**Stocks:** Checkered walnut, service.
**Sights:** ⅛″ serrated ramp front, fixed square notch rear.
**Features:** Heavy barrel, K-frame, square butt.

S&W Model 13

### SMITH & WESSON Model 14 K-38 MASTERPIECE
**Caliber:** 38 Spec., 6-shot.
**Barrel:** 6″, 8⅜″.
**Weight:** 38½ oz. (6″ bbl.). **Length:** 11⅛″ over-all (6″ bbl.).
**Stocks:** Checkered walnut, service.
**Sights:** ⅛″ Patridge front, micro click rear adj. for w. and e.

S&W Model 14

### SMITH & WESSON COMBAT MASTERPIECE
**Caliber:** 38 Special (M15) or 22 LR (M18), 6 shot.
**Barrel:** 2″ or 4″ (M15) 4″ (M18).
**Weight:** Loaded, 22 36½ oz., 38 34 oz. **Length:** 9⅛″ (4″ bbl.).
**Stocks:** Checkered walnut, Magna. Grooved tangs and trigger.
**Sights:** Front, ⅛″ Baughman Quick Draw on ramp, micro click rear, adjustable for w. and e.

### SMITH & WESSON MODEL 17 K-22 MASTERPIECE
**Caliber:** 22 LR, 6-shot.
**Barrel:** 6″, 8⅜″.
**Weight:** 38½ oz. (6″ bbl.). **Length:** 11⅛″ over-all.
**Stocks:** Checkered walnut, service.
**Sights:** Patridge front, S&W micro. click rear adjustable for windage and elevation.
**Features:** Grooved tang and trigger. Polished blue finish.

### SMITH & WESSON 357 COMBAT MAGNUM Model 19
**Caliber:** 357 Magnum and 38 Special, 6 shot.
**Barrel:** 2½″, 4″, 6″.
**Weight:** 35 oz. **Length:** 9½″ (4″ bbl.).
**Stocks:** Checkered Goncalo Alves, target. Grooved tangs and trigger.
**Sights:** Front, ⅛″ Baughman Quick Draw on 2½″ or 4″ bbl., Patridge on 6″ bbl., micro click rear adjustable for w. and e.

S&W Model 19

## SMITH & WESSON HIGHWAY PATROLMAN Model 28
**Caliber:** 357 Magnum and 38 Special, 6 shot.
**Barrel:** 4″, 6″.
**Weight:** 44 oz. (6″ bbl.). **Length:** 11¼″ (6″ bbl.).
**Stocks:** Checkered walnut, Magna. Grooved tangs and trigger.
**Sights:** Front, ⅛″ Baughman Quick Draw, on plain ramp, micro click rear, adjustable for w. and e.

## SMITH & WESSON 357 MAGNUM M-27 REVOLVER
**Caliber:** 357 Magnum and 38 Special, 6 shot.
**Barrel:** 4″, 6″, 8⅜″.
**Weight:** 44 oz. (6″ bbl.). **Length:** 11¼″ (6″ bbl.).
**Stocks:** Checkered walnut, Magna. Grooved tangs and trigger.
**Sights:** Any S&W target front, micro click rear, adjustable for w. and e.

## SMITH & WESSON 44 MAGNUM Model 29 REVOLVER
**Caliber:** 44 Magnum, 44 Special or 44 Russian, 6 shot.
**Barrel:** 4″, 6″, 8⅜″.
**Weight:** 47 oz. (6″ bbl.), 43 oz. (4″ bbl.). **Length:** 11⅞″ (6½″ bbl.).
**Stocks:** Oversize target type, checkered Goncalo Alves. Tangs and target trigger grooved, checkered target hammer.
**Sights:** ⅛″ red ramp front, micro click rear, adjustable for w. and e.
**Features:** Includes presentation case.

S&W Model 29

## SMITH & WESSON 32 REGULATION POLICE Model 31
**Caliber:** 32 S&W Long, 6 shot.
**Barrel:** 2″, 3″.
**Weight:** 18¾ oz. (3″ bbl.). **Length:** 7½″ (3″ bbl.).
**Stocks:** Checkered walnut, Magna.
**Sights:** Fixed, ⅒″ serrated ramp front, square notch rear.
**Features:** Blued

S&W Model 31

## SMITH & WESSON 1953 Model 34, 22/32 KIT GUN
**Caliber:** 22 LR, 6 shot.
**Barrel:** 2″, 4″.
**Weight:** 22½ oz. (4″ bbl.). **Length:** 8″ (4″ bbl. and round butt).
**Stocks:** Checkered walnut, round or square butt.
**Sights:** Front, ⅒″ serrated ramp, micro. click rear, adjustable for w. & e.

S&W Model 34

## SMITH & WESSON 38 CHIEFS SPECIAL & AIRWEIGHT
**Caliber:** 38 Special, 5 shot.
**Barrel:** 2″, 3″.
**Weight:** 19 oz. (2″ bbl.); 14 oz. (AIRWEIGHT). **Length:** 6½″ (2″ bbl. and round butt).
**Stocks:** Checkered walnut, Magna. Round or square butt.
**Sights:** Fixed, ⅒″ serrated ramp front, square notch rear.

## Smith & Wesson 60 Chiefs Special Stainless
Same as Model 36 except: 2″ bbl. and round butt only.

## SMITH & WESSON BODYGUARD MODEL 38
**Caliber:** 38 Special; 5 shot, double action revolver.
**Barrel:** 2″.
**Weight:** 14½ oz. **Length:** 6⅜″.
**Stocks:** Checkered walnut, Magna.
**Sights:** Fixed ⅒″ serrated ramp front, square notch rear.
**Features:** Alloy frame; integral hammer shroud.

S&W Model 38

## Smith & Wesson Bodyguard Model 49 Revolver
Same as Model 38 except steel construction, weight 20½ oz.

## SMITH & WESSON 41 MAGNUM Model 57 REVOLVER
**Caliber:** 41 Magnum, 6 shot.
**Barrel:** 4″, 6″ or 8⅜″.
**Weight:** 48 oz. (6″ bbl.). **Length:** 11⅜″ (6″ bbl.).
**Stocks:** Oversize target type checkered Goncalo Alves.
**Sights:** ⅛″ red ramp front, micro. click rear, adj. for w. and e.

## SMITH & WESSON MODEL 64 STAINLESS M&P
**Caliber:** 38 Special, 6-shot.
**Barrel:** 4″.
**Weight:** 30½ oz. **Length:** 9½″ over-all.
**Stocks:** Checkered walnut, service style.
**Sights:** Fixed, ⅛″ serrated ramp front, square notch rear.
**Features:** Satin finished stainless steel, square butt.

## SMITH & WESSON MODEL 66 STAINLESS COMBAT MAGNUM
**Caliber:** 357 Magnum and 38 Special, 6-shot.
**Barrel:** 2½″, 4″, 6″.
**Weight:** 35 oz. **Length:** 9½″ over-all.
**Stocks:** Checkered Goncalo Alves target.
**Sights:** Front, ⅛″ Baughman Quick Draw on plain ramp, micro clock rear adj. for w. and e.
**Features:** Satin finish stainless steel, grooved trigger with adj. stop.

## SMITH & WESSON MODEL 67 K-38 STAINLESS COMBAT MASTERPIECE
**Caliber:** 38 Special, 6-shot.
**Barrel:** 4″.
**Weight:** 34 oz. (loaded). **Length:** 9⅛″ over-all.
**Stocks:** Checkered walnut, service style.
**Sights:** Front, ⅛″ Baughman Quick Draw on ramp, micro click rear adj. for w. and e.
**Features:** Stainless steel. Square butt frame with grooved tangs, grooved trigger with adj. stop.

## SMITH & WESSON MODEL 547
**Caliber:** 9mm Parabellum
**Barrel:** 3″ or 4″ heavy.
**Weight:** 34 oz. (4″ barrel). **Length:** 9⅛″ over-all (4″ barrel).
**Stocks:** Checkered square butt Magna Service (4″), checkered walnut target, round butt (3″).
**Sights:** ⅛″ Serrated ramp front, fixed ⅛″ square notch rear.
**Features:** K-frame revolver uses special extractor system—no clips required. Has ¼″ half-spur hammer. Introduced 1981.

## SMITH & WESSON MODEL 586 Distinguished Combat Magnum
**Caliber:** 357 Magnum.
**Barrel:** 4″, 6″, both heavy.
**Weight:** 46 oz. (6″), 42 oz. (4″).
**Stocks:** Goncalo Alves target-type with speed loader cutaway.
**Sights:** Baughman red ramp front, S&W micrometer click rear (or fixed).
**Features:** Uses new L-frame, but takes all K-frame grips. Full length ejector rod shroud. Smooth combat-type trigger, semi-target type hammer. Trigger stop on 6″ models; 4″ models factory fitted with target hammer and trigger will have trigger stop. Also available in stainless as Model 686. Introduced 1981.

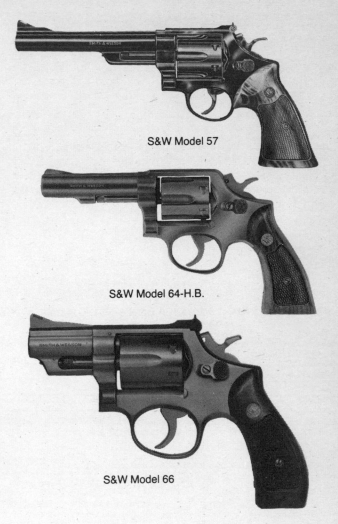

S&W Model 57

S&W Model 64-H.B.

S&W Model 66

S&W Model 586

## TAURUS MODEL 83 REVOLVER
**Caliber:** 38 Spec., 6-shot.
**Barrel:** 4″ only, heavy.
**Weight:** 34½ oz.
**Stocks:** Over-size checkered walnut.
**Sights:** Ramp front, micro. click rear adj. for w. & e.
**Features:** Blue or nickel finish. Introduced 1977. From International Distributors.

Taurus Model 82

## TAURUS MODEL 80 STANDARD REVOLVER
**Caliber:** 38 Spec., 6-shot.
**Barrel:** 3" or 4".
**Weight:** 31 oz. (4" bbl.). **Length:** 9¼" over-all (4" bbl.).
**Stocks:** Checkered Brazilian walnut.
**Sights:** Serrated ramp front, square notch rear.
**Features:** Imported from Brazil by International Distributors.

## TAURUS MODEL 73 SPORT REVOLVER
**Caliber:** 32 S&W Long, 6-shot.
**Barrel:** 3", heavy.
**Weight:** 22 oz. **Length:** 8¼" over-all.
**Stocks:** Oversize target-type, checkered Brazilian walnut.
**Sights:** Ramp front, notch rear.
**Features:** Imported from Brazil by International Distributers.

## DAN WESSON MODEL 9-2, MODEL 15-2 & MODEL 22
**Caliber:** 22LR, 38 Special (Model 9-2); 357 (Model 15-2), both 6 shot.
**Barrel:** 2", 4", 6", 8", 10", 12", 15". "Quickshift" interchangeable barrels.
**Weight:** 36 oz. (4" bbl.), 40 oz. (4" rimfire). **Length:** 9¼" over-all (4" bbl.,).
**Stocks:** "Quickshift" checkered walnut. Interchangeable with eight other styles.
**Sights:** ⅛" serrated blade front with red insert (std.), white or yellow insert optional, as is Patridge. White outline rear adj. for w. & e.
**Features:** Interchangeable barrels; four interchangeable grips; few moving parts, easy disassembly; Bright Blue finish only. Contact Dan Wesson for additional models not listed here. 10", 12" and 15" barrels also available with vent, rib. Rimfire specs. essentially the same as 357 models.

## DAN WESSON MODEL 8-2 & MODEL 14-2
**Caliber:** 38 Special (Model 8-2); 357 (Model 14-2), both 6 shot.
**Barrel:** 2", 4", 6", 8". "Quickshift" interchangeable barrels.
**Weight:** 34 oz. (4" bbl.) **Length:** 9¼" over-all (4" bbl.).
**Stocks:** "Quickshift" checkered walnut. Interchangeable with three other styles.
**Sights:** ⅛" serrated ramp front, rear fixed..
**Features:** Interchangeable barrels; 4 interchangeable grips; few moving parts, easy disassembly.

## TAURUS MODEL 82 HEAVY BARREL REVOLVER
**Caliber:** 38 Spec., 6-shot.
**Barrel:** 3" or 4", heavy.
**Weight:** 33 oz. (4" bbl.). **Length:** 9¼" over-all (4" bbl.).
**Stocks:** Checkered Brazilian walnut.
**Sights:** Serrated ramp front, square notch rear.
**Features:** Imported from Brazil by International Distributors.

## TAURUS MODEL 66 REVOLVER
**Caliber:** 357 Magnum, 6-shot.
**Barrel:** 3", 4", 6".
**Weight:** 35 ozs.
**Stocks:** Checkered walnut, target-type. Standard stocks on 3".
**Sights:** Serrated ramp front, micro click rear adjustable for w. and e.
**Features:** Wide target-type hammer spur, floating firing pin, heavy barrel with shrouded ejector rod. Introduced 1978. From International Distributors.

## TAURUS MODEL 85 REVOLVER
**Caliber:** 38 Spec., 5-shot.
**Barrel:** 3".
**Weight:** 21 oz.
**Stocks:** Smooth walnut.
**Sights:** Ramp front, square notch rear.
**Features:** Blue or satin blue finish. Introduced 1980. From International Distributors.

Dan Wesson 44 Magnum

## DAN WESSON 44 MAGNUM REVOLVER
**Caliber:** 44 Magnum, 6 shots.
**Barrel:** 4", 6", 8", 10", interchangeable, with or without "Power Control" gun levelling device.
**Weight:** 45 oz. (4" bbl.) **Length:** 12" (6" bbl.).
**Stocks:** Walnut or exotic wood. Two interchangeable styles, Target or Combat.
**Sights:** Serrated ⅛" front blade with red insert (yellow and white also available.) White outline rear adj. for w. & e.
**Features:** Interchangeable barrels, grips, front sight blades. Bright blue finish only. Only 6" and 8" guns are shipped from the factory—4" and 10" barrel assemblies available separately. Introduced 1981.

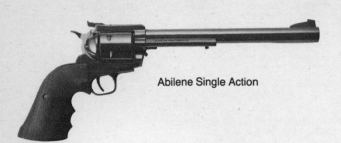

Abilene Single Action

## ABILENE SINGLE ACTION REVOLVER
**Caliber:** 357 Mag., 44 Mag., 45 Colt, 6 shot.
**Barrel:** 4⅝", 6", 7½", 10" (44 Mag. only).
**Weight:** About 48 oz.
**Stocks:** Smooth walnut.
**Sights:** Serrated ramp front, click adj. rear for w. and e.
**Features:** Wide hammer spur. Blue or Magnaloy finish. From Mossberg.

Colt Single Action Army

## COLT SINGLE ACTION ARMY REVOLVER
**Caliber:** 357 Magnum, 44 Spec., 44-40, or 45 Colt, 6 shot.
**Barrel:** 4¾", 5½", 7½" or 12".
**Weight:** 37 oz. (5½" bbl.). **Length:** 10⅞" (5½" bbl.)
**Stocks:** Black composite rubber with eagle and shield crest.
**Sights:** Fixed. Grooved top strap, blade front.
**Features:** See Colt catalog for variations and prices. Only basic models and prices listed here.

Colt New Frontier

## Colt Single Action Army—New Frontier
Same specifications as standard Single Action Army except: flat-top frame; high polished finish, blue and case colored; ramp front sight and target rear adj. for windage and elevation; smooth walnut stocks with silver medallion, or composition grips.

## COLT NEW FRONTIER 22
**Caliber:** 22 LR, 6-shot.
**Barrel:** 4¾", 6", 7½".
**Weight:** 29½ oz. (4¾" bbl.). **Length:** 9⅝" over-all.
**Stocks:** Black composite rubber.
**Sights:** Ramp-style front, fully adjustable rear.
**Features:** Cross-bolt safety. Color case-hardened frame. Available in blue or Coltguard finishes. Re-introduced 1982.

## F.I.E. "HOMBRE" SINGLE ACTION REVOLVER
**Caliber:** 357 Mag., 44 Mag., 45 LC.
**Barrel:** 5½" or 7½".
**Weight:** 45 oz. (5½" bbl.).
**Stocks:** Smooth walnut with medallion.
**Sights:** Blade front, grooved topstrap (fixed) rear.
**Features:** Color case hardened frame. Bright blue finish. Super-smooth action. Introduced 1979. Imported from West Germany by F.I.E. Corp.

## F.I.E. E15 BUFFALO SCOUT REVOLVER
**Caliber:** 22 LR/22 Mag., 6-shot.
**Barrel:** 4¾", 7", 9".
**Weight:** 32 oz. **Length:** 10" over-all.
**Stocks:** Black checkered nylon.
**Sights:** Blade front, fixed rear.
**Features:** Slide spring ejector. Blue, chrome or blue with brass backstrap and trigger guard models available.

## F.I.E. "LEGEND" SINGLE ACTION REVOLVER
**Caliber:** 22 LR/22 Mag.
**Barrel:** 4¾".
**Weight:** 32 oz.
**Stocks:** Smooth walnut or black checkered nylon. Walnut optional ($16.95).
**Sights:** Blade front, fixed rear.
**Features:** Positive hammer block system. Brass backstrap and trigger guard. Color case hardened steel frame, rest blued. Imported from Italy by F.I.E. Corp.

Freedom Arms Mini Revolver

## FREEDOM ARMS MINI REVOLVER
**Caliber:** 22 Short, Long, Long Rifle, 5-shot, 22 Mag., 4-shot.
**Barrel:** 1″, 1¾″.
**Weight:** 4 oz. **Length:** 4″ over-all.
**Stocks:** Black ebonite or simulated ivory.
**Sights:** Blade front, notch rear.
**Features:** Made of stainless steel, simple take down; half-cock safety; floating firing pin; cartridge rims recessed in cylinder. Comes in gun rug. Lifetime warranty.

### Freedom Arms Boot Gun
Similar to the Mini Revolver except has 3″ barrel, weighs 5 oz. and is 5⅞″ over-all. Has over-size grips, floating firing pin. Made of stainless steel. Lifetime warranty. Comes in rectangular gun rug. Introduced 1982. From Freedom Arms.

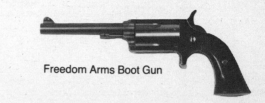

Freedom Arms Boot Gun

## MITCHELL SINGLE ACTION REVOLVERS
**Caliber:** 22 LR/22 Mag., 357 Mag., 44 Mag., 44 Mag./44-40, 45 Colt.
**Barrel:** 4¾″, 5½″, 6″, 7½″, 10″, 12″, 18″.
**Weight:** About 36 oz.
**Stocks:** One-piece walnut.
**Sights:** Ramp front, rear adj. for w. & e.
**Features:** Color case-hardened frame, grip frame is polished brass. Hammer block safety. Introduced 1980. From Mitchell Arms Corp.

Mitchell Single Action

## NAM MINI REVOLVER
**Caliber:** 22 LR, 22 Mag., 5-shot
**Barrel:** 1⅛″ (22 Short, LR), 1¼″ (22 Mag.), 1⅝″ (22 LR).
**Weight:** 4.5 oz. **Length:** 3.8″ over-all.
**Stocks:** Smooth plastic; walnut on magnum model.
**Sights:** Blade front only.
**Features:** Stainless steel, single action only. Spur trugger. From North American Mfg. Corp.

## RUGER NEW MODEL CONVERTIBLE BLACKHAWK
**Caliber:** 45 Colt or 45 Colt/45 ACP (extra cylinder).
**Barrel:** 4⅝″ or 7½″ (6-groove, 16″ twist).
**Weight:** 40 oz. (7½″ bbl.). **Length:** 13⅛″ (7½ bbl.).
**Stocks:** Smooth American walnut.
**Sights:** ⅛″ ramp front, micro click rear adj. for w. and e.
**Features:** Similar to Super Blackhawk, Ruger interlocked mechanism. Convertible furnished with interchangeable cylinder for 45 ACP.

Ruger New Model Blackhawk

## RUGER NEW MODEL BLACKHAWK REVOLVER
**Caliber:** 357 or 41 Mag., 6-shot.
**Barrel:** 4⅝″ or 6½″, either caliber.
**Weight:** 42 oz. (6½″ bbl.). **Length:** 12¼″ over-all (6½″ bbl.).
**Stocks:** American walnut.
**Sights:** ⅛″ ramp front, micro click rear adj. for w. and e.
**Features:** New Ruger interlocked mechanism, independent firing pin, hardened chrome-moly steel frame, music wire springs throughout.

### Ruger New Model 30 Carbine Blackhawk
Specifications similar to 45 Blackhawk. Fluted cylinder, round-back trigger guard. Weight 44 oz., length 13⅛″ over-all, 7½″ barrel only.

### Ruger New Model 357/9mm Blackhawk
Same as the 357 Magnum except furnished with interchangeable cylinders for 9mm Parabellum and 357 Magnum cartridges.

Ruger N.M. Super Blackhawk

## RUGER NEW MODEL SUPER BLACKHAWK
**Caliber:** 44 Magnum, 6-shot. Also fires 44 Spec.
**Barrel:** 7½" (6-groove, 20" twist), 10½".
**Weight:** 48 oz. **Length:** 13⅜" over-all (7½" bbl.).
**Stocks:** Genuine American walnut.
**Sights:** ⅛" ramp front, micro click rear adj. for w. and e.
**Features:** New Ruger interlocked mechanism, non-fluted cylinder, steel grip and cylinder frame, square back trigger guard, wide serrated trigger and wide spur hammer. Deep Ruger blue.

Ruger Super Single-Six

## RUGER NEW MODEL SUPER SINGLE-SIX CONVERTIBLE REVOLVER
**Caliber:** 22 S, L, LR, 6-shot. 22 Mag. in extra cylinder.
**Barrel:** 4⅝", 5½", 6½" or 9½" (6-groove).
**Weight:** 34½ oz. (6½" bbl.). **Length:** 11¹³⁄₁₆" over-all (6½" bbl.).
**Stocks:** Smooth American walnut.
**Sights:** Improved patridge front on ramp, fully adj. rear protected by integral frame ribs.
**Features:** New Ruger "interlocked" mechanism, transfer bar ignition, gate-controlled loading, hardened chrome-moly steel frame, wide trigger, music wire springs throughout, independent firing pin.

## SEVILLE SINGLE ACTION REVOLVER
**Caliber:** 357 Mag., 9mm Win. Mag., 41 Mag., 44 Mag., 45 Colt, 45 Win. Mag.
**Barrel:** 4⅝", 5½", 6½", 7½".
**Weight:** 52 oz. (4⅝", loaded)
**Stocks:** Smooth walnut, thumbrest, or Pachmayr.
**Sights:** Ramp front with red insert, fully adj. rear.
**Features:** Available in blue or stainless steel. Six-shot cylinder. From United Sporting Arms of Arizona, Inc.

## SEVILLE SHERIFF'S MODEL S.A. REVOLVER
**Caliber:** 44-40, 44 Mag., 45 ACP, 45 Colt.
**Barrel:** 3½".
**Weight:** 45 oz. (loaded).
**Stocks:** Smooth walnut. Square butt or birdshead style.
**Sights:** Sq. butt—ramp front, adj. rear; birdshead—blade front, fixed rear.
**Features:** Blue or stainless steel. Six-shot cylinder. Available with square or birdshead grip style. From United Sporting Arms of Arizona, Inc.

## TANARMI S.A. REVOLVER MODEL TA22S LM
**Caliber:** 22 LR, 22 Mag., 6-shot.
**Barrel:** 4¾".
**Weight:** 32 oz. **Length:** 10" over-all.
**Stocks:** Walnut.
**Sights:** Blade front, rear adj. for w. & e.
**Features:** Manual hammer block safety; color hardened steel frame; brass backstrap and trigger guard. Imported from Italy by Excam.

## TANARMI SINGLE ACTION MODEL TA76
Same as TA22 models except blue backstrap and trigger guard.

## THE VIRGINIAN DRAGOON REVOLVER
**Caliber:** 357 Mag., 41 Mag., 44 Mag., 45 Colt.
**Barrel:** 44 Mag., 6", 7½", 8⅜"; 357 Mag. and 45 Colt, 5", 6", 7½".
**Weight:** 48 oz. (6" barrel). **Length:** 11⅞" over-all (6" barrel).
**Stocks:** Smooth walnut.
**Sights:** Ramp-type Patridge front blade, micro. adj. target rear.
**Features:** Color case-hardened frame, spring-loaded floating firing pin, coil main spring. Firing pin is lock-fitted with a steel bushing. Introduced 1977. Made in the U.S. by Interarms Industries, Inc.

Virginian Dragoon

American Derringer AD

## AMERICAN DERRINGER MODEL AD
**Caliber:** 22 LR, 22 Mag., 22 Jet, 223 Rem., 38 Super, 380 ACP, 38 Spec., 9mm Para., 357 Mag., 41 Mag., 44-40 Win., 44 Spec., 44 Mag., 45 Colt, 45 ACP.
**Barrel:** 3″.
**Weight:** 15½ oz. (38 Spec.). **Length:** 4.82″ over-all.
**Stocks:** Rosewood, Zebra wood, walnut, or plastic ivory.
**Sights:** Blade front.
**Features:** Made of stainless steel with high-polish finish. Two shot capacity. Manual hammer block safety. Introduced 1982. From American Derringer Corp.

## C. O. P. 357 MAGNUM
**Caliber:** 38/357 Mag., 4 shots.
**Barrel:** 3¼″.
**Weight:** 28 oz. **Length:** 5.5″ over-all.
**Stocks:** Checkered composition.
**Sights:** Open, fixed.
**Features:** Double-action, 4 barrels, made of stainless steel. Width is only one inch, height 4.1″. From M & N Distributors.

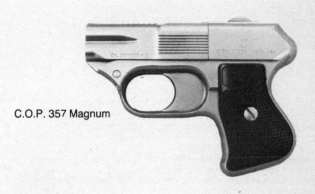

C.O.P. 357 Magnum

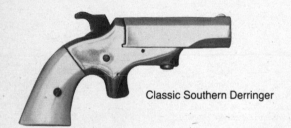

Classic Southern Derringer

## CLASSIC ARMS TWISTER
**Caliber:** 22 LR or 9mm Rimfire.
**Barrel:** 3¼″.
**Weight:** 18 oz.
**Stocks:** Pearlite.
**Sights:** None.
**Features:** Over-under barrels rotate on an axis for two separate shots. Spur trigger. 9mm Rimfire ammunition available. Made in U.S. by Classic Arms Ltd.

## CLASSIC ARMS SOUTHERN DERRINGER
**Caliber:** 22 LR or 41 Rimfire.
**Barrel:** 2½″.
**Weight:** 12 oz. **Length:** 5″ over-all.
**Stocks:** White plastic.
**Sights:** Blade front.
**Features:** Single-shot, spur-trigger derringer. Brass frame, steel barrel. The 41 RF ammunition is available from Navy Arms. Introduced in 1982. Made in U.S. by Classic Arms Ltd.

## HIGH STANDARD 9194 AND 9306 DERRINGER
**Caliber:** 22 LR, 22 Mag., 2 shot.
**Barrel:** 3½″, over and under, rifled.
**Weight:** 11 oz. **Length:** 5″ over-all.
**Stocks:** Smooth plastic.
**Sights:** Fixed, open.
**Features:** Hammerless, integral safety hammerblock, all steel unit is encased in a black, anodized alloy housing. Recessed chamber. Dual extraction. Top break, double action.

## F.I.E. MODEL D-38 DERRINGER
**Caliber:** 38 Special.
**Barrel:** 3″.
**Weight:** 14 oz.
**Stocks:** Checkered white nylon, walnut optional.
**Sights:** Fixed.
**Features:** Chrome finish. Spur trigger. Tip-up barrel, extractors. Made in U.S. by F.I.E. Corp.

## LJUTIC LJ 25 PISTOL
**Caliber:** 25 ACP.
**Barrel:** 2¾″.
**Stocks:** Checkered walnut.
**Sights:** Fixed.
**Features:** Stainless steel; double action; ventilated rib. Introduced 1981. From Ljutic Industries.

High Standard Derringer

Mitchell's Derringer

## MITCHELL'S DERRINGER
**Caliber:** 38 Spec.
**Barrel:** 2¾″
**Weight:** 11 oz. **Length:** 5¼″ over-all.
**Stocks:** Walnut, checkered.
**Sights:** Fixed, ramp front.
**Features:** Polished blue finish. All steel. Made in U.S. Introduced 1980. From Mitchell Arms Corp.

## REMINGTON MODEL XP-100 Bolt Action Pistol
**Caliber:** 221 Fireball, single shot.
**Barrel:** 10½″, ventilated rib.
**Weight:** 60 oz. **Length:** 16¾″.
**Stock:** Brown nylon one-piece, checkered grip with white spacers.
**Sights:** Fixed front, rear adj. for w. and e. Tapped for scope mount.
**Features:** Fits left or right hand, is shaped to fit fingers and heel of hand. Grooved trigger. Rotating thumb safety, cavity in fore-end permits insertion of up to five 38 cal., 130-gr. metal jacketed bullets to adjust weight and balance. Included is a black vinyl, zippered case.

Remington XP-100

## SEMMERLING LM-4 PISTOL
**Caliber:** 45 ACP.
**Barrel:** 3½″.
**Weight:** 24 oz. **Length:** 5.2″ over-all.
**Stocks:** Checkered black plastic.
**Sights:** Ramp front, fixed rear.
**Features:** Manually operated repeater. Over-all dimensions are 5.2″ x 3.7″ x 1″. Has a four-shot magazine capacity. Comes with manual, leather carrying case, spare stock screw and wrench. From Semmerling Corp.

## MERRILL SPORTSMAN'S SINGLE SHOT PISTOL
**Caliber:** 22 LR Sil., 22 Mag., 22 Hornet, 256 Win. Mag., 357 Mag., 357/44 B & D, 30-30 Win., 30 Herrett, 357 Herrett, 41 Mag., 44 Mag., 7mm Merrill, 30 Merrill, 7mm Rocket.
**Barrel:** 9″ or 10¾″, semi-octagonal; .450″ wide vent. rib, matted to prevent glare; 14″ barrel in all except 22 cals.
**Weight:** About 54 oz. **Length:** 10½″ over-all (9″ bbl.)
**Stocks:** Smooth walnut with thumb and heel rest.
**Sights:** Front .125″ blade (.080″ blade optional); rear adj. for w. and e.
**Features:** Polished blue finish, hard chrome optional. Barrel is drilled and tapped for scope mounting. Cocking indicator visible from rear of gun. Has spring-loaded barrel lock, positive thumb safety. Trigger adjustable for weight of pull and over-travel. From Rock Pistol Mfg.

Sterling X-Caliber

## STERLING X-CALIBER SINGLE SHOT
**Caliber:** 22, 22 Mag., 357 Mag., 44 Mag.
**Barrel:** 8″ or 10″, interchangeable.
**Weight:** 52 oz. (8″ bbl.). **Length:** 13″ over-all (8″ bbl.).
**Stocks:** Goncolo Alves.
**Sights:** Patridge front, fully adj. rear.
**Features:** Barrels are drilled and tapped for scope mounting; hammer is notched for easy cocking with scope mounted. Finger grooved grip.

## TANARMI O/U DERRINGER
**Caliber:** 38 Special.
**Barrel:** 3″.
**Weight:** 14 oz. **Length:** 4¾″ over-all.
**Stocks:** Checkered white nylon.
**Sights:** Fixed.
**Features:** Blue finish; tip-up barrel. Assembled in U.S. by Excam, Inc.

Thompson-Center Contender

## THOMPSON-CENTER ARMS CONTENDER
**Caliber:** 221 Rem., 7mm T.C.U., 30-30 Win., 22 S, L, LR, 22 Mag., 22 Hornet, 256 Win., 357 Mag., also 222 Rem., 44 Mag., 45 Long Colt, 45 Win. Mag., single shot.
**Barrel:** 10″, tapered octagon, bull barrel and vent. rib.
**Weight:** 43 oz. (10″ bbl.). **Length:** 13¼″ (10″ bbl.).
**Stocks:** Select walnut grip and fore-end, with thumb rest. Right or left hand.
**Sights:** Under cut blade ramp front, rear adj. for w. & e.
**Features:** Break open action with auto-safety. Single action only. Interchangeable bbls., both caliber (rim & centerfire), and length. Drilled and tapped for scope. Engraved frame. See T/C catalog for exact barrel/caliber availability.